The Methue
Book of New Am

The Methuen Drama
Book of New American Plays

Stunning
David Adjmi

The Road Weeps,
the Well Runs Dry
Marcus Gardley

Pullman, WA
Young Jean Lee

Hurt Village
Katori Hall

Dying City
Christopher Shinn

The Big Meal
Dan LeFranc

Edited and with an introduction by
Sarah Benson

Methuen Drama

Bloomsbury Methuen Drama

An imprint of Bloomsbury Publishing Plc

50 Bedford Square	175 Fifth Avenue
London	New York
WC1B 3DP	NY 10010
UK	USA

www.bloomsbury.com

First published 2013

ISBN
PB: 978-1-4081-5701-5
ePDF: 978-1-4725-0343-5
ePub: 978-1-4081-5702-2

Typeset by Country Setting, Kingsdown, Kent CT14 8ES
Printed and bound in Great Britain

Contents

Introduction

This collection includes six plays that represent some of the most exciting contemporary playwriting from the U.S. These plays, all produced within the last decade, range from the intimate to the epic, the personal to the national, and taken together explore a variety of cultural perspectives on life in America. The writers each have a distinctive theatrical vision, harnessing the power of live drama to create transformative experiences on our stages through some of the most exhilarating, challenging and exuberant playwriting today.

The first play, David Adjmi's *Stunning*, is an excavation of ruptured identity set in modern-day Midwood, Brooklyn, in the heart of the insular Syrian-Jewish community; Marcus Gardley's lyrical epic *The Road Weeps, the Well Runs Dry* deals with the migration of black Seminoles, is set in mid-1800s Oklahoma and speaks directly to modern spirituality, relocation and cultural history; Young Jean Lee's *Pullman, WA* deals with self-hatred and the pursuit of happiness in her formally inventive three-character play; Katori Hall's *Hurt Village* uses the real housing project of "Hurt Village" as a potent allegory for urban neglect set against the backdrop of the Iraq war; Christopher Shinn's *Dying City* melds the personal and political in a theatrical crucible, cracking open our response to 9/11 and Abu Ghraib; and Dan LeFranc's *The Big Meal* rounds out the collection: set in the mid-west in a generic restaurant, his inter-generational play spanning eighty years looks at family legacy and how some of the smallest events in life turn out to be the most significant.

The last decade in the U.S. has seen some of the most intense events of recent history – from 9/11 to the invasion of Iraq to economic collapse and the election of the first African American President. It has been a time of enormous change in America with a powerful sense of fragmentation, instability and evolution. In response we have seen a rich and fertile movement in playwriting trying to unpack this experience. The theatre, as always, is a vibrant place to reflect upon the

world around us, and these artists are portraying our new
environment through rage, compassion and generosity. As the
values of American identity shift around us – socially, politically
and economically – these writers are using new dramatic
forms to represent our splintering reality. The plays are
linking micro-events to the macro, transforming our perspective
on public events, and equally, how we think about our personal
lives. There are as many "languages" here as there are writers,
but there is a common dynamism as these playwrights each
grapple with how to respond to our contemporary lives. Not
one of them is suggesting an answer, but rather together they
are in conversation with one another. They pose divergent
responses to our shared issues, and as a group provide an
enriching, complex experience of U.S. drama today.

David Adjmi's **Stunning**, which opens the collection, is set
in the Syrian-Jewish neighborhood of Midwood, Brooklyn.
Lily, a teenage bride who has been married into a world of
material luxury with her much older husband Ike, hires a
housekeeper, Blanche, an African American woman. Both
women have lived in emotional isolation and the play deals
with the raw need of these characters through Blanche's
disruption of Lily's world as she presents an alternative way
of life, one that we later learn is masking her own reality.
    The play is written in the tradition of *Death of a Salesman* or
A Streetcar Named Desire, where we see individuals desperately
striving for a generalized version of success, and failing.
The title refers to the paralysis that sets in when people are
seen as moral failures by their communities, and Adjmi's play
captures these individuals trying to reconcile their schizophrenic
selves. *Stunning* also draws on American "screwball comedy."
It is a modern satire that uses fierce tonal shifts to create a
whiplash experience in performance, tapping into the inner
panic that underlies all the characters in the play. Adjmi uses
rapid-fire dialogue and interruption to convey this frenetic
energy with an uncanny ability to write about how women
behave, starkly setting this against the macho energy of his
male characters.

The play takes place in a "whitewashed" reality, in fact in a house so white there is a bucket of paint in each room that Blanche has to use for constant touch-ups. The hyper-sheen of this world that Adjmi is dismantling was brilliantly conveyed in production, first at the Woolly Mammoth Theater in D.C. and then at Lincoln Center's LCT3, both times under the direction of Anne Kauffman. The spaces demanded specific designs but each captured the veneer of the setting and a strong sense of Lily and Blanche's worlds collapsing in on each other in the third act. In performance the play is fierce and extremely funny, although ultimately *Stunning* is a tragedy looking at two individuals who, unable to reconcile their identities, obliterate not only each other but themselves too.

Marcus Gardley's **The Road Weeps, the Well Runs Dry** is the second play in his trilogy dealing with the migration of the black Seminoles (black and Native American people) from Florida, where they incorporate the first all-black town in Wewoka, Oklahoma. The first act of *The Road Weeps* takes place in 1850 and traces events leading up to the Civil War in Wewoka; the second act is set sixteen years later, following the war. The events of the war form a vital background for the play, but the time shift pivots around the birth of Sweet Tea's son at the end of Act One. There is an intense history between Sweet Tea's father, Number Two, the black "immortal" leader of the Freemen, and Trowbridge, the Seminole sheriff. Sweet Tea's baby is taken at birth to repay a blood debt between the families, and in Act Two we experience her homecoming where she meets her sixteen-year-old son, Wonderful. At the heart of the story is the test of identity and faith that comes for both families and the whole community when the town's water well runs dry. Mythically linked to the death of Goodbird, Trowbridge's son, some think it is an act of God or the weather, while others believe it is the local Creek Indians who are determined to enslave the community. The play charts the intense clash between these old and new cultures and belief systems in a bold interrogation of personal and communal spirituality.

Written in the tradition of Shakespeare and the Greeks, Gardley's style harnesses lush cadenced language and places the actor in a heightened theatrical world that thrives within a simple design. Several of the actors play more than one role, which enhances the theatricality and cyclical structure – resonating strongly with Gardley's fascination with memory and legacy. There are several songs in the play and a porous quality between the songs and the rest of the text that is always infused with musicality.

The Road Weeps is a poetic epic that ultimately taps into how our identities are intertwined with ancestry and place, focusing on the American concept of migration through the story of these two families. Gardley finally posits a positive view of people's ability to come together and accept all of who they are, as seen in the last scene of the play where they dance expressing liberty "only found in those who have freed themselves." Through the Lark Play Development Center's "Launching New Plays into the Repertoire Initiative" *The Road Weeps* is receiving a rolling premiere in four cities in 2013 (Los Angeles Theater Center, Perseverance Theater, Pillsbury House Theater and the University of South Florida).

Young Jean Lee's **Pullman, WA**, written in 2005, is writer/ director Young Jean Lee's exploration of the collision between self-preservation and self-hatred. There are no scene breaks in the play, but rather a series of sections defined by the characters speaking that oscillate between monologues or dialogue and a more fragmented poetic form. The three characters in the play are given the same names as the actors playing the roles in the production (in the case of the original Performance Space 122 production, Pete, Tory and Tom). The play is an expression of the struggle to live a happy life, tackling health, depression, relationships and love. It opens with a notional self-help talk, riffing on the prevalent self-help culture, on "how to live," which the character Pete directs to the audience. Pete wants to see himself as someone who is able to help other people, but as he begins to fail, Tory and Tom take over in the attempt, each using divergent strategies

and also failing. Pete's language is pedestrian, and this is set
in contrast to Tory's text, much of which resonates with
language from childhood stories and myths – a language of
escapism. Tom alternatively uses the language of religion to
soothe and comfort. Lee also weaves scatalogical imagery
throughout which gives the play a vital sense of the corporeal
nature of being human – considering the weight of material
reality against the levity of the spirit and a fulfilled life. The
play reaches beyond rationality and instead conveys, through
lacerating verbal rage and theatrical poetry, the emotional
reality of a salvage mission for happiness.

The play is transparent in its artifice, and demands
minimalist production values (Lee's stage directions state that
the actors should be dressed in ordinary street clothes and
that the house lights remain up for the whole show) to put the
actors and audience in the same space. In the tradition of
works such as Handke's *Offending the Audience*, *Pullman, WA* is a
consideration of the function of theater, asking what we hope
to accomplish by gathering together in a room. The play is
anti-genre and uses a range of shifting styles and language to
marry its form and content, constantly redefining the event
that is unfolding in front of us.

Pullman, WA is an early work of Lee's and one of the most
concentrated articulations of her concerns. She often tackles
the idea of accessing other people's minds asking, as the
character Pete exclaims: "I wish I knew what it was like to be
like you!" In later plays she examines prejudice, our sense of
identity and how we stereotype; and here we see her building
these ideas from inside by exploring the personal and social
pressures on an individual. The other constant in Lee's work
is an ongoing exploration of how the audience relates to the
performers, and in *Pullman, WA* we experience that starkly
honest impulse from the outset. As ever, Lee presents a thorny
problem rather than any straightforward answers. Her approach
is always to present the question in all its complexity to provoke
thought and reflection in her audience.

During the creation of *Pullman, WA*, Lee developed the
process she now uses in creating all her plays – writing with

a company of actors who are core collaborators in forging the production. The show was revived by Performance Space122 in 2010 and has since toured internationally.

Katori Hall's **Hurt Village** is set in the real housing project of "Hurt Village" in Memphis, Tennessee, at the end of a long hot summer. The project is slated for demolition through a government scheme (Memphis City received a large federal grant in 2000) that will result in the relocation of the vast majority of the project's residents, including Cookie, an aspiring teenage rapper, along with her mother Crank and great-grandmother Big Mama, the elderly matriarch. As the family packs up and prepares to leave, Big Mama's grandson Buggy unexpectedly returns from his tour in Iraq and tries to find where he belongs in his disintegrating community.

Hall deftly captures the urban wasteland of this northern Memphis housing project through her setting and characters. There is a potent force of what Crank declares to be "boredom and chaos" that infuses the world of the play and produces immense fall-out – from the crack epidemic sweeping through the Project to widespread youth pregnancy typified by Crank, who was thirteen when she had Cookie. Hall is turning inside out the forces of poverty and sharing a strident cry from these characters, trapped in a crumbling world and held there by societal forces which they had no part in creating. The bitter irony of Big Mama's effort to keep her family out of that very spiral of "boredom and chaos" is that her hard work to earn a living transpires to put the family just above the income threshold to qualify for a new apartment. Hall parallels the brutality Buggy has gone through in the war, where he was trained to depersonalize, with the faceless force that is obliterating a tight-knit community – potently suggesting that these two experiences are culturally and politically linked.

Hurt Village is a vivid portrait of how, as Toyia jokes, "needin' and havin' are two entire different things." Hall's language embodies the life-affirming force of personality of all her characters whose dreams are as clear as the forces working against them. There is a terse but high-spirited poetry, perhaps seen most vividly in the brilliantly virtuosic insult-topping scene and Cookie's deceptively simple raps that bookend the play. *Hurt Village* was produced by Signature Theater in New York in February 2012 under the direction of Patricia McGregor in a production that brought to fruition the duality of Hall's big-hearted and ferocious play.

Christopher Shinn's **Dying City** deals with the unsettling reverberations of the Iraq war, and in that sense is in powerful dialogue with the concerns of *Hurt Village*. The play focuses on the interrelated stories of newlyweds Kelly and Craig and of Craig's twin brother Peter. *Dying City* opens with Peter arriving at Kelly's apartment late one night, a year after the death of Craig in Iraq. The play jumps between this time setting and the eve of Craig's departure for the war. A central thread of the play, which we discover through emails between the two brothers that Peter shares with Kelly, is Craig's growing loss of faith in the war before his death. Through this discovery *Dying City* excavates the infection of 9/11, the war and the acute humiliation of Abu Ghraib. The cumulative impact of these events on the individuals, and the U.S. as a nation, is revealed such that the "dying city" is understood to refer as much to New York City as it does to shell-shattered Baghdad.

   The play is looking at cultural trauma as personal trauma, ultimately questioning our willingness or ability to reckon with our own history. Shinn explores the dichotomy between the state in which we live and our actions, looking at the chasm of hypocrisy that runs through all our lives as we try to line up the personal and political. Going back to the Greeks, the play is infused with the tragic implications of spiraling violence and the way in which the individual and the state are deeply entwined. *Dying City* powerfully mines this permeable territory between the personal and political by immersing us in the dreamy, hollow quality of loss. It lives in an in-between twilight space, as powerfully evoked in the middle-of-the-night opening.

   Dying City operates as a ghost story with an eerie and voyeuristic undercurrent, charged with the power of the unspoken text between this trio of characters. It begins as a mystery, as we seek to unearth what constituted Craig's "accident," but the play unravels as it progresses, suggesting that, in contrast with the neat formulaic structure of the "law and order" episodes Peter and Kelly joke about, these events are far too unruly for us ever to solve either personally or politically. Under the direction of James Macdonald, in the Lincoln Center Theater production I saw (Macdonald also first directed the play at the Royal Court in London), Pablo Schreiber superbly conveyed this fractured reality. By portraying both twin brothers he powerfully embodied the metaphor of the play and the question Shinn is asking: whether we can ever reconcile the personal and political duality of our lives.

Dan LeFranc's **The Big Meal**, the final play in the collection, is an inter-generational modern family story set in a generic chain restaurant in the mid-west. Sam and Nicole meet as a young couple in the restaurant at which she works and their relationship sets in motion an extensive story that traverses five generations. It explores the impact that seemingly small events can have on a large number of lives, using birth, courtship, parenting, divorce, death and economic hardship to express the pressures on the every-family in America today. As one family gather in a nameless chain restaurant for a series of ordinary meals, we experience the extremes of all our experience – the boundless joy of family, alongside the unavoidable tragedy of loss. As the characters age the actors playing them are replaced by others, creating a constant sense of a cycling reality that mirrors the experience of family and the relentless passage of time.

LeFranc is exploring emotionally raw material with non-traditional storytelling elements, writing acutely observed naturalism through a more formal lens. In conversation with the "new naturalism" of other contemporary writers such as Annie Baker, he is finding unfamiliar ways to tell familiar stories, depicting landmark life-events within an understated frame and enabling us to experience these stories anew.

There is an impressionistic quality to LeFranc's storytelling which puts front and center the details that might usually go by the wayside and in turn reflects the incomplete way we actually live. Formally, *The Big Meal* is written in a column structure, as you will observe in the layout. This creates a charged sense that any actor can enter at any moment and brings with it a broken, staccato and distinctly American rhythm. The approach effectively enables actors to capture the chaotic, often hilarious, unfiltered interactions of family and generates a scored, musical experience with the voices working as an octet. This rhythm is punctuated by characters being served a full meal, with dark undertones (as the play goes on we learn that this event always precedes their death). In the Playwrights Horizons production directed by Sam Gold we watched the characters eat a meal in real time as the feverish pace was put on hold.

The Big Meal is also in conversation with plays from the American canon such as Wilder's *The Long Christmas Dinner*, which traces a family across time through the touchstone of a holiday celebration. LeFranc speaks to a contemporary context by taking that conversation out of the home, or the dining room, and locating it in a chain restaurant – bringing private conversations into a public space. He is reflecting on how and where we spend our time together as a family, how each generation informs the next and we become who we are.

Together, these plays provide a visceral and vivid picture of playwriting in the U.S. today. These passionate and inventive artists give voice to the concerns coursing through our culture. They are questioning our collective identity in response to the last decade of social, economic and political turmoil. Beyond that, they are advancing our form, ensuring we continue to find ways in the theater to capture the impossible, messy, exuberant experience of life.

David Adjmi

Stunning

The history of the world is not the theater of happiness.
Periods of happiness are blank pages in it.

G. W. Hegel
Philosophy of History

Special Thanks

In no order: Rebecca Taichman, Lisa Portes, Morgan Jenness, Mark Subias, Adam Greenfield, Polly Carl, Stephen Willems, New York Theatre Workshop, Paige Evans, Andre Bishop, Emily Shooltz, Dartmouth College, Danny Mastrogiorgio, Quincy Tyler Bernstine, Laura Heisler, Charlayne Woodard, Cristin Milioti, Michael Goodfriend, Gabriela Fernandez-Coffey, Abby Wood, Clint Brandhagen, Lecy Goranson, Jeanine Serralles, Steve Rattazzi, Sas Goldberg, Nilaja Sun, April Yvette Thompson, Howard Shalwitz, Elissa Goetschius, Miriam Weisfeld, Woolly Mammoth Theatre Company, Kathy Sova, Paul Rusconi, Heidi Schreck, Kip Fagan, Jim McCarthy, Gloria Peterson, Anne Kauffman, Tory Stewart, Kath Tolan, Philip Himberg and all my friends at Sundance, Olivier Sultan, Corinne Hayoun. And to all the actors who participated in countless readings, workshops, etc., of this play who weren't mentioned here.

Thank you.

Stunning was developed by New York Theatre Workshop
(James C. Nicola, Artistic Director; William Russo, Managing
Director) and Manhattan Theatre Club (Lynne Meadow,
Artistic Director; Barry Grove, Executive Producer). The
world premiere was produced in Washington, D.C., by
Woolly Mammoth Theatre Company (Howard Shalwitz,
Artistic Director; Jeffrey Herrmann, Managing Director) on
March 10, 2008. It was directed by Anne Kauffman; set
design was by Daniel Conway, costume design was by Helen
Q. Huang, lighting design was by Colin K. Bills, sound design
was by Ryan Rumery; the dramaturg was Miriam Weisfeld,
the dialect coach was Sasha Olinick and the production stage
manager was Rebecca Berlin. The cast included:

Lily	Laura Heisler
Blanche	Quincy Tyler Bernstine
Ike	Michael Gabriel Goodfriend
Shelly	Gabriela Fernandez-Coffey
JoJo	Clinton Brandhagen
Claudine	Abby Wood

Stunning was produced at Lincoln Center Theater (LCT3;
Andre Bishop, Artistic Director; Bernard Gersten, Executive
Director; Paige Evans, Director of LCT3) in June 2009. It
was directed by Anne Kauffman; set design was by David
Korins, costume design was by Miranda Hoffman, lighting
design was by Japhy Weideman, sound design was by Rob
Kaplowitz; the stage manager was Megan Schwarz. The cast
included:

Lily	Cristin Milioti
Blanche	Charlayne Woodard
Ike	Danny Mastrogiorgio
Shelly	Jeanine Serralles
JoJo	Steven Rattazzi
Claudine	Sas Goldberg

Note on Style

The play shifts styles. While it is concerned with psychological reality, it only *intermittently* correlates with the detail or psychological consistency usually associated with Realism. There are deliberate *and drastic* alternations in tone, style, etc., that happen scene by scene, within scenes and *between beats* with *no* transition. It is therefore *critical* for actors to follow the rhythms of the play, as it is scored; the psychological truth can be extracted from this.

It is crucial that the shifts and transitions in the piece, no matter how abrupt, are rooted in an emotional reality.

Note on Text

A slash (/) indicates either an overlap or a jump – i.e., no break between the end of one character's speech and the beginning of the following speech (thanks Caryl Churchill).

Speech in parentheses indicates either a sidetracked thought – or footnote – within a conversation, or a shift in emphasis with *no* transition.

A [STOP] is a (*pause*) followed by either a marked shift in tone or tempo (like a cinematic jump-cut or a quantum leap) or *no* change in tempo whatsoever – somewhat like putting a movie on (*pause*) and then pressing play. These moments in the play are less psychological than energetic. They have a kind of focused yet unpredictable stillness, something akin to martial arts, where there is preparedness in the silence. Where a lunge or a swift kick can be delivered from seemingly out of nowhere: quickly, invisibly. Where the energy can shift dramatically in a nanosecond.

Setting

The play takes place largely within the confines of the Midwood section of Brooklyn – a very affluent, largely Jewish area; one that exerts a centripetal force on the people who live there. Despite the proximity to Manhattan, there's a provincialism to it, an insularity, but also an extremely tight-knit sense of community.

I know three things about the set for this play: (1) Continuing the homage to Douglas Sirk and Tennessee Williams (and Plato too, from *The Republic*), mirrors are very important to this world. It would not be out of keeping with the tenor of the play (and the themes of illusion, imitation, deception, whatever) to *selectively* stage whole scenes, parts of scenes, sections of the stage using full-length mirrors (think *Las Meninas* or even *The Lady from Shanghai*), keeping in mind, obviously, that this can't be used egregiously. (2) The world of the play is bleached-out, whitewashed – there's no color in it save for various shades of white and transparent surfaces, glass, mirrors, etc. (3) The set should have some kind of motility: it isn't stable; it wants to move, it wants to transform, whether with panels, walls, rollers, I'm not sure, but perspectives can shift.

Costumes

Monochromes. Of course Lily, Ike and JoJo (and eventually Blanche) are garbed in "JoJo Jeans" for much of the play – but there's not much color. Blanche's clothes should be, conversely, boldly colorful, but – like Rothko's canvases – get darker or more charged as the play progresses.

Time

Early 2000s.

Characters

Lily Schwecky, *cute, slight, waifish, something of an oddball. The "baby" — she's sixteen going on about eleven; she's a bit regressed. Her mind works quickly but her thoughts are incredibly scattered. A follower, but it's more out of a need for connectedness than an innate passivity.*

Blanche Nesbitt, *Lily's new housekeeper. African American; an extremely intelligent, voluble and terribly sensitive autodidact. Damaged, but maintains a great sense of irony and dry humor. She adapts to survive. She's performative, and the performance wears her down eventually. An outsider. Forties.*

Ike Schwecky, *Lily's new husband. Controlling brute, bumptious, but there's something fragile in him, broken — he's more transparent than he thinks. Mid-forties.*

Shelly, *Lily's big sister. A leader; she's got a stentorian quality, but naturalizes this by cultivating "girly" preoccupations. The laziness of her "r"s and "a"s feels calculated and somehow hostile. Early twenties.*

JoJo, *Shelly's uxorious husband. Basically a good guy but limited; rather put upon, has trouble sticking to his guns. Thirties/early forties.*

Claudine, *a bit hysterical; unselfconscious — even brutish — in her bids for approval. She has a desperate conformity. Nineteen.*

Act One: The Ambassadors

One

Claudine's *house.*

A card game.

Three girls sitting at a card table: **Shelly**, **Lily**, **Claudine**.

They all have nearly identical feathered hair modeled after the seventies "Farrah" look from Charlie's Angels. *They all have bangles – meretriciously loud bangles – on their wrists; this is an index of wealth.*

They all have variations of the same boots, clothes – one gets the sense that no one does anything in this world without the tacit agreement of the others.

Lily *is painfully, comically sunburnt and peeling for most of this act.*

The play opens with a virtuosic shuffling of the cards.

Rapid fire:

Shelly   Stick to the rules /

Lily   Where's / Tuni?

Shelly   Jacks or better nothing wild everybody / in?

Lily   We have to wait for Tuni but-h.

Claudine   Tuni's not coming she's getting a divorce:

Shelly   She's /

Claudine   Ye you didn't / hear she's

Shelly   Whaddayou*sketching?* /

Claudine   separating from (no I'm-not-sketching) she's separated / from

Lily   Oolie! /

Shelly   She just got married!

Lily   She had a baby /

Claudine   YE and the baby I think it has like a Down's *syndrome*?

Shelly   HEEE /

Claudine   (Aduknow) /

Lily   And she /

Claudine   (or like) /

Shelly   I /

Claudine   *and they hid it* /

Shelly (*to* **Lily**)   (Stop-playing-with-your-hands) /

Claudine   and Tuni had to take it in to see a *specialist* /

Lily   Wheh?

Claudine   in the *ity-cay* This *y-gay* /

Shelly   (You're-making-me-nervous-stop-it) /

Claudine   (I think it was Mount Sinai) /

Shelly (*fixes earring*)   (I-had-my-transplant-theh) /

Claudine   And like the husband / like

Shelly *pulls a packet of Juicy Fruit, puts down the cards.*

Lily   Did she have a / girl?

Claudine   he like /

Lily (*imagining a cute baby*)   Aboose.

Shelly (*to* **Claudine**)   (You want?)

Claudine   And then I (no-it's-not-sugahless) and I think he was rejecting the kid / or

Lily *accepts a stick of gum, chews.*

Shelly   I thought /

Claudine   or no, YEAH / and he

Lily   Heeee /

Claudine   goes "I don't want *you*? and I don't want this *kid*? and / gimme a divorce"

Lily   With the *Down's* syndrome / *kid*?!

Shelly   Dib Who's the husband.

Claudine   Morris Betesh /

Shelly   Piece a shit.

Claudine   No-Ye-He-is-a-piece- / a-shit

Lily   (Who's he related to?)

Claudine   Schweckies of Avenue P.

Shelly   That's not a good / family

Claudine   (*munching violently on a carrot stick*)   *Piece a shit* /

Lily   Do they own Duane Reade? /

Shelly   THAT'S YA SECOND COUSIN DUANE READE /

Claudine   (*vicious*)   *They have a bad* / *reputation*

Lily   (What do they own /

Claudine   (*finger-wagging tone*)   Bad family /

Shelly   And I go to her I go /

Claudine   (*vicious*)   BAD /

Shelly   I go don't marry this jerk /

Claudine   Me too!

Shelly   (And-remembah?!-and-I-go) /

Claudine   Me-*too*-everyone-her-mother – Debby /

Shelly   and now she's / screwed

Claudine   And-I- /go:

Shelly   fogettaboutit /

Claudine (*shaking her hand as if it's burned*)   *Yeah-oh-figget-* / it

Shelly (*mimicking her hand shaking*)   *Ooooolie figetiiiiiiit* /

Claudine (she / screwed herself)

Shelly   She's / finished

Claudine   She committed / suicide

Lily   (Oolie!) /

Claudine   RUINED!!

[STOP]

(*Crunching a carrot stick.*) I like the dip What's in this /

Lily   Chives.

Claudine (*bright*)   Heeee: I *like* chives. /

Lily   Should we / play?

Claudine (*quick*)   (Did you see Debbie's haih? She cut / it)

Shelly   I like your bangles /

Lily (*exhibiting her wrist*)   Sheri-got me for my-showah

Claudine (*muffled resentment*)   Your wrist looks thin.

Lily   I gained weight-h /

Shelly   Ca-an she's a *stick*!

Claudine (*a little too loud*)   You're BLACK!

Shelly   She's a Obdeh. /

Lily   From the panama jack.

Claudine   *Obdeh*

Shelly   She always / gets black

Claudine (*singsong*)   HOW WAS ARUBA-AAAAA?

Lily   Stunning.

Shelly (*singsong*)   Ye-eee-eeeee?

Claudine   Dibeh-you-nevah-said-nothing-You-got-back-when:

Lily   Yestiday /

Claudine   (Ack-blay) /

Shelly   You flew Delta? /

Lily   United.

Shelly   WITH THE TERRORISTS – ah?!

Claudine   LEAVE HAH.

Shelly   Whatditellyou:

Lily   Ikey bought the / tickets, I

Claudine   You look STUNNING.

Shelly (*chews gum efficiently*)   (Mommy wants you / to cawl hah)

Claudine   You look UNNING-STAY.

Shelly   cawl hah / cell

Lily (*juts out her arm*)   *I'm peeling: shoof*

Claudine   Was the sand pink. /

Lily (*peels an enormous swatch of skin*)   SHOOFIE.

Claudine   HEEEE. Put / cream!

Shelly (*mean*)   Dibeh ya hafta put cream!

Lily   I put-h!!

Claudine   Is the house finished Wheh's Ikey?

Lily   We just moved in /

Claudine   Did you go jetskiing? /

Lily   The water was choppy /

Claudine   But-it's-fun-right-isn't-it-I-TOLD-YOU-right /

Lily   I /

Claudine   Isn't it I know.

[STOP]

Shelly   You're *egnant-pray?*

Lily (*wide-eyed*)   Aduknow

Shelly   Ca-an.

Lily   He wants to start / soon.

Claudine   Is the house finished /

Shelly   Excited?

Lily   Ye.

Claudine   I want kids.

Shelly   You'll have-h!

Claudine   I'm sick of living with my mothah.

Shelly   I told you I would set you up

Claudine   with *Stevie* /

Lily (*revulsion*)   Ert /

Claudine   THIS IS HOW HE DANCES /

Shelly   He comes from a good / family.

Claudine (*practically hyperventilating*)   I'm nineteen-h! /

Lily (*gingerly*)   Ya bracelet is shahp

Claudine   (My-cousin-makes-bracelets-she-sells-them-at-flea-markets.)

Shelly (*blame*)   You don't go to parties /

Claudine   YOU SOUND LIKE *MY MOTHAH*.

Shelly   Do guys like whiney girls NO.

Claudine (*covers her face, emotionally exhausted*)   I'm old.

Lily   (I feel old.)

Claudine   Bonnie has four kids /

Shelly   (Three) /

Claudine   And she's two years younger than me I'm gonna be twenny.

Lily   (If I met someone you will.)

Claudine   But you're pretty.

Lily   You're stunning!

Claudine   I'M FAT!

Lily   Look at my / calves

Claudine (*looking in a mirrored surface*)   No-I-have- / crows-feet

Shelly (*re-applying lipstick*)   I like your / oots-bay

Lily   (I'm / fat)

Claudine   (I got those at Loehmann's) /

Lily   I feel old.

Claudine   SHUT UP YA FREAKIN TWELVE-ah.

Lily   I'm seventeen next week.

[STOP]

Claudine   I feel more secure in myself; don't you think I'm more secure in myself than I was this time lastchyee /

Lily   I like your bracelet /

Claudine   (*Errrrrt, I hate this bracelet, it's disgusting.*)

Shelly   How's the house?

Lily   Big.

Claudine   I heard it's stunning

Beat.

Lily   There's a ghost.

Shelly   Whadayou *tawking* about?

Lily   Ikey said there was, and then I saw it the other night.

Short pause.

Shelly   There's no ghost.

Pause.

Lily   I saw it. (*Beat; then to* **Shelly**.) I miss Mommy and Daddy.

Shelly   Don't be such a freakin baby.

Beat.

Lily, *somewhat abstracted, lifts her thumb to her mouth, grazing the tip of her lip;* **Shelly** *sees this – pushes it back down in her lap.*

Lily (*regaining awareness*)   It's weird. Aduknow.

[STOP]

Claudine   I saw Stevie on the holiday I saw Stevie I saw Ralphie / I saw

Shelly   Are we gonna play or what.

Claudine   Three card draw.

Lily   Deal /

Shelly   (Five.)

Claudine (*to* **Lily**, *regarding some pastry*)   Pass that –

Loud music cuts her off.

Two

Lily *and* **Blanche**.

An interview.

Lily *and* **Ike***'s home in Midwood, Brooklyn.*

The house is all-white – perhaps several shades of white, but white. There is no color in this set.

The minimalism **Lily** *espouses is that of the arid, philistine, nouveau riche – no art or anything – but terribly impressive in its own bombastic right.*

A vase of dilapidated chrysanthemums in a vase on a mantel.

Lots of reflective surfaces.

A fishbowl with a lonely confused little goldfish swimming in circles – a single charged node of color in an otherwise colorless room.

Lily *has a checklist in hand.* **Blanche** *stands out like a sore thumb.*

Lily   What's your name?

Blanche   Blanche.

Lily (*quizzical*)   Isn't that something you do to vegetables?

Blanche   I don't cook: /

Lily (*mild suspicion*)   Do you do windows?

Blanche   (Yeah and I iron) /

Lily (*vague panic*)   Tennis skirts?

Blanche (*desperate retraction*)   *But I could learn to /* cook

Lily   (Because-they're-white-and-if-you-burn-them-I'll-freak.)

Blanche   I won't.

Beat.

Lily   Are you detail-oriented?

Blanche   Uh-huh.

Lily   Like "orientated towards the details'?

Blanche (*nonplussed*)   (Isn't that what that / means?)

Lily   I play tennis Wednesdays and Fridays /

Blanche (*chummy*)   Oh I used to play *squash* /

Lily (*unbroken sentence*)   It's good for this (*points to arm*) feel this (*gestures*) it's a great spoht tennis.

Blanche (*feeling and talking at the same time*)   But that was a long time ago.

Lily (*points to hip*)   It's good for this.

Blanche   (Supple) /

Lily   But my backhand is suffering /

Blanche   *Pity* /

Lily   And you have to use bleach! I'm very meticulous about everything and I have ways I like things done; I like things a certain way, I'm meticulous. (*Aimlessly sprinkles fish food.*) "Hiiiiiiiieeee" (*To* **Blanche***; still sprinkling.*) that's Kitty / it gets fed once

Blanche (*looks for a cat*)   Where?

Lily   in the morning – "hiiiiii" (But-don't-overfeed-it-cuz-you'll-kill-it.)

Blanche   *The fish?*

Lily   Kitty – I know it's funny right? It's *gazzy* – it's from Anne *Frank?* That's her diary, did you ever read that book?

Blanche (*the whole thing is too much for her*)   Uh.

Lily   She kept a *diary?*

[STOP]

She forgets what she was saying. She jingles her bangles. Beat.

So-whatevah. (*Resuming her checklist.*) Do you know / how to

Blanche   Forgive me but I thought I had this job already.

Beat.

Lily   What-h.

Blanche   This feels like an interview.

Beat.

Lily (*indignant*)   Well I thought you would be *Porto-Rican!*

She pulls her gum out and makes shapes with it.

Blanche   Why'd you think that.

Lily (*darts a look*)   *Because we wanted a Porto-RICAN-h.*

She pops the gum back in her mouth.

Blanche   I'm confused.

Lily   I don't think this is gonna work out, lemme call you a car service. (*She goes to the phone, dials.*)

Blanche   But I have all my luggage with me.

Lily   Wheh do you live.

Blanche (*panicked*)   *Don't do that.*

Lily   I have a carry thing (*Into phone.*) Always Available? I need a cahr.

Blanche   Please don't call me a cab / I don't

Lily   Do you want to take the train?

Blanche (*we can see the despair*)   I'd . . . prefer. I. I don't have anywhere to *go.*

Lily   I'm more comfortable around Porto-Ricans. (*Into phone.*) Hello?

Blanche   LISTEN: I don't have anywhere to *go* and I'm tired, can't you just try me / out

Lily (*into phone*)   929 Ocean Parkway, it's between –

Blanche *grabs the phone, hangs it up.*

Blanche (*verging on tears*)   I DON'T HAVE ANYWHERE
TO GO!

[STOP]

Lily   Ya giving me a headeeche.

Beat.

Blanche (*manages a smile*)   Sorry.

Beat.

Lily   Ya meeking me very nervous-h.

Blanche   I'm – sorry. I'm . . .

Blanche *straightens up a few things to palliate – she assumes the comportment of some housekeeper* **Lily** *may have seen on television; she plasters on a smile.* **Lily***, vaguely soothed, produces a nail file.*

Lily (*files her nails; bright*)   It's just I had Porto-Ricans my
whole life, as maids? My mother had a Porto-Rican maid?
and then when I was a little girl I had a maid called Anna
Maria. She took care of me; I loved hah: she taught me
Spanish? She took me to the *park*, and pushed me on the swing
– *ella me decia: "Lily tú eres un angel, y tu pelo es de ceda / te quiero
como mi hija."*

Blanche   *¡¡Yo-tambien-te-puedo-mecer-en-el-columpio-vamos-al-
parque-AHORA-MISMO!!*

Beat.

Lily (*shocked, ecstatic, drops nail file*)   *¡¡¿TU HABLAS
ESPAÑOL!!??*

Blanche   (I studied languages.)

Lily   *Do you want a piece a gum? /*

Blanche   *Gracias!*

They chew gum and look at each other.

Lily   I've been chewing this same gum for three days.

Blanche   That's a lot of gum.

Lily *(quick)*   It is? No it's not because it's just one piece: I been *chewin* it fa three days. *Heeeee:* I *love* gum, you know what I like, Charms Blow Pops: OH MY GAWD. I used to get in so much *trouble?* in my *math* class? Oh my od-gay the *rabbi?* HEEEEEEE: because you're not allowed to chew gum? and he caught me? and I was gonna swallow it and I didn't? and he stuck it in my HAIHH!! *Ha ha ha ha ha.* Oh my goawd he was SO. SICK.

Blanche   Did /

Lily   Rabbi-Lerner-he's-SICK-oh-my-god-I-LOVE-him.

Blanche   You're in school?

Lily   Me no I quit /

Blanche   You / did?

Lily   Lastchyee, because I got married. I wanted to stay but my mother told me quit. Anyway I had a lot of planning with the wedding and everything.

Blanche *(pretending it's all normal)*   How long have you been married?

Lily   I had a long engagement.

Blanche   How long?

Lily   Three years.

Blanche   Wow.

Lily   I was twelve!

Beat.

Blanche   When you – got *engaged?*

Lily *(filing nails)*   Ye.

Blanche (*incredulous*)   You're *fifteen*?

Lily   Seventeen Well I'm gonna be My birthday's next week.

Blanche   But you said three years.

Lily   (I mis-did the math) We're goinna Tavern on the *Green*!

Blanche   That's quite a young age to be married.

Lily   What? Yeah. No. But I'm mature. (*Contemplative.*) I matured very fast starting when I was ten? I'm more matured since then, I was ten then I was a kid, I'm more matured now.

Blanche   Is that some kind of religious custom? To get married so young?

Lily   We're Jewish.

Blanche   You don't look Jewish.

Lily   How do I look?

Blanche   Middle Eastern.

Beat.

Lily (*perplexed and annoyed*)   Middle *Eastin??*

Blanche   You have Middle Eastern features. You know Dark Features?

Lily (*squinting in disbelief*)   I'm *tan.* I went to *Aruba*? /

Blanche   Not your complexion, your *features.*

Lily   I look *white.*

Blanche   Not to me.

Lily (*indignant*)   What do you mean not to you, *look at me* /

Blanche   I'm lookin.

A brief staring contest.

Lily (*sheepish*)   Well my family *they* are . . . I think from . . . the Middle East.

Beat.

Blanche   Where? /

Lily   Aduknow *the Middle East somewheh*!

Blanche   You don't know where?

Beat.

Lily   I think Syria.

Blanche   I didn't know there were Syrian / Jews.

Lily   But we're all *white*.

Blanche   Well technically you *aren't* white if / you

Lily   I tan easy? I have melanin in my skin?

Beat. Then playing along.

Blanche   *That's a nice tan.*

Lily   I'm peeling!

She gleefully peels a huge rectangle of skin off her arm.

Blanche (*horrified*)   You should use lotion for that!

Lily   I use! /

Blanche   Black people use cocoa butter, that's why we don't get any wrinkles /

Lily   (I'm getting / wrinkles)

Blanche   You know that expression "black don't crack"?

Lily   No.

Blanche   That's where that's from.

Lily   You don't have any wrinkles.

Blanche   I know and I'm forty-three.

Lily (*grabbing on to the sofa*)   HEEEE: THAT'S FREAKIN
OLD.

Blanche (*disconcerted*)   It's not *that* old.

Lily   (But-you-don't-look-it.)

Blanche (*pride-fully*)   "Black don't crack."

Lily   Cocoa butter.

Blanche   And you're *not* getting / *wrinkles*

Lily   And your skin loses collagen That's what happens
when you get old.

Blanche   Not you, you got great skin.

Lily   Your skin loses elastin, that's what happens, it's called
elastin.

She goes up to the mirror and examines her "wrinkles" while speaking.

So when people come to my house I want things to appear a
certain way, like I want everything to be spotless – you see
how everything is white that's how I want things to be
Stunning stunning *white* /

Blanche   Does this mean I have / the job?

Lily   And we have a bucket of paint in every room So if
things start to get dirty like if there's spots? Like on the walls?
or if you have nothing to do and there's down time you *repaint*
OK?

Blanche (*sigh of relief*)   *Thank you.*

Lily   Can I call you Anna Maria?

Blanche   Why? /

Lily   I just like that name /

Blanche   I was hoping you'd call me Ms Nesbitt /

Lily   *Who's that?* /

Blanche   Me.

Beat.

Lily   I-kinda-hoped-I-could-call-you-Anna-Maria (is-that-*okaaaay*-I-feel- / *baaaad*)

Blanche   I / kinda

Lily (*regressing*)   Anna-Maria-you're-so-nice-Anna-MARIA.

She hugs **Blanche***. She claps a tiny clap.*

Blanche   Where's my room?

Lily (*cheerful*)   It's in the basement!

Blanche   And it's safe?

Lily (*wide-eyed cheer*)   We took the asbestos out of the *ceiling*!

Blanche   Oh good (?)

Lily   There's an alarm /

Blanche   OK.

Lily   (Could you not track / dirt?)

Blanche   (I'll take these / off)

Lily (*single breath*)   When you're finished unpacking you can dustbust The kitchen's just around theh? you turn right and it's right there OK? I'm gonna get a facial here's my cell if you need it Oh wait I don't have a pen.

Blanche (*fear*)   And I have the job right?

Lily (*scrunches her face in the mirror*)   (I'm losing elastin.)

Blanche   (You look / fine)

Lily   OOLIE! I'm going to be late for my manicuah /

Blanche   *OK.*

Lily (*frantically grabbing her things*)   Down the stairs and the first door on your left That's your room.

Blanche   Down / the –

Lily   No second /

Blanche   What /

Lily   Door /

Blanche   On my left? /

Lily   *No right.*

Blanche *descends the stairs, hauling her heavy luggage with her.*

Lily (*chatters away in Spanglish after her*)   Oh and be careful, the steps Let me show you It's very steep. (*Spanish, speaks quickly.*) *Todavia estamos trabajando Anna Maria la luz está a tu derecha.* (*Runs after her.*) Switch the alarm off, *cuidado Anna Maria* careful don't fall . . . ANNA MARIA!!

She looks after **Blanche** *descending the stairs, her eyes glowing preternaturally. Arabic music cuts in.*

Three

JoJo *and* **Ike**.

They're both in fishing gear.

Both wear JoJo Jeans.

Ike *has a button that reads: "I like Ike."*

Lily *is carrying an enormous fish that's nearly twice her size and weight.*

Blanche *is in the periphery, repainting the walls with a roller, a paint trough nearby.*

Ike   You put it right on the grill /

Lily   With the bones?

JoJo (*points*)   Don't debone / it

Lily   Ert.

Ike   Grilled whole fish you never had that It's / unreal

Lily   (I nevah had / that)

JoJo   That's what gives it flava.

Lily   I never cooked fish.

JoJo   You put lemon You put salt You put garlic /

Ike   You put fresh oregano /

JoJo   Mint /

Ike   No / mint

JoJo   MY FATHER PUT / MINT

Ike   YOU DON'T PUT MINT!

They roughhouse for a few seconds. It ends just as suddenly as it started.

Lily   I'm taking lessons, cooking lessons, at the École, we're still on vegetables /

Ike   Gimmethebosses /

Lily   There's six kinds a / dice

Ike (*kissing her paternally*)   (Gimmethebosses / gimmethebosses)

Lily   No seven, brunoise, something a "m"? Lemme / get my

Ike   ALRIGHTAREADY

Lily   What?!

Ike   WE'RE / HUNGRY

Lily   ARAAAIGHT!

[STOP]

(Ooof.)

Lily *exits, galled, lugging the huge fish.*

[STOP]

The energy in the room shifts completely, becomes hyper-macho. Tableau.

JoJo   She p.g.? /

Ike (*makes a muscle*)   Workin on it /

JoJo   Honeymoon? /

Ike   Feel /

JoJo   You're working out?

Ike   I joined the gym, Gold's, I work out six days a week /

JoJo   I hired a trainer /

Ike   I run five miles a / day

JoJo   I run six /

Ike   I do crunches /

JoJo   I do squats /

Ike (*pointing finger*)   *You stretch?*

JoJo   I do bowflex /

Ike   *You wanna hurt your back?!* /

JoJo (*points*)   (Don't point.)

[STOP]

Ike *jogs in place.*

Ike   I'm in training.

JoJo   You gotta stretch the muscles.

Ike   I'm in pretty good shape / guy, my

JoJo   (Bowflex.)

Ike   age, look at Abie,

JoJo   Abie *yeah* / but

Ike (*stops jogging*)   Look at my stomach Jo, *flat* /

He lifts his shirt. **JoJo**, *in examining his stomach, punches it.*

Ike   DID I SAY PUNCH?

[STOP]

JoJo   (Good definition.)

Ike   Flat /

JoJo (*belated double take*)   (Wait-Abie-who?)

Ike (*strikes an Atlas pose*)   Feel: /

JoJo   Whaddayouon*steroids*?

Ike (*Atlas pose two*)   Creatine.

JoJo   That's bad fa ya kidneys You want *kidney stones*?

Ike   *I don't got kidney stones ya douchebag* /

JoJo   *DOUCHEBAG* /

Smack. Headlock. They get in **Blanche**'s *way.*

Ike   Uncle.

JoJo   NO!

Ike   I'll break ya fuckin neck.

Blanche   (I'll move.)

Headlock. **Blanche** *rolls her eyes.*

JoJo   UNCLE.

Ike *lets him out of the headlock.*

Ike   Power.

JoJo   Now my neck hurts /

Ike   Name of the game (*to Kitty*) Hiiiiiiiiiiieeeeeeeeeee
Kiiitty!

[STOP]

Energy in the room shifts again completely, an extempore business meeting.

JoJo   I'm hungry /

Ike (*shift*)   *Alright let's talk business:* /

JoJo   *Alright* (lemme get my / pad)

Ike   *Shoof:* outsourcing /

JoJo   Tawk.

Ike   We're at a time of expansion We need to leverage our capabilities Increase our profit margin /

JoJo   I / already

Ike   I know you don't wanna do / it but

JoJo   And then we gotta bring more *people* in, I don't / wanna

Ike   LISTEN TA MAY – We expand the market, PR, advertising /

JoJo   No –

Ike   (Plus with decreasing the labor / costs)

JoJo   (It's-not-actually-so-much-cheaper-I-saw-the-spreadsheet.)

Ike   LISTEN TA MAY!

JoJo   I don't want no sweatshops, I'm not into that (*He flexes some muscle.*) Ibe.

Ike   They're not sweatshops.

JoJo   (I'm starving / where's the fish?)

Ike   These people need work, they're dropping like *flies*, they're being barbecued *alive* they NEED WORK /

JoJo   I /

Ike   You wanna be a Nike You wanna be a Godiva chocolate?

JoJo (*points*)   JoJo Jeans!

Ike   Jo Jo JEANS /

JoJo (*moves to sofa*)   And they got *sweatshops.*

Ike   (Who?)

JoJo   Nike, Godiva, child *labor /*

Ike   My *grammotha* worked in child labor she freakin *oved*-it-lay /

JoJo   *CA-AN /*

Ike   "*CA-AN*" in a candy factory They gave her free candy bars /

JoJo   We already have a sizable profit margin.

Ike   What about our *skill set?*

JoJo   I /

Ike   We can leverage our capabilities CA-AN, Take it to the next level, we can be like a diesel, a Levi's, a Lee jeans (where's Brooke / Shields)

JoJo   I /

Ike   (Marky Mark The girl with the reversible mole) *not* this second-tier nonsense – if that's what you want fine I want MOAH!

JoJo   I want more / too.

Ike (*practically edging him off the sofa*)   No 'cause you're lazy /
move

JoJo   I'm / not

Ike   Spoiled bastard if (MOVE) if / you

JoJo   I'M NOT SPOILED /

Ike   SHADDAP (if-your-father-didn't-have-money-you'd-be-scraping-the-gutters-with-the-back-of-your-throat) /

JoJo   *What* /

Ike   SHADDAP (you're-too-lazy-to-even-understand-the-shit-life-you'd-have-if-you-weren't-so-spoiled) *That's* corruption /

JoJo   *I'm* corrupt? /

Ike   That's *repreHENsible* /

JoJo   I'M /

Ike   (You're-sitting-on-your-BlackBerry) / REPREHENSIBLE do

JoJo   (Wheh) /

Ike   you realize how much you have to work with Your *skill* set? Where's your ambition, where's your fire? – I'm like Vesuvius I'm like Magic Johnson I shoot hoops I have winged feet /

JoJo   I work my ass off. I *started* this company it's MY company /

Ike   ARE. YOU. IN?

Pause.

JoJo   You treat me like shit. I'm your partner.

Pause.

Ike   I love you like a brother; you know that.

Beat.

JoJo   Yeah yeah.

Pause.

Ike (*puts his arm around him*)   Remember we picked up non-Jewish girls together?

JoJo (*fond reminiscence*)   The chick with bad teeth?

Ike   (Deltoids, traps, rhomboids)

JoJo   Fucked up teeth is hot. . .

Ike   Now we're *arried-may* /

JoJo   (She p.g. yet?)

Ike   I *told* / you

JoJo   "Be fruitful and / multiply"

Ike   I want ten / kids

JoJo   KILL THE PALE-FREAKIN-STINIANS /

Ike   (oneafteranothah-boom-boom- / boom.)

JoJo (*quick*) I says ta-hah: "YOUR BRA DON'T EVEN FIT H" /

Ike   Who /

JoJo (*quick*)   She goes "I can't afford no bra" I go "I'll slip you twenty bucks if you show me your ass."

Ike   HA HA /

JoJo   HA HAHAHAH.

[STOP]

(*Beat; concession.*) Arite /

Ike   YES?

JoJo (*a little lost, abstracted*)   I don't know what I'm doing.

Ike (*preening happily*)   Cuz I'm alpha, cuz what I say goes, buddy

JoJo (*violent*)   BULLSHIT!

Ike   Alpha and the beta, the beginning and the end.

JoJo   (Omega.)

Ike   Who's got the power.

JoJo (*regretting everything*)   (I'm starved.)

Ike (*posing in the mirror*)   My arms are like *pistons*.

Four

Shelly *and* **Lily**.

They wear Fila Luxe tracksuits. Headbands too. Make-up: perfect.
Lily *is stretching her calves.* **Blanche** *is dusting inconspicuously in the periphery.*

Shelly   I used to get v's but now I do moons /

Lily   I have a French manicuah /

Shelly   You go to Linear Nails? /

Lily   No I used to go theh.

Shelly   With who Olga?

Lily   I don't go there / anymore.

Shelly   Was she fat?

Lily   I go to Ana Orsini.

Shelly   I used to go there.

[STOP]

Lily   I have a French manicuah.

Shows her.

Shelly   Heeeee: Stunning.

Lily   Let me see your v's.

Shelly   Moons.

Lily   I love / it-h

Blanche   Where's the Pledge?

Lily   What.

Blanche   I'm dusting.

Shelly   You use Pledge? It gives you waxy buildup.

[STOP]

Lily   I thought /

Shelly (*harsh blame*)   You use Pledge??

Lily (*meek*)   Ye.

Shelly (*to* **Blanche**)   LISTEN TA MAY: you don't use that, you wanna ruin all the furnitcha it's brand-new furnit-cha very expensivo *mucho dinero,* you wànna ruin this?

Blanche *shakes her head.*

Shelly   You don't use that on the furniture. (*To* **Lily**.) Did you tell her about the floors?

Lily   I /

Shelly (*to* **Blanche***; eyeing her suspiciously*)   You be careful with the floors araight?

Blanche (*restraint, but it's difficult*)   What would you have me use.

Shelly   *I can't remembah* it's this stuff / (*Snap, snap.*)

Lily   Anna / Maria

Shelly   *What's the freakin name?* (*Disproportionately angry.*) *I CAN'T REMEMBAH.* (*Snap, snap.*) It's much bettah.

[STOP]

Blanche   Well /

Shelly   I'll have you call my girl My girl is very good She'll give you the name.

Lily (*after an uncomfortable spell*)   Did you get the invitation / for

Shelly   Oh and I'm pregnant-h.

Beat.

Lily   *You're –*

Shelly   The-baby's-fine-no-disfigurement-I-got-the-
ultrasound-Tuesday.

Lily   HEEEEEE: SHEL / CONGRATS

Shelly   (I saw a little hand I saw little feet.)

Lily   When did / you

Shelly   I'm done with the first trimester they tell you not to
tell anyone before that, I can still do exercise, speedwalking
aerobics: *am I glowing?* /

Lily   Ye /

Shelly   (Badminton.)

Beat.

It's nice being pregnant just to glow.

Lily (*twirling her hair*)   Did you tell Jo?

Shelly   Yeah I mean no, I'll tell him, ca-an. Let's
speedwalk.

Beat.

Lily   Do I?

Shelly   What.

Lily   Glow.

Beat.

Shelly (*rhetorical*)   Are *you* pregnant?

Shelly *smiles a freakishly wide, teasing smile at* **Lily***; pokes at her
stomach.*

Blanche *looks disdainfully at* **Shelly**. **Shelly** *stares her down.*
Blanche *goes back to dusting, feigning interest in her dumb job.*

Lily   Let's speedwalk I have my thing.

Shelly *makes to leave. Hawk-like, she watches* **Blanche**, *her mouth curled into a snarl.*

Shelly   Shoof haddie.

Lily *looks up at* **Shelly** *who is still fixed on* **Blanche**.

Shelly   SHOOFIE.

Lily *jolts, looks to* **Shelly** *and then* **Blanche** .

Blanche *freezes a moment, then slowly pivots to see if she's being watched.*

Shelly *casually fingers the furniture for dust.*

Shelly (*looks out casually*)   Ooday ooyay ink-thay ee-shay eels-stay?

Blanche *stops for a moment;* **Lily** *doesn't get it on the first try.*

Lily   Uht-way?

Shelly   Do you think she *eels-stay*?

Lily (*slightly embarrassed*)   I don't ow-knay.

Shelly   SHOOFIE. (*Pause.*) My *last* aid-may ole-stay ings-thay.

Lily *looks at her.*

Shelly (*whispers loudly*)   And she wasn't an *igger-nay*.

Blanche *freezes.*

Lily (*deeply uncomfortable*)   When are we going already?

Shelly   *Iggers-nay eel-stay.*

Five

Ike *and* **Lily**.

The master bedroom, night.

Ike *does push-ups on the floor.* **Lily** *watches him, bored.*

Ike   Eighteen Nineteen.

Lily   She needs it to be off the books she said.

Ike   Twenny (sit-on-me) twenny-one.

She gets on his back while he does push-ups.

Lily   She doesn't want to pay taxes.

Ike   So.

Lily   So she doesn't want a check, anyways I need money.

Ike   Don't I give you money?

Lily   I had to pay the gardener.

Ike   Twenny-seven.

Lily   And Frieda's shower, I had to get her / a present

Ike   You don't have enough money?

Lily   I /

Ike   Look at this house, you don't like this house?

Lily   (No I like it.)

Ike   Those are dolomite floors.

Lily   Shelly has a credit card.

Ike   Use Shelly's I'll give you the money.

Lily *stands.*

Lily   Could I have my own bank account?

Ike   We have a bank account (thirty-six).

Lily   My name's not on it.

Ike   Why do you need your name on everything.

Lily   My mother says that she never heard of a husband /
who won't

Ike   Your mother should mind her own business.

Lily   DON'T TURN ME AGAINST MY FAMILY.

[STOP]

More push-ups. She brushes her hair and cries.

Ike   What the hell is wrong with you.

Lily   Aduknow.

Ike   Why are you *crying*?

Lily   I cry better than I speak.

Ike   Who says?

Lily   YOU.

Beat. He produces cash.

Ike   You need more I'll give you more.

Lily   I always need moah.

Ike   You buy gadgets.

Lily (*gravitas*)   I need gadgets.

Ike   No one / needs

Lily   You don't know what I need.

Ike *stands.*

Ike   I don't know what you need?

He grabs her. They kiss. It's not that sexy.

That's a good girl.

She looks up at him with her big, watery eyes. She chews her gum. She brushes her hair.

Lily   I'm bohed.

Ike   Your hair smells nice.

Lily (*cheered*)   There's no flakes *right-h*?

Ike   Who's my little girl:

Lily   Me.

Ike (*stroking her cheek*)   We'll talk about getting you a credit card.

Lily (*she sits on his lap*)   Also I want to take acting lessons.

Ike   You're already taking / lessons

Lily   At the École but that's cooking.

Pause.

Ike   I thought you wanted a family.

Lily   I can have / both

Ike   Because I want to have a family I thought that was clear.

Beat.

Lily   Maybe we / could

Ike   And I want it now /

Lily   But /

Ike   NOW I WANT IT NOW!

He kisses her violently, starts tearing off her clothes. **Blanche** *enters with laundry.*

Blanche   (Ooh I'll come back.)

Blanche *exits.* **Lily** *pulls away. Long pause.*

Lily   I got fitted for a diaphragm.

Pause.

Ike   Where is it.

Beat.

Lily   In the drawer.

Ike   Get it.

Lily   I just thought in / case

Ike   GET IT.

Pause. She goes to the drawer.

Flush it.

Lily   But I . . . I just got it.

Beat. He stares her down. She exits and returns.

Ike (*sweet*)   I didn't hear a flush.

Lily   You wanna check?

Ike   Don't use that tone with me.

Chews her gum. Pops.

Lily   We nevah do anything.

Ike   We just got back from Aruba.

Lily   I don't like being alone.

Ike (*gleeful*)   You're not alone – you got the ghost!

Lily   You shouldn't have told me about that.

Ike (*teasing*)   Awwwwwwww you scared of the ghost?

Lily   It's not funny /

Ike   BOO /

Lily   AAAAAAH

She screams, he laughs.

[STOP]

Ike   Honey there's no such thing as ghosts; don't be a dumbbell.

He ruffles her hair.

Lily   You told me the real-estate guy said it was haunted.

Ike   You gonna listen to some real-estate guy?

Lily   You said you believed it.

Ike (*gently, playful*)   Calm *down.*

Lily   I *saw* it. I saw it the other day. (*Beat.*) I saw a face.

Ike *looks at her, smiling curiously.*

Ike   You saw a *ghost!*

Beat.

Lily   In the living room – the other day.

Beat.

Ike   Honey, you're just seeing things.

Lily (*increasingly upset, a child's nightmare*)   It was looking right at me.

He looks at her – he's a bit spooked.

Ike   You saw somm?

Lily   The real-estate guy *told* you – I'm not making / it up

Ike   OK OK Look at me:

Lily   *I saw a face.*

Ike   Honey *look* at me.

Lily *looks at him.*

Ike   You think a ghost is gonna mess witchu when you got me protecting you?

Lily (*sad*)   When are you leaving?

Ike   China? I told you, Thursday.

Lily   Are you going to be gone for my birthday?

Ike   I leave right after.

Lily   How long will you be gone?

Ike   A few weeks.

Lily   Can I come?

Ike   Business.

Pause. She goes to mirror, brushes her hair.

Lily   I'm not a dumbbell.

Beat.

Ike   Who's my little girl?

No answer.

(*Seducing her.*) Daddy just has to be gone a little while and then he'll be home to take care of his baby.

Pause.

Lily (*vulnerable*)   I. I get panic attacks.

Ike (*making fun of her*)   "I get panic attacks."

Beat.

Lily (*shocked by his cruelty*)   It's not funny.

Ike (*thinks this is funny*)   Alright Alright.

Beat.

Lily   I want to go with you.

Ike   Who's my little gadget?

Lily (*frightened*)   Don't leave.

Ike   Gimmethebosses.

Six

Blanche *and* **Ike**. *The kitchen. Morning.*

Blanche *has just made a pot of coffee, she's playing waitress.* **Ike** *is eating – or slurping giant mouthfuls of cereal, alternating with drinking his creatine shake.*

Blanche   Refill? /

Ike   Just a few things, you come in, not a big deal I was thinking Sunday /

Blanche   That's my day off.

Ike   (Get me some milk.)

Blanche   Right / but

Ike   Yeah but I need you to do it Sunday see because I have stuff going on so it has to be Sunday It's no big thing.

Blanche   You want me to come into your office /

Ike   Cuz we're moving, Hong Kong, stuff What's this?

Blanche   What? Oh. Soy milk.

Ike   I want regular milk.

Blanche   But have you tried / soy?

Ike *(slams down milk, it spills)*   GET RID OF IT.

[STOP]

Blanche   But it's / very

Ike *(petulant, shouting)*   I WANT MILK REGULAH MILK.

[STOP]

Here's a sponge /

Blanche   I'll / clean it

Ike   (Where's-the-Splenda-we-got-Splenda?) /

Blanche   I /

Ike (*bright*)   So this Sunday aright.

Blanche   Where?

Ike   The warehouse? It's in Jersey, Hoboken, I'll give you carfare I'll give you twenny bucks Don' worry about nothin /

Blanche   This is making me uncomfortable /

Ike   (Where's-the-Splenda?) /

Blanche   Because. I, uh. I really don't clean offices?

Ike   You /

Blanche   Or. Well that's not what I was *hired* to do.

He gives her a dirty look. Downs some creatine.

(*Increasingly nervous.*) And. And I . . . The *boundaries*?

(*Beat.*) Do you see what I mean?

Ike (*strained cheer*)   An office is a house but with file cabinets.

Blanche   But. It isn't *really* a house.

Ike   Pretend it's a house.

Blanche   But /

Ike (*bright*)   Just pretend.

Blanche   Maybe we could organize it for later in / the week

Ike (*violent*)   I'M ASKING YOU TO DO ONE THING!

Blanche, *frightened, reflexively tries to shield herself.* **Ike** *looks at her, completely unaware of his effect on her. Beat.*

Ike   Whatsamatta?

Blanche   I – /

Ike   BOO!

Blanche (*terrified*)   AHHHHHH!

Ike (*delighted*)   I scahe ya? AH HAHAH.

Blanche *makes a feeble attempt to laugh along with him.*

Ike   Just do this for me, you're doing this for me. (I'll give you twenny bucks.) *What kinda music izzat?*

Blanche   Rachmaninoff.

Ike   It's giving me a headache BAH BAH BAH.

Blanche *shuts it off.*

Blanche (*a concession*)   I used to work in an office; I did book-keeping.

Ike   Good girl /

Blanche   I did a lot of office / jobs

Ike   You're gonna clean this up I gotta go.

He gathers his things.

You could make a lot of money book-keeping, why don't you do that?

Blanche   Capitalism, cubicles, it's not for me.

Ike   But if you got *skills* Your *skill*set?

Blanche   Offices make me claustrophobic.

Ike *Awffices?*

Blanche   The whole system.

Ike   Whaddayou a *commie*?

Blanche   Commie? No, more, uh /

Ike (*checks out her booty*)   Commie /

Blanche   democratic socialist? anyway I resist labels /

Ike   (What are those, Levi's?) /

Blanche   But the System wants to crush you.

Ike   "System"?

Blanche   The political truncheon? /

Ike   You got a good vocabulary.

Blanche   I got a PhD.

Ike   College, ye, not for me.

Blanche   I speak four languages.

Beat.

Ike   But there's only one language spoken in this world.

He looks right at her.

Blanche   Which is:

Beat.

Ike   Gold and Silver baby: Money talks. (*Beat.*) That's right.

[STOP]

Blanche   Are you still / hungry?

Ike   And I don't want you wearing no Levi's, *listen ta may.* I'll give you a closetful of jeans – the best – JoJo Jeans, a *closetful.* HOT. The *best,* you *listenna-may.*

Blanche   I don't got a closet.

Ike   Wha?

Blanche   My room, I use a suitcase.

Ike (*preening*)   I'll get you a closet.

Blanche (*irony*)   (Oo-that'd-be-nice.)

Ike   You like ya room?

Blanche (*tense smile*)   Well-I-feel-like-the-*walls*-are-closing-in-on-me-but-*yeah.*

Ike   You could take somethin for that.

Blanche (*finessing*)   I'm a little claustrophobic aha / ha

Ike (*a bit too loud*)   YOU LIKE HIP-HOP?!

Blanche (*jumps*)   I *yeah* I I like Tupac.

Ike   *Who?*

Blanche   They shot him? /

Ike   To me it's / noise

Blanche   (And Jay-Z got gunned down in that / video?)

Ike   I like it but it's noise /

Blanche   Well.

[STOP]

Ike (*swaggering*)   You're a hip-hopster.

Blanche   I like Sibelius best.

She watches him swagger. She doesn't know what to do.

Ike (*"rapping"*)
the hip
the hop the hip hip hippity hop
AND YOU DON'T STOP.

[STOP]

Blanche   Uh.

Ike   I know about hip-hop 'cause of my business, which is fashion Denim You like denim?

Blanche   It's – versatile.

Ike   You dress nice.

Blanche   Thanks.

Blanche *cleans.*

Ike   No I'm serious yo.

Blanche *cleans.* **Ike** *struts over.*

Ike   Is that a hip-hop shirt?

Blanche   I don't know.

Ike   "FUBU: for us by us."

Blanche   Mm.

Ike   Like that.

Blanche (*visibly uncomfortable*)   Yeah.

Ike   Nice.

Beat.

Blanche   You like Sibelius?

Ike   You like me?

[STOP]

(*Seductive.*) *You like me?*

He grabs her around the waist from behind. She carefully disentangles herself.

Blanche   I'll get the dustbuster.

She exits.

Seven

Lily, *wearing her party dress, holds a few helium balloons tied together. She stares in the mirror.* **Blanche** *is reading by lamplight in the living room. She looks up from her book and sees a forlorn* **Lily**.

Blanche   How was the party?

Lily   I'm old.

Blanche   Nice balloons.

Lily *plops down next to her, sighs dolefully.*

Lily   What are you reading?

Blanche   You wouldn't like this.

Lily   Could you read to me?

Blanche   It's theory.

Lily   What kinda theory? (*Grabs the book.*) I din know you liked to read.

Blanche   'Cause I'm a maid?

Lily   Ye.

Blanche   "Ye"?

Lily   YE!?!? (*Flipping through the book.*) What kinda book is this?

Blanche   Semiotics. (Can I have that back?)

Lily   What's *semiotics-h?*

Blanche   The science of sign systems.

Lily   Why are you *reading* it?

Lily *flips through it.*

(*Deeply offended.*) This is *retarded.*

Blanche   Well I have my degree in it. So. And I might have a teaching gig, I'm waiting to hear.

Lily *just looks at her, waits for the punch line.*

Lily (*squinting*)   What *degree?*

Blanche (*getting excited*)   I did my undergraduate work at Chicago? I studied Lit with (well-minored-in-philosophy) but with Saul Bellow?

Lily   Saul –

Blanche   He won the Nobel Prize?

Lily   *Heeeee!*

Blanche   And Paul de *Man* all these *guys.* They're mostly dead now, but nice dead white guys. And I did graduate work

at Brown in semiotics or – well under the rubric of critical /
theory

Lily   What's *Brown*?

Blanche   A college.

Lily   Is it a black school?

Blanche   It's integrated.

Lily   With what?

Beat.

Blanche (*confounded*)   White people (?)

Lily (*scrunching up her face; indignant*)   So why's it called *Brown*?

Blanche   I think we should avoid racial issues

Lily (*winsome*)   (I always avoid them) *So you went to college?
That's so shaahpl*

Blanche   And I even had a thing with Cornel West; well it
/ wasn't –

Lily   Who /

Blanche   He used to send me these letters? like love letters
and shit and he's all frontin he's all "your eyes your hips" /
And he's

Lily   Your teacher?

Blanche   He's like "I want to collapse you into the fold": I
was like "*un*fold me."

Lily   (?):

Blanche (*quick*)   Actually it's kinda ironic cuz I studied
representations of the African-American Domestic in Mass
Media with him and here I am – but I luuuv irony.

Lily   What's irony?

Blanche   This:

She circles a finger to **Lily** *and back.*

Lily   (Wha?)

Blanche   (Never mind.)

Lily   But if you went to college you can get a job –

Blanche   Well I need. I – I have to pay – my *loans*.

Lily (*clapping*)   And you're my *maid*?

Blanche   For the time being.

Lily (*sad*)   *But I don't want you to go.*

Blanche   But I might have this teaching job /

Lily (*earnest*)   But-you-clean-my-house-*stunning* /

Blanche (*produces pack of gum*)   Gum? /

Lily   (*Hee I love / Dentyne.*)

Blanche (*quick*)   And if I get it I can pay back my loans and it might lead to a tenure position Which can lead to making speeches and my book'll come out and I could maybe be a pundit Write for *Harper's* Start a blog –

Lily   Why couldn't you just get a teaching job to start with /

Blanche (*defensive*)   DO YOU KNOW HOW HARD IT IS TO GET A TEACHING JOB?! (*Compensatory girlish; quick.*) *A-ha-ha* I mean – no-but-the-academy is so *cloistered* I've applied for – I mean I cannot tell you how many jobs I've applied for –

Lily   Really?

Blanche   Oh I used reams of paper *reams* forests, whole *arbors*; but it's very white and it's hard as a black woman a lesbian I mean I like white guys *fine* but it's kind of a closed system and everyone wants to teach /

Lily   Why /

Blanche   Because what else are you gonna do with your worthless semiotics degree?!?! *Aha-ha just kidding.* No but they love the whole ivory tower thing *knowamsaaayin?* Because you're insulated from the real world: *That's* the academy. They won't look at *reality.* And of course it's all worthless I mean really does anyone give a SHIT about synecdoche or Kant's epistemological turn? *No!* / And the academy

Lily   You want taffy?

Blanche   wants you to believe that the life of the mind, critical thinking, that this is *worth* something but – SURPRISE – it's just more hucksterism, another trick (ye-ah-gimme-a-taffy) "Oh *take* out two hundred grand in loans" (but it's all part of the capitalist / machinery)

Lily (*proffering taffy*)   What's synecdoche? /

Blanche (*chews taffy, blithe*)   But on the other hand people have *agency* /

Lily   (I like / taffy)

Blanche   It's like Helen Keller said "I am only one person but I'm still a person." /

Lily   (I thought she was mute) /

Blanche   (I'm paraphrasin) /

Lily   (Oh) /

Blanche   But it's the same shit over and over: Absolute power corrupts absolutely History repeats like a bad case a reflux: "History is a document of *barbarism*" /

Lily   Who said that? /

Blanche   (This-guy-who-wrote-his major-works-on-toilet-paper-because-he-was-a-political- / prisoner)

Lily   (We're almost out of toilet / paper)

Blanche   (It's on my / list)

Lily   (Double ply) /

Blanche   *Yo me preocupo de esto / cálmate*

Lily   (Wait: *you're-a-lesbian?*)

Blanche   What.

Beat.

Lily (*a frisson*)   I feel like I heard you say you're a . . . "esbian-lay."

Blanche (*eating a taffy*)   Yeah.

Lily   Yeah you *are* or yeah you *said* it?

Blanche   *Yeah* I said it cuz *yeah* I *am* it.

Lily   You're an actual "lesbian"?

Blanche (*indignant*)   No: I'm an optical illusion /

Lily   But like: don't you think that like the *girl?* is supposed to go with the *guy?*

Blanche (*playing dumb*)   Why's that.

Beat.

Lily (*as if* **Blanche** *is mentally handicapped*)   Because the *man?* is *orientated* towards the *woman?*

Blanche   *Why?*

Beat.

Lily (*unbridled frustration*)   BECAUSE THE *GIRL?* IS *ORIENTATED?* TOWARDS THE *GUY.*

Blanche   (Not this girl) /

Lily   (Adunundahstan) /

Blanche (*only barely hiding her condescension*)   Adrienne Rich wrote an essay: that said that *all* women are lesbians. And there's a thing called: "compulsory heterosexuality"; and that first we're *all* dykes but it's the *system* that makes us straight.

Lily   What *system*?

Blanche   Forces of History Culture The usual vectors.

Lily   (Sounds like a dibeh) /

Blanche   (Well she ain't.)

Beat.

Lily   Girls are supposed to have kids and get *married*. That's life.

Blanche   *No*. That's *your* life.

Lily   Uhhhhh: Ya not very *bright-h* if you can't see what I'm saying?

Blanche   Uhhhhh: Actually I graduated Phi Beta Kappa with a 3.94 GPA. Don't tell me I'm not *bright*.

Pause.

Lily   I just don't agree with your lifestyle.

Blanche   Well it's not up for *consensus*.

Pause. **Lily** *takes another tack.*

Lily   In the *Bible?*

Blanche (*dismissive*)   Yeah what do you know about the Bible?

Lily   Uhh: I read it like a *hundred* times?!

Blanche   Where?

Lily (*vindication*)   THE YESHIVAH?!?!

Blanche   (Yeah so you know the Bible What do you know) /

Lily (*blunt textbook sanctimony*)   LESBIANS IS WRONG /

Blanche   (And they taught you grammar / too Nice)

Lily   And I know about Sodom and Gomorrah!

Blanche   What do you know?

Lily   They were *Sodomites*!

Blanche   And:

Lily   And they had *sodomy ca-an*? And God said to Lot's wife not to look back and she looked back.

Beat.

Blanche   Would you look back?

Lily   God said no.

Pause.

Blanche (*internal; faraway*)   I would.

Lily *looks at her.*

Lily   Fine but then you turn to a pillar of salt.

Blanche *turns to* **Lily**.

Blanche   You ever hear of a lose-lose proposition?

Beat.

(*Somewhat portentous.*) No. Not yet. But you will.

Silence.

Well I have some reading to do so . . .

Blanche *goes back to her reading.* **Lily** *stares at her, glum.*

Lily   Should I go to college?

Blanche *turns a page, ignoring her.* **Lily** *continues to stare mercilessly.* **Blanche** *blocks out* **Lily**'s *face with her hand.*

Lily   Maybe I shouldda finished high school. I wanted to stay but my mothah told me quit.

Blanche *forces a bright smile, clamps down on all her nervous energy; she makes a flash card.*

Lily   Do you think that's bad?

Blanche (*dryest sarcasm*)   No, I think it's a stroke of genius.

Lily   So you think I / should

Blanche *whips around, looks right in her face.*

Blanche (*terse*)   Honey, I can't fix you, I can't work out your problems for you!

Lily   I don't need you to / *fix* me.

Blanche   I can't control what you do!

Lily   But I wanna know what you *think* /

Blanche   I think we need a boundary, that's what I think.

Blanche *takes a breath, goes back to her book.* **Lily** *stares at her, chastened and a little offended.* **Lily** *tries to peek around the book, not getting the hint.*

Lily   I wanna go to college /

Blanche   Go /

Lily   I can't, Ikey wants to have kids, he said I have to start now. (*Genuinely sad.*) And I'm really mad 'cause my diaphragm fit me good, and then he made me flush it down the toilet.

Blanche *looks up from her book, sees* **Lily** *upset. She shuts the book, agitated, gets her things together.*

Blanche   I'm going to bed.

Lily   What's a matter?

Blanche   What's a matter, you're making some really bad choices and now I gotta sit here and watch you ruin your life and I don't wanna be involved, OK? *I told you that!*

Lily *looks at her, hurt and surprised.*

Lily   I'm . . . I'm not making bad / choices

Blanche   Did you hear what I said, I don't want to get involved.

Lily   Why? I'm making bad choices – because – I'm having a *family?*

Beat.

Blanche   You're *sixteen.*

Lily   I'm *married.*

Blanche   Maybe that was a mistake?

Lily   My mother got married at my age. Was that a mistake?

Blanche   You're a teenager and you're married to a middle-aged man – and now you want to have *kids*? /

Lily (*venom*)   I'm not a *lesbian* I can *have* them.

Blanche *grabs her book, switches off the lamp.*

Lily (*suddenly stranded*)   Where are you going?

Blanche   Just don't throw your life on the rubbish heap alright?

Lily   I don't think *this* is a rubbish heap.

Blanche (*gesturing to all the white stuff*)   Honey you live in an *igloo*!

Lily   So do *you.*

Blanche   Look: I'm grateful to have / this

Lily   Grateful means you keep your mouth *shut.*

Beat.

Blanche   No: *grateful* means you help someone who's helped you. (*Real feeling.*) Now you helped me, didn't you, you got me this job. (*Beat.*) And I need this job. I *need* this job. (*Beat.*) So now I want to help you.

Lily (*weakly*)   My family helps me.

Blanche   Your Family.

Lily   Ye.

Blanche   Is that what you believe?

Lily   Yes, they help me.

Blanche   Help you.

*She holds **Lily**'s face in her hands.*

Lily (*weaker*)   Yes.

Blanche   That's what you believe?

Lily *looks at **Blanche**; she's inexplicably and suddenly sad now. She nods yes weakly.*

Lily (*holding back tears*)   Why? You think they . . . they don't *like* me?

[STOP]

Blanche *very suddenly grabs **Lily** – tight. This is desperate, compulsive, out of measure – she's not in control of it.*

Blanche   Don't let these people decide your life for you, don't be a victim! *You* make the decision, *you* do it!

Lily *looks in her eyes, frightened and very curious.*

Blanche (*very, very vulnerable*)   You could make yourself a whole other person; it's right there Right in front of you . . . don't let them ruin / it.

Ike *has entered down the stairs, wearing only pajama bottoms. He watches them, unseen.*

Ike (*to **Lily***)   What are you doing?

Lily (*startled*)   Oh. I /

Ike   Why are you still up.

*He notices she's been crying. He looks at **Blanche** – caught.*

Long pause.

Lily   We were talking.

Ike   Come to bed.

Lily   Good night.

Blanche   And happy birthday.

Lily   Don't forget to. Uh. Pick up that stuff from – that cleaners.

Blanche *smiles a taut smile.* **Lily** *goes upstairs.* **Blanche** *stands there.* **Ike** *glowers at her – it's dreadfully uncomfortable. Eventually he turns around and walks upstairs.* **Blanche** *is left, solitary, still.*

Eight

Shelly *and* **JoJo***'s house.*

They have **Ike** *and* **Lily** *over for dinner*

They're eating pot roast with chopsticks.

Shelly   The tap water's not koshah!

Beat.

Ike   Wha??

Shelly   The rabbi said there's *crustaceans* /

Ike   in the *tap* / water?

Shelly   *micro*-crustaceans /

JoJo   Lobsters – Crabs – *Micro* /

Shelly (*to* **Lily**)   (Stop-playing-with-your-hands) /

JoJo   Only bottled water you / could drink

Shelly (*to* **Ike**)   You're not using your chopstick right.

JoJo   I'm using it / right.

Shelly   You hold it between this finger and this finger not that / finger and this finger

JoJo   I'm holding it between this finger and / this finger

Shelly   I said NOT that finger THIS finger.

[STOP]

They eat in silence. **Shelly** *monitors* **JoJo**.

Shelly   How's the baby situation?

Ike *looks at* **Lily**.

Lily   (Adunknow.)

They eat.

JoJo   I'll tell you one thing, my kids are movin to Israel; they're moving to Israel and they're joining the freakin Israeli army.

Lily *looks at him, then goes back to playing with her food, lost in thought and feeling deeply out of place. A beat.*

Ike (*bragging somewhat*)   You know what's not kosher?: Snickers bars.

They eat.

Shelly   Snickers and M&Ms.

Ike *darts a look to* **Shelly**, *scandalized*.

Ike   HEEE!

He covers his mouth.

JoJo   And Twix!

Shelly *looks over to* **JoJo** *dismissively*.

Shelly   Ca-an Twix.

Shelly *goes back to eating.*

Lily   You want your *kid* to be in the *army*!

JoJo   What?

Shelly   Israeli.

JoJo (*hip-hop posturing*)   Kill the palefreakin*sti*nians yo!

Beat. **Lily** *just stares at him, disbelieving.*

Lily   You're not even Israeli.

Ike *puts down his fork, turns to her.*

Ike   It's the Jewish *state.*

Lily   But we're Arabs.

Shelly (*makes a face*)   We're not Arabs you gazzcase.

Beat.

Lily   Gramma speaks *Arabic.*

Shelly   Ca-an she's a old lady.

Beat.

Lily   Well, would you kill your own relatives? Because that's / what

JoJo   WE'RE NOT PALESTINIANS IDIOT – ah

Lily   We're Ara – /

Shelly   They're *terrorists.*

Beat.

Finish your silvertip.

Shelly *picks up her chopsticks and eats. Pause.*

Lily (*quiet indignation*)   We're Arabs /

Shelly   We're *Jews* dibeh, you know what Jewish is?

Lily   We have melanin in our skin. We come from the Iberian *Peninsula.*

Beat.

Ike   The *what*??

Lily   WE'RE SPANIARDS FROM THE IBERIAN PENINSULA.

Beat.

Ike   Where are you learning this?

Lily   Don't you know your own *history*? that's who you *are*.

Ike (*sarcasm*)   Oh, really, so who *am* I?

Eyeballing her. A beat.

Lily   There was an inquisition /

Ike   *Yeah:* and they murdered JEWS /

Lily   And then we moved to Syria and became Arabs /

JoJo   I /

Ike   Who's telling you this.

[STOP]

Lily (*playing with her food*)   We're not white /

Ike   Shut up.

Beat.

Lily   We're Iberian / people fr –

Ike (*threat*)   SHUT: UP.

They eat. Long silence.

JoJo (*to* **Shelly**)   Did you get your passport?

Shelly *doesn't answer.*

Ike   I like the roast.

Shelly   Silvertip.

JoJo (*his mouth full*)   Tendah.

They eat.

Lily   What passport.

Shelly (*to* **JoJo**)   Don't play with that.

Lily   Where are you going?

Shelly   China *dibeh.*

Lily   You're going?

She looks at **Ike***. He doesn't look at her.*

Shelly   I wanna try kung pao steak. /

JoJo   IT'S NOT KOSHER I TOLD YOU!

Shelly   I wanna try certain restaurants, I wanna show you my fodors.

Lily (*to* **Shelly**)   You're going to China?

Shelly (*to* **JoJo**)   Djousee my fodors?

JoJo   "Buddha's delight."

Shelly   Oh I'm gonna miss my lessons at Padegat Could you tell Gerard? Oh and how's your backhand, is your wrist bettah?

Lily (*trance*)   My . . .

Pause.

Shelly   Your wrist?

Ike   Honey –

Ike *touches* **Lily***'s shoulder – she pushes him off and quickly exits.*

Ike   Whereyagoin?

He goes after her.

Shelly (*to* **JoJo**)   And I want a Mao suit.

JoJo   Aright.

Ike   WHERE YA GOIN?

Shelly   *You get bargains* /

JoJo   ARIGHT.

Shelly (*to* **JoJo**, *pointing at her book*)   Look at my fodors, *I want that!!*

Loud music.

Nine

Lily *and* **Blanche**.

Morning, a few days later, the living room.

Blanche *is looking out of the window, cleaning.* **Lily** *sits back on the sofa, listless and out of sorts.*

Blanche   Look at that cloud, it's like those cathedrals. I'd love to see those glistening white domes and minarets wouldn't you?

Lily   You want gum?

Blanche   Rome, Istanbul, I don't know I'd like to travel.

Lily   I thought you lived in Paris.

Blanche   I . . . I did.

Lily   So didn't you see em / then?

Blanche   I loved jogging the perimeter of the Jardin du Luxembourg and sometimes the Bois de Boulogne but I got shin splints 'cause the ground was unpaved it had rocks and things (oh, I miss bell) /

Lily   Who?

Blanche   hooks I told you about her She's a girl I'm friendly with she's like . . . well we were kind of close at one point.

Lily   Is she a philosopher?

Blanche   She doesn't believe in labels (neither does my other friend Luce).

Lily   Who's /

Blanche   A feminist, this other girl I know from France? You seem out of sorts.

Pause. **Blanche** *peers out the window.*

Lily (*glum*)   Did you get your teaching job?

Blanche   "I like a nice view but I like to sit with my back to it." That's a line from a book.

Beat.

Blanche *turns to see a rather enervated, depressed* **Lily**.

Blanche   What's wrong?

Lily   Headache.

Blanche   When's your tennis lesson?

Lily   You know any songs in Spanish?

Blanche   You gotta find something to do, Lily. Otherwise you're gonna fester. "Lilies that fester smell far worse than weeds." That's Shakespeare.

Blanche *produces aspirin, water, hands them to* **Lily**. **Lily** *takes the aspirin and drinks the water down.*

Lily (*plays with some taffy, stretches it out*)   Ikey's plane was delayed He called Something with the propellah.

Blanche   How long's he gonna be gone?

Lily   Two weeks, he went to China.

Blanche   Hip hip.

Lily (*sad*)   He said not to come.

Blanche   Will the mice play?

Lily   Will you read to me?

Blanche (*giving in*)   *Fine.*

Lily   Could I snuggle up on your lap?

Blanche   *No.*

Lily   *Please?*

Blanche   *Fine.*

Lily (*vulgar command*)   Play with my haih!

Blanche (*minstrelsy*)   Yes Miss Daisy /

Lily (*holds up* **Blanche***'s purse*)   I like when you call me that. Zat your bag?

Blanche   Uh-huh.

Lily   Stunning-h.

Lily *pushes* **Blanche***'s hand on to her head, and uses her hand to play with her own hair – as if to train her – then looks up admiringly.*

Blanche (*reads from Keats*)   "Ode on a Grecian Urn":

Lily   Ert.

Blanche   What "Ert"?

More hand training.

(*Reads.*)
  Thou still unravish'd bride of quietness,
    Thou foster-child of Silence and slow Time,
  Sylvan historian, who canst thus express
    A flowery tale more sweetly / than our rhyme:

Lily   You have nice cuticles.

Blanche   What? Uh – Oh – I bite them. (*Continues reading.*)
  What men or gods are these? What maidens loth?
  What mad pursuit? What struggle / to escape?

Lily (*speaking over her*)   That's from nerves. Sometimes I bite the inside of my cheeks – is that weeid?

Lily *pulls a little talisman out of* **Blanche***'s purse.*

Blanche (*continues reading*):
  What struggle to escape?
  What pipes and timbrels? What wild ecstasy? /

Lily (*holds up talisman*)   whatsat? /

Blanche (*grabs it, shoves it back in*)   *Stop goin through my things!* I thought you wanted me to read.

Lily   I do. What's this from?

Blanche   Keats.

Lily   It's boring.

Blanche   Oh *please* /

Lily   Poems and things: *ERT.*

Blanche   It's not *boring.*

Lily   It makes me tired.

Blanche   Is beauty boring?

Lily   Yes.

Blanche   Is *life* / boring?

Lily   I bought a new stunning belt with gold *pieces.*

Exasperated pause.

Blanche   You know what? You have to develop your aesthetics.

Lily (*abstracted*)   Why?

Blanche   Cuz the apprehension of beauty is an essential part of being *human,* that's *why.* "Beauty is Truth, Truth Beauty."

Lily   I know: but beauty is *boring* – like I look at like a flower and I go: "Ye, petals, ca-an!"

Blanche   It's not just / petals!!

Lily   And plants – I *hate* them, I hate watering them, you get dirt all over the place from the water from when it leaks out and you track it on the *floah!*

Blanche *stares at her in disbelief.*

Lily (*rifles through candy*)   Hee, I love gummy worms, I get naushus from them but-h. I like souah. (*Eats*) I like souah patch. I get naushus but-h.

Blanche *stares at her.*

Lily   What.

Blanche   Do you want me to read or not?

Pause.

   What pipes and timbrels? What / wild

Lily   Could you clean behind the refrigerator?

Blanche (*slams down her book*)   You have the *attention* span of an *aphid.*

Lily   Thehe's *mold*!

[STOP]

Blanche *bolts up to clean, picks up a rag.*

Lily   *What's a aphid?* /

Blanche   (Heard of a dictionary?)

Lily   Tickle my arm!

Blanche (*throws down the rag*)   *I gotta go on break* /

Lily   The whole day is your break.

Blanche   Excuse you?!

Lily   You're lazy You don't do any work.

Blanche   Because you keep dragging me over to read you poems and play with your frizzy hair /

Lily   (I'm-using-hot-oil-treatments.)

Blanche   I just want to get *by* – Is that alright?

Lily   I thought you said you wanted to help me.

Blanche   I just want to get by: Is that *OK* with you? Can I get *by?*

[STOP]

Lily   You have an attitude problem.

Blanche (*thrown*)   I have a *what*?

Lily (*crossing her arms*)   It's not workin out –

Blanche   Don't you know that ALL black people have an attitude problem.

Lily (*ingenuous*)   Yeah but why?

Blanche (*minstrelsy*)   Well, you know dat just how we are! Druggies, welfare mothahs, dat's just how it is for us black folk – *we sho don't know any betta*!

Lily   You don't have to be so whiney about everything. Oprah doesn't whine.

Blanche   You need to be *slapped* /

Lily   You leave grime on the bath / tile!

Blanche   *Where's Ike Turner when you need / him!*

Lily   Pack your / things

Blanche   And your damn husband needs to take anger management classes.

Lily   He has *mood* swings and I *love* him for his mood swings! And you're a very nasty *girl* /

Blanche   Actually I'm not a GIRL.

Lily   I /

Blanche   And I'm not YOUR girl, I'm my own *woman* and I kicked and bit and screamed and ripped people apart to BE that so do not FUCK: WITH ME.

[STOP]

(Sorry-I-don't-know-what-came-over-me.)

Lily *is breathing rapidly, she's not well.*

Blanche   Are. Are you –

Lily   (Could you get my Ativan.)

Blanche   Are you alright?

Lily *slumps, dizzy, over to the sofa, covers her face, breathes heavy. Almost a whimpering.* **Blanche** *runs to* **Lily**'s *purse, grabbing her Ativan, gets her water, etc.*

Pause.

Blanche   I'm sorry. I didn't mean to /

Lily *(looks up; she's terrified)*   I don't want to be alone.

Beat.

Blanche *(smiling kindly)*   We're *all* alone sweetie.

Lily   I'm *not.*

Blanche   OK.

Lily   I'm not alone.

Beat.

Blanche   You can rest your head on my lap.

Lily *does. Beat.*

Lily   Will you tickle my arm?

Blanche *tickles her arm.*

Lily   You're not really fired *Anna Maria.*

Blanche *smiles. She plays with* **Lily**'s *hair for a while.*

Blanche   Takin the pills?

Lily *nods.*

Blanche   And you popped em out and put em in the Midol bottle like I said?

Lily   Ye.

Blanche   Can't miss a day, even when he's gone, OK?

Lily *looks up at her lovingly.*

Lily   Thank you. Blanche.

Blanche (*smiles*)   What'd you call me?

Lily   You have such a nice face.

Blanche (*laughs; a little shy*)   Oh, please.

Lily   You do, you have good bone structure.

Blanche (*giggles awkwardly*)   Uhhh . . . whatever.

Lily   You have high cheekbones.

Blanche   Thanks.

Lily   Does that prevent you from sleeping in certain positions?

Blanche *looks at* **Lily***, laughs. The laughter subsides. Pause.*

Blanche (*surprisingly flirtatious*)   I'm adept at many positions.

Lily *has no idea what that means but knows it's some kind of pick-up line.* **Blanche** *snaps out of it, sits up.*

Blanche (*panicked, defusing*)   Uh. Oh – Oh You-know-who-has-good-bone-structure? Iman.

[STOP]

Lily *instinctively leans in and kisses* **Blanche***.* **Blanche** *leans in for a second, then pushes her off, stands.*

Blanche (*smiling awkwardly*)   Oh, OK, no thank you. Uh –

Lily*, like a magnet, springs up and is on her, glued to her face.* **Blanche** *tries to speak, her voice muffled by the kiss. She works to push* **Lily** *off. This doesn't work, not even a little.*

Act Two: The Pleasure of the Text

One

Blanche *and* **Lily**.

Blanche's *room.*

Music playing softly in the background, maybe something 1980s.

They're tasting wines. There's a bunch of wine bottles out – they're both slightly tipsy.

Their intimacy is significantly evolved here.

Blanche Swish.

Lily *swishes.*

Blanche Through the teeth. Slurp.

Lily *gargles.*

Blanche It's not Listerine, honey. Watch: *comme ça.*

She slurps. **Lily** *slurps.*

Blanche What do you feel?

Lily Firmness?

Blanche Are you asking me or telling me.

Lily Aduknow!

Blanche Feel it evaporate in your retronasal passage /

Lily (*wine in mouth*) OK /

Blanche (No swallow first.)

Lily I taste . . . burnt match?

Blanche Good /

Lily (And grass?)

Blanche What else?

Lily   Can we just drink?

Blanche   You don't want to get too drunk.

Lily   I do.

Blanche   The French don't drink to get drunk /

Lily   (I'm Jewish.) *What's this?*

Blanche   Châteauneuf du Pape.

Lily   S'it good?

Blanche   1950 that's a great year This is an excellent vineyard –

Lily   It is?

Blanche   Microclimatic Small yields No this is *incroyable* ooh grrrrrrl (here sniff).

She does.

Lily   It's . . . cheeky.

Blanche (*laughing*)   What's that mean?

Lily   I don't know.

Blanche   You're cheeky.

A whiff of sexual tension; **Blanche** *pulls back.*

That's a '99 Leroy.

Lily   Shoof.

Blanche   They're one of the great producers of white burgundy /

She sniffs.

Lily   You know so much /

Blanche   (Oak on the nose.) I make it my business to know. If you make something your business, you know it inside out.

Lily   I know you inside out.

Beat.

Blanche (*cynical laughter*)   That's what you think.

Lily (*playfully brazen*)   That's what I *know*.

Pause.

Blanche   Don't you know it's dangerous to trust people you don't know very well.

Lily   I feel light.

Pause.

Blanche   You want something to hold on to, that's all. You haven't found yourself, that's why. You don't know who you are, you haven't found yourself.

Lily (*drunken flirting*)   Who am I?

She gets close to her face.

Who am I?

She kisses her. **Blanche** *pulls away.*

Lily   What.

Blanche   Nothing; you remind me of someone.

Lily   Did she love you?

Pause.

Blanche   Not like that.

Pause.

Lily   Because *I* love you.

[STOP]

Blanche   *No.*

Lily (*almost weeping*)   I *love* you /

Blanche   You – ha ha. Y – you're just a tadpole /

Lily   I'm not a tadpole!

Blanche (*shooing*)   Swim away little fishie you're too young.

Lily   But /

Blanche   (Go find a nice Syrian girl / and)

Lily   NO.

Blanche   I am *forty-three*.

Lily   So?

Blanche   So I'm not going to take advantage of a sixteen- / year-old girl.

Lily   (Seventeen) you're not taking / advant –

Blanche (*resisting*)   It's not *ethical* /

Lily   I know you like me.

Blanche   Once is OK, but that's it; I'm not embroiling you in this.

Lily   In *what*?

Beat.

What about Adrienne Rich /

Blanche   She's passé.

Beat.

Lily (*assured*)   I think you're in love with me.

A shift.

Blanche   When's hubby comin back?

Lily   He's in the Orient.

Blanche   I know *that* but / when's he

Lily   A few days.

Pause.

Blanche   Let's just sit here with our little fluted glasses and chop it up alright?

Lily   Chop what up?

Blanche   Talk.

Blanche *downs a glass of wine, pours herself another.*

Lily   Where'd you grow up?

Blanche   Moved around.

Lily   No but – when you were adopted.

Blanche   I was twelve.

Lily   And / you

Blanche   And I moved to Philadelphia /

Lily   Liberty bell? /

Blanche   With the crack, yeah /

Lily   And then you lived in the homeless shelter?

Blanche *(regretting telling her this)*   That was later.

Beat.

Lily *(bright)*   I never met anyone from a homeless shelter!!

Blanche *(dry)*   Yeah, tick it off.

She downs some wine.

Lily   And were your parents nice? What were they like?

Blanche *(frozen smile)*   I don't want to talk about him.

Lily   Who?

Blanche   I mean *them.*

Lily   Why?

Pause.

Blanche   Cuz it's the past It's an illusion.

Beat.

Lily   But you said you have to know the past.

Blanche   Yeah but /

Lily   You said if you don't know history you become its victim – you're contradicting yourself.

Blanche   "I'm not contradictory: I am *dispersed*": Roland Barthes.

Lily   Ooh I got a flash card fa him /

Blanche   Keep up the flash cards.

Beat.

Lily (*waifish curiosity*)   What were their names?

Blanche   Who?

Lily   Your parents?

Beat. Then wearily:

Blanche (*sighing*)   Rich and Audrey.

Lily   "Rich and Audrey" /

Blanche   White /

Lily   "Audrey White" that's a pretty name /

Blanche   No: *They* were *white*.

Lily   Were they nice?

Beat. **Blanche** *doesn't look at her.*

Blanche   Will you stop *asking* / me that?

Lily   I'm / curious

Blanche (*snaps at her*)   NO they weren't nice they were fucking *horrible* is that what you want to hear?! Fingers on me middle a the night in my room night after night Think anyone did a goddamn thing to STOP it? "You're *black* You're a *woman* You're at the bottom of the *world*." Know how many times I heard that shit?!

Lily *takes a sip of wine, discomfited. Long awkward pause.*

Blanche   (*forcing a tiny smile*) So – so did you. Didja ever think about – girls before?

Lily (*softening*)   Not before this.

Blanche   Not even *once*?

Beat.

Lily   Well once.

[STOP]

Blanche   OK-wait-let-me-get-comfortable /

Lily   When I was in the dressing room /

Blanche   Where /

Lily   Loehmann's /

Blanche (*blunt*)   What's *Loehmann's* /

Lily   (You get bras and coats) /

Blanche   Oh.

Lily   There's a public dressing room /

Blanche (*swirling her wine*)   They say a public dressing room is a dyke's business office /

Lily   (Really?) /

Blanche   (No.)

Lily   So my mother used to take / me

Blanche   Loooooehmann's /

Lily   And I was really young, and I saw – you know; "that stuff."

Beat.

Blanche   "*Stuff*"?

Lily   That. Yeah.

Blanche (*amused*)   And you liked it.

Lily   Aduknow.

Blanche   Well *did* you or *didn't* you?

Beat.

Lily   I wasn't aware that I liked it? But . . . I think looking back? . . . Ye. /

Blanche (*mock warning*)   But don't look back /

Lily   *What?*

Blanche (*smiling at her inside joke*)   Pillar of salt, etceteras –

Lily   Oh.

Blanche   But we'll *all* go to hell now WHEEEEEE /

Lily   I don't feel good /

Blanche   (It could be the sulfites Are you asthmatic?) /

Lily   I feel like I could fall.

Blanche   You're just drunk.

Lily   You're not.

Blanche   I drink all the time. It's the law of diminishing returns /

Lily   Could you play with my haih?

Blanche (*drinks*)   (Needs more of a backbone) /

Lily   Tickle my arm.

Blanche *demurs at first, but eventually does. She grazes* **Lily***'s arm lightly with her fingernails. There's real longing.* **Lily** *starts looking through* **Blanche***'s purse.*

Lily   You have mints?

Blanche   I don't think so.

Lily (*pulls something out from her purse*)   Whassis?

Blanche   A pad. *Don't look through my stuff.*

Lily *pulls out a gun and sits up, alarmed.*

Lily   *What's that?*

Blanche   *Gimme that.*

She grabs the gun away from **Lily**.

Girl's gotta protect herself.

Blanche *shoves the gun back in her purse, moves the purse away from* **Lily**. **Lily** *settles back into* **Blanche**'s *lap.*

Lily   I'm drunk. I want a mint-h!

Blanche *goes back to grazing* **Lily**'s *arm.*

Lily (*relaxing a bit*)   I want a mint.

Blanche *looks at her, strokes her arm. It's love.*

Blanche   So were you in love at first sight?

Lily   With who?

Blanche   Hubby.

Lily   I was twelve. He used to buy me gum.

Blanche   Didn't the age difference bother your parents?

Lily   My father is much older than my mother.

Blanche   Where'd you meet?

Lily   My cousin's wedding, Julie, she drives a Mitsubishi Galant.

Blanche   That's nice.

Lily   (I like Jaguars) /

Blanche (*a bit of self-torture*)   And you started dating?

Lily   He took me for ice cream.

Blanche (*curled irony*)   And did you get all *excited* when you'd see him?

Lily   Aduknow.

Blanche (*playful mocking*)   Did you think, like, "*Oooh Pralines and Cream!*"?

Lily (*scrunched face*)   It was more I was nervous; my stomach hurt. I think I was excited, I was pretty young. I'm more matured now. Then I was a baby. Sometimes I would feel sick.

Blanche   A good sick?

Lily (*guileless, a bit more drunk*)   Well I'd throw up. But I'm more matured now; I don't throw up anymore; I got a lot of stomach viruses; my mother told me I had a sensitive stomach.

Blanche   And how did he propose?

Lily *is lost in thought. There's a shift into melancholy.*

Blanche   How did he propose / to

Lily   But I don't think it's right when people trick people.

Blanche   You / what –

Lily   I don't like that It's not right.

Blanche   Who tricked you?

Lily (*drunk*)   NO I didn't say that, you don't listen: What I said was I don't think it's RIGHT to trick someone.

Blanche *backs off. She takes a sip of wine.*

Lily   When did you first . . . have . . . like . . . sex or whatever.

Blanche (*lying*)   I can't remember.

Lily   How could you not remember. How old / were

Blanche   *I can't remember.*

[STOP]

Lily   Did. Did people tell you . . . what it was?

Blanche (*a dark undercurrent*)   I kinda happened upon it.

Pause.

Lily   I thought it was if you touched someone a certain way. Or. If someone *touched* you? (*Pause.*) I was ignorant.

Blanche *looks at her.*

Blanche   No one talked about it to you?

Lily   And he said I wasn't a *virgin* anymore? So then I said that I *would* marry him. Because . . . my reputation would be ruined.

Pause.

(*Tearing up.*) But then I *was* a virgin . . .

Blanche's *expression slowly turns steely.*

Long pause.

Blanche   And you never said anything?

Lily (*still shaken*)   My reputation would / be

Blanche (*punishing*)   So you're a victim.

Lily   No . . . I /

Blanche   Yeah you are.

Lily   I'm not a /

Blanche   You think cuz you ain't equipped to handle life you ain't accountable?

[STOP]

You think people are gonna feel sorry for you? "Oh poor baby, no one raised her, no one gave a shit, so now *we* gotta help her?" – because *nobody* cares if you lose, the world's full a losers! Losers get *punished* for being losers, nobody fucking cares – it's the *winners* people care about! You gotta rip yourself up and start / over – !

Lily *shudders, jerks her head to the left, sharp intake of breath – it's the "ghost."*

Lily   It's here –

Blanche   What?

Lily (*panic*)   *That* – it's – It's in here The – I just saw it again.

Blanche   Where?

Lily *is still, alert; her eyes dart nervously.* **Blanche** *looks at* **Lily***, gets increasingly spooked. She looks out, sensing a presence in the room. Her breathing gets unsteady. The silence is fraught with terror; they're both too frightened to move. It goes on like this for a bit.* **Lily** *tentatively relaxes her posture a little bit.*

Lily   I . . . I think it's gone now.

She approaches **Blanche** *from behind, touches her lightly on the shoulder.* **Blanche** *gasps, shudders, jerks her head.*

Lily   It's only me.

Blanche *turns to see her.*

Blanche (*denial*)   I don't believe in ghosts.

She turns away from her; ineptly tries to make light of it.

You givin me the creeps.

Lily (*hurt*)   But . . . I . . . I *saw* it.

Beat.

Blanche (*feigned indifference*)   They can't haunt you if you don't acknowledge em; pretend it's not there.

Lily *looks at her, not quite comforted by this.*

Lily   Will you sleep with me tonight?

Blanche *hesitates. Eventually she nods yes.*

Lily   We can sleep here in your room. I don't like to be alone.

Blanche (*throws her a T-shirt*)   Sleep in this.

They get dressed for bed. **Lily**'*s having some trouble with the T-shirt.*

Lily   I don't like it when you yell at me.

Blanche   I didn't yell at you.

Lily (*drunk*)   You did, you said "I'M AT THE BOTTOM OF THA EARTH I'M BLACK."

Blanche   (Sorry) /

Lily   I don't like that I get scahed.

Blanche   I'm just worried about stuff; it's not you. I have a lot of. Uh – things on my mind.

Lily (*a caper*)   Like what-h? maybe I could help!

Blanche (*lying*)   My. My – loans and stuff are due.

Lily   From college?

Blanche   I used up my deferments they said. They're coming after me.

Lily   But we're paying you

Blanche   Yeah enough for food and *c'est tout*. (*Bright.*) I'll be OK – I'm just

Lily   (You'll pay them back.)

Blanche (*forcing a smile*)   I'll get a teaching job soon enough.

Pause.

Lily   Well. I have this checkbook – why don't I write you one.

Blanche   One what?

Lily   *Check* dibeh!

Beat.

Blanche   *No.*

Lily   I *want* to.

Blanche   It's not your responsibility.

Lily (*sincere, lovingly*)   *You're* my responsibility.

Long pause.

Blanche (*moved, despite herself*)   You don't even *know* me.

Lily   He said I should write you checks, how much is it for?

Lily *opens her purse and pulls out her checkbook.*

Blanche   You're crazy, I'm not taking *money* from you!

Lily   You helped me; now let me help you.

Blanche *looks at her.*

Lily *fills out and signs a check.*

Lily (*girlish*)   Look Don't I forge his signature good?

Lily *hands the check to her.* **Blanche** *looks at it. Slowly she takes it, looks down at it. It's real. She laughs. She looks at* **Lily** *and shakes her head. She looks down at the check again. She begins to weep – the tears come from a deep, deep, wounded place.*

Blanche   That's eight thousand dollars.

Lily (*bright*)   Now you can stay!

Blanche   I can't take this from you!

Lily   Yes you can.

Pause.

Blanche (*embarrassed laughter*)   *Gracias* Lily.

Lily   *De nada.*

Blanche   *Ojalá no se enoje.*

Lily   *El no se enterará.*

Blanche (*laughs*)   I hope you're right.

Lily *kisses* **Blanche** *on the cheek, a quick peck.* **Lily** *fluffs a pillow.* **Blanche** *gets under the covers.*

Lily   Let's go to bed I got a tennis lesson in the morning –

Blanche   I got laundry.

Snap blackout.

Two

Five days later, morning. The living room.

Blanche *is repainting the minimalist walls.* **Ike***'s back from China, doing the crossword. He's wearing a suit; he looks especially groomed. He is wound up and angry.*

Lily *enters, she's on cloud nine, a woman in love.*

Lily   I finished unpacking your stuff.

Ike   What?

Lily   Welcome back!

Ike *continues with his crossword, not looking at her.* **Lily** *looks at him, cheery.*

Ike   Stop looking at me.

Lily   What?

Ike (*not looking up*)   You keep lookin at me funny.

Lily   You look nice. You never wear suits to work.

Ike (*weirdly uncomfortable*)   I got a meeting.

Lily   With Jo?

Beat.

I gotta meet with some people.

Beat.

Lily   So how was it? did you see the wall?

Ike   That's Germany /

Lily   *Yeah* and also CHINA.

Beat.

I like that suit / on you

Ike (*fillip of hostility*)   WILL YOU SHUT UP ABOUT MY SUIT, I CAN WEAR A SUIT IF I WANNA WEAR A SUIT!

Lily *looks at him, smiling indifferently.*

Lily (*irony*)   Sexy when you get mad.

Ike *knows he's insulted her but can't figure out how.* **Blanche** *smiles to herself and continues to paint.* **Lily** *picks up a book: Barthes's* S/Z. *She reads.*

Ike   Hear any news? /

Lily (*terse, not looking up*)   I'm not pregnant.

Beat.

Ike   You spoke to the / doctor?

Lily (*perfunctory*)   There's nothing wrong with me /

Ike   Well there's nothing wrong with *me.*

She reads. **Ike** *glowers at her.*

Ike   Did you hear what I said /

Lily   "There's nothing wrong with me."

Ike (*turns to face her*)   Where were you last night?

Lily   Here.

Ike   I woke up you were gone.

Lily   I couldn't sleep.

Blanche (*repainting, cheery*)   We're running outta "snowball."

Lily (*gets up to exit*)   I'll get more.

Ike   Let the G get it.

*A little flirtatious pantomime behind **Ike**'s back:* **Lily** *winks seductively at* **Blanche**.

Blanche *smiles flirtatiously and licks her lips.*

Ike, *sensing something, turns his head;* **Blanche** *instantly resumes her default painting position;* **Lily** *tries to act casual.*

Lily   What –

Ike   Why don't you –

He cuts off mid-sentence. They resume flirting. He quickly shifts back around, eyeballs them.

Lily (*caught*)   I'm not doing anything –

Ike   *What was that?*

Lily (*innocently*)   *What?*

Ike *slowly pivots back and resumes the crossword.* **Blanche** *giggles to herself.* **Lily** *pretends to be interested in* **Ike**. **Blanche** *flashes her tit as* **Lily** *exits.* **Lily** *tries to stifle her laughter.*

Ike, *sensing something, shifts abruptly to look at her and* **Blanche** – *who narrowly escapes exposure. He's getting angry.*

Ike (*punishing her*)   Get me cream.

Blanche   It's on the table.

Ike   It's not on the table.

Blanche *walks over and takes the cream, which is three inches away from him, and positions it two inches from him – then flashes her best "innocent helper" smile. She goes back to painting.*

Ike *gets up to feed the goldfish.*

Ike (*to Kitty*)   Hiiiiiiiiiiiiiiieeeeeeeeee. Hiiii honey!!
Awwwwwwwwww.

Blanche *looks over at him. She rolls her eyes. He senses her looking at him and quickly jerks his head to catch her. She deftly resumes painting. He sidles over to her. He leans against the wall, almost hovering.*
Blanche *continues to paint.*

Ike · Nice bracelets. .

Blanche   What, oh these Oh they're bangles.

Ike   Very sharp, where'd you get em?

Blanche (*lying*)   The mall.

She continues to paint.

Ike (*to* **Blanche**)   You didn't by any chance mention anything to anyone did you?

Blanche   Bout what?

Ike   When you were in my office . . . ? You didn't happen to see anything?

Blanche   When I was cleaning?

Ike   Mention anything?

[STOP]

You wouldn't screw me would you?

Blanche *looks him up and down.*

Blanche (*dryly*)   I wouldn't.

Ike   Did you open your big mouth?

Blanche *notices that half his suit is covered in white paint.*

Ike   You look nervous.

Blanche   I. Your suit –

Ike (*facetious*)   What I don't MATCH?

Blanche   No – You –

Ike *realizes he has paint on his suit.* **Lily** *enters holding a paint can.*

Lily   I can't find the – (HEEE.)

Ike (*points at* **Blanche**)   Why does she have to do that?

Lily (*recites dutifully*)   It's minimalism.

Ike   You think it's funny?

Lily   The decorator / said

Ike (*upset*)   IT'S NOT FUNNY!

Lily   I don't think it's funny!

Ike *exits.*

Lily (*calls after him*)   I-don't-think-it's –

She and **Blanche** *lock eyes. They laugh and laugh mischievously, but there's real intimacy.*

The laughing grows uncontrollable, hysterical. Eventually it is drowned out by the sound of a woman speaking French – a language-lesson CD.

Three

Bedroom, night.

Ike *is going over receipts,* **Lily** *is practicing French. The CD overlaps their conversation.*

Tape   I am hungry: *"J'ai faim."*

Lily   *"J'ai faim."*

Tape   I am thirsty: *"Jai soif."*

Lily   *"J'ai soif."*

Tape   I am frightened: *"J'ai peur."*

Ike   I'm missing / money.

Lily   *"J'ai peur."*

Tape   I am cold: *"J'ai froid."*

Lily   *"J'ai"* /

Ike   I'm *missing money.*

Tape   I am hot: *"J'ai chaud."*

Beat.

Lily   From where?

Ike   The *bank.*

Lily   You gave / me a checkbook.

Tape   I am afraid to take the plane: *"J'ai peur de prendre l'avion."*

Ike   You spent eight *grand* in one shot?

Lily   *"J'ai peur de prendre l'avion."*

Ike *slams the CD off.*

Ike   Whaddayou spending eightthousanddollars for.

Pause.

Lily   I needed it.

Ike   For what

Lily   I don't have to tell you.

Ike   THAT'S MY MONEY

Short pause.

Lily   What's yours is mine Right? Isn't that what a marriage is? I take what I want from you and you take what you want / from me.

Ike   Why are you acting this way.

Lily   Because you're a liar.

Ike   How am I a liar?

She turns to him.

Lily   Because I talked to my sister and she told me you stole money from Jo and that they fired you last week. And that's why you're wearing a suit and screaming at me because you keep lying to me. Because you can't bribe me with money because we don't have any money. And no one's gonna hire you because everyone knows you're a thief.

Pause.

Ike   That's bullshit.

Lily   You *knew* she'd tell me.

Beat.

Ike   I didn't steal money. I. I re-allocated it.

Lily   Yeah.

She turns the CD on again; he slams it right off.

Ike   And don't you fucking tell me off. I won't be spoken to by my own wife like this and I'm – HEY. (*Grabs her.*) I'm having a rough week, I don't need to come home to you calling me names.

Silence.

And there are plenny a people who'd kill to work with me so shut your mouth You don't know what you're talking about. You hear me? I know how to run a *business*. That's why you live good because I know what I'm doin.

Lily   Like your father, like how he ran a business?

Ike (*hoarsely*)   Don't talk about him.

Lily   My sister / said

Ike   Your sister's a fucking liar, alright?

Lily   No, you're a liar. You.

Pause.

(*Quiet and so sad.*) You tricked me . . .

[STOP]

He kisses her hair. She's momentarily helpless – he's got power over her.

Ike   I'm gonna take care of you.

Lily   Stop it /

Ike   I'm gonna take care of you . . . daddy's gonna take care of his baby OK?

Lily, *in a single gesture, disentangles herself. She opens a drawer and grabs a bottle of expensive wine.*

Ike   What's that?

She grabs a corkscrew and opens it expertly.

Lily   Keeps the cork intact /

Ike   You don't *drink* /

Lily   I do now, *Pouilly-Fumé*, medium-bodied white /

Ike   Since when do you drink?

Lily   I started a wine cellar.

Ike   IN YOUR DRAWER?

Lily   Anna Maria taught me about *tasting* /

Ike   *Who?!*

Lily (*squinting*)   She's an oenophile.

She swishes; slurps some wine. He looks at her.

Ike   *I don't want you drinking wine* /

Lily (*swirling*)   Honey, cantaloupe /

Ike   You're not old enough / to

Lily   Oh I'm not *old* enough? *Really?* Talk more about that.

Long pause.

I think we should. Get an annulment.

Ike What?

Pause.

She turns, looks right at him.

(*Terrified.*) Who's putting ideas in your head?

Lily I have my *own* ideas.

Ike Is it that *nigger*!

She looks at him, enraged.

[STOP]

Ike Where's my money?

Lily You are an ignorant. Old. Man /

Ike *grabs the glass of wine as she's about to drink it and throws it in her face.*

Ike (*leaning in*)   And you're turning into a spoiled little *brat* I don't like it.

He does push-ups. She's brewing.

Fifteen. Sixteen.

She starts attacking him, hitting him. It barely affects him. She kicks him, etc., but she's slight. He waits until she's out of breath. She's miserable, frustrated, humiliated, angry. He's impassive and his impassivity makes her angrier.

Seventeen. *Don't do that again.*

Pause.

Eighteen. Nineteen. Twenty (I'm warning you.)

Lily *attacks him.* **Blanche** *enters with the laundry.*

Blanche (*smiling obliviously*)   I forgot the whites /

Ike *bolts up.*

Ike WHADAISAY?

Lily *eyeballs him; quiet and confident.*

Lily   You don't have power over me.

[STOP]

He smacks her across the face.

She smacks him right back.

[STOP]

In a single move, he punches **Lily** *square in the face.* **Blanche** *is terrified, paralyzed.*

In the next section they speak quickly over each other, it's a bit chaotic.

Ike   Do NOT touch my person do you hear me, you don't EVER touch me, EVER, do you hear / me

Blanche   I /

Ike   And YOU you just bought a ticket to your own funeral *did you / hear me.*

Lily *(cups her hand over her eye)*   You / hit me

Ike *(to* **Blanche** *)*   You're DEAD, did / you hear me

Blanche   Who / me

Lily   *¿Me lastimó, / viste lo que hizo?*

Blanche   *¿Estas / bien?*

Ike   WHAT DID / YOU SAY TO HER?

Lily   *Tengo que irme de aquí; promete que nos iremos.*

Blanche   I promise /

Ike   WHAT DID / SHE SAY TO YOU??

Lily *(still stunned)*   You hit / me.

Ike *(shame; then to* **Blanche** *)*   Good-bye, back in your / cage

Blanche   I /

Lily   (You / hit me.)

Ike   Get / *out*!

Blanche   Lily /

Ike   GET OUT!!

Snap blackout.

Four

Sounds of tennis balls being lobbed about.

The lounge area of an indoor tennis court.

Lily *and* **Shelly** *in tennis outfits, headbands, sweaty.* **Lily** *is twirling her racquet.*

She has a black eye.

Shelly   The silks were nice. We saw a silkworm farm. A place where they make silkworms. (*Beat.*) I mean not silkworms I mean, HA HA, where the silkworms are. Where they *make silk.* (*Beat.*) I was gagging from the smell. ERT.

Lily   Does it smell?

Shelly   (The silk is nice but-h.)

Lily   My backhand's improving Gerard said.

Shelly   My knee hurts.

A pause as **Lily** *adjusts a string on her racquet.*

Lily   So, how are you feeling?

Shelly   When I was carrying Ricky I was bad, when I had Joey – *Stevie* – but / aduknow

Lily   Do you want something else to drink?

Shelly   I wish they had Sprite; I don't like this OTHAH CRAP-ah.

Beat.

Lily   Do you know anything about Chicago? /

Shelly   Windy /

Lily   You were never theh? /

Shelly (*picks up glass*)   Wisconsin, Ohio, aduknow. (*Sips.*)
You know who's theh – Oprah. (*Sips, then pushes glass away with
histrionic disgust.*) ERT I'm NAUSHUS. You want my lemon?

Pause.

The sounds of tennis balls being lobbed.

You need to be pregnant.

Lily   Yeah.

Shelly   "Yeah."

Beat.

What's with you?

Pause.

Lily   I'm getting an annulment.

Shelly *laughs at her.*

Lily   It's not funny.

Shelly (*dismissing*)   Oh please. The string on my racquet
broke look at this –

Lily   (He stole money.)

Shelly   We'll get the money back.

Lily (*after a beat*)   He *lied.*

Shelly   You're not getting an *annulment.*

Lily   I'm bisexual. I was talking to Blanche that's what she
said.

Lily *sucks on the lemon wedge innocuously.*

Shelly   What's what who said?

Lily   I'm not a lesbian.

Shelly   Who's *Blanche*?

Lily   My maid.

Shelly   Why is your *maid* telling you you're a bisexual?

Pause.

Lily (*regretting telling her*)   Tell me more about the silk farm.

Shelly   Is your *maid* a bisexual?

Lily (*sucking the lemon*)   Lesbian.

Shelly   *Back up /*

Lily   You want gum?

Shelly   NO I DON'T WANT GUM.

Pause.

Lily   I'm moving to Chicago.

Shelly (*laughing*)   With who your *maid*?

Lily   She has tenure track

Shelly (*giddy*)   *Op*-stay already I *caaan't.*

Lily   Northwestern. It's the ivy league.

[STOP]

Shelly *is speechless.*

Lily   She has connections /

Shelly   What is she gonna teach toilet scrubbing?

Lily   Semiotics /

Shelly   OK: *you're not a lesbian /*

Lily   Which is /

Shelly   I-DON'T-WANT-TO-KNOW-WHAT-IT-IS.

Lily   She has a PhD.

Shelly   Yeah she's a freakin genius.

Lily   She quotes poetry do you?

Shelly   No I don't quote POETRY Lilian I'm too busy cleaning up my kids' VOMIT. (*Pause.*) I gotta go to my jeweler It's almost six –

Lily   Wait /

Shelly   You smell: go shower.

Lily (*very tender*)   I love someone; I never had that before.

Shelly *scrutinizes her like meat.*

Shelly   *Shame on you.*

[STOP]

She gets up to leave. **Lily** *grabs her arm.*

Lily   Shel /

Shelly   *I thought you wanted kids.*

Beat.

Lily   I'm on the pill.

Shelly   You're *what*? I thought /

Lily   Don't tell him.

A recognition of **Lily**'s *duplicity slowly registers on* **Shelly**'s *face.*

Shelly   I have to go /

Lily   Please / don't

Shelly   No I don't want to hear this *shit.*

Lily (*heartbroken*)   *Why?*

Shelly   Why, because it's making me SICK. (*Beat.*) I'm *pregnant* and you're making me *sick.*

Lily   I /

Shelly   I was doing you a *favor*. You think JoJo wanted to go
into business with your low-life husband – *that was from me*!
(*Beat.*) And then you spit in my *face*?

Lily   I'm sorry.

Shelly   *Pig.*

Pause.

Lily   I appreciate everything you / and

Shelly (*shaking her head; to herself*)   No I don't *want* your
appreciation Don't *waste it on me.*

Lily *zips up her tennis racquet in its case.*

Lily   I thought we could be . . . *close.*

Shelly (*looks at her – steely*)   You're. Committing. Suicide.

Lily (*feigning bravery*)   People can think what they want /

Shelly   You're not a *fucking* lesbian /

Lily (*quiet tears, but trying to stay composed*)   I'm /

Shelly   And we'll see how you don't care what people think,
we'll see. And don't you DARE come crawling to me on your
hands and knees because I'll kick you right in the throat.
You'll get *nothing.*

Lily (*stunned*)   Don't talk to me like that.

Shelly   How should I talk to you? What do you feel you
deserve? You feel proud of yourself?

Lily   I – I thought I could come to you.

Shelly   *Why?* You think you can bring your filthy news to
me? Do you have such a *low* opinion of me?

Silence.

Lily (*a plea*)   But. I'm. I'm . . . not *happy.*

Shelly   *So be unhappy.*

Lily   Like you?

Shelly   That's right. Like me. You're damn *right* like me –

Lily *exits.*

Shelly   I feel sorry for your husband.

Five

Blanche *and* **Lily**.

The living room, daytime.

Blanche *is dustbusting.* **Lily** *is eating candies and little confections and chatting excitedly.*

Lily   And there were peonies and hydrangeas / and

Blanche   And were they just *petals?*

Lily   No.

Blanche   See?

Blanche *gives her a peck on the cheek.*

Lily   And I became a member of Channel 13!

Lily *produces a tote/duffel bag with the PBS logo emblazoned.*

Blanche   Nice /

Lily   (And-also-they-gave-me-a-comb) /

Blanche   Did you make your / flash cards?

Lily   And there was a flower shaped like – oh what's it called? *(Snap, snap.)* OOLIE.

Blanche   A forsythia?

Lily   No.

Blanche   A daisy?

Lily   A *hyacinth.*

Blanche   Oh "the hyacinth girl."

Lily   What?

Blanche   What? Oh that's / from

Lily   Yeah a flower.

Blanche   Shaped like a hyacinth?

Lily   No.

Blanche (*dustbusting under her feet*)   (Lift.)

Lily (*lifting her feet up*)   No it was – insects – it was like insects, like these. Uh. *Bright* insects, and they were green, and they would form themselves like that, it was very mysterious

Blanche   To escape predators.

Lily   YES.

Blanche   It's not mysterious it's nature survival of the species.

Lily   Oh.

Beat.

Blanche   (Down) How's your eye?

Lily (*putting her feet down*)   Better /

Blanche   Where's Rich?

Lily   What?

Blanche   I mean – hubby.

Lily   Aduknow he stays out late.

Blanche   He's watching me. I keep thinking he's gonna turn a corner and appear outta nowhere He scares me.

Lily   He thinks you got him fired.

Blanche (*laughs, exasperated*)   I was there *one* day.

Lily   Where?

Blanche   His *office*, I'm not *that* good at book-keeping!

Lily   He's paranoid.

Beat.

Blanche   You goin to your sister's?

Lily *doesn't respond, a shift.*

Lily   I'm not talking to her.

Blanche   Why?

Lily   No reason.

Blanche   She loves you.

Lily   She doesn't like *you.*

Blanche (*chipper*)   'cause I'm black and she's racist it's perfectly consistent.

Lily   She said the n word.

Blanche   I heard, I don't mind. It's just a signifier – and what are signifiers?

Lily   Arbitrary /

Blanche   And what is all language?

Lily   Metaphor.

Blanche   Because /

Lily   There's no relationship between things and words /

Blanche   "Necessary" /

Lily   (Necessary) but you keep telling me that she *doesn't* love me.

Blanche   Well – her love is *degraded* but she has good intentions.

Beat.

Lily   She said I was a pig.

Blanche   Why would she say that?

Pause.

Did you quarrel?

Beat.

Lily   I told her.

Blanche   Told her what?

Beat.

(*Senses something.*) Told her what.

She freezes.

Why would you do that.

Beat.

Lily   I wanted to prepare her.

Blanche   For:

Lily   When we go /

Blanche   *Go?*

Lily   To *Chicago*.

Beat.

Blanche (*faint exasperation*)   I don't have that job yet darling.

Lily   You basically have the job.

Blanche   I don't have the job, I told you / I'm –

Lily (*smiles confidently*)   But you'll get it, or you'll get something, it doesn't matter /

Blanche (*snaps*)   It *matters*.

Pause.

You understand what you did? The ramifications? He's gonna haul me right out on my ass the second he finds out.

Lily *looks at her, bemused.*

Lily   But – you don't even *want* to stay here.

Blanche   *Want?* What I "want"? what does that have to do with anything?

Lily   But we can't stay, not after he –

Blanche   Do you know what it is to have nothing? You know how many times I packed my suitcase in the past six months?!

Lily   But – he hit me /

Blanche (*snaps*)   So *what* You think I ain't been *hit* before?!

Lily *tentatively goes to* **Blanche**.

Lily (*deep, profound tenderness*)   I won't let anything happen to you.

Blanche *slowly turns to* **Lily**; *those eyes; it's heartbreaking. A short pause.*

Blanche (*toughness beginning to melt*)   How you gonna protect me. You just a kid.

Short pause.

Lily   I *will.*

Blanche *looks at* **Lily**. *She touches* **Lily**'*s cheek. Softens.* **Blanche** *sees herself in* **Lily**'*s eyes. It's mesmerizing. She smiles a faint smile, tinged with sadness.*

Blanche (*undercurrent of deep worry*)   Know how stupid I was at seventeen? That's when I left home . . . took me years before I figured out what I was doing with my life.

Beat.

Lily (*sweetly encouraging*)   And now you're almost *there.*

Blanche *snaps back into the moment. Nods affirmatively, but it's detached. Her eyes fill with worry, her voice gets a bit higher here.*

Blanche (*deep fear, almost a whisper*)   But the world's a dangerous *place.*

Lily   I'm not scared.

Blanche *is faraway.*

Blanche (*gently and not just pain, sorrow*)   You *say* that but you don't know what it's like. (*Beat.*) You can be hurt and *never* recover. (*Pause; then to herself.*) You think you can end it but it don't end.

Lily   But – you're telling me I have to make *choices.*

Blanche (*snapping out of it*)   But / not

Lily   You're saying don't be a victim – /

Blanche (*a shift*)   I'm. No – /

Lily   That's what *you* / said!

Blanche *turns on* **Lily** *quite suddenly; it's ferocious but she is very still, focused.*

Blanche (*taut, tense*)   *No* I'm saying *stay* – stay *and fight* for something. You gotta take up the damn cudgels, not run away! (*Beat.*) You can walk out that door but you never really leave! You think you do – but you come back to the *same thing* again and again! You need to meet it head on!

Pause.

Lily (*imploring, confused*)   You promised me we'd leave.

Blanche *looks at* **Lily** *– another shift, 180 degrees. Her heart melting, she's instantly filled with guilt over her outburst.*

In a single gesture, she grabs **Lily** *tight, holds her for dear life.*

[STOP]

Blanche *quickly, hungrily covers her with kisses; she's filled with need. Then – abruptly, she stops, looks at* **Lily***, holding her shoulders.*

Blanche (*pain still seeping through, fearful*)   I know honey I know . . . but we gotta look at reality here.

Lily   You're the one not looking at reality!

Blanche   We can't just leave, sweetie.

Lily (*desperate to convince her*)   I have money saved up. We can live on that /

Blanche   Yeah and then what?!

Pause.

Lily (*shakily*)   But . . . I have to make the right choice now . . . That's what you told me, I have to take the right actions.

Blanche *cannot make eye-contact with her.*

Blanche (*impossibly vulnerable*)   I just can't . . .

Lily   Of *course* you can. (*Grasping at straws.*) This is – this is just *irony* . . . You don't need to be here . . . It's – it's just . . . *funny*.

She forges a tiny smile, wishing away the whole nightmare.

Blanche (*almost in tears, very tiny*)   I c-can't – I can't – make myself into what I – w-what you need me to *be*.

Pause. **Lily** *looks at her, perplexed.*

Lily   But . . . I don't want you to *make* yourself – into / anything I

Blanche   LOOK AT ME! I'M A FUCKING FAILURE, WHAT DO YOU WANT FROM ME?!

Lily   That's not true . . . I look up to you /

Lily *goes to comfort her;* **Blanche** *flinches, angry.*

Blanche   Because you don't know anything! Of course I glitter when you look at me! You don't have anything to compare it to! *You have no life experience.* Are you *joking*? (*Pause.*) You *child.* (*Beat. She grabs her face.*) Look at me: I'm

forty-fucking-three years old I'm cleaning *houses* on my hands
/ and knees

Lily   But you're working / on

Blanche   *No! NO I can't work anymore!* I'm at the *end* of it, do
you understand? I can't *do it anymore* I'm *tired*!

Lily   But /

Blanche (*a quick explosion*)   I'M TIRED!

A deafening silence. They both stand, frozen.

Lily (*quiet humiliation*)   I'm . . . trying to have more . . . life
experiences.

We see a smile spread slowly across **Blanche**'s *face. Her countenance
changes completely. They're saved.*

Blanche   It's fine. We don't gotta make a deal out of it.
(*Bright.*) As Bubbles Sills used to say: leave the drama on the
stage.

Lily *looks at her.*

Blanche (*forced smile, girlishness*)   We just have to call your
sister, tell her it was a joke, kay?

Lily   She won't believe that.

Blanche   Say it was a gag /

Lily   But –

Blanche   Say it was a / gag then kissy kiss make

Lily   No.

Blanche   up and drop the whole / thing

Lily   She won't believe that /

Blanche (*strained sweetness, smile*)   Just call her.

Lily   I /

Blanche (*spasm of rage*)   CALL HER!

Long pause.

Blanche *stands there, closes her eyes; she's exhausted. It's as if her entire history has finally caught up with her here. She grasps on to a piece of furniture, to stabilize herself.*

Lily (*sweet, sad*)   I don't want to drop the whole thing.

[STOP]

Blanche   We can't do this.

Lily (*tearful, crushed*)   We can

Blanche   No. We can't.

Lily (*soft*)   *Why?*

Pause.

(*Paralyzed with grief and confusion.*) So what was what was this? You were telling me things. Why? because I'm – gullible?

Blanche   That / ain't it

Lily   Taking my money? / You knew I'd

Blanche   This is not a sustainable *relationship.*

Lily (*hurt*)   WHY?

Blanche (*passionately*)   Because I want you to be HAPPY and you WON'T with ME.

Lily   I am happy with you.

Blanche (*gently*)   It's not real. It's fake.

Lily   It isn't fake!

A tortured and very ashamed **Blanche** *looks away from* **Lily** *as she starts to crumble.*

Blanche   I can't fix you, I can't f-fix myself –

Lily *is lost, in disbelief. A long unbroken silence.*

Lily   I. I just told my *sister.*

Beat.

Blanche   Call her and tell her you / were

Lily   SHE WON'T BELIEVE THAT!

[STOP]

Blanche   She will. She will – just –

Lily *gets her coat, etc.*

Where are you going? /

Lily   I don't know.

Blanche *(increasing panic)*   Sweetie – don't – don't leave. Let's – we can figure something out.

Lily *(weakly, barely able to speak)*   Why.

Blanche *(urgent, grasping for words)*   Let me – Let me help you.

Lily   You want to "help me." "I help you . . . and you help me."

In an instant **Lily** *jumps to the conclusion that she's unearthed the whole horrible truth about this relationship. Something's dying in her. Pause. The whole thing slows down.*

Lily *(weakly, quiet)*   Could I get my money back.

Blanche *looks at her, startled. A pause.*

Blanche *(fearful)*   What?

Lily   The money I gave you. I need it back.

Blanche *(grasping)*   I can't – I can't get that I already used it.

Lily   For what.

Blanche *(panicked)*   You know that – I used it, I paid my loans.

Pause.

You gave me a check.

Lily *slowly lifts her head to meet* **Blanche***'s gaze.*

Long silence.

Then, finally.

Lily (*quiet, through tears*)   You are *so. Dead.*

Blanche *looks at her, terrified. A pause.*

Blanche (*fear*)   What are you talking about? You gave me a *check.*

Pause. **Lily** *slowly turns away from* **Blanche***. She's palpably alone.*

Lily (*completely helpless*)   You're *tricking* me.

Lily*, in a daze, tries to gather her things.*

Blanche (*frenetic*)   Wait /

Lily (*vulnerable*)   You're *tricking* me I / know you are

Blanche (*desperate, pleading*)   Lily come on –

Lily *storms out.*

Blanche *just stands there, very still. Long, long silence.*

Blanche *dazedly looks around the room, tries to orient herself. She sees a rag, picks it up, trying to snap out of it.*

She looks for the caddy, sees it, walks to it, picks up the Windex, still unsteady.

She walks to a mirror, sprays the Windex, wipes it with a rag.

As she is wiping, she catches her reflection in the mirror.

She is transfixed by her own image.

She stretches out her arm as if holding a gun.

She sprays the Windex, watches the liquid drip down, waits a moment.

She sprays again, waits another moment.

Sprays again.

Again.

Again, again, faster and faster as the liquid drips down the mirror and her face becomes a blur.

Six

A diner. Muzak is playing lightly in the background. We hear the muffled voices of other diners, clanking silverware. **Lily** *is sitting alone at a booth. She is miserable. She wears sunglasses and a fur coat.*

Shelly *enters with* **Claudine**. *She's wearing a "Chairman Mao" suit she purchased in China.*

A pause.

Shelly (*brusque*)   What.

Pause.

I'm here, what.

Lily   I . . .

[STOP]

Shelly   WHAT.

Lily   I. I just.

Lily *takes off her sunglasses. Her eyes are completely red, tears are streaming down her face. Her voice sounds oddly high; she speaks from the back of her throat, very frail.*

Shelly   You what?

Lily   I stopped taking (*Pause.*) I –

Shelly   WHAT.

She's crying and can't get the words out.

Lily   I stopped taking . . . my . . .

Shelly   You what?

Lily   My . . .

Shelly   I can't hear what you're saying.

Lily   I / s-s-sstopped

Shelly   OK, look I'm gonna / go

Lily   My PILL.

Beat.

I stopped taking . . . my . . . my pill . . . stopped – I stopped
taking my *pill* I . . .

Lily *attempts a hopeful smile, even a conspiratorial giggle.*

Shelly *just looks at her.*

Lily *earnestly takes* **Shelly***'s hand.*

Shelly *just stands there.*

Lily (*trying, to no avail, to be conversational*)   I . . . I . . .

Lily *releases quiet, helpless sobs. She looks down, ashamed.* **Shelly**
*stands, observing: neither cruel nor compassionate, but almost anthropo-
logical, as if this is a new, unfamiliar, alien specimen.*

Lily *weakly releases* **Shelly***'s hand. It drops back to her side. The
lights dim very slowly on* **Lily***'s sobbing.*

Act Three: Para Los Muertos

One

Living room. The vase of dead chrysanthemums is replaced by fresh flowers, bright green in color, and supplemented with a few other vases, also of brightly colored flowers. **Blanche** *is listening to music.*

Ike *enters. She senses someone – turns, thinking it's* **Lily**. *It's him. He picks up the remote, turns off the radio.*

Ike   Whatcha doin?

Blanche   I was listening to that.

Ike   Chillin? (*Snaps his fingers.*) Chillin out? (*Snaps his fingers.*)

Blanche   I'm taking a *break*. I'm legally entitled / to

Ike   Legally /

Blanche   Breaks, yeah, that's right you're legally entitled to things.

Ike   Are you interested in the Law, Anna Marie?

Blanche   The name's Blanche.

Ike   Ya know. My dad loved the Law: *true.* (*Pause.*) He was a very great man.

Blanche   (Want somm to / drink?)

Ike (*produces a picture of him*)   He's my spittin image.

Shows her.

That's a derby hat, from the old times, check that out: he was a sharp dresser wasn't he? He used to work in textiles. He built himself from the ground up and then they wrecked him. They pillaged him, they stole the rug out from under him. He died with nothing; and he had greatness in him. (*Beat. Saccharine smile.*) But that's how people are. Wouldn't you agree?

Blanche   Uh-huh.

She smiles a strained smile, looks away. He puts the photograph back in his wallet.

Ike   I get the sense you don't like me.

He walks to the fishbowl.

He feeds Kitty.

Kitty likes me. (To Kitty.) Hiiiiiiiiiieeeeeeeeeee.

Blanche *anxiously watches him feed Kitty.*

Blanche *(attempting to finesse it)*   Kitty likes the new algae I can tell.

Ike   Look at that look That's love.

Blanche *(trying to impress him, nervous)*   You know actually goldfish *can't* love. Neuronally speaking I mean They aren't wired for it.

Ike *(quiet, coiled)*   Do-you-know-what-love-is?

Blanche *(plastering on a smile)*   It's – so / subjective

Ike *(explosion)*   SO-DON'T-SPEAK-FA-FISH!

Blanche *holds the smile, rather tensely, slowly swivels back.*

[STOP]

Blanche   I / think

Ike   Why don't you go out on dates?

Beat.

Blanche   Pardon?

Ike   *Dates?* With *boys?*

Beat.

Blanche   I don't know that that's relevant to my job.

He scrutinizes her. She thumbs through a magazine, noticeably unnerved.

Ike   You won't look me in the eye; why's that?

She turns to him.

Blanche   Look you / in

Ike   You look my wife in the eye Why's that.

[STOP]

Blanche   I'm sorry?

Beat.

Ike   Are you?

Blanche   What?

Ike   Sorry?

[STOP]

Blanche (*laughs*)   OK, this is slightly – uh /

Ike (*shift, more intense*)   See these *rivets*? On these jeans? These are like *eyes*. My eyes are *rivets*. I have eyes all over my *person*. I can see everything . . . There isn't a THING you can hide from me.

Blanche (*tense smile*)   Uh. I don't know what you mean.

Pause.

Ike   So you a *college* girl, huh?

Blanche   That's right.

Ike *looks at her, smiles.*

Ike   Nope!

Blanche   What?

Ike   Never went to college.

Beat. She smiles brightly, heightening the performance.

Blanche (*glib*)   Uhh: I went to Princeton then Brown Got a PhD /

Ike (*plainly*)   Don't waste my time, arite? I had you checked out.

Beat.

Blanche (*laughs*)   Um. I think *you* a little checked-out, cuz this is kinda over tha top.

Ike   Why you cleanin my toilets you got a Ph fuckin D, huh?

Blanche (*rolling her eyes*)   I wuz in Paris a bunch a years; I'm not acclimatized / to

Ike (*hard sarcasm*)   Oh not / "acclimatized"

Blanche   I reject / establishment –

Ike (*laughing*)   You know you act like you're so much better than me You're not even *educated*!

Blanche   I speak four languages /

Ike (*unfettered exasperation*)   YEAH! *BULLSHIT!* AND THREE OTHAHS!

[STOP]

Blanche *artifices a Cheshire cat smile. A shift here.*

Blanche   Sounds like you a little jealous.

Ike   Of what.

Blanche   Me.

Ike *laughs softly.*

Ike (*sarcasm*)   Well . . . now that you mention it I actually always *dreamed* a bein a career criminal / so

Blanche (*plainly*)   But you *are* a criminal.

[STOP]

Ike (*staccato, quiet*)   (You got a big mouth You know that.)

Blanche (*shakes her head no*)   Ain't my fault. Tried to make yourself inta somethin and ya failed. It happens.

Ike *chortles to himself.*

Ike (*tries to make a joke out of it*)   I'm a failure?

Blanche (*a shift from caustic to a bit more plaintive*)   You thought you could be anything you wanted. Tried to make yourself a whole other person. Kicked screamed all you wanted Din matter It's the System. (*To herself.*) You don't got a choice in it. Don't matter what you do Gonna crush you anyhow.

Ike *looks at her – this all resonates uncannily with him. It freaks him out – he pushes back whatever fear she draws out of him.*

Ike (*bravado, smiling*)   I'm a failure? You're funny. I made two hundred grand in one year: NET! You think you'll ever see money like that? You're a joke. Look at this HOUSE –

Blanche (*pointed, almost prescient*)   This *house*. You know what this house is? A *casket*. A big *ugly* casket That's what you built. (*Beat.*) An you'll die in it.

His smile fades. Pause.

Ike (*pretends to be impervious*)   What about you? How you gonna die Huh? (*Beat; then steely.*) Bet I can guess.

An impasse. She turns to leave, he stops her.

Oh, and by the way? We *are* white; people of Spanish descent are *Caucasian*, I looked it up.

She turns to him.

Blanche (*sarcasm*)   Congratulations.

She starts to exit.

Ike (*fake pleasantry*)   Oh one more thing:

She stops in her tracks.

Doesn't turn to look at him.

Blanche   What's that.

Ike (*coy*)   How do I say this: uh – do you know a guy named Richard Nesbitt?

On the words "Richard Nesbitt" **Blanche** *becomes very still. Her breathing becomes unsteady. She doesn't look at him.* **Ike** *takes in her reaction. She slowly shuts her eyes, the cells in her body are dying, one at a time. Her composure begins to crack.*

Ike   From Philly? Rich Nesbitt? (*Pause.*) It's kinda sad actually. Couple months back his own daughter tried to shoot him, just left him there. He coulda died. Cops are lookin for her.

He walks to her very very slowly, a spider trapping its prey.

(*Gets very close to her.*) Why do you think she'd do somethin like that huh?

Pause.

Blanche (*deep sadness, almost a whisper*)   Thought I could end it . . . (*To herself, a recognition.*) but it don't end.

Ike (*clueless*)   End what?

Long pause. A smile slowly spreads across his face; he's openly gloating.

Guess you just got that criminal instinct, huh?

Her expression changes. Her lips curl into a tiny, taut smile. She turns to him.

Blanche   Criminal instinct Yeah That must be it. (*Smiles ironically.*) Must be a relief fa you Huh? I make sense to you now? (*Tiny laugh.*) Oh I know what you thinking. Think I don't? Guess what: I built my whole LIFE around what you think a me ALL OF YOU! (*Tiny smile again; then quick.*) You-think-I-don't-see-it? Think-I-don't-bash-my-*head*-against-the-wall-seein-it-every-damn-day-a-my-*life*?

[STOP]

(*The pain mounting here.*) That's why I made my own raw materials, *had* none Had to make somm up What else I *got*! No wallpaper on my walls *Flash cards* . . . Kant . . . Aristotle . . .

Ike (*affectless*)   Wow great story Maybe when you get to prison you can write ya memoirs – /

He walks determinedly to the phone, picks up the receiver. She goes after him, lunges impulsively – grabs the phone from him. She's shaking, panicked, not sure what's next.

[STOP]

(*Looking out, quiet but tense.*) Gimme the phone.

Blanche *just stands there, shaking, terrified, cornered. It's a complete impasse. An extremely tense silence.*

Blanche (*faking bravery, but it's hard*)   She *loves* me.

A beat. He slowly turns to her, dumbfounded – it's true and he knows it, sees it in her. Just saying the words jolts her out of the moment, slowly transports her. A realization:

(*Almost radiant.*) Don't matter what you do . . . cuz she loves me.

Blanche *smiles softly.* **Ike**'s *humiliation starts to morph into a quiet, frightening rage.*

[STOP]

Ike *grabs* **Blanche** *by the hair. Hard. In a single gesture he jerks his arm to his side; she goes crashing down with it, screaming, dropping the phone.* **Ike** *drags* **Blanche** *over to the paint trough.*

Blanche (*terrified*)   I'm – NO!!

In one gesture he shoves her face in it. Hard. He holds her head down – suffocating her.

She tries to scratch his face, hit him, but he pins her hand down. He finally lifts her head up.

Blanche   NO! NO –

He shoves her head back into the paint trough, pushing her face hard into the pan.

After a long while **Blanche** *stops struggling.*

He pulls her head out, releases her body.

She's coughing, spitting out paint, no energy, shaking, wiping white paint out of her eyes, her face, her hair.

Ike *slowly rises, facing a mirror. He's numb. He sees his reflection. Grows transfixed by his own image here – he's a stranger. Slowly the recognition builds, the guilt starts to surface, the awfulness.*

Blanche *starts to move. He turns to look at her.*

He can't look at her.

Ike (*gruff*)   I live good.

(*Feeling welling up.*) I got a nice house.

(*Pushing back tears.*) I don't want nothin from nobody.

Blanche *looks out, reaching for transcendence with all her might.*

Blanche (*a sad smile*)   Candle in the window.

Ike (*denial, anger, pushing off guilt*)   I don't hurt *nobody.*

Blanche (*immersing herself in the beauty of her own vision*)   House in Wicker Park. Books homes trees.

Pause.

Stars in the sky.

The space has transformed. We're in **Blanche***'s room.* **Blanche** *sits alone. It's dark except for a soft light.*

Two

We hear footsteps descending a staircase into the basement. **Blanche** *hears it. She looks toward the door, wipes paint off her face, sits up expectantly. She is working to push past her humiliation, but it won't leave.*

Lily *opens the door to* **Blanche**'s *room.*

A shaft of light illuminating the two of them.

Lily's *hair is different – swept up.*

She tries to make herself impervious to **Blanche**'s *pain here but keeps being thrown off balance by the fierce longing and sadness welling up in her.*

Blanche (*smiling expectantly*)   I wuz hoping you'd find me.

Pause.

Lily (*breathing unsteadily*)   The decorator's coming tomorrow. We're turning your room into a nursery.

Pause.

Blanche   You're. (*Pause.*) That's /

Lily   He'll be here at ten. Pack up.

Blanche (*flicker of hope*)   Wait – I –

Lily   We're not calling the police.

Pause. **Blanche** *summons the courage to speak.*

Blanche (*with difficulty; comes from a wounded, raw place*)   I *love* you.

Silence.

Lily (*not looking at her*)   You left this in my room.

She tosses a book on to the bed.

Blanche (*painful admission*)   I never *been* in love before . . . I'm forty-three years old I never been in love wit *nobody*.

We see **Lily** *look at her. Her heart is breaking. Slowly, we watch her work to stamp back the feeling.*

Lily   Do you have my money.

Pause.

Blanche   I'll. I'll get it for you I – here I got . . . some of it I /

She rushes to her wallet – holds up a wad of cash – extends her arm.

Long pause.

Lily *starts to melt a bit.* **Blanche** *looks at her, hopeful.*

Lily (*tentative*)   What was the money for?

Beat.

Blanche   I . . . borrowed from the wrong people . . . they were threatening / me They

Lily (*snapping back*)   Do you know what you are?

Pause.

A good *teacher*. I was *lacking*: I never learned any *lessons*.

The emotion starts to build.

Now I have Life Experience.

[STOP]

Blanche (*quick*)   I'll get you the rest a the money I / just

Lily (*quiet, raw pain, looks down, fists clenched*)   I-don't-give-a-shit-about-the-money.

[STOP]

Lily *composes herself; stands erect, like a statue.*

Blanche (*speaks quickly*)   I'll tell you anything you wanna know – *ask* me – anything . . .

Beat.

Lily   The decorator's coming tomorrow at ten, you have to clear out.

Lily *won't look at her – she could crumble, but she won't.* **Lily** *quickly makes her way to the door.*

Blanche (*desperate plea*)   *Look back!*

Lily *freezes.*

Blanche   *Look: BACK.*

Beat.

(A whisper) Mira hacia atrás, no me conviertas en piedra.

A long pause. **Lily** *hesitates, then leaves.*

Coward.

Beat.

I DON'T NEED YOU.

Silence.

(To herself, deeply unconvinced; she's sinking.) I'll come out on top. I always knew I was meant for greatness. Deep inside A little voice I knew . . . I knew . . .

She looks around at the cage she's built.

(Quiet.) Help me.

She smiles a sad smile.

(Plainly.) I made bad choices . . . *(Fighting tears.) I made bad choices.*

Three

A split scene.

On one part of the stage: **Ike** *and* **Lily**.
That same evening.
Their bedroom.
He is finishing his push-ups; **Lily** *is at her vanity, combing her hair.*

On another: **Blanche** *is alone in her basement room, packing her things, but very laxly. As she packs she composes a letter in her mind to "bell."*
Bits of white paint still caked on her face.
She puts on a CD, a piece of Sibelius's, which plays softly in the background; a beautiful, lush, sad piece of music.

The realities overlap and merge here – there are no more discrete spaces, levels, it's all collapsed.

Lily *brushes her hair, counting the strokes, beginning at forty-two, under her breath.* **Ike** *is doing push-ups, counting, beginning at seventy.*

Lily   Sixty-four, sixty-five, sixty-six /

Ike   Ninety-two, ninety-three /

Lily   Sixty-seven /

Ike   Sixty-eight, sixty-nine /

Blanche   The food at Gagnaire was perfect that night wasn't it, bell? / He does wonders with radishes wouldn't you say? *Wonders.*

Ike   *Seventy.*

He slumps to the floor exhausted. The music plays.

Lily   Seventy-one, seventy-two, seventy-three /

Ike *(frustrated; down to* **Blanche***)*   Fuckin *music* Turn that shit off!

Lily   Seventy-four, seventy-five /

Blanche   I prefer him to Robuchon (although the potatoes at Robuchon oh my / *god*)

Ike *(gingerly, very careful)*   Whadja do today?

Lily   Seventy-six, seventy-seven, seventy-eight, seventy-nine, eighty, eighty-one /

Ike   Honey?

Lily   Eighty-tw – *(Beat. Abstracted.)* What.

The music continues to play. **Ike** *looks at* **Lily***.*

Ike   Did you have a good day?

Lily   I went / to the

Blanche *(rapt)*   Oh / and *remember*

Ike (*screams to basement/***Blanche***; fillip of rage*)   SHUT-THE-*FUCK*-UP.

Nearly, but not quite simultaneously: **Blanche** *jerks her head to the left, gasps, frightened – it's the ghost. The physical vocabulary here is identical to* **Lily***'s earlier in the play. She looks about the room, jarred.* **Lily** *jumps, drops her brush. Her face remains oddly expressionless.*

Ike (*super-sweet smile*)   Oh, honey did I scare you? I – I'm so sorry I didn't mean to do that . . . I don't ever want to scare you.

He picks up her brush, hands it to her.

Whaddayou say sweetheart?

Beat.

Lily   What? (*Pause.*) It's not important.

Blanche *calms herself down, returns to the fantasy.*

Ike (*working to be attentive*)   No no no – it's important. I wanna know, I'm interested in what you do.

Lily (*not responsive*)   I had lunch.

Blanche   And the wines / (aha-ha)

Ike   Who'd you go with?

Lily   No one. I went by myself.

She's staring in the mirror holding her brush.

Ike   You OK?

Lily   I like being by myself.

Blanche *smiles – laughs quietly to herself for a moment.*

Ike   You look nice /

He smiles. **Lily** *doesn't.*

Blanche   But that waiter He told me it was a Crozes Hermitage C-R-O and AHA-HA and I must have looked / confused because

Ike   What'd you do somethin to ya hair I like it.

Blanche   because he . . .

Blanche *mumbles the rest to herself, giggles to herself quietly, packs.*
Lily *looks at* **Ike**.

Lily   I don't want a live-in.

Ike   What.

Beat.

Lily   A girl. (*Beat.*) I can clean my own house.

Ike   We could get a day workah.

Lily   People steal.

Beat.

Ike   Whatever you want, it's . . . it's your decision, honey.

Lily (*abstracted*)   Thank you.

Pause.

Ike   You're letting em get to you.

Lily   No.

Blanche (*bright*)   I think Luce has a mind like a magnet.
And we're like little iron filings she draws to her /

Ike (*jarred*)   People got short memories /

Blanche   We're / helpless

Ike   It'll all be in the past.

Lily *turns to him. She looks at him.*

Lily   No. It *won't*.

Blanche   We're helpless but / that's

Ike (*screaming, upset, no control*)   YEAH-IT-WILL.

Blanche *gasps, jerks her head left; looks around the room, terrified.*

Recovering himself, **Ike** *gets behind* **Lily***, talking to her reflected image in the mirror.*

Ike   Anyways-screw-them-we-don-need-them-you-think-we-need-them? We don't need nothin from nobody.

Beat.

We got each other . . . Love is powerful . . . *Power /*

Blanche (*a terrified whisper*)   *What-are-you?*

Lily *jerks her head quickly to the side − she's seen something.*
Blanche *jumps.*

[STOP]

Lily   I just saw it again. (*Beat.*)

Ike   Saw / what

Blanche   *Who's there?*

Beat. In the short silence **Blanche***, in a single gesture, pulls the gun from the suitcase. She holds her arms at her side. Stands very still, alert.*

Lily   A face I saw it . . . it was . . .

Ike *starts laughing.*

She turns to him, looks at him − his cruelty is astonishing.

Ike   Ya didn't see anything.

Lily *looks at him, not quite understanding.*

Lily (*somewhat dazedly*)   I saw a face . . .

Ike *walks over to her; her discombobulation makes him laugh harder.*

Ike (*through laughter*)   Honey: I was playin a trick on you.

Lily *just looks at him. She's sinking.* **Ike** *tries to stifle the laughter.*

Blanche *shudders.*

Blanche   WHO'S THERE?

Points the gun.

Ike   There's no ghost.

Lily (*dying inside*)   *What? /*

Blanche (*terrified*)   *Get-outta-here! You-don't-exist!*

Ike *laughs – a private joke with himself.*

Blanche *pivots, points the gun.*

Ike (*laughter building*)   I was having fun witchu!

Lily *looks at* **Ike** *– practically looking through him. Her loneliness is palpable, she's far away.*

Ike   Wha? *Don't look at me like that.*

Blanche *shudders, gasps audibly, as if someone's grabbed her from behind.*

Ike   C'mere – /

Blanche (*deep frustration, exhaustion*)   *I ain't scared a you!* YOU-DON'T-EXIST!

Ike *kisses* **Lily**'s *neck from behind. Music fades.*

Blanche (*ferocious, desperate*)   *I-AIN'T-SCARED-A-YOU!*

Ike *slowly removes* **Lily**'s *clothes – she is very still. Her eyes are frozen.*

Blanche's *bravado falters.*

She releases the gun weakly, it falls to the ground. She covers her eyes with her hand, weeps helplessly. The lights begin to fade.

Blanche (*to herself, weeping*)   It don't end . . .

We hear a car horn faintly in the distance.

It don't end – I can't end it I can't . . . I can't I can't . . .

On the last "can't" we hear the car horn again, louder this time, two short beeps.

I can't . . .

I can't . . .

I can't . . .

We hear the car horn again, much louder, one long beep − it cuts off her last "can't," as the lights go to black.

Once we hit total darkness there's a beat. Then:

Two loud beeps.

A pause.

One loud long beep.

On the last beep, lights come up on **Lily** *halfway down the stairs.*

It's the next morning. Bright.

As **Lily** *approaches the door to the basement we see:*

Blanche *lying on the floor in a corner, face down, gun not too far from her hand. Blood pooling around her head. She looks incidental to the surroundings, insignificant.*

Lily *lingers in the stairwell, outside the door, she stands tentatively.*

Lily (*through the door, tentative*)   I heard something break, did you break something?

Pause.

Your car's outside

Pause.

(*Strained hauteur.*) You better leave your address. So we can find you if we need you to − to pay for something. Th-th-there's expensive things in there.

In the silence she starts to fall apart − she loses her comportment. All her emotion comes to the surface for this one instant, and it's pulverizing.

(*Almost a whisper.*) Don't f-f-forget. Don't forget / to

The car horn honks.

She freezes back into her old rectilinear posture. Her face is a mask.

(*No effect, faraway.*) Your car's outside.

She slowly walks to the foot of the staircase.

Then she looks up, ascends.

Lights fade to black as she reaches the top stair.

Darkness.

We hear the car horn.

Glossary of Syrian-American Terms

aboose "Oh how sweet and adorable."

ca-an ("ca" as in "cat" and "an" as in "ann") Spoken when challenging the veracity of something. Has a vaguely sarcastic connotation, as in "Yeah, right!" Sometimes serves as phatic punctuation.

dibeh Slang for idiot (female); dib (male).

ERT An exclamation of disgust or revulsion.

gazz Silly and fun.

gazzcase ("a" as in "lair") Playful term for someone who is mentally disorganized, a kind of screwball.

gimmethebosse "Give me a kiss."

HEEE Not a word but a sharp intake of breath indicating shock, concern, surprise or worry.

ibe (with a hard "i," silent "e") Comment on shameful or inappropriate behavior.

obdeh, female; *obid*, male ("ob" as in "obverse") Person of African descent.

oolie An exclamation of shock, worry, horror, discovery – spoken with correlative intonations (reverential worry: "*ooooollllliiieeeee?*", "OOlLIE!", "*OOLIER*," etc.).

shoof, shoofie A command – "Look!" As in, "Shoof had-die!" ("Look at her!")

sketching Slang for kidding or joking.

Translations from Spanish

Spanish   Ella me decia: "Lily tú eres un angel, y tu pelo es de ceda / te quiero como mi hija."
English   She told me: "Lily you are an angel, and your hair is silk I love you like a daughter."

Spanish   ¡¡Yo-tambien-te-puedo-mecer-en-el-columpio-vamos-al-parque-AHORA-MISMOH!!
English   I could push you on the swing too, let's go to the park right now!!

Spanish   Todavia estamos trabajando Anna Maria la luz está a tu derecha.
English   We're still working Anna Maria, the light is on your right.

Spanish   Yo me preocupo de esto cálmate.
English   I'll take care of this calm down.

Spanish   De nada.
English   You're welcome.

Spanish   Ojalá no se enoje.
English   I hope he doesn't get mad.

Spanish   El no se enterará.
English   He won't find out.

Spanish   ¿Me lastimó, / viste lo que hizo?
English   He hurt me, did you see what he did?

Spanish   ¿Estas / bien?
English   Are you alright?

Spanish   Tengo que irme de aquí; promete que nos iremos.
English   I have to get out of here; promise we'll leave.

Spanish   Para Los Muertos
English   For the Dead

Spanish   Mira hacia atrás, no me conviertas en piedra.
English   Look back, don't turn me to stone.

Marcus Gardley

The Road Weeps, the Well Runs Dry

The Road Weeps, the Well Runs Dry will be produced at four theaters across the country as part of the Lark Play Development Center's Launching New Plays into the Repertoire program funded by the Mellon Foundation. Perseverance Theater in Juneau, Alaska; LATC in Los Angeles, CA; Pilsbury House in Minneapolis, MN; and the University of Southern Florida in Tampa will share the world premiere.

Them

Number Two, *a black god*
Young Number Two, *his memory. The same actor plays*
　　Potter's Clay, *an army scout*
Mary South, *his wife, a full-blood Seminole*
Sweet Tea, *his daughter, black and Seminole*
Trowbridge, *the sheriff and a full-blood Seminole. The same actor*
　　plays **Red Kyote**, *a stranger, and* **Seminole Chief**
Half George, *Trowbridge's wife, black and Seminole. A witch*
Goodbird, *his son. The same actor plays* **Wonderful**, **Young**
　　Trowbridge *and an* **Echo**
Horse Power, *town elder and medicine man, black and Seminole*
M. Gene, *his granddaughter, the first lady of the church. The same*
　　actress plays **Wind Song**, *the music of nature*
Fat Rev., *her husband*
Colorado, *an orphan, the town Casanova*

There

Indian Territory. Present-day Wewoka, Oklahoma.

Then

Winter 1850 and 1866. The action takes place over two
twenty-four-hour days.

This

The stage is seasoned in golden desert. In the rear stands the
shadow of a mountain and a wood with trees the shape of
warring gods. At their feet flows a silver creek, to the right a
chapel; a well stands center and to the left a trade store with a
sign that reads: HALF GEORGE'S TRADE OR BUY.

Author's Note
The scenes are meant to move at a steady pace. The stage
direction *Time* refers to a change of thought or a short pause.

Prologue

NUMBER TWO WRESTLES HIS ANGEL OR BLACK
BEAR EMBRACES RED COYOTE

Night. The white eye of heaven falls on two men in a standoff, their eyes locked to kill or fuck. One is **Number Two**, *forty-three, black, built like a mountain. The other is* **Trowbridge**, *forty-five, Seminole, built like a tree. He wears a sheriff's badge. It is 1850.*

Trowbridge   One of us is 'bout to die.

Number Two   Figured as much.

Trowbridge   My sum figures you on count ya killed my boy.

Number Two   Meant to bruise 'im.

Trowbridge   Don't matter.

Number Two   Meant ta nick him but he kept at me. Made me mad and I got happy with my blade.

Trowbridge   Ya cut him round like cake: a slice in every direction.

Number Two   He shouldna got into my Sweet Tea. I saw 'em both in the creek – evenin past. He had her rollin. He had my daughter like she was a whore.

Trowbridge   What'in no matter. You knew to come to me if you had a problem with mine. You knew to come to me if you had a problem at all. I'ze the law in this town, Number Two. I say what gets killed.

Number Two   Just 'cause you sheriff don't mean you massuh. Dem days is dead. I'm a free man now and I ain't got to get your permission to kill somethin. Even if that somethin be your son.

Trowbridge   Come close then so I can kill ya. My woman wants your head to make a soup, told me not to come back till I had it.

Number Two   And you are your woman's wife?

Trowbridge   Yeh and she be my man. Figure she already got my balls, gal just needs your head.

Number Two   How you doin it then Trowbridge? Bring you a rope?

Trowbridge   Nawl, ain't got time to watch you hang round. Got to kill ya natural: bare hands to crack your neck. Axe off ya head then leave your body for birds.

Number Two   Well, it's a way to go. No hard feelings though if I protect myself and kill ya first.

Trowbridge   Do what ya must. Though if you do end me, promise me you'll go and end my wife. Don't let a woman live without somethin to live for.

Number Two   Dat on my word and soul.

Trowbridge   Then ya was good till the hell of the devil got in ya. Now I been sent to put out the fire.

Number Two   And God give you the strength to do it. You'll surely need Him.

Trowbridge *and* **Number Two**   Ahhhh!

The men collide like bulls, their hands horns. They clinch one another's necks then freeze. Their bodies form the mouth of a cave. Enter **Horse Power**, *seventy-two, holding a lantern and his staff. He enters the cave followed by* **Wonderful**, *sixteen, red as honey with beautifully wild and nappy hair. Flashforward, 1866.*

Horse Power   We rest here. This cave be the mouth of the mountain. We sit here on its lip and wait for heaven's freckles to burn through the blanket of night. It's them starry freckles that will tell you your history, Wonderful.

Wonderful   Way up there? How my history get way up there in the sky, ole Horse?

Horse Power   At night every man can see his story writ on God's black face. During the day God hides it behind His hot smile and cloudy beard but at night . . . while He keeps His white eye open, His freckles glow a sparklin gold. So that if a man seeking God's face reaches his hand to the sky – he'll cause a spark. It's with that spark that a man can chart his story. He can trace his past, find his callin, and if he's wise he can foretell his fate.

Wonderful   Wo-ah, that's a lot. I don't know if I want to know all that. I'd rather hear a bedtime tale or an old joke.

Horse Power   Joke!? You think this s'pose to be funny?

Wonderful   Uh, nawl, I –

Horse Power   – You think I ain't got nothin better to do than to sneak you out of the house knowin how vengeful and bitch-dog evil your grandma can be? I'm reading the stars for your benefit, boy. You fifteen!

Wonderful   Actually, I'm sixteen –

Horse Power   – Same thang, you just carried a one! My point be you're at a fork in the road in life. You could go left but you might get left, you could go right but it might not be right. Only the stars can chart your course. You need your history and you need it now.

Wonderful   But what if I don't like it? What if my story's bad?

Horse Power   Piss and shit, ain't no such thing as a bad history. There's only a bad way to tell it. You need to know where your fathers came from so you don't go down the same roads they got lost on. You need to know what's in your blood, Wonderful.

Wonderful   Yeh, I s'pose you right.

Horse Power   Course I'm right, I'm seventy-two years old. I'm wise as books. Now give me your hand so I can wake up your star. I ain't got all night.

Horse Power *lifts his cane and wraps* **Wonderful**'s *hand around it. He guides the cane to a star. The star burns into a comet. Then other constellations cruise across the sky as we fall back into time.*

Wind Song:

Horse Power (*softly singing, offstage*)
Fuslanoji ca-pozi.
Nika cal-scan caha-ni.
Hopwa paya ti fuslanoji.
Fuslanoji ca-pozi. (*Continues humming.*)

[*Translation*: Grandmother is a yellow bird. Put her on my shoulder so she can teach me things. I have been looking for her, my little yellow bird. Grandmother will teach me how to spread wings.

Horse Power
We came here
Twenty years ago from Florida swamps.
When fightin for freedom had taken its toll
And we had grown old of being some Indian chief's slave.
Though it took us forty-five days
We traveled the road called West
Where rocks chewed through our deerskin shoes
Through our meat and bone
Breakin our walk into limps, our dead stares into a trail
    of tears
Like the Choctaw, Chickasaw, Cherokee and Creek:
Fierce engines blowin steam
We came here: three hundred free black Seminoles up
    from three hundred years on our knees
Drownin in the heat and burn of the desert stretch and sun
Walkin 'pon our dead whose heads felt like soft mud under
    our feet.
We came here cursed.
Weak and guilt-ridden for not dancing their souls to sleep.
So we made one promise: no longer would we weep
In honor of those we lost on the trail.
We promised to hold up our heads
And not show grief
The last of our tears we left in a well.

Number Two *and* **Trowbridge** *unlock their grip on one another.*

Trowbridge   Look there in the East! A creek! I found my land!

Horse Power   When we got to Indian Territory, Trowbridge was the first to find water. He was a full-blood Seminole, the son of our former chief Long John. But he came West with us Negroes to make sure the neighboring Creek Indians didn't try to enslave us. Back then the government had signed a treaty declaring every man in Indian Territory was free. But the Creeks didn't consider it law so Trowbridge came to enforce it. Unlike his father and the chiefs before him, Trowbridge denounced slavery. He helped us escape and we all loved him for it. Well, all 'cept Number Two.

Number Two   What you mean, your land? You know that ain't how the wind blow in Indian Territory, Trowbridge. Here it's a land grab. First man to stick his pike in unclaimed earth owns it.

Trowbridge   Sounds like we got to race for it then, Number Two. Though I feel bad ridin against you knowing I got a horse built like a train. And all you got is that suck-egg mule Marvelous Jack.

Number Two   Don't matter. I didn't come all this way to let an Indian take the only good land left. Horse Power, count off. If Trowbridge wants this creek land, he's going to have to ride me for it. Count off!

Horse Power   And so I did. TOOT-CHI-NIN-GIN! HO-GOH-LIN! HAM-GIN! RIDE!!

Number Two *and* **Trowbridge**   Yah!!

They pull reins that are nailed to the stage floor. They move as if on horses.

Watchin them ride was like watchin fire chase lamp oil. Trowbridge had the lead 'cause his horse was younger and a better breed. But Number Two had an edge 'cause his mule knew that if he didn't win, he was gone be served for supper right side a biscuit.

Ha!!

They ride even harder.

Horse Power   Now no one saw who reached the creek first.
It was too far away for even good eyes to see it from where we
stood. Number Two said he got there first but soon as he
hopped off his mule Trowbridge knocked him down ridin his
horse then stuck his pike in the land. But Trowbridge said that
was a lie. He said Number Two rode his mule so hard it
collapsed on top of him and he just a poor loser. Either way,
Trowbridge's pike was stuck in the mud and Number Two
was wounded so I had to do what was right. I declared
Trowbridge "land owner."

Number Two *falls defeated.* **Trowbridge** *sticks his pike into the
land and does a victory dance.*

They ride even harder.

Horse Power   And this liked to had kill Number Two. He
spent most of his life buyin his freedom and this was his one
chance he had to own somethin worth slavin for. He spat
blood from the bitter taste in his mouth, took his wife Mary
south and moved crossed the creek, into the woods . . . till the
day he got a taste for sweet revenge. And this, my boy, is how
your story begins . . .

The scene fades as the wind song hums. We return to 1850.

Act One

THE OLD TESTAMENT OR WHY THE WELL RAN DRY

Enter **Sweet Tea**, *sixteen, a vision in a patchwork skirt. She walks through the woods at a fast pace, as if being followed. Suddenly, her father jumps out from behind a tree.*

Number Two Daddy's baby!

She screams.

Sweet Tea Awl Paw! You scared me!

Number Two So, you lucky it's me and not those slave-catchin Creeks. I thought I told you to be in the house come sundown.

Sweet Tea You did, but Maw needs me to pick up powdered milk at the trade post. I'll be just a breath.

Number Two Breath or not, I don't like you out here at night –

Sweet Tea – Yeh, but you want you peach pie, don't you, Paw? Can't make peach pie without powdered milk, now can I? (*Time. She smiles.*) Can I, Paw?

Number Two Oh. Well you right. Hurry back then. And don't stop for nothin. Hear me?

She walks off.

Sweet Tea Loud and clear.

He exits. We hear and see a silver creek in the wood. Then an echo.

Good Bird (*offstage, singing*)
  KI MO NARO! KI MO NARO! KI MO NARO!

Sweet Tea (*offstage, singing*)
  CAPN CARO! CAPN CARO! CAPN CARO!

Goodbird, *sixteen, angelic, takes off his shoes and steps into the creek.*

Goodbird   SIMMON AITCHEE! SIMMON AITCHEE!
SIMMON AITCHEE!

Sweet Tea   VERMIN AITCHEE! VERMIN AITCHEE!
VERMIN AITCHEE!

Enter **Sweet Tea**.

Goodbird   Wo-ah God, there she is. Heaven in the flesh.
And the reason my flesh be so weak. You're late, gal.

She steps in the water.

Sweet Tea   'Pologies, it was hard for me to get away. My
paw been on me lately like I'm sticky. Askin me off questions
and starin at me for no reason 'cept I guess to try and look
into my soul. He say he nervous that some Creek Indians gone
snatch me but I know better. I'm 'fraid he know about us,
Bird, and it's breakin his heart.

Goodbird   Awl, he's a big man, Sweet, if he gets broken
he'll heal. We can't be worried 'bout our folks no more, we too
young for it. Plus it's them that got the bad blood. Our duty is
to love and make love and make love last.

Sweet Tea   Yeh, I s'pose. Just sometimes I wish we'd up
and leave here. Pack our bags, hitch a wagon and walk into
the ocean to live as fish. We'd spend our days neck to neck,
lookin into each other's big ole eyes and swimmin. And we'd
have a whole school of children too.

Goodbird   A whole school?! Who's gone feed a whole
school?

Sweet Tea   The ocean. And we'd forget about this dusty
town, and the heat and the farm and Creek Indians tryin to
slave us or bad blood 'tween our paws. We'd be happy. We'd
be fishy.

Goodbird   You somethin strange, gal. I don't want to be
no fish. Hell, I just got the hang of being a man. And I likes it.
I likes being your man. And you know what else I likes?

He grabs her by the waist.

Sweet Tea   Boy, you a mess.

Goodbird   Yup. And I likes gettin in your mess.

He picks her up.

Dang you got heavy. What you been eatin?

Sweet Tea   Anything I can get my hands on. But it ain't the food that's got me big, Bird. I got to tell ya —

Goodbird   — It don't matter, I likes ya round. Just more meat for me to lay my lips on.

He bathes her in kisses. They make nature.

A stir. A figure lurks in the shadows.

Sweet Tea   Hold, you hear somethin?

He continues to kiss her.

Goodbird   Nawl, I don't hear a thing. Not a thing at all.

Sweet Tea   There was a stir, somebody's here. (*Beat.*) You best go. You best go home now.

Goodbird   But I thought we was gettin fishy.

Sweet Tea   Not tonight. I got a bad feelin in my gut. Let's meet tomorrow. There's somethin I been wantin to tell ya. Somethin I got to lay on your heart.

She rises from the creek.

Goodbird   But you just got here —

Sweet Tea   — Yeh. (*Touching his heart.*) And if I'm in here, I'll never leave.

She kisses him and exits.

Goodbird   Well hens! What a way to kill a rooster!!!

He rises from the water and leans against a tree to dry off. Time. A figure snatches him from behind the tree and drags hims into the woods. We hear the swift stab of fork into flesh and the flap of wings. A stream of blood slithers into the creek. All goes dark. **M. Gene** *enters, drawing the curtain of a glorious dawn over the night sky. She wears a flounced skirt and a cape made from flour sacks.*

M. Gene (*singing soft first, then it rises*)
I need thee
O i need thee
Ev'ry hour i need thee
O bless me now my Savior
I come to thee.

She fetches water from a well, lifts the pail, drops it. Out pours blood. It forms a road.

Come, sweet Jesus . . . blood . . . There's blood in the well! Huz?! THERE'S BLOOD!

Fat Rev. *runs in with his rifle. He wears a black suit with specs.*

Fat Rev.   Dear heart, what is it?

M. Gene   In the well! In the well! Blood! Our water's been messed with, huz. I sent down a pail and it came up with blood. There's blood in the well, huz! Lord help us . . . blood!!

Fat Rev.   What you mean "blood"? You sure the water just ain't dirty?

M. Gene   Nawl I said! The blood was fresh . . . and red as tongues. BLOOD!

Rev. *sends a pail down.*

Fat Rev.   Alright, alright calm down –

M. Gene   – Can't be calm. Somebody's been meddlin. Somebody's been up to no good. It's time to call on God. It's time to seek His face . . .

She circles the well, dashing holy water.

Heavenly Father, help us down here! *YA HOLA-HO-YA!* We need ya, Jesus, our well water's turned to blood. *LA-CO-YANKA-HA-YA!* How will we drink, Lord? How will we quench our thirst . . . (*Continues in a whisper.*)

The pail returns to **Rev.** *dry. Enter* **Colorado**, *combing his hair with an antique brush. He is dark, fine as hot gravy.*

Colorado   Mornin, Rev. (*Beat.*) Say, what's gotten into your wife?

Fat Rev.   The Holy Ghost. It's got her speakin in tongues 'gain. She went to fetch water and found blood in her pail so now she stirred. I sent the pail down and it come up with air, so I reckon the well's run dry.

Colorado   Run dry?! But how I'm s'pose to keep waves in my hair with no water. It's my wavy hair that makes the women wet. Though I bet my bones them Creek Indians had somethin to do with this.

Fat Rev.   Slow ya ride, young buck. You jumpin to conclusions –

Colorado   Where else am I s'pose to jump? You know them Creeks been tryin to get at us since we moved here. If we didn't outnumber them three to one they'd have us enslaved already.

Fat Rev.   Calm yaself, this is an act of nature. We'll just have to fetch water from the creek. Though Lord knows Number Two hates it when folks go near his land.

M. Gene *wakes from her prayer.*

M. Gene   The Lord has spoken! He told me He drunk our well as a warnin. And till we turn from our wicked ways will thirst for His water that never runs dry.

Fat Rev.   Hold a hallelujah, you sayin God drunk our water, wife?

M. Gene   Ev'ry last drop. And He said He won't fill it up till every man in town confesses that He is Lord.

Colorado   God said all that, M. Gene? Sound like to me you was the one doin all the talkin.

M. Gene   Don't start on me this mornin, Colorado –

Mary South (*loud, offstage*) – Mornin! Mornin all!

Colorado   Shucks and clucks, here come that full-blood Mary South. I sho don't feel like hearin her "how do" this morn –

Enter **Mary South** *in a blouse and skirt that was once a Confederate flag, followed by* **Sweet Tea**.

Mary South   – How do? How y'all do!! Sho is good to see y'all early this morn. I was just sayin to my husband Number Two how we rarely commune at the square – 'cept on Sunday's course and Wednesday's prayer meetin. Truth told, if it whatin for the well bein in the center of town we'd hardly ever run into each other. Sho is a healthy place for meetin – the well. We could do lady teas here I reckon and the mens could gather for farm talk. Course sometimes the well do smell the devil's bowels and that would be somethin to get over. But we womens, meanin me and Sweet Tea, get awful lonely without y'alls company. And I tell ya further, my skin starts to itch if'n I go too long without good gossip. Ha! (*She giggles.*) Good gossip cleans my teeth. Healthy gossip that is. Something you can suck on like cane. Bad gossip makes your breath stink and God don't like stink. God keeps a clean house. How y'all feelin?

Fat Rev.   Thirsty. The well done run dry.

Mary South   What you mean, run dry? It was more than half full yesterday –

M. Gene   We know. God drunk it as a warnin.

Colorado   No he didn't. The Creeks put a spell on it –

Fat Rev.   That's ain't so. It's just nature.

Sweet Tea   – Maybe it was the sun.

Time. Everybody stares at her.

Mary South   Wo-ah, Sweet Tea, stay out of grown folks' business now –

Sweet Tea   – But it's true, Maw. It's been hot as biscuits since last Sunday when Horse was by the house readin Paw his story. The ole man had a heat stroke. It got hot that day and been hot ever since, I think we havin a drought.

Colorado   Drought? Now that's just ig'nant. It's winter. How we gone have a drought in winter.

M. Gene   'Cause it's God!!

They all bicker. Time. Enter **Horse Power**.

Horse Power   Chil'ren! Tell me why y'all doin more cocking than the crow? It's too early for all this noise.

Mary South   Father Power, you just in time, it appears the well has run dry. And you know we rely on you to explain the nature of the supernatural. None of us can figure it out but . . . perhaps you can reason the "why and how-to" so that we may drink from this well again. After all, you are our wise elder.

He bathes himself in the compliment then examines the well. Time.

Horse Power   Well . . . it's a well. Wells keep water, they keep folks' wishes. I figure . . . somebody threw a wish down the well and it drunk up all the water. That mean they had a big wish. Either way the well's thirsty and needs rain. Now if I give a dance the Breath Maker will laugh, lean his head back and weep tears into it. But I gots to get paid first, I don't dance for free.

Colorado   Fair 'nough, what's your price?

Mary South   Right, Sweet Tea, hand me some button coin from my sack.

They hand him coins.

Horse Power   Sixty-six be my age. Be the price for my dance. Pay it now and you won't regret it later. Let's see: two some, three some, four, five, then six some. Five more is what's due.

M. Gene   Excuse me, Christians, but remember we do not pay for dances. It's old Indian lore like rain dancin that angers God and it don't make sense.

Horse Power   It make sixty-six cents. Be my age, be my price for my dance. Come on, M. Gene, I know you and the Rev. know how to tithe. Pay an old man.

M. Gene   We ain't even payin you mind Grand Paw. God brought us all the way from Florida and we like the chilren of Israel, still scrvin other gods. We will never pay you –

Fat Rev.   Here's five buttons for a two-step, Paw.

M. Gene   Huz, don't you dare!

Fat Rev.   Be sweet now, peach. Your Grand Paw knows how to read the sky. If he say he can solve the matter with the well then we should let him dance.

Horse Power   Why thank ya, Rev. I always did like you better. Now if y'all stand back, this olc Horse is gone kick up a dust storm. See if hc can't get the sky to cry.

He circles the well tossing oil over his head. Ironically, his dance is akin to **M. Gene**'s. *It's a stomp dance.*

Horse Power   Sweet Breath Maker! *YA HOLA-HO!* Bring us rain. If I had a turtle: king of the water world, I would scratch his belly till he cried us a river. But all I have here on this dusty land is my feet and the mouths of my chilren. *CO-LAKKO OP YANKA.* Give them water, Breath Maker. I can't bear to lose no more kin to thirst and tears. Bring us rain, I beg you! *(Beat.)* Wait, y'all hear that?

They all lean over the well. Time.

Enter **Trowbridge** *from behind.*

Trowbridge   MORNIN!!

Everyone jumps.

Colorado   Oh, sheriff, it's you.

Trowbridge   'Tis. How come y'all ain't at work!?

Fat Rev.   It appears the well's run dry, suh. Horse just givin us a rain dance to fill it –

Trowbridge   What 'bout business? Colorado, ain't Number Two 'spectin you 'cross creek?

Colorado   Yeh, boss, but I waitin for some water to brush my hair. I got to put these naps on my head to sleep.

Trowbridge   Boy, you fine enough for a Friday, get goin. If you get any prettier I'm a make you wear a dress. Fat Rev., how come you ain't rung the church bell? Folks rely on you to wake they rumps up, so move yours. And M. Gene, when you plan on openin the school?

Fat Rev. *exits.*

M. Gene   School don't start till high noon, sheriff. When the childers come back from farm work.

Trowbridge   – Don't matter. It's high enough for light, which means ya need to teach. Our chilren ain't gettin no smarter on account of you . . .

M. Gene   Yes'm, suh. Mary, if you will . . .

M. Gene *exits.* **Mary South** *follows.*

Trowbridge   Damn shame I got to reminds folks they job ev'ry morn. Last thang I want to be is somebody's massuh, and look at me, I done turned into my paw. Horse Power?

Horse *is still listening to the well.*

Horse Power   What, boy? I'm busy.

Trowbridge   You're needed at the trade post. Goodbird didn't come home last night and my wife got a shipment come in from Kansas. She needs you to help her unbox.

Horse Power   So? What I'm s'pose to do about this well?

Trowbridge   There's nothin you can do but wait for rain. In the meantime, we'll use the creek: we won't go at night and we won't go alone. We'll be like the wind and do our own sort of dancin. So spread the word! The well's run dry and the creek is now our nurse mother.

Trowbridge *exits.* **Sweet Tea** *passes* **Horse Power***, who stops her.*

Horse Power   Hold. Ya should be ashamed.

Sweet Tea   Pardon?

Horse Power   Your bird's wish drunk up the well. Now ya got to cry. To save our town you got break the law and weep.

Sweet Tea   But why? I don't understand.

Horse Power   Ask the well. I'm just an echo. Ask the stones.

He exits. **Sweet Tea** *looks in the well.*

Sweet Tea   Um . . . (*Beat.*) Hello?

Time.

Echo   I'm hell . . . low.

Sweet Tea   Oh. (*Beat.*) Well . . . well, why are you dry?

Echo   Why . . . why won't you cry?

Sweet Tea   Oh, are you thirsty?

Echo   Lo. I thirst thee . . .

She looks around.

Sweet Tea   Well, I can try . . . . and weep for you well.

Echo   And I . . . I will reach for you gal.

Sweet Tea *lifts her head.*

Sweet Tea   Let's see, I haven't cried since I was five so . . . I s'pose I should think of a sad thought. I can make it in my mind, send it to mine eyes and . . . they'll well up, spring forth a tear. Yes, I'll weep. Hold on, well, I need to "mind" some sadness. (*Time.*) Here. There. A drop.

She sheds a tear. **M. Gene** *and* **Mary** *sit on the chapel steps.*

M. Gene   The Lord spoke to me this morn while I was prayin, sister. He said he's fed up with our heathen ways and was moved to drink our water. Next he'll send plagues.

Mary South   Plagues?! I can't deal with no plagues. It takes me three weeks to recover from a dust storm. What kind of plagues? Is it frogs? I can fry frog legs if it's frogs.

M. Gene   He showed me the image of a man crawling out the belly of a whale.

Goodbird *crawls out of the well, wet and cut up.* **Sweet Tea** *screams.*

M. Gene   It was Pharaoh's firstborn. And he was dying.

Sweet Tea   Goodbird? Bird, that you?

Goodbird (*raspy*)   Sweet?

M. Gene   And Egypt cried over him like a child.

Sweet Tea   Goodbird, what happened!? How'd you get in there?

Goodbird   I . . . luh . . . .

Sweet Tea   I love thee oh-so, Bird . . . Wait, where you going?

His eyes close.

Hey, Goodbird. Hey . . . Good. Don't leave me 'lone. Please! Don't go without us growing old. Stay on my eyes . . . Bird. If you go . . . go in my eyes.

M. Gene   And he died. Just like he came: wet, curled up in some woman's breasts.

Goodbird's *spirit flies.*

Sweet Tea   Hesaketv emese.

She closes his eyes.

M. Gene   His death would bring new life. The Lord was tellin me to pick up the rod, sister. He said I've sat idle way too long while leaders like my grand paw and the sheriff have kept our minds in bondage. Until they turn from their ways, they'll be plagues, sister. There will be floods.

Mary South   Well, I'm on your side, First Lady, but what can we do? This Trowbridge's land and Horse Power's our elder. They just doing what they think is best –

M. Gene   Man can't serve two masters, Mary South. You got to pick a side. God has anointed me to be Moses, to lead his people. Now all I need is a help-mate.

Mary South   What about your husband? The Rev. –

M. Gene   – He's a glutton and a yeller-belly. I'm gone need a woman to stand 'side me. Paul had Silas. Moses had Aaron. And although I wouldn't likely choose a full-blood Seminola, God has chosen me to choose you, sister. Won't you answer the call?

Sweet Tea   – Momma! Momma!

Mary South   Oh, that's my girl. I'll think on it and get back to you, sister.

M. Gene   Alright then, go forth. And be blessed.

Mary South   And you. Be blessed . . . prophetess.

She runs to her daughter.

Sweet Tea   How'd I lose you when everything was good? When everything was right.

Mary South   My sweets, what's the matter?

Sweet Tea   Goodbird. My Goodbird's gone.

Mary South   Sheriff's boy? That's the sheriff's boy?

Sweet Tea   Yeh, Ma. I can't feel my heart.

Mary South   He's cold. I best get his father.

Sweet Tea   Mother, stay. He's dead.

Mary South   Merciful . . . How, daughter?

Sweet Tea   I can't figure. He came here, half out of himself . . . out of the well . . .

Mary South   The well?

Sweet Tea   Like he was comin up for air. I s'pose he climbed up but I don't know how long he was down there. Maybe who cut him threw him down.

Mary South   Lord, his mother can be a foul, evil thing. When she finds out she'll gut an appetite worst off than a pack of kyotes. Best we make sure we have no part in this spill. Be a good girl and help me drag the body to the bush.

Sweet Tea   Like a dog!? He was mine! My beloved.

Mary South   Your beloved what?

Sweet Tea   My one. My man, and I'm not ashamed of it and won't be.

Mary South   Wo-ah. This Goodbird's yours? You got a man gainst your paw and I'ze want and this one? You know how your father feels about his kin –

Sweet Tea   – What do it matter now, he's gone! And I don't much care what my paw feels. I loved him. And I won't have you shamin us over his body.

Mary South   Nawl babe, course. Best we not tell your paw and let things die then, hunh?

Sweet Tea   Don't know how I can keep it.

Mary South   If'n you kept it this long you can. Let's move him 'fore he gives a stink. And careful of his side, there's somethin stickin there, below his wing.

Sweet Tea *pulls the tooth.*

Sweet Tea   What is it?

Mary South   Tooth of a pitchfork looks like. Come, we'll take him to the chapel but we won't cry. For this our way. We women labor out the bodies of the world . . . only to have to bring 'em in.

Mary *pockets the tooth. They pick up* **Goodbird***'s body and exit. Near the creek,* **Number Two** *combs his cornstalks with a pitchfork. It's missing a center tooth.* **Colorado** *leans against a tree.*

Colorado   Brother, when it gets this hot I just want to make love in the creek. Lay a whore down in the water, wrap her legs round me, lean her back 'gainst a willow and rub my trunk deep into the soils of her nectar land. I want to feel round in her forest like wind, shake the fruit from her branches, make her moan so loud father bear wakes from a nine-week nap and a flock of bill horns fill the sky. Brother, I want to lift her . . . rush my waves with more and more rapids, more and more winds. Rustlin! Whistlin! Whoosh! Then I'll bet I burst. Like the golden poppy when sweet pollen pops from the stem. I bust nut. And shiver. Like all hard men do. And the sweet whore will have carved my name into the bark behind her: Colorado, it will read. Co-lo-road-do. The colored road. The black adventure. The long dark, rocky way.

Number Two   Niggah, are you ever gone work?

Number Two *hands him a pitchfork.*

Colorado   Can't work while I'm horny, Number Two, it messes with my head. Won't get nothin done that way. Got to wait till my pipe blows steam.

Number Two   I ain't got to wait till shit. It's hot as hell. Ain't gone be waitin till you soften to stack hay. You get hard at the sight of a hen walkin fast.

Colorado   Yeh, you right. I figure I stay hard 'cause I'm a lover by nature. God told me my callin is to answer the natural needs of women and someday spread my seed like wild fire. It's 'cause I was lost from kin when I was a babe and now God wants me to make up for it. Populate like Abraham. He was a lover too, you know? Man had it with a woman at the age of a hundred and somethin. Now, that's how I'm gone be. Makin 'em moan till I die.

Number Two   And you gone be short-lived you don't pick up a fork and help me stack. Cows be round shortly. And we still got some pails to fill creek-side, plus I want to try and gather fence for keepin hunt from my chicks. You want to be a lover, shoulda got a woman's job like the sheriff. Sittin up, actin like he own everybody 'cause he a full-blood. Me and you is cut from the blanket of night. Means we got to work. Means we got to slave the land.

He takes a drink in the creek and spots his reflection. It sparks a memory. Enter **Young Number Two**, *sixteen and shackled. He too takes a drink.* **Young Trowbridge** *enters with a spear; wearing nothing but a loincloth.*

It is 1823, Indiantown, Florida.

Young Number Two   Uh . . . 'scuse me –

Young Trowbridge   – Shh.

Young Number Two   What you mean "shh"? I can see ya ass.

Young Trowbridge   – Shh, said. I'm huntin the black bear.

Young Number Two   Where? Ain't no bear come through here –

Young Trowbridge   – He's just beyond those trees, in the bush eatin beauty berries.

There's a stir in the bush.

Young Number Two   Oh. Is that how you got naked? That bear ate your clothes?

Young Trowbridge   – Nawl and I ain't naked. This the warrior's armor, it's called a sackcloth.

Young Number Two   Well, if that's a sack it ain't holdin much and if it's a cloth you didn't got your money's worth. Ain't you cold as a well-digger's butt?

Young Trowbridge   I'm the son of a Seminole chief, I don't get cold. Now shh. I must face the bear and run my spear through his heart.

He creeps closer.

Young Number Two   Well, ain't this head-scratchin. I ain't never seen a half-naked man sneak up to a bear. Be like a chicken with no feathers walkin up to a wolf. Where I come from we call that free food.

Young Trowbridge   Shh! There must be silence when I kill him. It's my rite of passage: to leave the *talwa* in quest of the *éco*. I must bring the black bear home to feed my tribe for the Green Corn Festival. This is the beginning of my story.

Young Number Two   It looks like it gone be a short story. You can't kill no bear with that twig you call a spear. You need to set a trap. I'll help you for a horse and somewhere to lay my head for the night.

Young Trowbridge   Nawl, don't need it. 'Sides, I can tell you a runaway by them shackles on ya feet. It's against the law to give a runaway slave a horse in these swamps.

Young Number Two   Fine, but you wastin my talents. I know how to squeeze a bear and what to sing in his ear so he sleep, even where to lay him down. My massuh was a Creek Indian and taught me the secret song.

Young Trowbridge   Don't matter. Only Indians can wrestle the wild with secret chants. Niggras ain't got the blood for it. My paw says y'all good for makin nature grow 'cause ya got strong hands. But it means you b'long in the field.

Young Number Two   And what he know? Ya paw ain't God. I know God and He say I can wrestle any nature come my way. He give me a gift for it.

Young Trowbridge   Bully! God made you dark 'cause you b'long at the bottom. Even when a man look under his feet he find blackness. Now that mean somethin.

Young Number Two   Yeh, it mean he dirty and need to clean his feet!

Young Number Two *wrestles him. Time. The shadow of a bear appears. A growl!*

Young Trowbridge   He lickin his lips, let's run!

Young Number Two *grabs him.*

Young Number Two   You crazy!? Stay still. You can't run from no bear. We got to look into his eyes. If we stare him down, he'll let us see into his soul . . .

Young Trowbridge   Then what?

Young Number Two   Then I sing.

They turn toward the bear's shadow. The bear growls again! They stare.

(*Singing.*)
   MAT-KI-MATAH. MAT-CAT-CAH CA-LI-PAT-CA
   MAT-CA-CAH . . .

In shadow the bear bows and exits.

Told ya. Niggras can wrestle the wild just like Indians.

Young Trowbridge   Blood. You something else. You . . . say, maybe I found my black bear after all.

Young Number Two   What you mean? (*Beat.*) Why you lookin at me like that?

Young Trowbridge   'Cause.

He points spear at **Young Number Two**.

Young Trowbridge   You gone be mine.

Mary South   My man.

Number Two *wakes from his memory, as lights fade revealing* **Mary South**.

Number Two   Woman.

Mary South   May I talk with you a spell?

Number Two   I'm workin.

Mary South   It's urgent. There's been a happenin. And I needs to give you this alone.

Number Two   Colorado, go purchase that fencin at the trade post. Go with speed. Come with speed.

Colorado *exits.*

Number Two   Now you, speak with speed.

Mary South   Goodbird, Trowbridge's boy. We found him dead in the well. Don't know how he got there but we moved him to the chapel. And our hands been on the body.

Number Two   How you find a man in a well dat deep?

Mary South   He climbed out s'pose. You know it ain't no water in it now. He woulda drowned if it was. Somethin lifted him. A wanting.

Number Two   There was water in dat well yesterday. Somebody's been meddlin.

Mary South   Husband, what if his mother thinks we had some part in the act? The killin?

Number Two   Who said he was killed?

Mary South   I figure he musta been 'cause of the cuts. Plus I found a prod . . . some tool's tooth pierced in his side. From there I reason he was stabbed.

Number Two   Stabbed? Who said that?

Mary South   His body said. Somethin went at him with hate – bold and blind. My guess: he was cut up and tossed in the well to be lost in darkness. But the killer whatin so bright. Most birds don't drown, ya know. Most can swim.

Number Two   That so?

He lifts pitchfork showing missing tooth.

Mary South   Course. Everybody knows birds . . . (*Sees missing tooth.*) Lo, help me, Jesus.

Number Two   What is it? What you see, Mary?

Mary South   Nothin. I don't see nothin, I swear it.

Number Two   Then you not lookin good enough! Look closer woman. What you see?

Mary South   I see a gap. I see there's somethin 'tween us I didn't know. And don't want to now.

Number Two   That bird was makin nature with our daughter. Did you know that?

Mary South   Only recent. Only this morn.

Number Two   And you weren't gone tell me?

Mary South   Was. Soon as you would have . . . You killed him, Number Two? You killed the sheriff's only child?

Number Two   And woulda got away with it 'cept for you takin the body from the tomb.

Mary South   Merciful savior . . . Why?!

Number Two   That bird was makin nature with our daughter! The seed of my enemy plottin his own in the soil of my girl. Couldn't sleep with the thought of him flyin off with her in my dreams. Couldn't get no work done. But it's quiet now. Just listen. It's ever so quiet.

Mary South   His mother will bite down on us. That Half George will torture us slow as ticks in time. Can you be that foolish? Don't you know her power?

Number Two   That witch may have tricks in her bag but she knows 'bout me. She can't even breathe on me and cause a chill. I'm godly.

Mary South   Maybe in your own eyes, but I've layed with ya. If you were a god certain things would be magnificent.

Number Two   I don't like your mouth now, wife.

Mary South   If she lays a hand on my child, if she plucks even a strand of hair I will match my daughter's pain with yours. Twofold. If she merely scratches her, I will cut your neck while you sleep. Quiet. It will be ever so quiet.

She starts to exit but he stops her.

Number Two   Hold.

Mary South   Let me be.

Number Two   Hold, I said! I am your man. If I hold you – love it. If I touch you, be still. I bring peace, woman. Your needs are to please me. To make lust and children for me, not to lay threats. No, Mary South, you lay your body on me and perhaps a blanket when I am cold. I'm your god. You are to serve me.

Mary South   What this? What has this hate done to you? Where's my man?

Number Two   I put him to sleep. What you don't know about me is that I was a twin. I shared my mother's womb with a brother who wrapped his cord round my neck and fought me in my mother's belly for space. We were as alike as a pair of hands. Only he came out Number One, big and laughin. And I came out Number Two: blue as deep water and with a white mark 'cross my chest. I s'pose this caused everyone to treat me like such. I always got the seconds. Always walked behind, was always forgotten. Till sixteen years when the mark took the shape of a fist and somethin grew inside me I could no longer keep down. Till I was forced to take action, take the lead and push my brother from a top a tree. To quiet it. He was no rock, my brother. He burst into pieces at first crash. I figured that's what killed my momma. Drove my father crazy and forced me to run away. This mark. You and I both know it grows still. It charges me, urges me to be Number One. Horse Power says it's the mark of the white sun. Its shape means my life has no end and I can only be killed by my own blood. No blade nor gun or curse can take me down. I tested it, last Sunday when Horse read my story. I climbed a mountain, leapt into the sky, swallowed the sun and did not die. It's true, wife. I'm immortal.

Mary South   If you believe that, then that I married a fool. And that makes me a fool's wife. And that makes me laugh. And that makes me think life is funny. And that makes me want to cry. I have to tell Half George 'bout her child. You best tell Trowbridge you killed his son. You best solve this. Or you'll need to swallow more than the sun to calm her revenge.

Mary *exits.* **M. Gene** *and* **Fat Rev.** *walk to the well as people pass carrying pails from the creek.*

Fat Rev.   Now M. Gene, I must preach against this proclamation. Public broadcasts is why we have a church. I can say all what need be said in my Sunday sermon. Perhaps even make room for your need so that folks is sho to listen. Wife will you stay put and listen.

She stops.

Callin the sheriff and ya grand paw heathens is not the way to go about this. They good men . . . even if they is going to hell. I figure grand just been worshipin the olden spirits so long he can't get used to Jesus. And the sheriff . . . .well, he ain't never had to slave so he don't know how to treat us like we free. But they good men –

M. Gene   – You they shepherd, husband, and they your sheep. If they go to hell and you let them, it means you they wolf. How you live with yourself? Bein a wolf?

Fat Rev.   Well, I don't live with myself. I live with you. Now stop this, I mean it. You my wife but you got to mind me.

She pushes past him.

My foot is down M. Gene. See! Look at it! It's down. Down on the ground like so. Look at it!

She stops, looks.

M. Gene   I see it. It's pretty, but it don't walk over me. I'm led by God. And if you try and stop me, I'm gone cut you. I'm gone cut you in the name of Jesus –

Fat Rev.   – That's blaspheme! I'm your husband, but I'm a preacher. You can't talk to me any old way. You done blasphemed, M. Gene!

M. Gene *gets on a soapbox and blows a ram's horn. It hardly makes a sound. The townsfolk gather.*

M. Gene   Beloveds! Barking Water folk! Gather round. Gather round in the name of God. Women! Children! Theyz men! Gather round! Gather round in the name of God! (*Dramatic.*) Darkness! Locusts! Frogs! God spoke to me this mornin and told me we were bound. Bound by the old ways of witchcraft and slavery. Bound by our sheriff and grand paw Horse. And until we set ourselves free from them . . . there will be plagues.

They whisper insults about her.

The first was blood, which fell from my pail. The second was drought that drunk up the well. The last in the Bible is our third instead. Goodbird, the firstborn in this town . . . is dead.

The townsfolk gasp. In the chapel, **Sweet Tea** *sings over* **Goodbird**.

Sweet Tea (*singing*)
    KI-MO-NARO . . . CAPN-CARO . . . VERMIN-AITCHEE . . . SIMMON AITCHEE

Trowbridge *enters.*

Trowbridge   Where's my boy?! Where's my Goodbird?

Sweet Tea   He's here, sheriff.

Trowbridge   Breath Maker, don't let that be my child. NO, Heaven! Some God, give me back my boy! Some nature, give me my bird. How'd he go!? How'd he fly!!

Sweet Tea   Don't know. Found him in the well. Cut.

Trowbridge   Cut, how?! And by who?!

Sweet Tea   Ya questions are mine. I was his beloved. Me and your son, we were together for sunsets . . . (*Soft.*) He was my one.

Trowbridge   He was your what!?

Sweet Tea   My man. Your bird was mine.

Time.

Trowbridge   Course. He tried to tell me he was in love.
No wonder he kept it. There's hate between me and your
paw. That's why he couldn't say your name.

Sweet Tea   Don't hate me, suh, I luh –

Trowbridge   – I know. I knew such a love once. (*Beat.*) But
worry not. His death will take a life. I'll hunt the killer out and
cut off his head.

We return to the square.

M. Gene   But the next four plagues will be worst! Pestilence
will consume the sky! Beasts and flies will eat our livestock and
grain! Boils will pop from our skin! And hellfire will fall down
like rain!

A rock hits **M. Gene** *in the head. The crowd is silent. People at the sky
then run off. Inside the trade store,* **Half George** *cans tobacco. She is
a thick, handsome woman with hair white as George Washington's wig.
Enter* **Mary South** *with a fruit basket.*

Mary South   Evenin, Half George, how you? (*Time.*) My,
the trade store so pretty you'd think it was springtime in
November. Is this new calico? I'll take three yards of this and
some red ribbon when it moves ya. Sweet Tea is due a new
blouse though Lord knows I can't afford it. May I also have
some coal oil, a jar of molasses and powdered milk? (*Beat.*) You
lookin healthy t'day, Half George. I likes that color on you, it
brings out your womanly features. (*Time.*) Yeh, well, I was just
passin through, plum pickin and carryin on. Thought you
might be needin some fruit for your preserves.

Half George   Who said I preserved? I likes my fruit to fit
my nature: hard and rotten.

Mary South   Well, I believe God makes us all different.
Some of us is soft and peachy. Others are hard and rotten but
we all got good centers. Sometimes ya just got to peel away
the rotten parts to get at the sweet, but we all good. And got
good centers.

Half George   You sound like you think you done made some golden discovery. I can look and tell folks got good centers. I figured that when I was five. You one dumb woman, Mary South.

Mary South   Awl, go on . . .

Half George   Fine, I will. I wanted to tell you it before but didn't care enough to make it plain. Guess I do now. Here it is: I thinks you the dumbest bell ever rung in this dustball town. I thinks you hollow. Thick. Clangin. And if I had my way I'd silence your chime. I'd stick a nice-size rock down your throat then stitch your two lips together to make a hem. And if you choked it would be an "oh well." Life is hard 'nough with a rooster's cock-doodle wakin me every morn and sometimes sky thunder wakin me in the dead of night but havin to endure your empty talk, you comin here actin like we friends but needin somethin makes me want to beat ya. Knock ya down. Makes me want to stand on your head like a cliff to get a better view of the ocean.

Mary South   You seem in a mood. What's say I come back once you had a breather?

Half George   What's say you buy or trade now? You look like you need somethin.

Mary South   Yeh. Well, in truth I do need a thing.

Half George   I don't barter in fruit and cake. You can leave that basket for my Goodbird though. He's got a sweet tooth.

Mary South   Your Goodbird, you say?

Half George   Yeh. What you got he can drink, smoke or fuck with?

Mary South   You haven't heard.

Half George   Heard what? Nobody ever talks to a witch.

Mary South   Your boy . . . your boy is gone.

Half George   Gone? (*Beat.*) Oh. This 'bout your Sweet Tea, ain't it? Well, chicks come home to roost. What can I say that

I ain't thought before: my boy has a sweet tooth. Couldn't
keep him from your fawn. He's sprung and so is his dickie. Did
she run away with him? They'll be back. Goodbird don't stay
gone long. He picky and don't eat any woman's bread. Plus,
I heard yours don't know how to knead. Where they run to?

Mary South   They didn't. Though I wished they had. For
he's dead, Half George.

Half George   Not dead. Missin. He flies 'way for long
periods of time. His father does the same when he gets mad.
Men. Always runnin. It's 'cause they got fears of bein forced
off land. It makes 'em antsy –

Mary South   – I saw the body. Had it. Brought it to the
chapel myself. I even got some of his blood on my dress.

She shows a bloodstain.

I didn't want to break your heart, good woman. But no man
was man enough to do it. He's dead and 'twas his body that
cursed the well.

Time.

Half George   . . . My gut told me to keep him in. Told me
to mind him.

Mary South   Take my time for his. What he would have
given you in love, I'll give in labor –

Half George   Why come?

Mary South   No reason. I just feel sorry for ya and wants to
offer my hand.

Half George   Hand for what? You ain't never offered it
before.

Mary South   You ain't never needed it. But we the same.
Outcasts in our own town. Folks looks down on me 'cause I'm
full-blood Indian and married to a Negro. They look down on
you 'cause you a Negro married to a full-blood. But we the
same: two sides of the same hand. We got to help each other up.

Half George   – Bullshit! I smell bullshit, Mary South. You been eating bullshit?

Mary South   Nawl, ma'am, but I will if it please ya –

Half George   – IT WON'T! FEED ME TRUTH! –

Mary South   – It was an accident. Number Two stabbed him out of fear. He was drunk, angry, but he didn't mean it. Don't hurt him, Half George. I know you have great power and I believe in it. I believe in the old way but our new God teaches us forgiveness. He teaches us mercy and I need yours. Let me work for you is what I'm sayin. I know your man don't have time to since he gots to keep justice in the town. And now that your boy's gone . . . Look, I got strong hands. I can till. I'll sow so you can reap.

Half George   Reap: Corn Harvest. (*Thinking.*) Summer: a swallowed sun. Winter: a dead bird. Means: the spring of a new life. (*Beat.*) Your Sweet Tea's pregnant.

Mary South   Can't be. Sweet Tea's pure.

Half George   Woman, you that dumb? They were rollin since your gal grew hills. I want the child: night of the birth. And I won't harm yours. That's our deal.

Mary South   But Half George, there's no child, I swear –

Half George   – He will be raised by my hand. And his heart will be dead to your kin. You came to seal it. Let it be sealed.

She burns a needle under fire.

Mary South   Yes 'm.

Mary South *offers her hand.*

Half George   The time has come for the old smoke, Mary South. Go, tell your man. The time has come for a little sweat.

She burns "the pact" on **Mary**'*s hand with a needle.* **Mary** *gasps. In the square,* **M. Gene** *paces carrying a sign that reads: "Who stoned God's own?"* **Fat Rev.** *follows.*

Fat Rev.   M. Gene, you whatin stoned. You was pebbled. And it was one pebble. And sugar, it grazed you. Whoever threw it got bad aim or merely meant to scare you. Let's go home now.

M. Gene   A pebble was all it took for David to kill Goliath. How ya think it did me?

Fat Rev.   You're not Goliath, M. Gene. You're not even a Philistine.

M. Gene   "He that cast the first stone. Let him be without sin." Somebody in this town don't think they a sinner. But wait till I find him out.

Enter **Horse Power** *squeezing blood from a stone. He circles the well.*

Horse Power
   KI- YO-LA-HO-YA! YA HOLA-HO-YA!
   CO-LAKKO OP YANKA!

Fat Rev.   Good Lord, it's ya Grand.

M. Gene   What he doin? Is he bloodlettin? What a heathen. Grand Paw, come here!

He hands **M. Gene** *the bloody rock.*

M. Gene   What's this . . . it was you? Paw, you stoned me?

Horse Power   Yeh, I threw it. Threw it 'cause you're hard-headed and I wanted to see if your hard head could take a rock. Ya bled, so I figure it can't. Serves ya right for tellin folks tales. I tell the tales in this town! Me. I keep the stories. You cursed our town by tellin folks dem biblical lies. You got them livin in fear of nature when you know nature be God! Even your Jesus would be ashamed. You cut us off from the spirit's protection, M. Gene. You cut your gene gal. Now you're just an M.

He continues to dance round the well. **M. Gene** *falls to her knees, stunned.*

Fat Rev.   Alright, Grand Paw, get ya goin. Otherwise
I'm gone have to beat ya 'gainst the whippin tree. Ain't no
man gone be throwin stones at my wife. Don't care if she
deserve it or not. I'm the only man that's gone touch her. And
that's the Word. So get you gone.

Townsfolk pass carrying pails of water.

Horse Power   Y'all hear that! The Rev. is kickin ya paw
out of town. He gone feed him to whatever lurk beyond the
wood. If the Indians don't slave me, the coyotes gone have a
lean meal with my meats. Can y'all stand for that?

Fat Rev.   Paw now, I don't want there to be no mess.

Horse Power   – Can y'all walk by and let him kick me to
the grave?! Ya own paw.

The townsfolk stop to protect him.

I didn't think ya could. They not standin for it, Rev. You
might be their leader but I'm the one they'll always follow.
You forget . . . this my town!

He dances round the well.

M. Gene (*singing, full of anger*)
Satan is a liar and a conjurer too
If you don't watch out, he'll conjure you
If I could, Lord, I surely would
Stand on the rock where Moses stood.
Elijah rock!!! Shout! Shout!
Elijah rock, I'm comin up Lord!!

M. Gene *exits. Drawing the curtain of dusk over day, she climbs the
mountain. Women pour water into a tree stump then grind kernels to make
sofki. Men cover their faces with warrior paint and load guns.*

Trowbridge *carries the body of his son into the trade post where*
Half George *cleans.*

Half George   There's garfish and a bowl of meal on the
stove. You should eat. Horse'll be here at dawn to start the
burial.

Trowbridge   – Don't matter. I ain't hungry.

Half George   Still, ya should eat. Your heart may be heavy but your gut still needs attention. I'll heat you a plate.

Trowbridge   Don't bother, I'm going out for air.

He grabs his gun.

Half George   You don't need your gun for air, huz.

Trowbridge   I do if I can't breathe. And I won't be able to till I kill somethin. A group of menfolk are forming a posse at the foot of the mountain come sunset. To avenge Goodbird's death, they're going to raid the Creek Indian camp and kill the chief. With or without me they'll have his head.

Half George   For what? Can't you use yours, you know the Creeks didn't have nothin to do with this.

Trowbridge   They been threatenin us for sixteen years, Georgia. Creepin round our town at night, watchin us like hawks. I could feel their eyes on my back.

Half George   Those weren't Creek eyes. (*Pointing to the body.*) Just look. Look at your son and see who left their mark on his body. Who got hands strong enough to choke a neck? Who carries a pitchfork?

Trowbridge   It's not him. I know him. He would never do this.

Half George   Ever since we moved here he's been stewin. His hate for you havin grown so hot, he won't even cross the creek. Man sends his wife and his gal to fetch goods or packages. He can't even stand to look at you long enough to buy a box of tobaccah. And you think he won't kill your boy?

Trowbridge   You don't know him like I. We go back sunsets. Days and nights: just us for years. We only chose to hate each other 'cause our love was so strong it would have killed us. But he'd die for me. He'd never kill mine.

Half George   For his gal he would. If he saw your boy with his girl and felt that love was going to wound her like it did him. He'd kill yours to save his. I know for a fact, huz. His wife came and told me. She even left his tooth.

She shows him the tooth. Time.

Trowbridge   I'm a kill him.

Half George   Can't. He's got the mark. Horse Power says he can only be killed by his own blood. We got to get at him another way.

Trowbridge   Don't matter. Got to kill him tonight. While I'm thirsty.

Half George   You not listenin. You the sheriff. You got to be the law and arrest him. You got to call off that raid 'fore sundown. For those men go killin the wrong one or worst yet get killed.

Trowbridge   But I want to hug him.

Half George   You do and you gone be dead.

Trowbridge   Don't matter.

Half George   Don't matter? You dead and it don't matter. What about me?! I matter?

Trowbridge   I ain't strong as you, Georgia. It's the one thing that keeps me in your arms. Your awesome strength. Perhaps, you're my man and me: just kisses. But I can't live without my vengeance quenched. I gots to touch him.

He kisses her forehead.

Half George   Listen to me, you go and stop that raid. You look me in the eyes and tell me you're going to stop that raid, Trowbridge.

He grabs his axe and a sack.

Trowbridge   It's been so long since I touched him . . . So long . . .

He exits. Outside, bowls of sofki and fruit are left on the porch.

Half George   You stop that raid, Trowbridge!! Don't leave a woman lonely in this world like most men do! Like most kin! Like even most gods.

She unveils her child's body, she prays.

Mary *and* **Sweet Tea** *in the chapel.*

Mary South   You could have come to me. I would have taught you how to keep that ugly muscle from spittin 'tween your legs. I know tricks! How far long are ya?

Sweet Tea   Long 'nough.

Mary South   What that mean? Two months?

Sweet Tea   Longer. Been hidin it for close to eight.

Mary South   Eight?! Gal, I thought you was just fattenin up for winter. Jesus! We got to keep you healthy and I got to start knittin, carvin a cradle and . . . . (*Beat.*) Lord, how quick I forgot. How quick as if nothin had happened . . .

Sweet Tea   What is it, Maw?

Mary *packs articles in her basket.*

Mary South   Nothin. Nothin, love. We just got to get you out of town – that's all. We got to get you out of town quick as possible.

Sweet Tea   But why? I can't be travelin while I'm pregnant.

Mary South   Don't matter, we got to get. They're plagues here. Plagues that will try to take your firstborn. You heard the first lady –

Sweet Tea   – Maw, you don't believe that lore?

Mary South   I've seen things, Tea. Beautiful things that your eyes can't hardly fathom. I've seen children cured by kisses. Old women made beautiful by scratching their heads. I've seen people sprout wings. But I've also seen horrible things. Boys killed for their father's crime. Father's turnin their backs on their chilren. Babies ripped from the arms of their mothers to pay a debt. I've seen plagues in people far worst than those in nature. And I'm afraid these plagues are destroying our town. Now I never ask you for much, babe. But this one thing you got to do for me. Let me take you 'way from here. To the ocean. I know it's your dream, Tea. Let me keep you Sweet.

Creekside. **Number Two** *tends to his corn.* **Colorado** *enters with a gun.*

Number Two   Where you been, Colorado, I thought I said come with speed?

Colorado   I tried, boss, but there were distractions in town. Some Creeks killed the sheriff's boy and we formin a posse. We gone raid the Creek camp tonight. I just came by to see if you want to join us. I know you ain't one to partake in town affairs but . . . well, everybody knows you're quite the warrior. We've all heard the legends 'bout you and the red kyote and you fightin that whole army at Fort Gibson. We need you, Number Two –

Number Two   Is you askin or is the sheriff?

Colorado   You know the sheriff don't ask for nothin. He ain't a man, he a massuh. He been treatin me like a dog all my life and part of me don't care to fight for his son since I hate him but . . . I figure I hate the Creeks more.

Number Two   No, you don't. Hate don't exist. Only love is real. Figure, hate be love misled but it's love nevertheless. Can't hate nothin you don't love. Can't love nothin you don't somehow hate. You love the sheriff?

Colorado   Hell and naw.

Number Two   Then you don't hate 'em. But me. I love 'em. I love 'em like I love a woman. Like I love my wife. Just with bad directions. Lost like. Like I could soon as kill 'em to kiss 'em on his lips.

Colorado   Wo-ah, ya revealin lots. We just partners. I ain't got to know your sickness –

Number Two *shoves him against a tree.*

Number Two   While you work for me, Colorado, best learn what kind of man I am. Best learn when it's best to test me. Trowbridge crossed me. Misled the love I had for 'em. That whatin good. Now, I didn't stop lovin him, love don't die. It sometimes gets misdirected and grow round like undergrowth but love always grow. Maybe even choke somethin. In plain, this my meanin: best not test me. If I tell ya to come back with speed, best do like I tell ya or I might get a hold of ya . . . and choke.

He releases **Colorado** *who exits.* **Number Two** *skips a rock in the creek. It sparks a new memory.*

Young Number Two *is revealed under sunlight skipping rocks in the water. Enter* **Young Trowbridge**.

Young Trowbridge   I can show you how to skip rocks, Number Two. I'm a master at it.

Young Number Two   Show me how to leap off a cliff you want to show me somethin.

Young Trowbridge   Ooo, somebody's hot. You mad ' 'cause I'm going West with old Horse?

Young Number Two   Nawl, what I care? Likes to be on lonesome anyways. And with you gone I'll finally be free. Be my own massuh.

Young Trowbridge   That's what you want, ain't it?

Young Number Two   Been what I wanted all my life.

Young Trowbridge   Then why you hot?

Young Number Two   Don't know! Maybe 'cause of the heat . . .

Young Trowbridge   Oh. Figured you'd be used to Florida swamp by now. Maybe its 'cause I'm so close to ya. Maybe I make ya heated.

He puts his arms around **Young Trowbridge**'s *waist. They wrestle.*

Young Number Two   Don't touch me. It ain't normal.

Young Trowbridge   So, neither is your aim. You want to skip a rock, best lead it to water. And use your hips more. Ain't you ever made love?

Young Number Two   I've made plenty things.

Young Trowbridge   Hm. That mean no. I could teach you a swing or two. But you'd have to come West and help me build a town with old Horse –

Young Number Two   – Why would I do that? Like you said, I'm free.

Young Trowbridge   And you'd still be. You'd just be free with me. Might as well . . . I know ya got the hots for me –

Young Number Two   – Ha! ya been dreamin. Stay sleep –

Young Trowbridge *kisses him.*

Young Trowbridge   Hm. Now looks like we both woke.

Sun and moon move into the same house: a solar eclipse. The creek turns black. **Number Two** *wakes and sees* **Trowbridge**. *Moonlight falls, we return to the stand-off.*

Trowbridge   I been sent to put out your fire!!

Number Two   Then God give you the strength to do it. You'll surely need Him.

Trowbridge *and* **Number Two**   Ahhhh!

They collide, choke each other. Time.

Number Two   Take this breath, Trowbridge.

Trowbridge   No! Won't. Won't sleep!

Number Two   Take it, I said! Be with your son.

Number Two's *hands meet.*

Trowbridge   No . . . bird . . . air . . .

He takes his last breath. We hear a wind song. He dies. **Number Two** *lays him in the creek, cuts off his hair braid and pockets it. He walks into the wood and comes upon* **Horse Power**.

Horse Power   Your fated day is here, Number Two. The mark of the white sun that grows on your chest, the Breath Maker's fire has risen. Stolen by rabbit, swallowed by your paw, it lives holy in you now. Only you can keep us from being made slaves. Bring the heat, Number Two. You hear them cries in the night. Follow 'em and put them Creek Indians on their knees. You are the sun! So burn!! Set them massuhs on fire!

A scream. In the woods, **Sweet Tea** *lies against a tree. She's in labor.*

Sweet Tea   I can't do it here, Maw! I can't have my babe in the wood.

Mary South   Yes you can, you strong. You come from good stock. Just breathe for me.

Sweet Tea *breathes.*

Mary South   That's it, babe. Keep breathin for Maw. That's it.

An owl flies to a nearby tree.

Half George (*as the owl, wobbling her neck*)   Whooo . . . Whoo . . . Whooo . . .

Sweet Tea   I think he's comin . . . O God . . . God blood . . .

At the camp, **Rev.** *and* **Colorado** *take shelter from gunfire.*

Colorado *is cut.*

Fat Rev.   You gone be alright. Just hold this kerchief to your wound.

Colorado   We're outnumbered, Rev. Trowbridge never showed and the Creeks got the upper hand. It's over. We're good as dead.

Mary South   Nawl, just push, babe. He gone be fine. Just push for Maw.

She screams, pushes.

Half George   Whoo . . .

Mary South   There you go . . . that's it! I see a head! I see him comin!

A loud rumbling.

Fat Rev.   Who's that? There in the East.

Colorado   Don't know. Is it the sheriff?

Fat Rev.   Nawl. Nawl, look it's . . .

Number Two   *HO-YA!!!*

Colorado   Number Two and he got a glow on 'em. He got a glow! Look at 'em. Those Creeks can barely touch 'em. He poppin they necks like peas from pods. Good God, he's . . .

Mary South   Beautiful. Look at your son, Sweet Tea.

The owl flies off.

Number Two   *LAKKO OP YANKA!!*

Mary *takes the baby and cleans him.*

Half George   I heard a cry in the night, looks like my gift is here.

She appears in a feathered neckpiece.

Mary South   He just arrived, Half George. Let my girl have one day with him.

Half George   What for? Ain't no better time than the present to get a gift.

Sweet Tea   Maw? Maw, who's out there?

Mary South   Nobody, Tea.

She hands **Half George** *the baby.*

Mary South   Take him then. This must be God's will.

Half George   Ah, just look at him. He's got Trowbridge's eyes.

Fat Rev.   He killed every last one. Number Two killed every last one of 'em.

Colorado   Will have half their tribe after us now.

Fat Rev.   Come. Sweet Jesus.

Half George   And he shall be called . . . Wonderful.

Number Two *walks out of the moon, dancing.*

Number Two   *YA HOLA – HO-YA!*

He blows the moon out.

Prelude to Act Two

THE GOSPEL OF FATE ACCORDING TO RED COYOTE,
OR THE SILENT YEARS

*Dusk: the moon and sun are making love. She bleeds milk and smoke, he
spews fire and cold light.* **Number Two** *and* **Half George** *meet at
the creek. It is 1866, sixteen years later.*

Number Two Come out from behind those trees, Georgia.
Don't let this body fool ya. I'm bleedin like a cut pig but I'm
still a god.

He spits blood.

Half George Don't matter. I knows your secret, Number
Two. Horse told me your weakness.

Number Two Liar. He'd never tell it. You just tryin to get
in my head like ya been doin for the last sixteen years.
Meddlin my mind. Poisonin me every chance ya get.

Half George I suck poisons, I don't sick 'em. My way to
kill a man is quick, fast, out the water like a 'gator, mouth
open to bite down then watch your eyes roll.

Number Two Nawl, you been creepin to my window at
night. Shootin needles in my neck, droppin petals of mornin
glory in my coffee. Bet ya even sold my woman them cherries:
givin me these shakes and stenches. Ya rippin me apart but
I won't burst. I got a gift and ya knows it. Just came by to tell
ya, you clever for a bear and I wants to give you a hug.

Number Two *tries to grab her but feels a sharp pain in his gut. He
falls to his knees.*

Half George Folks been sayin you been bleedin for weeks,
Number Two. They say you got the runs so bad you can
hardly walk. Say you smell of dog shit too, but worst 'cause
you ain't a dog. Myself, I figure it's the Breath Maker's way of

makin you the butt of jokes. Ya paw named ya Number Two so I guess He figure you might as well smell like it.

Number Two   It ain't God, it's you! I know you been cursin me out your black bag but ya days are numbered. It's time for you to follow ya man back to hell.

He rises as night falls.

Half George   And God give you the strength to do it! You'll surely need 'em.

The moon opens her eye.

Number Two *and* **Half George**   AHHHHH!

They collide like rivers, their hands tides. They form the mouth of a cave. We return to the present where **Horse Power** *is showing* **Wonderful** *his star.*

Wonderful   Mercy! Is he gone kill my maw? Is the sheriff gone kill my maw, Horse?

Horse Power   I don't know, Wonderful. I can't quite make out that part of the story. Figure that part of the story you got to find out for yaself. A star can only shine on so much. You gots to be the harbinger of your own fate now.

Wonderful   Then I got to kill him. I gots to kill the sheriff fore he kill my maw.

Horse Power   Careful. The worst thing a man can do is kill one of his own. It be damned enough when somebody else kills your kin but when a man kill his own, its worst than him killin himself. The stain of a blood relative don't come off your hands, it just leaves a mark that grows. 'Sides, Number Two is mean but he got a good heart. He just need help putting it in the right place.

Wonderful   Oh, I'm a put it in the right place. Right 'tween my fist and squeeze it. He's a walkin plague! He killed my paw and my grand, cursed the well. Killed hundreds of Creeks and is makin a killin off the land. Land they rightfully belongs to me.

Horse Power   Land don't belong to no man. This here
Earth be God's breasts and it's for our milking not our rape.
The minute a man claims a part of Mother Earth's flesh he
gets fucked. He goes mad for her meat like a dog at the first
taste of blood. Chewin everything in his path – nature, people,
histories – till all that's left is bones and the spirits of bones
that haunt him past apologies. Carvin your name into land be
the biggest curse in Creation. You do better to cut off your
own head.

Wonderful   And I surely would if it meant his death. Don't
you feel the heat, Horse? It's getting hotter in town by the day.
And the hotter it gets, the stronger he becomes. The well's still
dry and the creek is dryin up. Folks is dyin of thirst and what's
worst, the sheriff is cold. He taxes us and treats us worst than
dogs. Makes folks work in his cornfields for little to no pay. He
don't even observe Sundays. Somebody's got to put him
down, no matter the cost. And we both know I got the blood
to do it.

The scene fades as **M. Gene** *walks down the mountain, humming.*

Act Two

THE NEW TESTAMENT OR WHY THE ROAD WEEPS

Fat Rev. *and* **Colorado** *build a wall near the creek.* **Colorado** *is ugly. It's hot.*

Fat Rev.   Buildin this wall in front of the creek don't make no kind ah sense. Them Indians just gone climb over it. Ya can't kept folks from water.

Colorado   I know it, but Number Two the sheriff. And if he wants a wall built in front of the creek, he gets a wall built in front of the creek.

Fat Rev.   There's been ten years of peace though. Why he want to stir things? Man said he planned to charge them Creeks too if they want to take a drink. Like he own the water.

Colorado   He might as well, he own everything else. His sweetcorn alone bring in a hundred dollars a season. Course we only got one season: so you can imagine how heavy his wallet must be. Man even got folks from Fort Riley ridin out here just to take a bite.

Fat Rev.   Don't matter. It ain't Christian to cut folks off from water.

Colorado   They shoulda thought about that 'fore they killed Goodbird and cursed our well. I don't feel sorry for them Creeks. If they die of thirst it be God's will.

Fat Rev.   Awl, quit ya gummin: you spittin sixteen years' worth of hogwash. I know for certain them Creeks didn't kill Goodbird. The Lord told my wife who did it in a dream. He said it was a black bear.

Colorado   Toes! You mean to tell me a black bear killed Goodbird, threw him down the well and drunk all our well water?

Fat Rev.   Yup. We was fighten them Creeks for nothin all those years. Good thing God spoke to my wife though. Ain't she just a wonder?

Colorado   Yeh, Lord, I often find myself wonderin 'bout her. Then I gets itchy.

Fat Rev.   Awl, don't be jealous, Colorado. God gone send you a godly woman too. Just hold fast now and pray.

Colorado   Nawl, ain't no woman want a man with a face like mine. I used to be God's gift but been fightin too much. And losin. Got too many scars coverin my beauty, figure. Now you can't even give me away.

Fat Rev.   Ya just shy 'cause you ugly. I can teach ya what to say to a gal, make her forget you hard to look at. Don't let this fat fool ya. I used to be a heart-breaker way back when. Had enough loose women to start my own church choir. Well, till I found Sister Moses and got saved.

Colorado   Is that what you call it? Don't you mean damned? I don't want to hurt ya heart, Rev., but your wife is wearin your pants and holdin ya pecker.

Fat Rev.   Bite ya tongue! She mean but I won't have ya buryin her name in the mud –

Colorado   – Like she do yours. What you think she sayin 'bout you behind your back? She got curses for you I ain't never even called the devil. And the way she run the church and boss the menfolk round. She do all but preach ya sermons and any man with half a mind can tell she write 'em.

Fat Rev.   You know 'bout that?

Colorado   The whole town know 'bout that.

Fat Rev.   Jacob slept! Folks must thinks I'ze yeller?

Colorado   As churned butter.

Fat Rev.   Awl, I could cry.

Colorado   And be the first to weep since we moved here. Thirty-two years we been on this land, ain't a man wept once. Don't you do it, Rev. If anybody should cry it should be your wife. I bet I could teach you how to make her mind.

At the square, **M. Gene** *preaches before women who fan themselves with hats.*

M. Gene   God ain't meant for Eve to have to mind no Adam. It's s'pose to be the other way 'round. Only thing is man ran faster and got to God's book 'fore woman could. She was no doubt pregnant at the time and could only get so far. So man grabbed the book and changed the scripture to fit him. That's why some of the good book don't make no sense. Man been meddlin in it. But God really mean for women to lead. Just think on it, we more like God than any man. We love easier, more patient, long sufferin and we the creators. We give men life. That there is plum proof we more like God and he's given me eyes to see it. And I sho aim to spread it as gospel. Far and wide, wide and free. And you do the same, my daughters. Go and be like God . . . for you all our goddesses.

The women applaud and disperse.

Mary South   My, that was some sermon, sister.

M. Gene   Why thank ya, Mary. And don't you look like you done touched the hem of God's garment, stole it, then put it on for church service.

Mary South   Well, you know I had to look smart for my Sweet Tea's homecoming. Her letter say high noon but I didn't want to miss her in case she got here early. She might feel a little lost after sixteen years.

M. Gene   Lord today, why she chose to get an education then be some nurse for the union army I'll never fathom. Tendin to colored soldiers, being round all those savage, sweaty menses and ain't got no husband. It's a lot on a gal.

Enter **Horse Power**, *pulling a wagon.*

Horse Power   – There she is, just the woman I want to see and my, she is as beautiful as a cactus in the desert of my soul. How you be, gal?

Mary South   As peachy as pie and how are you Paw Power?

Horse Power   Well, in truth I'm a little thirsty. Life got me plum out of button coin and I need a drink. Does your pocket still jingle, gal? Let me hear it.

M. Gene   Paw, we are not feedin your drunken spirit with our hard-earned buttons. Leave us. You know better than speakin to ladies 'fore you had a bath.

Horse Power   Lady? Is that what you callin yaself these days, M.? Any man get a good look at your face will throw a rope around it and saddle it up to a trough. Don't you ever tell me who to speak to and when. You my dead daughter's only child, if it whatin for me you'd still be a seed swimming in my nut sack.

M. Gene   Niggahs and flies –

Mary South   – Alright now, today's my Sweet Tea's homecoming. Y'all be sweet.

Horse Power   You right, daughter. I just needs a drink to calm my nerves. Been dancin round the well all night, it's got my head spinnin.

M. Gene   Then stop dancin, heathen. It ain't rained in sixteen years. The land's cursed –

Horse Power   You should know since you cursed it! *(Soft.)* Mary did I tell you, you look beautiful as butter cake t'day? You don't even need frostin. You go good with air. Have I told you that?

Mary South   Every day, Paw, but I appreciate it. You go soft on the First Lady now.

She gives him two buttons.

M. Gene   He need to come to church and let me lay hands on him. Cast that demon from the pits of his soul.

Horse Power   Never! I ain't never lettin you put your hands on me. You still just an M. And an M. ain't much –

M. Gene   – In the name of Jesus!

She touches his head, he spits on her.

Christ! He spat on me.

He exits into the trade post.

Mary South   Mercy. He actin outside himself t'day. Must be somethin in the wind.

M. Gene   No . . . it's the final plague. God has hardened his heart like he did Pharaoh's. Next, he'll send a flood. All these years and we still ain't learned God wants us free. He's drunk our well water, sent a dry spell, killed a firstborn, kept us in battle with the Creeks, and now . . . niggahs is spittin. He's the cause, Mary. My grandpaw is Egypt. It's time for Moses to take up her rod.

Mary South   You don't mean that, sister. He's just old and drunk –

M. Gene   – I got to. Otherwise, we'll never keep this Promise Land. I must part the sea along his back till he bleeds a river. So we can cross. Be free.

In the store, **Horse** *counts for* **Half George**.

Horse Power   Here it is: two sum, three sum, four sum and six.

Half George   I know what ya got, Horse and it ain't enough for a bottle of whiskey. Why don't ya buy a glass and take it slow – it's morning yet.

Horse Power   'Cause it's gone be a long day! I feel it in my bones. This day gone go on for years. Cut me some slack, Georgia. You know I'm good people.

Half George   What's good people got to do with the price of whiskey? Three sum and four more is what you need, pay it or get you gone.

Horse Power   Ain't this a dog's shame! You forgot I saved ya from that medicine man back pass Molly's bend. He had ya growin rice in the marshlands, half clothed, drinkin black drink, and you carryin him on your back like you was his mule. He had you so shocked your hair turned to the white of bird droppins. But it was I who snatched you from that pit, Georgia Mae. When your black kin turned their backs on ya for being witchy, it was me who took you on my hip like a babe, fed you out of my mouth and put you on the road with the rest of my chilren. But you forget!!

Half George   So what ya sayin?

Horse Power   I'm sayin ya owe me.

Half George   Well, blood and shit. Didn't realize you been holdin to my debt all these years. Fine, I'm a pay ya. T'day in fact, pay you in full. I'm a give you anything in this store you want. You been holdin to my debt all these years then you gone get what you got comin. But after this don't come back. Ever.

Horse Power   What you talkin 'bout? You can't keep me from buyin and tradin.

Half George   Who say I can't? Read the sign 'bove the door. It say: "Half George's Trade or Buy." And guess who I be?

Horse Power   All I want is some whiskey. This done got out of hand now. All I want is a drink.

Half George   Too late. You done already put in your order, now you gots to get served. Boy! We got a tall order for a small man.

Wonderful *enters from the back.*

Half George   Get him a box and give him his whiskey. Then bag him this brandy wine, some canned beans, these four beets. Give 'em this cordial, that sack of almonds near the churn.

Wonderful   But Maw, those your favorite.

Horse Power *drinks from the bottle.*

Half George   I know, but I'm payin a debt. Give 'em these herbs: this sallyfoot, a pinch of nightshade, mint leaves for his breath.

Wonderful   You going away, old Horse, or having a Thanksgivin?

Horse Power   Neither, your maw just lost her mind and wants me to help her find it.

Half George   And put in some dry milk, he got bad bones! Oh! And don't forget the rest of this crow! He sho 'nough gone eat that.

Horse Power   I can't take these goods, Georgia. I got a bad back and legs. I can't lift this.

Half George   No matter, I'll take 'em. It's my debt to pay. I'll carry 'em myself.

She exits with the food.

Horse Power   Damn the devil, it's hot as hell t'day. The demons is risin, boy. They rippin my chilren from my arms and the chilren slippin. I can't hold to 'em no more. I'm too old. It's time to be wise.

He exits. **Wonderful** *picks up his spear and practices fighting techniques.*

Sweet Tea (*singing offstage*)
   I was in bloom
   Like tulips in June
   Till I found you . . .

Enter **Sweet Tea***, in a petticoat, grand hat with a ruby pin and gloves.*

Sweet Tea   Well, ain't this enough to pout lips? Where's my welcome wagon? Ain't nobody even here on a mule waving their big toe and whistlin Dixie. Where folks at?

Wonderful   Gone.

Sweet Tea   Gone where? Didn't they know Sweetly Tastin Freeman was comin to town. Been on the road for half a month since the war. Shoppin, shuckin, eatin and carryin on. What ya think of my hat?

He hardly looks, continuing to joust.

Wonderful   It's big.

Sweet Tea   Course it's big. I'm a big woman. Was a gal when I left but . . . where's Half George?

Wonderful   Gone.

Sweet Tea   Gone to where and who in God's name are you?

Wonderful   Wonderful.

Time. She realizes who he is.

Sweet Tea   That so? Well, what's so wonderful about ya?

Wonderful   Can't say, it's a secret.

Sweet Tea   Course. This Indian Territory: everything here is put under a rock.

He stops maneuvering with his spear.

Wonderful   Good God, you sho is perty, ma'am.

Sweet Tea   Aren't you a gentle soul?

Wonderful   Yes'm. I'm gentle . . . but I can be rough if you likes that.

He gets close to her, she moves.

Sweet Tea   Lord, I sho am hungry. Would you believe I been cravin peaches and butter biscuits for sixteen years? Left this town in a rush. Didn't even take my maw's recipes – just had to see the world. Had to touch the ocean.

Wonderful   You been to the ocean?

Sweet Tea   Plenty ah times. It's truly Mother Earth's greatest bounty. Don't let nobody keep you here too long, Wonderful. Every man must see the ocean one day. I reckon it's why God put us here in the first place. Simply to admire His watercolors. You wanna hear her? I stole the ocean's song and put it in a shell. Come listen . . .

Sweet Tea *puts a seashell to his ear.*

Wonderful   Wo-ah, what she singin? She sound sad.

Sweet Tea   Yeh, she misses her sun.

Wonderful   Fancy that. The ocean got a boy.

Sweet Tea   Course. Her boy is the sun. She gives birth to him every morning only to watch him leave her and rise 'cross the sky. They say she sings a sad song till he returns. So it's best to capture her song at night. She sings a high tide then. A song of rejoicing.

Wonderful *falls in love. He tries to kiss her.*

Sweet Tea   Hey now, take that horse around the bend. Don't you know who I am, boy?

Wonderful   Yes'm. You my destiny.

Sweet Tea   Yeh. (*Beat.*) I'm ya maw.

He's hit with lightning. He grumbles, then tears rain from his eyes. He runs into her arms for shelter.

Number Two (*singing offstage*)
    Daddy's baby is a sweety
    The sweetest honey she can be
    He spoils her with cakes and candy
    And choco from the cocoa tree.

High noon: **Number Two** *walks out of a ray of light and into the square wearing a double-breasted suit and Stetson hat. His badge is gold. Folks greet him in passing.*

Number Two
    Yeh, daddy's baby loves her mommy
    But no one's sweeter than her pappy be
    He rocks her like the sea and hobby
    He prays to God she'll never leave.

He is the only one in town not bothered by the heat. He leans against his statue on the well and lights a cigarette. A wind sings.

Red Kyote (*whisper*)
Ki mo naro! Ki mo naro! Ki mo naro!

A wind takes his light, a figure drifts by.

Number Two   Trowbridge?

He chases the figure and runs into **Fat Rev.** *and* **Colorado** *carrying pails to the chapel.*

Fat Rev.   Heaven come a cropper! Sheriff, you look hot enough to put on a plate.

Number Two   Say, y'all get a look at that man that just ran through here?

Colorado   Ain't no man run through here. Just been us. We takin a break from workin on the wall. It got so hot Rev. here started sweatin grease. Do Lord, I can't muster how you able to wear that suit, sheriff, and not even break a sweat.

Number Two   Don't know, guess it's my mood. This gone be the best day of my life: my Sweet Tea comin home.

Colorado   Oh that's right. I forgot your Tea was comin to town. Gal whatin nothin but a sprout when she left, shave-tail and sass-saaaay. Ooo that gal used to get under my skin quick as gin, when the devil come out she go in.

Fat Rev.   That's 'cause you treated her meaner than a cooter. Fact she was 'bout the only woman in town who hadn't lost they skirts in your wagon.

Colorado   Yeh Lord, those were the days of Jubilee! But now I'm ugly as homemade sin.

Fat Rev.   Now that's the gospel truth, you is ugly. (*Beat.*) Say sheriff, you alright? You lookin offish for the best day of your life.

Number Two   Nawl, I'm fine. Just got my head in a twist. That Half George been whisperin little nothings in my ear

again. Got me playin outside my character, Fat Rev. I sho
could use a shave if it please ya. Don't want my Tea thinkin
her father's turned into a grizzly.

Fat Rev. *retrieves tools and gives him a shave.*

Fat Rev.   Sit on down then, it'd be my pleasure. And
Colorado, I don't want to hear no more 'bout you're ugly.
Consider yaself bless. Least now a gal will have to love you for
your heart.

Colorado   Some good that'll do me. My heart's beat up
worst than my face.

He exits. **Fat Rev.** *shaves* **Number Two**.

Number Two   Sho hurt me to see that boy with his head
bowed low. Hidin himself from eyes, talkin soft when gals pass
and him not even tryin to pinch they cushions. I got to give
him somethin to lift him . . . somethin sweet.

Enter **Potter's Clay**, *an Army Scout.*

Potter's Clay   Pardon me, I am looking for Freedman. (*To*
Number Two.) Are you Mr. Freedmen?

Number Two   Yeh, but so is everybody else in town. We
all related if not by blood by name. It be our law: every man
here is free and thus called Freedman.

Potter's Clay   Right. But you are the sheriff, right? A Mr. . . .
(*reading from a letter*) Trowbridge Freedman?

Number Two   Nawl. Trowbridge left our town sixteen
years back. Up and left without a word. I'm the new law.
Name's Number Two.

They shake hands.

Potter's Clay   Well, it's quite an honor to meet you. I'm
First Lieutenant Potter's Clay. I served in the first Kansas
Colored Infantry during the Civil War and now work as a
scoutsman at Fort Gibson. And sheriff, I must tell you that this
town is nothin short of a miracle. It's somethin my eyes ain't

never seen before, my mind ain't thought possible and my heart could really get used to. Negroes! A whole town full of nothin but Negroes. It's like heaven but it's so hot you think you're in hell and wants to get sinful. Y'all got Negro blacksmiths, cattlemen, carpenters, grocers, schoolteachers. Hell, it seem like even the dogs here be Negroes.

Fat Rev.   Well, hold on now, we ain't nobody's dogs . . .

Number Two   – He didn't mean that, Rev., the boy's just sprung. He been fightin in a war for freedom but ain't never seen it up close. Not real freedom. Here, we put the word free to good use. Even the land be free. It belong to all of us and grows the sweetest corn far as the eye can see. Plus it brings in more money than we know what to do with.

Fat Rev.   Well, I don't know about that, I sho could use two nickles to rub together –

Number Two   – Hush Rev.! Welcome to Freetown, Mr. Clay. Now how can we help ya?

Potter's Clay   Actually, I was hoping to come and help you. I was told that this land was cursed by the chief of the neighboring Indians. He said the sun hung heavy over this place, making ya'll crazy and dying of thirst. I was hoping to bring you good news, tell you that help was on the way but . . . I'm afraid to report the government has given your land to the Seminoles.

Number Two rises. *The scout is frightened.*

Number Two   That must be an error! We were told by the government we could settle any land we found here! We were told this land was ours by right. They gave us their word!

Potter's Clay   Forgive me, but a word hardly suffice when compared to a letter. I have one, sir. Would you like to read it –

Fat Rev. *takes it and reads.*

Fat Rev.   "Dear Sheriff Freedman. Due to the war a few land settlements have come into question and a delegation of chiefs have met to decide what to do with the land you and Negroes occupy. Because the Seminole chiefs cannot be expected to take reservations on land that will not grow good crops or neighbor cool streams they are requesting that you provide homes for them and their families in your town. Knowing the abolition of slavery to be a fact throughout the United States, the Seminole leaders are willing to live in cohabitation with Negroes but cannot be expected to incorporate them on equal footing. Because as they have learned from the white man, the Negro is undoubtedly inferior. The emancipated Negro must, of necessity, be suitably provided for and governed by the Chiefs from this day forward. We, the United States government, trust that this decision will be met with your full accordance. Our sincerest appreciation, Major John B. Sandborn." *(Beat.)* Governed by the same chiefs that enslaved us. The same men we ran away from. God help us . . .

Number Two   Mr. Clay, tell your major we don't have hearts for masters here. If the Seminole chiefs want to live in our town, they may but as equals. Here, there is only room for one chief. And that chief is me.

Potter's Clay   Are you sure, sir?

Number Two   We have our own law and the treaties of the United States government cannot stand against it. We will be free or will go to war fightin for our freedom.

Potter's Clay   I understand your frustration, but as one Negro to another you don't want to go against the United States Army. They will crush you.

Number Two   Good. Let 'em come. It's been a long time since I had a crush.

Potter's Clay *exits and* **Number Two** *continues his shave. At the trade post,* **Sweet Tea** *ravages food. The store is a mess.* **Wonderful** *listens to the shell sing.*

Wind Song (*singing offstage*)
 I was in bloom
 Like tulips in June
 Till I found you

 You brought the moon.
 Luring the sea to swoon
 I drown without you

 I was so blue
 Drownin in blues
 Till I found you

Wonderful   My grand maw said you was gone for good.

Sweet Tea   Well she wrong. I come back.

Wonderful   Yeh. But why'd you leave?

Sweet Tea   Had to. Had to make sense of the world. Couldn't quite get my head round it. You weren't my child though I gave birth to you and no one would tell me why. They just took ya as if they owned ya. I looked up one day and you were gone from my arms and all that I was left with were two options: I could chew nails and be mad at the world or find my place in it. So I left.

Outside, **Half George** *kicks* **Colorado**.

Half George   Stop layin round my store, Colorado. I don't shelter dogs or fleas, I sho ain't gone shelter no ugly-ass man!

Wonderful   Oh God it's my grand! She comin . . .

Sweet Tea   Wonderful, meet me at the creek at midnight. It's our only chance to get away from here. I'll have a coach waitin. Promise me you'll meet me. (*Beat.*) PROMISE ME!

Wonderful   Yes'm.

Half George   Heat and bone: looks like a tornado blew through here.

Enter **Half George**.

Wonderful   I'm cleanin it up, Maw. Don't have a hissy. I'm cleanin it up.

He cleans.

Sweet Tea   She got you callin her maw, ain't this thick as horse shit.

Half George   Course he calls me maw, I'm his ma'am. Wonderful, hurry and clean then go upstairs.

Sweet Tea   That's a lie. You been tellin him a lifetime of lies, Half George –

Half George   – Wonderful, go upstairs.

Wonderful   But I thought you said clean first –

Half George   GO UPSTAIRS NOW!

He exits.

Ya lookin healthy, Sweet. Thought you'd be gone for longer but it figures. It's the first lunar moon of his sixteenth year.

Sweet Tea   Been gone for his entire childhood, that whatin long enough for you?

Half George   Mine's gone forever. Got any idea how long that is?

Sweet Tea   I didn't come to pay a visit so you know. I came to get my son –

Half George   – You ain't got no son.

Sweet Tea   Oh but I do, and he has his father's sweet tooth and his grandfather's eyes. And I'm takin him or gone be dead tryin.

*Enter **Mary South**, out of breath.*

Mary South   Sweet Tea?! Baby! I told myself I whatin gone be late for your arrival and look at me: late as sinner for altar call. Jacob crept, come hug my neck! Ain't nothin harder for a mother than to go ages without seein her child. Just look at ya grown. Turn round, girl, let my eyes have their fill! Ha!

Heaven done come from my loins. Turn 'gain, girl! Don't she make you smile, Half George?

Half George   Yeh. Somethin like that.

Mary South   Where's ya sack? How long you been waitin? Did you eat? Ya tired? Ya must be comin all the way from Boston. Girl, look at ya. You done put on weight in all the right places. Ya look good if ya tired –

Sweet Tea   – Mother, don't fuss.

Mary South   I know, I know, I'm just sorry for being late. First lady was in need, you know how that is . . . let's get you home. I'm makin a feast! Is this ya hat? It sho is big.

Sweet Tea   You like it? Go ahead, try it on.

Mary South *puts on the hat.*

Mary South   Grace and mercy, Tea. This here's a crown of glory. I'm 'bout to go show off.

She exits.

Sweet Tea   Here. This should more than pay for the food. I'll be expectin my son at dusk. If I don't see him, I'll be comin here and carryin more than a gun.

Sweet Tea *exits, crashing* **Colorado**.

Sweet Tea   Heaven!

Colorado   Hell! Watch where ya . . . (*He falls in love.*) going . . .

Sweet Tea   Colorado, is that you? Ooo, you got ugly. Pardon me, but age played a number on you. God help Job, it's good to see you though. Bye.

Colorado   Yeh. Yeh, it's good to . . . see . . .

She walks off.

You thief. What a sweet thief she's become, quick as death. To snatch my heart and break it whole in the whisper of her breath.

A loud echo shakes the mountains.

Red Kyote (*offstage*)
CAPN CARO! CAPN CARO! CAPN CARO!
SIMMON AITCHEE! SIMMON AITCHEE! SIMMON
    AITCHEE!

Colorado   Wo-ah, what call is that?

Red Kyote
VERMIN AITCHEE! VERMIN AITCHEE!
    VERMIN AITCHEE!

Number Two *pushes past* **Colorado** *and storms into the trade post where* **Half George** *drinks coffee, rocking in a chair.*

Number Two   Where is he, Georgia! Where is Trowbridge?

Half George   Dead.

Number Two   Don't lie to me! I just heard him hollerin our song in the mouth of the mountain. I know you hidin him. Tell me where he is or I'll turn this store upside down.

Half George   Go 'head. It ain't clean enough as it is.

Number Two   GIVE HIM TO ME!!

Half George   I would if I knew where his body was, Number Two! But somebody buried him without a dance, didn't even leave a marker or stone. And now he's walkin round ghostly.

Number Two   Nawl. Nawl, you tryin to get me out my head but I won't go. I know what I heard and it whatin no ghost. You cursin me.

Half George   Nawl but I did try to curse ya, it just didn't take 'cause ya already marked. A curse ain't nothing but a bad story somebody bought into and you already been sold. I tried everything in my bag on ya but nothing stuck. 'Cause you fucked good and ain't a thing a witch or a god can do about it. Ya curse is writ right cross ya chest. It say "everything you love you gone kill."

He grabs her by the throat.

Number Two   If you didn't owe me so much, I'd kill you,
woman. Ya had the best years of Trowbridge's life. You had
his heart and he had mine and that left me with leftovers.
I only keep you alive to watch you long for him like I do.

Half George   Is that what you think I been doing all these
years – longing? Bull and shit, I did enough of that when I was
young. When Trowbridge kept crawling out my bed at night
to cross the creek so he could lock arms with you and wrestle
down y'all's lust. Longing. You too old to be a fool. I don't
long for nothing in this world but a cup of coffee and a little
light dancin. Sth.

*She throws a spider on him. It crawls down his back and he dances. She
drinks.*

Number Two   Get it. Get it off me. Get it off me, Half
George.

We hear cicadas. He screams and in a fit knocks **Half George** *to the
floor. The coffee spills. He runs off as* **Wonderful** *enters.*

Wonderful   Maw! Maw, you alright? Maw!

She groans.

I'm a kill 'em! Jesus, I swear . . . tonight. I'm a put an end to
all this.

At the square, **Horse Power** *drinks before* **Fat Rev.** *and* **M.
Gene***. Townsfolk pass with pails.*

Fat Rev.   You shouldn't have spat at my wife, Paw.

M. Gene   Not at. On! He spat on!

Fat Rev.   Will ya let me handle this!? Ya can't spit on a
man's wife, it ain't healthy.

Horse Power   She was my gal 'fore she was your man.
Means I can do what I want to her.

Fat Rev.   Nawl you went too far. Now I got to tie ya to the
whippin tree.

Horse Power   Ha! What I look like an old man whipped? These folk ain't gone allow that.

M. Gene   Oh but they will. For I have led them to salvation. You been drunk too long to pay attention. But I'm the new law. They do just what I tell 'em.

Fat Rev.   Wife, get a hold.

M. Gene   Nawl you get a hold! You ain't a man if you can't keep this town Christian. If you can't whip a man for spattin on your own wife and in the face. In the face like she a boot that need shinin. You get a hold!!

Fat Rev.   Fine! This your want? Hold on then, Paw, here it goes!

Fat Rev. *ties him to the tree.* **M. Gene** *reads a Bible.*

M. Gene   "And the Lord said to Moses, go to Pharaoh: for I have hardened his heart."

Horse Power   Y'all gone let him hit an old man! Ya gone let him whip me just for spittin!

The townsfolk motion to help **Horse Power**.

M. Gene   "And Moses said to his people STAND STILL and see the salvation of God!"

They stop and bow their heads.

Then Moses lifted his rod.

Horse Power   You been my boy, Rev. How can a boy whip his own paw?

M. Gene   And stretched his hand over the sea.

Horse Power   Argus . . .

M. Gene   And divided it!

Fat Rev. *releases the first lash.*

Horse Power   GOOD GOD!!

He falls. Folks turn their faces.

M. Gene   "And the Egyptians shall follow them and be troubled." Trouble him!

Another lash. It sends him to the ground.

Horse Power   Jesus . . .

M. Gene   "And all the host of Pharaoh that came into the sea were tossed." Toss him!

This lash nearly kills him.

Horse Power   Holy . . . .

Fat Rev. *drops his head. Townsfolk exit.*

M. Gene   Now, Paw . . . accept the Lord into your heart, hunh? This was for your own good. Now take Jesus. He waitin . . . you see him, Paw? He waitin.

He turns away from her. **Fat Rev.** *breaks the rod against his knee and exits. At* **Number Two***'s cottage,* **Sweet Tea** *rubs aloe on her father's bites.* **Colorado** *wears a suit.*

Number Two   You ever seen anything prettier than my Sweet Tea's face?

Colorado   Nawl, I don't reckon.

Number Two   Course you ain't! And smart. Dog and bone, this here fawn 'bout the smartest thing God let breathe. Did I tell you how well she did in nursin?

Colorado   Only about a thousand times.

Number Two   First in her class and she colored too.

Sweet Tea   They were all colored, Paw. It was a colored school.

Number Two   Don't matter. If it was a white school you'd still be first. 'Cause ya my seed and mine always lead. She a catch hunh, Colorado? Smart as a whip, pretty as petals, Christian as Christ and pure as snow. Ain't ya, Tea?

Sweet Tea   Pure as possible.

Number Two *laughs.*

Number Two   Look at him! You got Colorado blushin. He fancies you, Sweet. Man had nothin but curses to bathe you in when ya was young. Now he can't keep his eyes off ya. Ain't that just like life? Always hell bent on teachin you a lesson, even when you late for school.

Colorado *rises, embarrassed.*

Number Two   Sit down, boy. We getting ready to eat. Mary done made a whole spread. Ain't that right, woman!

Mary South *yells from the kitchen.*

Mary South   Sit down, Colorado, I'm just getting ready to bring out the meats!

She enters with food. A knock.

That's the First Lady and her huz. Colorado, will you let them in? Number Two, put out that smoke and come sit at the table.

M. Gene *and* **Fat Rev.** *enter.* **Mary** *returns.*

Mary South   Evening First Lady and Rev., y'all have a seat. Number Two, I'd wish you put on your boots. This is our daughter's homecoming.

Sweet Tea   Maw, I don't care. Let him wear what he wants.

Number Two   Yeh, woman, I let your mean-lookin friend come in my house. I didn't say nothing 'bout her face, don't say nothing 'bout my feet.

M. Gene   Come on, sheriff. Ya wife asked ya to put on ya boots. She a woman which mean she know somethin 'bout attire. Ya should bless her and cover them nasty toes.

Number Two   Fat Rev., tell your jaw-jackin wife to mind her business. This ain't no church. I don't need her amen when my wife starts preachin foolishness. Mary, hand me them beans.

Mary South   We got to pray over the food first, Number Two.

Number Two   Like hell. Rev., pass me dem beans.

M. Gene   Husband, don't move a muscle. If Number Two wants to act like a child, then let him serve himself.

Number Two   Fat Rev., I done asked you to pass me them beans now. I don't want to have to kick you out my house with all this good food sittin up here waitin for you to devour it. Pass me them beans!

Fat Rev. *picks up the pot of beans.*

M. Gene   Husband, don't you dare!

He puts them down.

Number Two   Pass 'em!!

M. Gene   HUSBAND!

Sweet Tea   PAPPY!! (*Soft.*) Let's say grace first.

Number Two   You right baby girl. I'll wait.

M. Gene   Husband, if you please . . . pray. And speak with diction and clarity. After all it is called grace. Therefore be graceful.

Fat Rev. *tightens his lip.*

Fat Rev.   Let's all bow our heads and close our eyes. Lord, we thank you for this food we are about to receive for the nourishment of our bodies for Christ's sake . . . and Lord we thank you for teaching us long suffering, for you said you would not put anyone on us who we could not bear. So Lord we thank ya for you are our Father which art in Heaven. Hallowed be thy name. Thy kingdom come, Thy will be done on Earth as it is in Heaven.

> And give us this day, our daily bread.
> The corn rolls and maize that keep us well fed
> The sweets and meats we are eager to eats
> The neck bones and chitterlings, hog maws and pigs' feet

The fried chicken, sweet beef and delicious pork chuck
Them hush puppies so good they make your dog shut up.

M. Gene   Husband . . .

Fat Rev.
The rice and beans, the collard greens.
Candied yams, that dressin with ham
These mashed tators pipin hot with gravy
The tator salad and slaw, somebody save me!

Everyone save **M. Gene** *signify his sermon.*

M. Gene   Have you lost your mind!?

Fat Rev.
Them fried okras, and black eye peas
The corn on the cob sprinkled with cheese

M. Gene   That's enough!

Fat Rev.
The moon shine for wine, pot liquor to sip
Cha cha to season, hot sauce for dip

M. Gene   Reverend!

Fat Rev.
Whiskey to get wasted and sweet tea to drink
Lord I get your holy ghost every time I think
'Bout catfish and fish cakes. Turtle soup, salmon baked
    to a golden crisp.
Carrots cooked in butter and cinnamon dipped
'Scuse me if I skip when I see apple turnovers turned
    over in sugar
Peach cobbler with cream and cream a top whatever
Plum puddin can't stay long on my plate
Put it in my mouth watch me salivate
Over teacakes and chicory tea,
God if ya don't have mercy on me, Lord –

M. Gene   HUSH!!

Fat Rev.   No, you hush! You ain't my god! You will not tell me what to say or do anymore. You're my wife, which means you are to mind me. So mind!!

M. Gene *holds back tears.*

Number Two   Guess that mean it's time to eat.

Everyone prepares their plate.

Mary South   First Lady, you alright?

Number Two   Leave her alone, Mary. M. Gene been havin that tongue-lashin comin to her thirty years. Now Rev. pass me them beans.

Rev. *passes the beans.* **M. Gene** *rises.*

M. Gene   I feel the Lord callin me for a baptism. Mary, won't you join me!? (*Beat.*) Please, Mary, I need you.

Mary *rises.*

Number Two   Sit down, wife. You know I'm not 'bout to let you leave this house and we got company. M. Gene, you leave. Mary, you finish makin my plate.

Mary *sits.* **M. Gene** *exits.*

Fat Rev.   Well, amen.

Fat Rev. *eats. At the trade post,* **Wonderful** *tries to leave unnoticed, but* **Half George** *senses him. She sits in her rocker molding a doll.*

Half George   There's some garfish and meal on the stove.

Wonderful   Obliged but I ain't hungry, I'm goin out for air.

Half George   Is that why you carryin your suitcase?

Wonderful   Yeh, I'm gone put some air in it. Ocean air. I won't be gone long, Maw –

Half George   How many times have I heard that tune from a man? Course it sound promisin at first but then it fades into one long note, that they never write.

Wonderful   Not me. I'll write you every day, and send dime
novels and lace, perrty broaches. You'll see. I won't let ya miss
me long enough to notice I'm gone –

He puts one foot out the door.

Half George   – Wonderful! I just want you to know I don't
regret what I done. Though I know it was bitch-dog evil, I still
can't bring myself to feel bad about it. Course I know I should,
havin been takin' from my own maw. I know what it's like to
long for an embrace that no other woman's arms can fold, to
suck a tit with milk made for your mouth and then get snatched
and thrown into a world where her heartbeat can no longer
rock you. If God made a woman to despise slavery and curse
the takin of babes from their maw's arms it be me: Half
Georgia and the other half I never knew.

Wonderful   Then why'd you do it, Maw?

Half George   Don't know: had lost my child, was losin my
man. I came all this way West through tears, blood and starvin
so I could put my good wish down in somebody. Somebody
I could call mine. So that when I gave my last breath, I could
look God dead in the face and say: see there. That's some of
me. Go ahead look God, that there somebody got half of me
in 'em. Now I'm full Georgia. Y'all up here in heaven gots to
call me Georgia 'cause I ain't half of nothing no more, I'm big
as a state. 'Cause I put my good wish down in somebody and
he Wonderful.

He gets his other foot out the door.

I put some button coin in ya case. And some food in ya jacket
there . . . case you get hungry. Send me a word every blue
moon, hunh?

Wonderful (*holding back tears*)   Let me go, Maw.

*He exits. She extends the limbs on her clay doll and a figure rises from
shadow – it is **Red Kyote**. She maneuveres the doll and he walks –
enchanted by her craft.*

Half George   We best make sure he leaves town safe, huz.

Red Kyote   Yes'm wife. I'll get my good axe.

In the dining area everyone eats in silence.

Sweet Tea   I got news. I ain't stayin.

Mary South   Ain't stayin? What you mean?

Number Two   Yes, ya is.

Sweet Tea   Nawl, Paw, I ain't. I only came back 'cause I left a part of myself here. And now that I found it, I can't find a good reason to call this place home.

Number Two   Yeh you can. You marryin Colorado.

Colorado   Wo-ah?! Ain't she been through enough ugly?

Sweet Tea   You haven't changed, have ya, Paw, still hard of hearin.

Number Two   I know what's best for you, Tea.

Mary South   Number Two, let her do what she wants.

Number Two   She too young to do what she want. She's marryin Colorado.

Mary South   He don't even love her!

Number Two   The man's wearin a tie! When ya known him to wear a tie? He's in love!

Colorado   It don't matter, I ain't worthy. You got a beauty in you, Tea, that lips can't quite speak of. Let alone touch.

Number Two   – Don't matter. She ain't got but one choice. Mary, get the pie.

Mary South   Jesus. How'd I ever love you?

Number Two   You ain't! Ya felt bad for me 'cause I was born a slave. Been carryin the guilt of ya kin for sellin mine and wants to get rid of it. That's why ya married me, to erase the stain. I figure I'm black enough to wash it and you red enough to pay me what's due. Now get your rump up and get me some pie.

Mary *leaves to get the pie.*

Number Two   I let you be gone sixteen years from me, Sweet. Sixteen and I didn't force ya back once but I need you now. As you can see, I'm gettin bitter. I need you to stay.

Mary *returns with his pie. He eats.*

Number Two   I built this town for you, fought hundreds so you could carve your name in this land, Tea. You got to stay. You my one –

Sweet Tea   – Nawl. You save that number for somebody else. I'm not yours anymore –

Number Two   – Merciful!

He grabs his gut, falling.

Sweet Tea   What's wrong? Paw, what is it?

He reaches for **Mary**.

Mary South   It's his bowels again. They turnin on him.

Number Two *spits up blood.*

Colorado   Mercy, Rev., I think it's time to call it a night.

Fat Rev.   Yeh, look like you right. Sister Mary, mind if I make myself a plate first.

Mary South   Course not, you and Colorado help yaself to what's left in the kitchen.

They exit.

Number Two   Mary, where'd you get this fruit from? These cherries . . .

Mary South   From the trade store.

Number Two   It's poison. Got an off-taste. That witch Georgia's up to her tricks again.

Sweet Tea   Maw, make him root tea –

Mary *does not move.*

Number Two   Done had enough of this! (*Groans.*) Just when a man gets settled in his nest here come the claws. What a clever bear she is. I need to hug her where it hurts. I need to hug her now . . .

Sweet Tea   No, Paw, sit. You need to . . . Paw!

He exits.

Jesus, what's gotten into him?

Mary South   He sick. Been sick awhile. Had a fever in Spring. Said Half George was blowing poison pricks at him through our window but I ain't seen her. Week later he started bleeding from the mouth. Said she was putting poison petals in his coffee and it was givin him the shits, makin him spew blood. But it didn't harm me. Guess today he figure she done messed in the cherries but I think he losin his mind.

Sweet Tea *wipes up the blood.*

Sweet Tea   His blood. Look, it's sparkling . . . you ever seen such a thing? (*Time.*) What did you put in his pie, Maw?

Mary South   Sugar. He likes his pie extra sweet. I may have sprinkled sugar on it – that's all.

Sweet Tea   Maybe I should taste it then. See what it do me.

She lifts the pie to her mouth.

Mary South   Hold! It's glass. There's the tiniest shards of glass spread like sugar 'cross his piece. I been feedin it to him so that he quiets. His temper's gotten so bad lately. He's not been himself, Tea. Been killin men like they flies. Bossin folk, runnin the town like he God. And he just might be. 'Cause I can't kill him. God know's I've tried: the pricks, the coffee – it's all been me. But he won't die. He just ain't of this world.

Sweet Tea   That so? Hm. Sound like to me he got this whole town poisoned.

At the wall, **M. Gene** *stands on a rock and sings loudly as tears fall. She is offering herself to the Creeks.*

M. Gene (*singing*)
 When I'm in trouble
 I can call him day or night
 He'll always go with me
 To the battlefield to fight
 Elijah Rock! Shout! Shout!
 Elijah Rock, I'm comin home, Lord!!

M. Gene *closes her eyes. A figure snatches her, carries her over the wall as dusk falls. She drops her Bible.*

Number Two *arrives at the creek in pain and drinks. It sparks a memory.* **Young Number Two** *and* **Young Trowbridge** *tumble on wrestling. They have pikes.*

Young Number Two   I got here first, Trowbridge! This creek land be mine.

Young Trowbridge   You cheated! Ain't no way you coulda rode that fast on a mule.

Young Number Two   Bully. I got it fair and square. Now get off me!

Young Trowbrige *pins him and kisses him till the wrestling turns into love-making.* **Young Number Two** *pushes him off.*

Young Number Two   I know what you're doing, Trowbridge, and it won't work.

Young Trowbridge   I bet it will. You know you love me.

Young Number Two   Ha! Love ain't nothin but another massuh. Ya don't know 'cause you ain't never been slaved like me. Starved and whipped and made to work for another man's gain. That's love. And I don't want it.

Young Trowbridge   Yeh, you do. 'Sides, ain't you read the stars? We'ze made for each other. And by the will of God made to make love.

They kiss. **Young Number Two** *pushes him.*

Young Number Two   We can't do this!! We ain't youngins no more . . .

Young Number Two   We men.

Number Two   We men.

Young Number Two *fades away by sinking into the creek.*

Number Two   They'll never let us love and you know it. Not this town. They been through too much to turn a blind eye to anything that could curse 'em or challenge their new faith. They need us to be men, Trow. Folks can't wrap they head around us this way.

Young Trowbridge   Don't care 'bout other folk's heads. God gave me one for a reason.

Number Two   Don't matter. We got to do what's best for our people. We got to end this.

Young Trowbridge   You don't mean that.

Number Two   Look at me! (*Soft.*) I don't love you.

Time.

Young Trowbridge   You planned this all along, didn't you? You got in my head, crawled in my heart just so you could take my land –

Number Two   Don't do this.

Young Trowbridge   Well, I ain't lettin you take it. This land's mine.

Young Trowbridge *takes his pike and exits.*

Number Two   Don't do this! You come back!!

He runs after him but falls, spitting blood.

Come back to me. You can have it, just . . .

He groans. Time. Enter **Wonderful** *with a suitcase and spear.*

Wonderful   Sheriff?

Number Two   Trow?

Wonderful   Nawl. It's Wonderful. I come to kill ya, suh.

Number Two *laughs.*

Number Two   You never stop, do you, Trow? I knew you'd come back for me.

Wonderful   I ain't Trowbridge, suh. I said my name is Wonderful –

Number Two   I know. I know who you are, you're my one.

He opens his arms.

Come kill me, one. Come try.

Wonderful *moves holding the spear.* **Number Two** *closes his eyes.* **Wonderful** *lifts the spear and lunges –*

Sweet Tea   – WONDERFUL!!

He freezes. Enter **Sweet Tea**.

Sweet Tea   Don't do it. He's my paw. I know you hate him but he's mine. Put it down.

Still trembling, he drops the spear. She embraces **Wonderful**, *whose back is toward* **Number Two**. **Number Two** *lifts the spear.*

Number Two   You must sleep, Trowbridge. You must stay slee –

Sweet Tea   DADDY!!

She pushes her son out of the way and takes the blow. She opens her mouth. We hear ocean. She falls into **Wonderful**'s *arms.*

Wonderful   Oh God . . . Oh . . . .

Number Two   Tea?

Wonderful   Maw . . .

Sweet Tea   Shhh. Forgive my paw. (*Smiling.*) He just a man.

Number Two (*dazed*)   Tea, what I tell you 'bout being out late?

Wonderful   O Jesus. Keep me. Keep my secret 'fore you go, Maw.

Sweet Tea   Course.

Number Two   Go in the house now, Tea. Go in 'fore you catch a cold.

Wonderful   My grand said you was the sweetest thing to taste. She said you was so happy when I was born, you got lifted and flew away like a bird. That's what makes me Wonderful, Maw. (*Whispers in her ear.*) I can fly.

Sweet Tea   I know, babe. Your paw was a good bird . . .

Sweet Tea *dies.* **Number Two** *sees his daughter dead and goes wild.*

Number Two   GEORGIA!!

At the well, **Fat Rev.** *and* **Colorado** *put sassafras on* **Horse Power**'s *back.*

Horse Power   I told Number Two the wrong story but he needed somethin. I wanted to give him a wish but instead I gave him a curse. I told him his mark meant he could never die and he took it to heart. And forgot how to live.

Number Two *rises.*

Number Two   You come out from behind those trees, Georgia! Don't let this body fool ya. I'm bleedin like a cut pig but I'm still a god.

He spits blood.

Half George   Don't matter. I knows ya secret. Horse told me your weakness.

Number Two   Liar! He'd never tell it. It's time for you to follow your man back to hell.

Half George   Ha! And God give you the strength to do it! You'll need him.

The moon opens her eye.

Number Two *and* **Half George**   *AHHHHH!*

Number Two *charges toward* **Half George**. *When he reaches her she moves and he falls into the arms of* **Red Kyote**.

Number Two   Trow? You did come back?

Trowbridge   Yeh. I come back for you.

Wonderful *rises and stabs* **Number Two** *in the back. The god screams pure sunlight. At the square,* **Mary** *walks to the well.*

Mary South   They took her . . . the Creek Indians. I found her Bible near the wall. They snatched M. Gene.

Fat Rev.   No God, not my peach . . . O God, not my one . . .

He tries to go but **Colorado** *embraces him.*

Mary South   They shoulda took me. I'm the one with the stain.

Horse Power   What stain? I don't see no stain, Mary.

Mary South   'Cause it run deep. It be in my bone. The bloodstain of my paw's slaves.

Horse Power   Nawl. You say what eats at you, gal. A stain ain't no mark on your life. It be there to make a point. It be there to say you ain't washin yaself 'nough. Ain't lovin you. But you can wash, girl!

Mary South   With what paw –

Horse Power   – Tears! What else God gave us to clean with? Been holdin our rain back for thirty-two years 'cause of the trail. Holdin tears so we wouldn't remember how long we wept. But to stay strong you gots to let yaself get weak. Weep, Mary. Ya guilt done made ya a slave but I'm telling ya to live free. Weep! Weep for your kin! Weep for M. Gene!

Mary South *weeps: it is a wailing song.*

Horse Power   And Colorado – you kiss! Kiss your hands. Then kiss your legs and thighs. You fall in love with you. Your beauty ain't skin deep, your beauty is your skin. Black, beautiful as heaven itself. You kiss you. And you! Rev.! Laugh.

Life don't add up to sense. Don't you get mad at God and go
to some dark place just to spite life. You laugh.

Fat Rev. *grins. It grows into laughter.*

Horse Power   And you . . . (*To audience.*) Sing!

M. Gene *saunters across the land. She is in another place – dazed, her
hair and clothes mangled. She bears a tattoo across her face.*

M. Gene
  I need thee O, I need thee
  Ev'ry hour, /I need thee
  O bless, me now my Savior
  I come to Thee . . . Yes . . .

Everyone
  Yes . . .
  Yes . . .
  Yes . . .
  Yes . . .

M. Gene (*church*)
  O . . . yes . . .

Horse Power   Yes. Shake the stones. Rock 'em. We be
tellin the wrong stories, chil'ren. We dry 'cause we forgot how
to be sad. But God's gonna open the window of Heaven and
pours us out a blessing we ain't got room to receive. I said
weep. For weeping endureth for a night but Joy! *Ya –ho-la!*
Comes in the morning! I said weep! Weep and dance! Dance
and sing. Sing and love! Love your face, love your tongue,
your kin, love ya hist'ry.

Tears fall from the statue of **Number Two** *and form a road. The
well spills over and it rains. The people get soaked. They laugh, some cry
and the Holy Ghost falls. Most dance in a wicked ecstasy.* **Potter's
Clay** *enters with the* **Seminole Chief.**

Potter's Clay   This is it, Chief. The town of the Freeman.
As you can see: they're heathens. It won't be no problem
taking this land.

Seminole Chief   Nawl. I can't let my people settle here. The Creek Chief was right. The land must be cursed. Look at how it's raining directly on the square and nowhere else. And look at how that water keeps comin out of the statue's eyes, out of the well – like a fountain. These people are either evil or crazy or . . . got a magic beyond my thinkin.

Potter's Clay   It doesn't matter, suh. If you don't take this land, eventually the Creeks will.

Seminole Chief   Well, if that's true they'll have their hands full.

The people lift their hands, laughing and dancing. This is a freedom found only in those who have freed themselves. The praise rises and cools off. All goes dark except for the moon. In its eye **Wonderful** *cocks his head and bends. Suddenly black wings reach out from his back like arms reaching out from a womb. He writhes – then stands tall. Above,* **Number Two** *and* **Trowbridge**'s *spirits wrestle for all time, even after their bodies burst into stars.*

Wonderful *kneels. He prays to Jesus and the olden spirits.*

Wonderful   Yo-hoya! Ho-ya-la! Hallelujah!

He blows out the moon.

Amen.

Young Jean Lee

Pullman, WA

Pullman, WA premiered in 2005 at Performance Space 122 in New York. It was co-created and performed by:

Thomas Bradshaw	**Tom**
Pete Simpson	**Pete**
Tory Vazquez	**Tory**

Written and directed by Young Jean Lee
Lighting design by Eric Dyer

Characters

Pete
Tory
Tom

Note
"Pete," "Tory" and "Tom" were the names of the performers of *Pullman, WA* in its original production at PS 122. The characters should be named after whoever is playing them.

Setting
Bare stage except for two chairs off to the side facing the audience, which is the "giving up area" (i.e. the place where the characters go when they've given up). House lights remain up throughout. There are no lighting or sound changes. Everyone wears ordinary street clothes.

In general, lines between characters are directed both to each other and the audience.

Pete *enters.*

Pete   I see you out there.

I see you out there and I can see that you are all different kinds of people.

You are all going through different kinds of things.

Some of you may be happy. Others of you may be in hell. I don't know. But what I do know is that I know how to live.

Pause.

I don't know what all different kinds of people are like.

There are too many kinds, so I don't know what each one is like.

You are sitting in your seat. You have come to the theater, and you are sitting in your seat, and you are someone.

Everything you are, sitting in that seat and being where you are, is what you are.

I wish I knew what it was like to be you.

But you are sitting out there, in your seat. And, probably, you are listening to and watching me.

What are you doing here?

I don't even know why I'm asking these things, but somehow it seems important. It seems important but maybe it's not because I'm going to tell you how to live.

I know how to live.

I don't know if you ever felt this way, but sometimes life feels confusing. For me, personally, a lot of times, life feels confusing. A lot of times in my life I have felt that I did not know what I was doing and that everything was fucked up. That is a familiar feeling for me, so I know what that feels like.

And during those times when I felt so unhappy and confused, I would wish that someone would tell me what to do. That

I could pick up a recipe book, and it would be a recipe book for life, which would tell me what I should do to live a good life and be happy.

There are books and people who claim to give you these things, but none of them work.

But now I know, I've figured out how to live, and this is not a joke.

We are in this room. We are in this room together and I am speaking to you, and I am going to tell you how to live.

I am confused now.

But now I am clear again.

I keep coming back to the main point, which is that you are sitting in your chair and I don't know who you are or what you are like. But I know how to live, so I can tell you that. And maybe you already know how to live, so this will be old news to you, but no human being is perfect so maybe it will still be useful for you.

Okay, so the first thing for you to know is that *you* are *you*. Some of you already know this. Some of you know it so well that you don't even have to think about it. You have always been you and that was that.

But for some of you, and I know how it feels because I'm like this too, the idea that you are you is more shaky.

You think that you are too unproductive or do stupid things, and this makes you not you.

Okay, I'm not being very clear. Let me try to give you a personal example. For me, I have never felt like I was me. There was always something wrong with who I was so that I was always thinking of myself as some future-existing person, someone who – like an outline of someone . . . oh shit, it's hard to talk about this stuff.

OK. There is this idea that some people have that they don't count if they are fucked up in some way.

Like this idea of being fat. If you're fat, then you're not who you're supposed to be. You're supposed to be thin. So when you're fat, it's like you don't count, like you're not you. Does that make sense?

It is very difficult to believe . . .

Pause.

Do you know what other people look like to me? They look so sure of themselves, so settled in their identity. "I am this, and this is my life, and it is good." A kind of absolute certainty about themselves that enables them to be completely honest in everything they say. You know, it's a weird thing, but I always assume that the people I talk to are being one-hundred-percent honest with me. Even though I know that I myself am frequently dishonest, I believe that other people are honest because I feel they have nothing to lie about. But that seems kind of unlikely, huh?

Sorry I'm taking so long to get to the how-to-live part, but this is all part of it. This is all how it gets set up.

So anyway, when you look at other people and they seem to have such stable identities, the fact of the matter is that you have a stable identity as well.

I know you don't want it, but you have it and it's there.

There are all kinds of gifts that get doled out in this life.

I look out there at you and there's a whole range of physical graces that got bestowed upon you.

And being born with certain gifts makes life a lot easier in many ways. If you were born beautiful, and rich, and smart, and charismatic, to a loving family, then you are not going to endure the same kind of suffering as someone who was born ugly, and poor, and awkward, and stupid, to an abusive family.

And a lot of this has to do with social skills. Social skills are one of the most important things in the planet. It is possible for someone born with few gifts, but gifted with social skills, to be better off than someone who is born with many gifts but is bad at social skills.

And by social skills I don't mean the ability to talk a lot and schmooze at parties. By social skills I mean an intuitive sense of how to act around other people so that they want to keep being around you. Like if you're in a subway station and someone is sitting at one end of an empty bench, and you're the kind of person who would go sit right next to that person instead of leaving at least two or three spaces in between you, then you're pretty much fucked for life. Even homeless people know better than to do that.

But then again I don't know how much looks and things factor in.

Pause.

I feel like I'm not doing a good job of explaining things.

Misery is not always such a straightforward proposition of you saying, "I feel miserable." Sometimes it comes out in other weird ways, too. You know those health problems you have, those weird health problems that the doctors can't diagnose? The inexplicable skin problems, back problems, knee problems, problems with your genitals, things like that? Chances are pretty high that those are psychosomatic.

You may not know it, but some of you hate yourselves. You hate yourselves for not being the thing you're supposed to be, for not having the life you're supposed to have. And the distance between you and that thing you're supposed to be is killing you. It makes you break out in these weird health problems and it makes you do bad things that are bad to yourself.

A lot of us seem to have contempt for happiness. It's cooler to be destructive and chaotic and romantic and extreme – and that's always what I've valued my whole life and still do. I love all that stuff – the violent, the crazy, the extreme. I think it's great. But the thing is, it has a negative backfire that leaves you feeling like shit.

But let's talk about something important, which is the idea of suffering. When I think of suffering in the world, I think of the obvious things. People who are being tortured, victims of natural disasters, people living under oppressive regimes in poverty-stricken countries, kids who are being abused . . . all that stuff sucks.

But these are not things that you're dealing with. There is all kinds of self-inflicted pain that you are doing to yourself, and some of you have no idea that you are doing it.

The biggest self-torturing device I see around me are people having obsessive bad thoughts. Whenever you make a mistake or something bad happens, you start obsessing about it over and over in your mind in this private internal freak-out. But think about it this way. If you saw some parent relentlessly picking on their kid in the same way that you pick on yourself whenever everything's not perfect in your life, you would probably feel really fucking afraid for that kid.

We have this idea that we need to whip ourselves into shape, without realizing it's the whipping that's causing us to be fucked up in the first place.

And stop thinking of all of this as being for pussies and still trying to cling to all your stubborn little notions about your current situation. If it worked for you that would be one thing, but it doesn't even work.

Now, this theory that I have . . .

OK, I've been talking for a while, and much of it has been repetitive and a good portion probably unconvincing.

Here is one convincing thing. As an experiment, try doing the following things for one day:

1) Eating only healthy food.
2) Getting some exercise.
3) Not drinking alcohol.
4) Going to bed early.

Then wake up the next morning. You will probably feel better!

Everyone is born with *something*, and it's important to develop whatever parts of yourself you want to develop. Like if you're good at science, it's a good thing to study science more and more to the point where you're getting better at science and knowing more about it.

Wow, that's a boring example.

But you get the general idea. And it's not a moral thing. It's just that you're hurting yourself. You keep doing things that hurt yourself – things that you might not even suspect as hurting yourself. You drink too much, you have unprotected sex, you stay in bad relationships, you let yourself get over-burdened with responsibilities, you don't get enough sleep, you smoke, you watch too much TV, you don't do the things you want to spend your time doing.

It doesn't matter, all this judging that goes on between people, all this intuitive sensing of weakness and criticism of it. There is no big shining ideal that matters either. The only thing that matters is feeling good. And if it makes you feel good to help people and make a difference in the world, then you should do that. And fuck anyone who says that you're an asshole if you're not out there tending the sick and feeding the poor. That's just another unrealistic delusion of what people are supposed to be.

If you can wake up sober after a good night's sleep, it should feel good. I guess that's the meaning of life. Being able to walk down the street without physical pain and without being chased by the police. If you're being tortured, if you have squalid poverty, if you're some kid cowering in the basement as their psycho parent rampages throughout the house, it's hard to feel good. Feeling good is a luxury. Stop torturing yourself.

But now I'm being repetitive again. Let me tell you something new.

Okay, this isn't new at all. It's going to be exactly what I said before in a different format, but it's an important point to hammer in.

Holding up a fist.

This is you.

Holding up second fist above first fist.

And this is the you that you're supposed to be.

And this is what you do whenever you feel like you're not meeting the expectations of your higher self.

Slowly pounds second fist into palm of other hand with an agonized expression.

Tory *runs onstage and shoves* **Pete** *to the floor, smiling happily.*

Pete *goes to the giving-up area.*

Tory (*to audience, smiling*)   You are sitting in the middle of a giant puffball.

It's your birthday, and the sun is out. The sun is warming the outside of your puffball.

You have . . . All your friends look like mushrooms, except for the ones who look like unicorns.

There is a long drama with one of your friends. She was originally your sister, but then you were separated by wickedness and she flew away, I mean she died, she was killed, and flew away to heaven. But then years later you were reunited through a chain of unforeseen circumstances.

It was a great birthday party. We blew up the pool and put in the waterslide and had watermelon cake. It is summer.

You saw an old man in the middle of the road and invited him to the party, and it turned out he was a magician, so he did tricks. He made people's heads float on top of the pool like apples without hurting them.

And then we played all of our owl music on our owl record players and played the same song on both players so it was like double stereo.

Last summer we had some good parties. We tied all the unicorns together and had a unicorn race where nobody could win because they were all chained together, which was fine because unicorns are not a competitive animal.

Last summer there was also a troll who kept eating people, and we had to – he ate a chunk out of *your* unicorn – and he had to be killed.

We are not afraid to kill if the need arises.

The biggest thing about us is that we are strong. We are a strong people and nothing can crush us.

Pete (*from giving-up area, to audience*)   You are a failure!

All of the following until **Tom**'s *entrance is directed at the audience.* **Tory** *smiles happily throughout.*

Tory   You are in a canoe on a lake, with swans floating all around you. The swans are quacking out all kinds of songs to you. The swans spell out the words to the songs by swimming in formation with their bodies so you can remember the lyrics and sing them to yourself later on.

Pete   Everyone thinks you suck!

Tory   You are flying in a rainbow-colored balloon in the sky that is filled with jackrabbits. The jackrabbits keep jumping out of the balloon, hitting the earth, and bouncing back up to wave at you. Sometimes they bounce off the side of the balloon and fly through space until they bounce off the moon and ping-pong through the stars.

Pete   Nobody will ever truly love you and you will never truly love anyone.

Tory   You are on the inside of a stapler. The outward casing is protecting you until it is time to do your job, which is simple and straightforward.

Pete   You tell people you like their art when really you think it sucks.

Tory   You constantly talk shit about people behind their backs, even people you don't know.

Pete   You act like you're still in high school.

Tory   You are flying over a rainbow on the back of a unicorn. As you get close to the rainbow you can see that it is made of millions of smiling otters. The otters are hooting in welcome, and the hooting is filling your head and pushing out your brain until it falls out and nothing is left but their soft hooting.

Pete   You reveal deeply personal information about your friends to other people.

Tory   You want to be famous.

Pete   You accuse other people of wanting to be famous.

Tory   You are lying in your bed, surrounded by angels. The pattern from your blanket has floated up into the air and the angels are blowing it back and forth at each other above your bed. You fall asleep to the image of plaid floating in front of your eyes.

Pete *leaves the giving-up area and stands next to* **Tory**.

Pete   You pretend to be interested in boring things in social situations.

Tory   You are constantly trying to make yourself a better person, but this never involves helping anyone else.

Pete   You're kind of unexpectedly prissy.

Tory   You have a fake laugh that you use all the time.

Pete   You are full of self-righteous political wrath but do nothing about it.

Tory   You are much more mundane than you lead others to believe.

Pete   You are obsessed with saving small sums of money.

Tory   You think your bad moods should swallow the whole world.

Pete   You're so judgmental of other people, it's kind of awful. Who the fuck cares, why can't you just leave people the fuck alone? Everyone is doing their best, they're just trying to do whatever they can to live an OK life and feel a little better about themselves every once in a while, but you're so mean about it!

Pete *returns to giving-up area.*

Tory *goes through the audience directing each of her following lines to a different person, while smiling.*

Tory   You have taken on way more responsibility than you can handle.

There are a million things you need to do that are not getting done.

Other people are not helping you in the ways that they should be.

Your feelings of anxiety are fucking up your focus and productivity.

You keep wasting time that you cannot afford to lose.

You are incompetent.

You have no idea what you're doing.

You've fooled other people into thinking you're an adult.

People are trusting you to do a good job.

The whole premise behind what you're doing sucks.

You've made a series of incredibly bad decisions.

Everyone is mad at you.

(*To whole audience.*) This is going to be a total disaster.

Tom *enters.*

Tom   I am an angel of the Lord.

I have flown vast distances over pure white fields.

I have come to bring you rest.

I will stand watch over you in the night.

I will guard your path in the daylight hours.

Have no more fear.

I will shelter and protect you.

Amen.

Tory (*going to giving-up area*)   This is a total disaster.

Tom (*to* **Pete**, **Tory**, *and audience*)   Stop freaking out.

I know you feel totally scared and confused right now but it's OK, I can help you.

It's OK.

Calm down.

You are not a failure.

Calm down.

I don't want you to get so unhappy like this anymore.

There were two shepherds, and the Lord asked them to protect and watch over his lambs in the field.

The shepherds said, "Yes, Lord, I will obey," and tended the lambs with gentleness and care.

But soon the shepherds grew weary of their task and began to beat and flay the lambs with their staffs.

The Lord descended upon them and asked, "Did I not ask you to protect and watch over my lambs in the field?"

"Yes, Lord," said the shepherds.

"And did you not say to me, "Yes, Lord, I will obey?"" asked the Lord.

"Yes, Lord," said the shepherds.

"Then why do you not obey?" asked the Lord. "Why do you beat and flay my lambs with your staffs?"

"We did not beat and flay your lambs with our staffs," lied the shepherds.

The Lord replied –

Pete (*leaving giving-up area, to audience*)   You know what? Fuck this!

You are fucked up! You might not know it, but you are. And you think that everything that goes wrong in your life is because other people are fucking things up, but actually it's because *you're* fucked up!

Fuck you!

Tory (*from giving-up area, to audience*)   Go fuck yourselves!

All of the following until **Tom**'s *speech is directed at the audience.*

Pete   You are alone!

Tory   You are completely alone!

Pete   Nobody can ever feel what you feel!

Tory (*leaving giving-up area*)   If you looked into your mind you would see mess upon mess!

Pete   There is nothing but failure!

Tory   I can't help you!

Pete   Nobody can help you! You should have been born different!

Tom *is horrified.*

Tom (*to audience*)   I'm the King of All Kings.

Bring your sufferings unto me.

Speak unto me your troubles, child.

(*To* **Pete** *and* **Tory**, *indignantly.*) There's a bad thing inside you, and you don't even know it.

There's . . .

Tom *suddenly howls in pain.* **Tory** *and* **Pete** *follow suit.*

Tory *calms down. As she speaks the following lines,* **Pete** *and* **Tom** *become happy.*

Tory   It's OK. It's . . . there's a field. A green field. And on that field are unicorns, white unicorns. They are soft and gentle and they are singing through their nose a silent song, an airy whistle, and there are white clouds in the sky. This is the way the world works. Green field, white unicorns, blue sky, white clouds. You are safe. I will protect you.

Tom   I will protect you from all harm.

No harm will come to you.

If you deliver your heart unto me, you will be forgiven.

(*Pointing to a person in the audience.*) Stop crying, child. Rise and walk again.

Rise up.

Have no fear.

Pete   A few minutes from now, an army of soldiers will come marching over the side of that hill, and you will be saved. All you have to do is wait behind this rock. Keep very still. Put your head down, like this.

He hides his head with his arms.

Tory *hides her head with her arms.*

I can still see you! Hold very still. Don't look up. Don't look up at that –

Tom   Have no fear. *I* know you feel alone. *I* know you feel that you are surrounded by traitors.

Pete   Whatever you did, however bad it was, it's OK. It's OK. *I* forgive you.

Tom   *I* want to help you. *I'm* going to help you.

Pete (*to* **Tom**)   Maybe they don't need help.

Tory (*to audience*)   You are a loser. You're a loser because you were born that way. You will never be anything other than what you are. This is the way the world works. I am helping you by telling the truth. You are a loser and you will lose.

Pete (*to* **Tory**)   Ow.

Pause.

Ow!

Tory   Shut up.

Pete (*to* **Tom**)   Help!

Tom (*to audience*)   I will never leave you alone

(*To* **Pete** *and* **Tory**.) You guys are assholes.

Tory   I don't care.

Pete (*to audience*)   What if everything started spinning until it became a little round owl-face on a record player? Would that make you feel better?

Imagine it. A little round owl-face on a record player that goes around and around without stopping, forever.

Tory (*to audience*)   If you drive out far enough into the fog, eventually you'll go flying off into another world. You have no idea what that place is like.

Tom   I want to say something.

Pause.

(*To* **Pete** *and* **Tory**, *angrily.*) You are sitting in the middle of a lake, and the lake is on fire! The trees around the lake are on fire, and you are on fire!

(*To audience.*) And everything spins out the wrong way and then goes back in. It swirls and swirls, spinning in an endless sea of light, and then the bull comes over the horizon with its little horns and saves everybody, because that is the nature of the animal. That is the nature of the animal within.

Let me tell you about my childhood.

When I was a kid, I wasn't allowed to go trick-or-treating.

When I became a young man, I wanted my penis to turn into a turtle, but it never did.

Pause.

I think you need my help.

Pause.

I will save you.

It's OK.

It's OK, I will save you.

There's a place in the woods, and we can go there.

Pete (*dreamily*)   There's a fog at the end of the road.

Tom (*to* **Pete**, *angrily*)   You don't know what that place is like!

You have a bad thing inside you, and you don't even know it.

(*To audience.*) Come unto me.

I am you are the meek and the lamb.

Everything will be OK.

Everything will be OK. I know things.

I know . . . things.

I don't know shit.

Pete (*to audience, businesslike*)   We'll do it in steps.

Tom (*falling apart*)   I don't know. I don't know shit.

Tory (*to audience, businesslike*)   This is how to live.

Pause. **Tom** *silently freaks out.*

Pete   Be good.

Tory   Be good.

Pete   Do things.

Tory   Do things.

Pete   Don't do bad things.

Tory   Don't do bad things.

Tom   OW! OW! OW!

I fucked up!

I fucked up!

(*To* **Pete**.) Sorry. (*To* **Tory**.) Sorry.

Tom *goes to giving-up area.*

Pete   Eat healthy.

Tory   Eat healthy and exercise.

Pete   Don't smoke.

Tory   Don't drink.

Pete   Get lots of sleep.

Tory   What else?

Pete   Don't use drugs.

Tory   What else?

Pete   Don't do it because of morality. Do it because it's selfish for you. Do it because it brings lots of good rewards to you personally.

Tory   OK, what else?

Pete   I don't know.

Tory   Do what makes you feel good.

Pete   Don't hurt anyone.

Tory   Hurting people is an egotistical high.

Pete   Which has a negative backfire on _you_.

Tom (_leaving giving-up area_)   All right. All right.

There was a pack of wolves with two female wolves in it. One was powerful and the other had no power. One day, the weak female gave birth to a bunch of baby wolves, and for the first time in her life she knew what it felt like to be happy. That night, the powerful female went into the mother wolf's den, dragged out her pups one by one right in front of her, and killed them.

Pause.

Nobody likes his story. He tries again.

You were sitting in a white field, and everything was white. The sky was white. There was nothing but emptiness and white and quiet.

Pete (_happily_)   And unicorns.

Tom (_to_ **Pete**, _angrily_)   There were no unicorns there!

Pete _makes an irritated gesture._

Pete   The unicorns are flying over the rainbow!

Tom (_to_ **Pete**)   I must confess.

You are a bad person.

Pete _gets mad._

Tory (_interrupting their fight_)   You are in a space ship made of donkey balls. You are flying around and around the earth. The stewardesses are serving you cocktails that are red and green and blue and purple, and you are looking out your window.

Tom (*pitifully*)   I don't see it.

I think I'm dying.

I'm dying.

My liver. My penis.

Tory (*to audience*)   I can see you out there. I can see you sitting out there with your little pinched lips and your prissy face, sitting there all high and mighty with your little squeezed-up, pinched-up prissy disapproving face going, "I don't like this." Well, the reason why you're sitting up there all unhappy with your little, pinched, disapproving lips is not because what *we're* doing sucks, but because *you're* lacking. You're lacking in something. We all know people like this, who have some part of their brain that's gone dead, who can't understand anything and want to be left alone in their little bubble of vacuity to carry on their stupid life without ever having to think about anything, ever. You're a judgmental, negative priss who accuses other people of being judgmental and negative. Why don't you go home, you fucking hypocrite.

Pete   I am on an underwater planet in the belly of a whale, which is populated by fish. The fish go to school, where they learn about fishing. There is a glass tank in the belly of the whale, and every time the whale eats a fish the carcass comes drifting down into the tank for anatomy class.

Tom   You are on a field in a forest.

Tory   You are on a field in a forest and you are singing, you are riding a horse.

Tom (*to audience, kindly*)   Just . . . go ahead and be pathetic. It's OK. It's not pathetic.

Tory (*to audience, very mean*)   You should have been born different.

Tom   It's not pathetic.

Tory   It's completely pathetic.

Pete   Shut up!

Tory   What's wrong?

Pete   I didn't get to say any of the things I wanted to say!

Tom   Don't say them.

Tory   Shut up! Everyone shut up!

Pete   You shut up! I didn't get to say anything!

Tom   You can say anything you want.

Tory   Say it now.

Tom   Say it!

Pete   I want to say . . .

Tory   What? Say it!

Tom   Say something!

Pete   I . . . know something.

Tom   What?

Pete   I know . . . how to live.

Tory   How do you do it?

Pete   Somebody else say it.

Tom   This is how to live.

Tory   Be born different.

Tom   Somebody else say it.

Pete   I'll say it.

Tom   Say it!

Pause.

Tory (*going to giving-up area*)   I think you just have to be born different.

Pete *and* **Tom** *look at each other and awkwardly get into "Jesus/God" positions, standing next to each other facing the audience.* **Pete** *is Jesus and* **Tom** *is God.*

All the following lines are directed to the audience until **Tom**'s *sudden howl of pain.*

Pete   Fear not, for I will walk upon the land.

Tom   I will walk upon the land, in the hills and the valley below.

Pete   I will walk upon the land and shout my name.

Tom   I will shout my name in the desert.

Pete   Over the plains and in the valley, you will hear my name echoing.

Tom   You will hear my name echoing into the hills.

Pete   You will hear my name echoing and fall down.

Tom   You will fall down groveling upon the earth.

Pete   You will weep and curse my name.

Tom   You will curse my name and I will smite you down.

Pete   I will swing my balls like a Santa Claus sack around my head.

Tom   The sons of my sons will run in circles around me, each holding one of my ball sacs.

Pete   The sons of my sons will run around and around me until I am trapped in a prison of my own balls and flesh.

Tom   I will shout at them as they run away with my balls in their hands.

Pete   I will comfort you in your pain.

Tom   Deliver your heart unto my hand.

Pete   My shepherd will guide you in the field.

Tom   There will be no more cause for sorrow.

Pete   You will sleep with the lambs upon the earth.

Tom   Amen.

Pause.

Pete (*chanting – "hai" and "fai" are pronounced like the word "hi"*)
Hai, hai, a-shing-a-shing hai, a mekka-lek hai mekka shing-a-shing fai.

Tom   Hai, hai, a-ding-a-ding hai, a wokka-wok hai mekka fikky-fock fai.

Pete   Hai, hai, a-fing-a-fong hai, a wikka-wok hai mekka ching-a-chong hai.

Tom   Hai, hai, a ching-a-ching hai, ma-lekka-lek hai donga fing-a-fing hai.

Pete   Hai, hai, a-shing-a-shing hai, a likka-luk hai mekka ching-a-ching fai.

Tom   Hai, hai, a-ding-a-dong hai, a likka-lik hai mekka fikky-fock fai.

Pete   Hai, hai, a-fing-a-fong hai, a fikka-fock hai mekka ching-a-chong hai.

Tom   Hai, hai, a ching-a-ching hai, ma-likka-lek hai donga fikky-fock hai.

Tom *suddenly howls in pain.*

Pete   What's wrong?

Tom   I think I'm dying.

Pete   Why?

Tom   My eyes hurt.

Pete   You should get eye-removal surgery.

Tom   No!

Pete *howls in pain.*

Tom   What?

Pete (*casually*)   Nothing.

Tom *howls in pain.*

Pete   Shut up, dude! You're not even hurt.

Tom   Yes I am.

Pause.

Pete   Help me.

Tom   You help me.

Pete   You help me first.

Tom   Some pretty sad things have happened to me. Do you want to hear about them?

Pete   Tell me about it tomorrow.

Tom   When I was five –

Pete   Do you know what's a good thing to do when you're sad?

Tom   Get drunk?

Pete   No.

Tom   Do cocaine?

Pete   No!

Tom   What then?

Pete   I don't know.

Tom   You're kind of an idiot.

Pete   You're an idiot! I know how to live!

Tom *howls in pain.*

Tom   Fuck!

Pete   OK. I can help you.

Tom   How?

Pete   I can tell you how to live.

Tom   I already know how to live.

Pete   No, OK, this is it.

Pause.

Do unto yourself as you would do unto another for whom you cared very deeply.

You have to be nice to yourself. For example, if your room is a total disaster area and you need to clean it but can't bring yourself to start doing it, just imagine that you're cleaning it for a really good friend who just found out they have cancer. But really, that friend is you.

Pause. **Tom** *is baffled.*

Pete   I'm trying to say that you should be motivated by compassion to yourself. Instead of telling yourself that you're a lazy slob for not cleaning your room, you should tell yourself that you deserve to have a clean room and that cleaning it is a nice thing to do for yourself.

Tom   That sounds like something for pussies.

Pete   See! That's the *opposite* of how to live. You think you can roll around in your sea of jellyballs like a big jelly whale, but eventually the jellyball fluid is going to leak out and kill you!

Tory *leaves the giving-up area and sings to* **Pete**, *calming him.*

Tory (*sung: double "h"s at the end of a syllable indicate that it is held for an extra beat*)
    Hikk-en yaa, chunken yaa, moo-oo-kohh-oh-ko chunyeh.

Pete
    Hikk-en yaa, chunken yaa, moo-oo-kohh-oh-ko chunyeh.

Tory
 Saylekah-malikka-chah-mahah-maluk-alukohh-oh-ko-
chunyeh.

Pete
 Saylekah-malikka-chah-hah.
 Maluk-ohh-oh-ko-chunyeh.

Tory
 Hikk-en yaa, chunken yaa, moo-oo-kohh-oh-ko chunyeh.

Pete
 Hikk-en yaa, chunken yaa, moo-oo-kohh-oh-ko chunyeh.

Tory (*spoken*)   A-shee-shee.

Pete and Tory (*singing together*)
 Sayleh-kah-malikka-chah-mahah-maluk-alukohh-oh-ko-
    chunyeh.
 Sayleh-kah-malikka-chah-hah. Maluk-ohh-oh-ko-chunyeh.

Tom   This is a seminar on how to be cool.

Tory   I want to crack open a monkey's ribcage and dump a
pile of worms on top of its internal organs to see how they all
interact.

Pete   There are many ways of being cool.

Tom   I'm obsessed with things getting stuck into people's
eyeballs, like that precise moment of when the foreign object
pierces the jelly of the ball. I can imagine it over and over
again in my mind for hours. Like the idea of being able to
give someone a paper cut on both eyeballs with one swipe.

Tory   What else is cool?

Pete   This sucks! I hate this!

Pete *exits.*

Tory   On my farm, there are some ducks.

Tom   I love all God's creation, to the smallest hair on their
head.

Tory   Do you love my ducks?

Tom   I love all God's creation.

Tory   I love my ducks' duck-meat.

Tom   I will protect their duck-meat.

Tory   From what?

Tom (*pause*)   Wolves.

Tory   There are no wolves on my farm.

Tom   You're going to hell.

Tory   Why?

Tom   Because you don't have Jesus in your heart.

Tory   How come?

Tom   Because you didn't invite him. It's like with vampires – you have to invite him or he can't come in.

Tory   What happens if he comes in?

Tom   What do you want to happen?

Tory   I want to be a mermaid.

Tom   If you invite Jesus into your heart, then you can be a mermaid.

Tory   How?

Tom   Because when you die you'll go to heaven, and heaven is a mermaid fairyland.

Tory   Are you serious?

Tom   Absolutely.

Pause. **Tory** *is overjoyed. She takes* **Tom**'s *hand.* **Tom** *smiles a big, forced smile.*

They smile and hold hands. **Tom**'s *smile disintegrates and he lets go of her hand.*

Tom (*to audience*)   I don't know how to live. I don't know how to act around other people. I have no idea what the fuck I'm doing.

And it scares me to look out there at you, because I'm afraid that you are all living your lives on instinct and feeling totally fine, while I'm all alone in my fucked-up state.

(*To* **Tory**.) Sorry.

Tom *exits.*

Pause.

Tory *walks downstage, smiling at the audience.*

Tory   One summer, I drove across the country. I wasn't driving, so I actually ended up sleeping through a lot of it. It was ridiculous how much I slept. I think I slept like twelve hours a day for six days straight, which was weird because normally I'm not a big sleeper. I remember constantly half waking up to the feeling of the air-conditioner combined with the feeling of heat pressing down on the outside of the car. The first thing that would register was the brightness through the windows, and then the radio. I could stay in that half-awake state for a really long time, like an hour, without any kind of interruption. Whenever we stopped at gas stations I was usually half-asleep and remember stumbling through the heat and then suddenly getting all alert when I got in the store and saw all this stuff I wanted to buy, like something to drink or a magazine or cassette tape. When we got back on the road I'd drink my drink and look at the different landscapes going past the windows.

I was surrounded by mermaids. I was lying on soft green grass and they were standing on their flippers in a circle around me. I looked up and saw a bright blue sky criss-crossed with rainbows that arched from one puffy white cloud to another. As I sat up, the mermaids started hopping away and I could see that the landscape around me was composed almost entirely of chopped-up mermaid parts.

There were mountains of mermaid-tail fish-slices and mermaid torsos planted like bushes all around. Mermaid-guts hung from all the trees and the lakes were clogged with mermaid-hair. The fields were littered with squirming mermaid babies who lay unattended as hundreds of frolicking mermaids played kickball with hundreds of mermaid heads.

As I walked to my waiting rainbow-coach, squashing a mermaid baby-head with each step, I realized how fortunate I truly am.

Katori Hall

Hurt Village

Hurt Village had its world premiere at the Signature Theatre Company, New York City, on February 27, 2012 (James Houghton, Founding Artistic Director; Erika Mallin, Executive Director). The cast was as follows:

Cookie	Joaquina Kalukango
Crank	Marsha Stephanie Blake
Big Mama	Tonya Pinkins
Buggy	Corey Hawkins
Toyia	Saycon Sengbloh
Cornbread	Nicholas Christopher
Ebony	Charlie Hudson, III
Skillet	Lloyd Watts
Tony C	Ron Cephas Jones

Directed by Patricia McGregor
Set and Projection Design by David Gallo
Costume Design by Clint Ramos
Lighting Design by Sarah Sidman
Sound Design by Robert Kaplowitz
Wig and Makeup Design by Cookie Jordan
Original Music by Luqman Brown
Fight Direction by Rick Sordelet
Choreography by Daniel Price

Characters

in order of appearance

Cookie   Thirteen years old, Crank and Buggy's daughter, precocious and gifted, a wannabe rapper, just wants to get out

Crank   Late twenties, three years clean off of crack, hustles the government and does everybody's hair in the neighborhood, cranky, has been taken in by Big Mama, used to date Buggy

Big Mama   Fifty-five years old, the matriarch of the family and respected hard-working pillar of the community, Buggy's blood grandmother

Buggy   Late twenties, a soldier returning home from the Iraq war with a haunting secret

Toyia   Late twenties, the fast-talking, loudmouth upstairs neighbor, works as an exotic dancer at the local "shake junt," Cornbread's "babymama," calls herself a feminist

Cornbread   Late twentics, mixed-race or "high yella," FedEx employee and small-time drug dealer (also called "doughboy"), not-so-secretly in love with Crank

Ebony   Late teens, neighborhood comedian and small-time doughboy, a Tony C crony

Skillet   Mid-teens, badly scarred from a childhood accident involving a skillet, speaks really slowly

Tony C   Early forties, The "Kang" of the doughboys who controls the crack houses in Hurt Village

Setting

The end of summer. Hurt Village, Memphis, Tennessee. Second Bush dynasty.

Prologue

Dusk. Somewhere the sky is falling into the ground. Bits and pieces of magenta, peach and coral hues make the broken bits of beer bottles and crack vials glow with a stardust twinkle. No grass. No one. Dust rolls across this beautiful broken land like wisps of cotton candy blowing in the country wind. Except cotton candy does not exist in this modern-day wasteland. Nothing even remotely related to sweetness exists here. A crooked, dinted, weather-beaten sign that says "Hurt Village" sways in the wind. A two-tiered housing project served up Southern-style. Shattered windows. A constellation of garbage and debris. Broken-down, burned-out cars. Dingy, tattered shirts and socks hang on for dear life to sagging clothes lines. The ghosts of hopscotch marks fade into the ground.
A fading graffiti tag which says "Das Haus des Jammers" is splashed across one of the crumbling walls of the project. It looks as if a wrecking ball has already slammed through the sides, exposing the units. The faint outline of the Memphis Arena Pyramid glistens into existence in the distance. In the emerging darkness, a chorus of children sweetly sings:

Children
Hurt Village is falling down, falling down, falling down
Hurt Village is falling down, my fair bitches
Hurt Village is falling down, falling down, falling down
Hurt Village is falling down, my fair bitches.

Lights up on **Cookie**, *a thirteen-year-old flat-chested woman-child with a colorful array of barrettes hanging onto her greasy plaits. She is beating on the army-green electric utility box in the front yard area with her small fists. She provides a steady bass accented by a quick rat-tat-tat at the end. As she flows, the sky drops further into the land, until – one by one – the unit lights of the housing project flicker on to light the night.*

Cookie
This be the war / ungh / this be the war / ungh
This be the war / ungh / this be the war / ungh, ungh
This be the war / ungh / this be the war / ungh
Ungh /

You can't see the stars no more /
Just the bling from the dreams of souls searching for
   the same thing /
For a lift of light from cavin' ceilings /
This my ode to project people strugglin' /
Mamas and fathers hold yo' daughters /
I'm precocious / most here know this and they know
   I spit the illest shit /
I spin ghetto tales that'll make you weep /
My lyrical lullabyes'll knock yo' ass to sleep /

'Cause I be the street storyteller /
Runnin' crackers through my hellah /
Ringin' the bells and yellin' through the wire like Mariah /
Having CNN on fire /

Bye-bye to crumblin' walls /
Bye-bye to Auction Street /
Bye-bye too many sold /
Bye-bye too many beat /

They makin' niggahs extinct /
Too many drugs in the jail meat /
Chickenheads ain't comin' home to roost /
And Welfare man stopped sellin' Juicy Juice /

Ain't gone have nobody to play with afterwhile /
. . . while . . . while

Shit! I done got off my rhyme.

She looks out into the audience.

Remember when the candylady used to live on the Seventh
St. side of the complex? You could get them pink chewys for
two cents a dollop. You can't buy shit for two cents no mo.
E'erthang cost nearbout a dollar. Inflation. Fuck Bush!
Remember when we use to play curbball? Object of the
game: you had to stand on yo' porch and hit the curb of yo'
neighbor's porch with a ball. If you hit they curb, you got a
point. If it bounced back and hit yours, you got a double.
Hell, yeah! I was the queen of muthafuckin' curbball. Wun't

nobody betta than me. Or how 'bout when folks'll be outside
playin' "hide the belt"? You'd take yo' mama's most favoritist
belt she whip you wit, and somebody like Ray-Ray or Peaches
would go behind the complex and hide it. When they fount it,
e'erbody would break for the base 'cause whoever got the belt
could beat the shit out of e'erbody! Base'll be somebody
porch that had a couch on it so you could sit down and catch
yo' breath after runnin' so hard. I still got welts till this day.
I couldn't run for shit. Us project kids cleverah than a
muthafucka, maine. Mmph, mmph, mmph, them was the
days. Fo' it got bad. I mean Hurt Village always been bad,
but it done got bad-bad, like you-betta-move-yo-Big Mama-
out-these-muthafuckin-projects-fo-she-get-gang-raped-
robbed-and-murdered-by-her-gangsta-disciple-crackhead-son
bad. Yeah, we done seen some thangs livin' on the Old
Thomas side. Folks from all over Memphis know our street as
the Million Dollar Track. You can get yo' crack, smack, dro,
and you can catch a bullet. Children can't even go outside to
play no mo'. I ain't played curbball in I don't know how long.
They done already moved a lota folk out. We the last ones.
That why Big Mama been bein' cheap. She been savin' up
her scrilla for a minute for when we move to our new house.
Oooooo, Big Mama know she been bein' cheap as hell.
Memphis be hot as a muthafucka in the summer and she
don't be lettin' a niggah turn on the air conditioner for mo'
than fifteen minutes at a time. Always yakkin'. "You gone run
up the light bill." She 'en even have to pay for 'lectricity!
They give that shit to us for free! But I guess po' folk always
gotsta be savin' they scrilla. Like take Dawn dishwashin'
liquid for instance. That's stuff the shit, ain't it? It's for more
than just dishes. It body wash, washin' detergent, Windex,
bubble bath, Barbie shampoo . . . Yeah, maine. Folks 'round
here so po' we can't even afford the "r" at the end. Project
niggahs have to think fast, cry later. Livin' o'er here can try
you sometimes. I done had fun though. But I'm thirteen, and
I'm a grown-ass woman now.

Crank, Cookie*'s mother, enters, striking a clenched-fist-on-hip pose
on the cracked concrete porch.*

Crank   Cookie! Get yo' ass up in here. You know you supposeta be in this house befo' them skreet lights come on. When them lightnin' bugs start lightin' they asses, yo' ass need to be lightnin' up in here. I'n gone tell you no more, nah!

Cookie (*indicating the broken street light*)   The skreet light broke. How I'm supposeta know when it time to come in?

Crank   You know you got yo' first day of school in the mornin'.

Cookie   So!

Crank   Cookie! Don't make me come out there and yank you! And keep on sittin' on that 'lectricity box. Yo' booty gone blow up.

Cookie   Yes, ma'am! (*To the audience.*) Maine, I can't wait to move on up out of here.

Act One

Scene One

Inside the unit. Cardboard boxes are scattered everywhere. They are packing. It is sparsely furnished with that black lacquered rent-to-own furniture made out of more sawdust than actual wood. The television is on its last leg, hence the aluminum foil to give a signal. Black Entertainment Television (BET) is on – as usual. There are cracks in the cement walls, which are painted a deep, peeling burgundy. There is the drone of crunk music blaring from car speakers outside, classic Three Six Mafia. You can hear an occasional bottle thrown to the ground accented by yells from the guys outside.

Cookie I don't wanna get my hair did!

Crank I'dn know why you whinin' for.

Cookie I wanna go outside and play!

Crank No child of mine gone be runnin' round like a cat been suckin' on her head.

Cookie Ma!

Crank You hear 'bout that lil' girl on Seventh Skreet?

Cookie Naw . . .

Crank Had a little girl over there didn't like to get her hair did. Jus wouldn't let her mama comb her head. Braids was just a' hangin' on by a strand. So her mama left her braids in for two years. One day, da girl come to school and say her head hurtin'. Nobody believe her. Next week she was dead. Come to find out a spider came in the middle of the night, set up a nest in her head and sucked all the blood out.

Cookie That's a urban legend!

Crank That ain't no legend. Bet!

Cookie You just a lie –

Crank *smacks* **Cookie** *on the head with the comb. Enter* **Big Mama**, *the matriarch, who rules her house with a sharp tongue and an iron fist.*

Big Mama   Don't be callin' yo' mama a lie, even though she can't tell the truth worth shit. I should pull one of her gold teeth out e'ertime she lie. Call her a "story."

Cookie   You a story!

Big Mama   Just look at that chile head. Look like a cat been suckin' on it.

Crank   I tolt her! If she would just sit down, her head would done been combed by nah. Next time, I'ma let you go to school nappy-headed.

Big Mama   Girl, I'll stomp a cone in yo' ass you let that girl go to school lookin' like that.

Crank   Ugggh! I'm so glad y'all goin' back. So I can go on my vacation.

Cookie   Ma, seem like you always on vacation. Whatchoo gone do when I'm at school?

Big Mama   Sit on her narrow behind and collect a check. That's what she gone do. I done been on my feet all damn night. I ain't gone work that night shift no more. Folks down at the VA 'bout to run me ragged.

Crank   If you didn't work so much, yo' check'll be more.

Big Mama   Honey, that welfare ain't 'bout shit. And I'm too young for some Social Security. I gotta work. What I need to do is collect me a muthafuckin' crazy check. 'Cause y'all about to run me crazy. Speakin' a' crazy. You crazy you thank you gone lay up here all day watchin' TV and not work. You need to call yoself findin' you a job.

Crank (*irritably*)   I'm finna go to cosmetology school –

Big Mama   "Finna go" don't put no food on the table. Shit! I don't know why somebody wanna waste money on cosmetology school when everything you need to know you can learn in that kitchen.

Crank   If I'ma have my own shop, I'ma need a license to practice.

Big Mama   What you need a license for? You might work on folk heads, but you ain't no muthafuckin' brain surgeon. You still needs to get yoself a job.

Crank   I make 'nuf money fixin' folks' hair. I gets my cash under the table, then my welfare check, and a crazy check. I'm rollin'. All – what them folks be sayin' – "tax exempt." Besides, Oprah say –

Big Mama   Don't pull that Oprah-follow-yo-dreams bullshit on me. I had a dream once. I had a dream that by the time I was fifty-five I'd have my house to myself and wouldn't have to feed and raise no more chillen. I done already had mine, and I'm still raisin' chillen. And Crank, you ain't even none of mine. I took you in 'cause you had a baby by my grandson, but as long as you live under my roof, you gone do as I say. I might nota brought you in this world, but I sho as hell –

All   " – can take you OUT of it."

Big Mama   I sho'll will. Nah, how come y'all ain't rippin' through these boxes? Y'all know them housing folk comin' to move us by next Friday.

Crank   "Movin on up! To Raleigh! We finally got a piece of the piieeeeee!"

Big Mama   Is you back on crack?

Crank   No.

Big Mama   Betta not be. You get on that shit again, I'll really stomp a cone in yo' ass.

Cookie *looks out the lone window.*

Cookie   Where all these niggahs gone go?

Big Mama   Honey, the hell if I know. The city suppose to move us everywhichaway but the right way. But they movin' us the right way. We movin' out to Raleigh, the best 'burb in M-town.

Crank   Niggahs just gone move over to the white folks' neighborhood and fuck they shit up.

Big Mama   Well, white folks can keep on movin' out east till they nearbout fall in the ocean. Fuck 'em. Ouch!

Cookie *has dropped a big-ass box on* **Big Mama***'s foot.*

Big Mama   What the hell wrong with you droppin' that big-ass box on my gotdang toe! Y'all know folks with sugar feets be hurtin and some more shit.

She takes off her shoe to inspect her feet. Sucks her teeth.

Need to get my damn foot shaved. Cookie, hand me a beer out the 'frigerator.

Cookie *goes and gets the beer for* **Big Mama***.*

Cookie   It's hot.

Big Mama   That 'frigerator just stay broke.

Cookie *kicks the refrigerator. It turns back on again.*

Big Mama   Where my mail at? My J.C. Penney catalogue come?

Crank   Cookie was sittin' on it.

Big Mama   Well, I hope you done washed yo' booty. Betta not be no crabs crawlin' on it.

Crank *covers* **Cookie***'s ears.*

Cookie   What she talkin' 'bout?

Crank   Nothin'.

Big Mama   I am talkin' 'bout somethin! S – T – D –

Crank   Shhheee don't need to know 'bout all that!

Big Mama   How come she don't? Hell, you had her when you was thirteen –

Crank   Ain't it time fo' you to go to bed so you'll be ready fo' yo' shift tonight?

Big Mama   Not befo' I make my list. When they move us out to Raleigh, this what I'ma have in my house. Y'all need to learn how to make ya' goals. Write that shit down on paper. When it wrote ain't no denyin' it. (*She gazes at the catalogue.*) Ohhhh, look at that recliner . . . Gone look good in my new livin' room. We is gone have a livin' room and a dinin' room, ye'en know? Oooooo! I got my "Publisher's Clearin' House"!

She fans a yellow envelope in the air.

Crank   There she go . . .

Big Mama   We gone win our million dollars if I keep on sendin' these jokers in!

Crank   You and yo' bougie dreams.

Big Mama   Hell, one day I'ma win! And y'all ain't gone get na'an one penny! I'ma get me a house out by the white folk by my damn self. Cookie, go get me my pocketbook for me a stamp.

Cookie   You'd think that'd let you mail it in for free they got millions of dollars.

Cookie *goes to get* **Big Mama**'s *pocketbook on the counter.* **Crank** *continues to shift through the boxes.*

Crank   These junts is heavy.

Cookie   Books?

Crank   How it's gone be some books?

Cookie   I don't know. You said it was heavy. I ascertained it might be some books.

Crank   You ass-a-wha?

Cookie   Assumed. Divined. Hypothesized –

Crank *pops* **Cookie** *upside the head.*

Crank   Come over here and help me move it! / Tryin' to be all smart and shit.

Big Mama   Crank, don't you hit that chile in my presence.

Beat. **Crank** *looks at* **Cookie** *who holds her head in pain.*

Crank   Fine. Go clean up that room fo' you go to school. Look like a damn tornado done ripped through it.

Cookie   Maaaaiiiiinnnneeee!

She stomps off.

Crank   I don't wanna hear no nothin' comin' out yo' mouth! I'm tired of you back talkin'', nah.

Beat.

She just done got to bein' hard-headed. Don't wanna mind nobody.

Big Mama   She just don't wanna mind you. That's what y'all get for havin' 'em so young. Hell, Cookie might as well be yo' lil' sistah.

There is a knock on the screen door.

Crank   Who dat is?

Big Mama   Clearly, the Prize Patrol or somebody that wanna get shot.

Big Mama *goes to the screen door, but she stops dead in her tracks. Her eyes change. The harsh glaze her eyes hid behind has dropped – curtain down. We see this strong woman cave into herself – sag like the branches of a weeping willow – but just for a moment.* **Buggy**, *her long-lost grandson, opens the screen door and walks inside the unit. He wears a wife-beater sticky with sweat. His muscles are squished like sausages into a shirt that can barely contain his chest. He is a man. He lifts his marine jacket off his shoulder. His pants are cuffed into sandy black boots that have been attacked by ghetto dustballs. The one that got* *out. Gorgeous, he is: deep bronze skin with the slanted eyes of an Angolan warrior. He stands there.*

Big Mama   Lawd, have mercy on my soul . . . We done thought you was dead.

Buggy   No, ma'am. They sent me home . . . rightfully so.

Big Mama   How come you ain't tole nobody? We coulda picked you up from the airport. Got Cornbread 'nem to pick you up.

Buggy   I thought I'd save y'all the trouble. So I walked.

Big Mama   Boy, how you gone walk all the way from 'cross town in this heat? You gone have a stroke.

Buggy   I done been to some hotter places, Big Mama. Heat ain't never kilt nobody.

Big Mama   How come it ain't? Them high-school boys be fallin' out at football practice all the time playin' in that hot-ass sun –

Buggy   Ain't nobody playin' football, Big Mama –

Big Mama   Come here and let me look at ya.

Buggy *hugs his grandmother.*

Big Mama   My grandson . . . Yo' mama woulda been so proud of you. Servin' yo' country, boy. Makin' niggahs over here proud. How come you ain't tell nobody you was comin'?

Buggy   Didn't know I was comin' back till it happened.

Big Mama   Yeah, life'll do that to you.

Beat.

Buggy   Crank.

Crank   I'm surprised you 'member me.

Buggy   Always.

Beat. **Big Mama** *breaks the uncomfortable silence.*

Big Mama   Damn, you done got swole. What they feedin' folk over there?

Buggy   They sho'll don't feed nobody no pig feet, hog mogs or collard greens.

Big Mama   Ooooooo, that what we gone have tonight!

Crank   Big Mama, I done already packed up the big pots.

Big Mama   So! We gone have us a party. Tell everybody my lil' Buggy done come on home.

Buggy   Awwww, Big Mama, don't call me that. That ain't befittin' a soldier.

Big Mama   I don't care what they call you over there, Artelius. Here you "Buggy"! Cookie, come on in here and see yo' daddy.

Cookie (*offstage*)   I'm a freak of nature; I ain't got no daddy.

Buggy   I know that ain't who I thank it is.

Cookie *runs in and stops at the door.*

Cookie   Who the hell he?

Crank   You'un 'member him?

Buggy   She done got stout. She wun't nothin' 'bout three when I seen't her last.

Crank   That was right before . . .

Big Mama   Yo' mama passed.

Buggy   Yeah.

Crank   Yeap.

Buggy   You look just like yo' mama.

Big Mama   Honey, two peas in a pod. Can't barely tell one from the other. They wear the same size shoe, too.

Cookie   I hope you brought us somethin' from overseas like other folks do. I heard you can get some fresh Air Force Ones on the low-low, you know though.

Buggy   How old you now?

Big Mama   Honey, thirteen goin' on thirty.

Buggy   Well, kids 'round here grow up fast.

Big Mama   Sho'll do. Unh, unh, unh. I need to get on yo' exercise program. Done left and went and got fine on ya' grandmama. I'ma have to starve myself. They need to lock the 'frigerator up 'cause I done got to lookin' bigger than a barge!

Cookie   Ain't nothin' up in there to eat no way. We woulda had somethin' up in here, if Crank hadna popped off the food stamps.

Big Mama   Who you done popped off my food stamps to?

Crank   Don't worry 'bout it. You gone get yours. I done got fifty dollars for a sixty-five-dollar book.

Cookie   How you gone pop off a sixty-five-dollar book for fifty dollars? That don't make no sense.

Crank   Cuz nobody wanna use them fucked-up ass food stamps.

Cookie   I suppose they less attractive, but check this. They savin' more 'cause a sixty-five-dollar book is really worth seventy dollars of groceries 'cause you ain't gotta pay tax on a book. They gettin' seventy dollars' worth of food for fifty dollars. That's just stupid business right there. That's why niggahs be broke right now. They don't know howta handle they business.

Buggy   She smaaaart. Know how to make a dollar, huh?

Cookie   I'm tryin' to save me up a little cash pot. I got a album comin' out.

Crank   She be lockin' herself up in the bathroom. Rappin' into her little funky Fisher Price tape recorder.

Cookie   That all I got, maine.

Buggy   So you a rapper? You gone flow for me?

Cookie   I'll think about it.

Buggy   Gone spit me a couple of bars.

Cookie *blushes.*

Crank   Don't be shame, nah!

Buggy *starts beating on the cement wall.* **Cookie** *finally gains some confidence.*

Cookie
  Lil' bitches be rappin'
  Fingers poppin' on the corner
  Be poppin' they pussy
  But they don't really mean it though
  Niggahs tryta look at me
  But can't step to me correctly
  Niggah don't perpetrate
  I'm just trying to percolate
  Whut! Whut! Whut! Whut!
  Straight up off the dome, son.

She starts jookin' in circles.

Big Mama   Why these young folks don't sing no more. Just be boppin' they gums.

Cookie   I'm expressin' myself! Hell, it's war out on these skreets.

Crank   You don't know what war is.

Buggy   That was awesome!

Uncomfortable silence.

Cookie   Why you talk funny?

Crank   'Cause he a oreo. Always been one. You gone be one too in a little while 'cause you finna be bussed over to them cracker schools.

Cornbread, *a mixed race or "high yella" old friend of* **Buggy***'s, knocks on the screen door. Then he comes in. Decked out in navy blue and orange, he sports "FedEx" proudly on his shirt.* **Toyia** *enters with him, his "babymama." They are so engrossed in their fight that they don't notice* **Buggy** *standing in the kitchen corner.*

Toyia   Girl, I need to borrow a cup of warshin' powder.

Crank   For what?

Toyia   I need to douche this niggah sperm out my muthafuckin' pussy. What you thank!

Cornbread   Ain't nobody done put they dick up in you.

Crank   Don't be talkin' like that 'round my chile.

Toyia   She gone find out soon enough. See, Cookie listen to me 'cause this here a cautionary tale. Don't let na'an one niggah trick you into havin' a baby that even they don't want 'cause, you see, they be the first ones to keep on steppin' down the line when you need some Pampers, some Similac, some shoes or some bail. Always screamin' and hollerin' 'bout how, "It too expensive! It too expensive!" but when you axe him for four hundred dollars for a abortion, niggah don't wanna give it, but that's yo' fault, niggah. I told ya so! That's yo' fault, niggah. That's yo' fault, so hell, yeah, you gone take care of me now. Don't pay up then, you pay ten times later. Wha! Wha!

Cornbread   Somebody please put a dick in her mouth.

Toyia   I done already had one and it wun't yo's –

Big Mama   Ay! Ay! Ay! It's called a condom!

Toyia   My bad, Big Mama. I didn't barely see you over there.

Big Mama   Well, get some muthafuckin' glasses then.

Toyia *finally notices* **Buggy**.

Toyia   I'm sorry, ma'am. But bump some glasses. I needs me a muthafuckin' microscope.

She sashays over to **Buggy**.

Toyia   Who this fine speci-man chillin' up in the cut?

Cornbread   Keep yo' project paws to yo'self. It ain't nobody for you. This my niggah. My niggah! Awww, playa president, wha! Wha!!

Buggy   Cornbread!

Cornbread   You been shipped outta here for more than a Memphis minute!

Buggy   Yeah, but I'ma be back for a while.

Toyia   You done come back for the high-school reunion?

Cornbread   Toyia, you ain't even graduate.

Toyia   Niggah, you ain't neither! (*Looking him up and down.*) You look real different from high school, though. Don't he Crank?

Crank   He look . . . betta.

Beat. She busies herself, continuing to pack. **Crank** *picks up* **Cookie**'s *dolls' house.*

Cookie   Unh, unh! You can't throw that away.

Crank   Why not? You don't play wit' it no more.

Cookie   It's a testament to my childhood.

Cornbread (*to* **Cookie**)   Don't mind her!

Crank   Cracker be gone.

Cornbread   I ain't white, twitchy-ass girl! I don't know how many times I gotta tell y'all funky ass.

Crank   You betta be nice, or I'ma tell Toyia where I seen't you last Saturday.

Toyia   Where you seen't him?

Crank   On Beale lookin' drunker than a skunk. Believe that, playa.

Toyia *smacks him upside the head.*

Toyia   Just tell me when you cheatin'! That's all I axe, that's all I axe!

Cornbread   Maine, you got a Kool on you?

Buggy   Always, always.

They begin to light up.

Big Mama   Unh, unh. Parliaments the only thang I let be smoked up in here. Take that menthol shit on somewhere.

Buggy *and* **Cornbread** *exit the unit to smoke.*

Cornbread   I love me some pussy, but it's just too much up in there.

Beep. Beep. **Cookie** *runs out past them.*

Cookie (*to* **Cornbread**)   I need some lunch money.

Cornbread *digs into his pocket and pulls out several bills. She takes one and begins to run off.*

Cornbread   Ay, girl.

She comes back, kisses him on the cheek. Runs off again.

She gettin' so big.

Buggy   Yeah . . .

Cornbread   So, fuck witcha boy for a minute. What you been eatin'?

Buggy   What *you* been eatin'?

Cornbread   I been eatin' real good since I got me a job on the "plantation."

Buggy   Awww, damn, maine.

Cornbread   Yeah, FedEx 'bout to have me throwin' my muthafuckin' back out. Liftin' they heavy-ass boxes. Makin' five dollars and a quarter on the hour.

Buggy   Might as well be bent over pickin' cotton.

Cornbread   That what I know. But they the only ones hirin' niggahs wit' a charge so . . . you know? Damn, niggah. It sho'll is good as hell to see you. Glad I got to see you fo' they move us all out.

Buggy   Glad I came, too, hell. Y'all wun't gone tell nobody?

Cornbread   Hell, niggah, you the one that done stopped writin' folk, tellin' folk where you was at. We just thought the good ole boy was in heaven.

Buggy (*looking around*)   This some sad shit –

Cornbread   Ain't it? But I guess it's for the best. They, uh, gone flip these units. Memphis done got this thang – the HOPE grant. Thirty-five million to make these here units into "mix income" 'partments, they sayin'. Hurt Village gone be turnt to uptown condos!

Buggy   How dat gone work?

Cornbread   I dunno. Bougie ass niggahs don't like to stay nexta poor-ass niggahs, and white trash don't like to stay nexta niggahs, so how they gone brew that pot of stew, I don't know. If you axe me, look like they tryin' to mix shit up that don't need mixin'. Just ask my ma and pop. Hell, I coulda told 'em that little recipe ain't gone work.

Buggy   You always talkin' food.

Cornbread   Hell, I'm always hungry. Don't tell the missus, but, uhm, I done saved up enough money off that hustlin' . . .

Buggy   Still on that track.

Cornbread   But, see, I'ma 'bout to be out the game, bra. *This* the week I quit.

Buggy   Yeah, niggah, whatever.

Cornbread   I'm fo' real! Playa, I'm workin' me a legit now. Fuck this shit. What Whitney Houston say? "Crack is whack!" The game ain't nothin' like it useta be. It useta be 'bout makin' a coupla dollars. Now, niggahs wanna kill ya' over a porch. I been doin' this shit e'er since high school. I'm tired, niggah. I asked God to let me hustle till I made it and I done did it. Gone get me and homegirl a mansion out in Mississippi. As crazy as she is, maine. I swear fo' God, this my last week. Hell, tell ya what. You come in be my right-hand man. The faster I sell it the faster I'm gone. I'll give you fifty skraight off the prof.

Beat.

Buggy   Niggah, I'm the protector of the United States. How I'ma be lookin' like slangin' rock on the porch?

Cornbread   'Scuse me then, ole-Ninja-Turtle-lookin' ass niggah. Well, tell me about the war, then. You kilt some folks?

Beat.

Buggy   Yeah . . .

Cornbread   You look like you done kilt twenty niggahs whitcho bare hands and shit. Look at you, maine. Ye'en like us, maine, you done did somethin' withcho life. Maine, make me 'bout to cry up in this bitch. I heard you been stationed all over the world. Germany, Philippines, hell, now, Iraq.

Buggy   Yeah, my tour of duty over, so . . .

Cornbread   You probably got so much action out there, maine. Poppin' them Muslim maniacs in they head.

Buggy   Naw, it wun' like that, really.

Cornbread   Maine, you went over there to free that country. That some brave-ass shit. And I bet you can get pussy easy with that uniform.

Buggy (*reluctant to divulge*)   Well . . .

Cornbread   Don't tell me you been bumpin' some niggah booty?

Buggy   Hell, naw!

Cornbread   Hell, niggah, well I ain't know! You ain't answering me skraight so I'm askin' ya is ya crooked.

Buggy (*deepening his voice*)   Hell, naw!

Cornbread   Just makin' sho'! It done got to be a epidemic down here. Now, I don't mind if a girl do that shit. That's sexy as hell. I went to the shake junt one night and saw two freaky deaks lookin' for that chewin'. Hell, that's what I'm pursuin'. Lesbianos bes my favorito thingos, ye'en know? Toyia, know. We got some funny niggahs runnin' round out here, now. All out in the open. It's terrible.

Buggy   Why you so concerned with it?

Cornbread   Hell, somebody gotta be! Somebody gotta make sho' folks livin' right, ya know what I'm sayin'?

He looks **Buggy** *up and down.*

Cornbread   A solja. Done made it out. So to celebrate yo' homecomin' we gone have to take the boys out to the shake junt. Take you on that Pure Passion trip, ya know what I'm sayin'? Get you some pussy and some new tennie shoes 'cause it's toooo hot for some boots.

Broad daylight. There are the sounds of gunshots in the distance. **Buggy** *jumps.* **Cornbread** *smiles.*

Cornbread   Welcome home, niggah.

Scene Two

THE RING SHOUT

The snapping ring. **Ebony** *and* **Skillet** *are in their respective corners on the concrete, ready to duke it out.* **Buggy** *is watching his welcome-home festivities, leaned against someone's car, eating off a styrofoam* *plate.* **Crank** *is on the porch eating popcorn.* **Toyia** *is on the upper level keeping score with her "ohhs" and "ahhs." In one corner there is* **Skillet** – *a skinny tall, lanky boy with slurry speech, gold teeth and a pick in his afro. He is badly burned on his face and legs, but he wears his scars proudly: his ghetto badge of honor. He is always putting cocoabutter on his burns. He speaks very slowly, so he can barely get a word out edgewise. In the other corner is* **Ebony,** *the king of the checkers. He's the absolute don of the checking ring. He'd make Jesus cry. He has a greasy wave nouveau (jheri curl wave at the top with shaved sides), gold teeth, shorts so long they could be his pants, a wifebeater, tattoos and K-Swiss trainers so white a helicopter could spot him from the sky. His rapid-fire rollin' delivery keeps the crowd entertained.* **Cornbread** *is barbecuing on a poor man's grill – a hinged oil barrel. And, as usual, he is instigating.* **Cookie** *is jookin' (a kind of Michael Jackson-esque urban ballet) in the dirt. Everyone watches the game.*

Cornbread   We have in one corner – Skillet, otherwise known as the Coca-Butter man.

All   Ooooohhhhhhh!

Cornbread   And in the other we have, the king of the checkers, Ebony. Let's get ready to ruuuummmmble!

Ebony   Bumpy-gum lookin' ass, old broke ass mo'fo niggah.

Skillet   Yo' Mama so fat . . . when she wear a Malcolm X jacket . . . helicopters wanna land on her.

All   Boooooh!

Cornbread   You gone let him talk to you like that?

Ebony   Is that all you can come up with? Niggah, that cocoa-butter ain't gone help you, it's gone make you crispier than you already is, you Krispy Kreme-ass crunchy black-ass niggah. Check this out, y'all. Skillet house so stanky dat that when you go up in, it smell like *The Twilight Zone,* "Doo, doo, doo, doo. Doo, doo, doo, doo."

All   Oooohhh!

Cornbread   Where is yo' balls, Skillet! Where is they?

Skillet   Niggah . . . fuck . . . you . . . and yo' . . . mama!

Ebony   I can't, my mama died when she looked at yo' face.

All   Ooooooh!

Cornbread   It's gettin' crunk up in the Hurt.

Toyia   Whut! Whut!

Ebony   You soooo broke that when niggahs break into yo' house, they *leave* you money.

All   Ooooohhhhh!

Ebony   Wearin' them broke-down fake-ass Adidas them Mexican niggahs be wearin'. Fajitas.

All   Ooooohhhhh!

Toyia *pipes in with a small baby balanced on her hip.*

Toyia   You leave him alone. I don't know why you always be pickin' on Skillet. You know he slow.

Ebony   Shut up withcho WIC Weetabix weave wearin' ass.

Toyia   Yo' mama!

Ebony   Yo' mama, bitch . . .

Toyia   You just mad 'cause you can't get none of this, witcho greasy hair ass. Can fry a bucket a' chicken all that Canola in yo' hair.

Ebony   Bitch, don't nobody want you. You so ugly, when niggahs come to the shake junt they don't give you dollars, they put pennies in yo' panties.

Toyia   Midnight-blue lookin' niggah, fuck you.

Ebony (*to* **Cornbread**)   You can't turn a hoe into a housewife.

Cornbread   Ay, ay, ay –

Toyia   And you can't make yo' lil' ass dick longer than yo' belly button.

All   Oooohhh!

Skillet   Niggah ... you ... so black ... you ... piss ... coffee.

Cornbread   Niggggah, booo!

Ebony   Naw, niggah, 'least my blackness is natural. Yo' momma so stupid she thought leavin' a skillet of grease on the stove would warm up the house, but she burnt you up instead. Stupid ass bitch.

All (*low rumble*)   Oooooo.

Cornbread   It's gettin' personal up in the Hurt!

Toyia   Unh, unh. That just ain't right.

Skillet
I might be slow wit' my spit
But I'm quick to hit a bitch
Like yo' hoe sistah Peach
She ain't nothin' but a snitch
Yo' sistah is a lesbo
I fucked her real good
And so did everybody
In the whole damn hood.

*He literally pats himself on the back, gives himself a pound. He has never released something so quickly before. Someone provides a beat for **Ebony**. **Ebony** runs around the circle beefin' himself up.*

Ebony   Louder y'all! Turn it up! Check this out!

Rat-tat-tat-tat-tat-tat

Niggah, niggah on the wall who the fairest of them all
It ain't you, 'cause it's me, kang of checkin'', Ebony
I'ma tear you to the roodoo tooda. I'm gone wreck this place
'Cause you in my crunk-ass circle, muthafucka

All
Kill yo'self, fool!
Kill yo'self, fool!

Ebony   In my circle, I swear fo' God you'll be stomped fool!

All

Kill yo'self, fool!
Kill yo'self, fool!

Ebony   You steppin' up too close to the checkin' King. Fool!

These words are like tornados, my breath like earthquakes
I see yo' chest pumpin' hard, yo' knees beginnin' ta shake
Babies are scared of you. Niggah, I'm scared of you
It ain't nothin' new about it, you'se a ugly-ass dude

You so ugly look like the Devil done shit on yo' face
You ain't never gone get pussy, betta start yo' paperchase
'Cause you can't ever step up to me wit' whack-ass rhymes
That don't cost a goddamn dollar, a quarter or a dime

This is skraight off the dome, this spit fire crunk-ass poem
Don't step up to me, I'll run yo' monkey ass home
Fry you like a piece of bologna and pop you in the middle
Then burn you up again and flip you in my fuckin' skillet.

Cornbread   Whut! Whut! WHUT! WHUT! WHUT!
WHUT!

Ebony *has won the verbal match (as usual). The women dance and make ululationesque sounds. They all start gangsta walking. And they break out into their well-known chant, the "Hurt Village Anthem." They pick up various props: a metal barrel, a pole, empty glass bottles from the trash surrounding the complex. This garbage becomes ad-hoc instruments in their own makeshift orchestra pit.*

All

We gone keep it real crunk
Keep it, keep it real loud
Bump all you bitches
Bump, bump all these fake hoes
We know how to keep it real crunk
Keep it real loud
Fuck all you niggahs who don't know what we talkin' 'bout
.

We gone keep it real crunk
Keep it, keep it real loud
Bump all you bitches
Bump, bump all these fake hoes
We know how to keep it real crunk
Keep it real loud
Fuck all you niggahs who don't know what we talkin' 'bout.

Cornbread Who run this?!

All We do!

Cornbread Who run this?

All We run this!

Cornbread Who run this?

All We do!

Cornbread Y'all scared?

All I'n' scared!

Cornbread Y'all scared?

All I'n' scared!

Cornbread Who gone get crunk in our muthafuckin' circle?

Cookie *jumps in.*

Cookie
I'm sick n' tired a' bein' sick n' tired
A' walkin' through the skreets
Fellahs starin' or they glarin'
Some grinnin' past gold teeth
Now, they say they wanna take care of me
'Cause I'ma victim of real bad case of TB

Titties and booty, it's double duty, I'm thirteen
The corner boys never stop talkin' rude and
They either call me a bitch or hoe
Cuz to they toe up ass car, this bitch won't go

Y'all know the type that be in his brother's ride
Like to lean to the back and then lean to the side
Always be bumpin' the latest Triple Six
"Bitch, come over here and suck my dick!"

And dis here be the killin' part 'bout it
Y'all just playin' hopscotch on the Hurt Village lot and
This niggah come and fuck up ya concentration
You ignore his fellatio verbal penetration

But then he try to get out the car
"Niggah, do you really wanna catch a rape charge?"
"Fuck you then, you siddity ass bitch."
Got the nerve to get mad
'Cause he the one done flipt the script

I don't care about the scrilla
Runnin' 'roun' in yo' pockets
Or that ya got a dingaling
That's as long as a rocket
Yo' wee-wee won't take me there
And yes, niggah this is my rullll hair

So there, keep runnin' yo' fake-ass game
Fo' I say somethin' that'll make you feel real shame
Whut! Whut! WHUT! WHUT! WHUT! WHUT!

All
    We gone keep it real crunk
    Keep it, keep it real loud
    Bump all you bitches
    Bump, bump all these fake hoes
    We know how to keep it real crunk
    Keep it real loud
    Fuck all you niggahs who don't what we talkin' 'bout!

Buggy   That's my girl !

Crank   That's *my* girl!

Ebony   That shit don't count. Lil' bitches can't step up up
in the ring! I couldn't half understand what she was sayin'!

Toyia   Niggah, 'cause you ain't gotcho GED.

Cookie   I used a dictionary *and* a thesaurus on yo' ass.

All   Check!

Ebony   That ain't fair!

Cornbread   Don't matter, niggah. Can't help it ye'en know what she was sayin'!

Skillet   I could understand it shorley. You got punked by a little girl, muthafucka!

Ebony *rises to confront* **Skillet**.

Skillet   What niggah! You ready to die today?

Ebony *puts a finger in his face.*

Ebony   Ain't nobody gone do nathan but penetration to yo' ass.

Skillet   That's you son. I don't bend over and let nobody up in my booty, but I hear yo' daddy punked you for five years skraight before bein' shipped out to the state pen. Sold his own son booty for a couple of crack vials. That's penetration for *yo'* ass.

If looks could kill from **Ebony***,* **Skillet** *would be buried twenty-five feet underground. This is the best check of the day.*

Silence for a long-ass time.

Toyia   Check!

Crank   Hell, that's five checks!

Cornbread   And he's the winner!

He raises **Skillet***'s damaged hands above his head. Everyone celebrates.* **Ebony** *seethes.*

Ebony   You know what we do to lil' doughboys like you?

Skillet   Niggah, don't nobody care you second in line to the doughboy crown round here. I might spit slow, but ain't no hoe up in me, maine.

It's kiss or kill.

*A slow drone wafts from an approaching car: Elvis Presley's "In the Ghetto." Everyone freezes. While **Ebony** seems to grow taller, the others shrink. **Crank** takes **Cookie** by the hand and goes inside. **Toyia** tiptoes back into her unit. **Cornbread** looks down to the ground. **Skillet** continues to stare into **Ebony**'s eyes. **Ebony** smiles.*

Ebony   Niggah, keep on yappin'. (*To* **Buggy**.) You know I'm workin' for Tony C, now.

Buggy *stares at* **Tony C** *approaching.*

Buggy   He still 'round?

Ebony   Yezzir. That's a real OG for ya.

Tony C, *a forty-year-old original gangster, steps out of his Escalade all pimped out in the freshest doughboy gear. Doo-rag, ace-bandages round his wrist. Bling. Wifebeater, long shorts. **Tony C** gives **Ebony** the customary hug/dap.*

Tony C   Whassup mofo?

Ebony   Ain't nothin' much going on.

Tony C   Sorry to interrupt y'all . . . party – Who dis swole-ass muthafucka?

Ebony   Awww, this Buggy. You 'member him, don't it?

Tony C   If I knew him, I wouldn' be axin'.

Buggy   I'm Big Mama grandboy.

Tony C   Yeah . . . I 'member you. Tiffany lil' boy. Question is, you 'member me?

Buggy (*spitting on the ground*)   Yeah.

Tony C (*to* **Ebony**)   Glove compartment, maine.

Ebony *walks off, smirking.*

Buggy   So you the crown 'round here?

Tony C   Skillet, this niggah axin' me a question?

Skillet *stays silent.*

Tony C   Cornbread!

Cornbread *jumps.*

Tony C   I see that house you runnin' out in South Memphis comin' 'long.

Cornbread   It's good. It's good.

Tony C   Long as you ain't got none up in this here complex –

Cornbread   Tony C, you ain't gotsta worry 'bout me. You do North Memphis, I do South . . . It all breezy-breezy on my end.

Tony C   Well, my boys gone need to post up on this here porch for the week. Folks gone want they goin' 'way presents. Ya feel me?

Buggy   Ain't no need to bring this round my porch.

Tony C   Niggah, how this yo' porch?

Buggy   I'm livin' here now.

Tony C   Yeah, well, niggah, you might live here, but you don't own this porch.

Beat.

Hate to hear what happened to yo' mama. Got to wonder why folk kill they self. That's usually somethin' most niggahs don't do.

Buggy   They usually kill each other.

Beat.

Tony C (*smiling*)   I see you done learnt somethin' in yo' lil' life. (*Shaking his head.*) How a hero gone come home to some shit like this? That's how it be for a niggah, though.

Ebony *comes back and hands* **Tony C** *a package.*

Tony C   Look, you a big-ass niggah. I'm lookin' for some new soljas. You need some work?

Buggy   Work?

Tony C   I ain't stutter na'an one time now, did I, niggah? Could use somebody like you witcho skill set. You'd be a good muscle man. I bet you done kilt folks.

Buggy   A couple.

Tony C   Me, too.

Skillet   Me, three.

Tony C   Niggah, you ain't done shit! Shut yo' punk-ass, sissy-ass, skirt-wearin' ass up, you slow-ass muthafucka. (*To* **Ebony**.) He gone get my blood pressure up.

Ebony   I know, maine. He done already got mine up.

Tony C *tries to hand* **Buggy** *a package.*

Tony C   Take it.

Buggy   What I'ma do wit' that?

Tony C   Take it. A lil' present. From a hustler to a hero.

Buggy *doesn't.*

Tony C   Niggahs comin' back from overseas usually need to get they sniff on, smoke on. Hell, these 'Nam vets my bestus customers.

Ebony   See this shit right here, this shit right here. *This* shit righ' *here*'ll take you to another muthafuckin' level, maine. Ask Funky Ricky.

Tony C   That 'Nam niggah been comin' to me for over twenty years now.

Buggy   I don't need it.

Beat.

Cornbread   Hell, I'll take it.

Tony C   You bet' not touch that shit, you fat-ass high-yellah honkey monkey.

Silence.

I don't need it neither, but what I am needin' is a new recruit. (*To* **Ebony**.) You thank we could trust him?

Ebony   Tony C, he seem like a good recruit, you know what I'm sayin'? Bet he speak Iraqi and shit. Help us wit' our code –

Tony C   Niggah, what the fuck is you talkin' 'bout ?

Ebony   I don't know maine. I'll be quiet.

Tony C   Yeah, niggah, why don't you do that?

Buggy   I'll think about it.

Tony C   You know I run all North Memphis. I run the Hurt, Lamar Terrace, Dixie Homes, Smoky City, Scutterfield. This shit prime muthafuckin' real estate.

Buggy   Seem like these developers thank it's prime muthafuckin' real estate, too.

Tony C   Naw, naw, soljah boy. All this shit mine. And don't let nobody tell you no different. (*Beat.*) I'ma be needin' somebody like you. Disciplined and shit. (*Indicating* **Ebony**.) Not like these other knuckleheads. Think on it.

He snaps at **Ebony**, *who jumps to attention. Blows a kiss to* **Toyia**, *who has come out of the unit. She nervously smiles at him. The Elvis drone dissipates as they get into their car and drive off.*

Toyia   I hate that song.

The television is on and music videos are playing. **Toyia** *begins to dance and snap her fingers to the beat.*

Scene Three

FLEAS IN A JAR

Next day. Inside **Big Mama**'s *unit.* **Toyia** *is standing at the screen door. She ain't playin'.*

Toyia   Tilapia! I know you ain't sittin' on my brand new muthafuckin' Camero. I can't tell! Well, pop yo' ass right back off it then. These project kids don't know who they messin' wit'. Can't wait to move up out this muthafucka.

She begins to dance and snap her fingers to the beat.

Oooooo! I hate this song!

Crank You hate every song BET play.

Toyia 'Cause I'ma muthafuckin' feminist.

She makes her booty clap on the beat.

"Caught in the Closet" was good though. But I got that shit free from the Bootleg man, don't play. You won't catch me buyin' not a na'an 'nother Pied Piper CD. I ain't got time to be puttin' no scrilla in no pedophile's pockets. I'm a muthafuckin' feminist! Is that niggah ever gone go on trial?

Crank They say they waitin' till the girl get old enough. But wifey say she standin' by him, though.

Toyia Awww, hell to the naw, naw, naw! That bitch just don't wanna give up her allowance. Hell, can't say I would either, but that niggah need to be put on punishment, or somethin'. She can't let him get away with that shit. She need to put him on "pussy punishment."

Crank She did. That probably why he goin' around pissin' on fourteen-year-old girls.

Toyia True that!

Crank I heard despite it all, she 'bout to have a Pied Piper, Jr.

Toyia Unh, unh! Wouldn't be me. Shit, "pussy punishment" the next birth control. Cornbread ain't 'bout to burn my shake-junt body out. Awww, hell to the the naw, naw, naw. But the folks up at the hospital really know about pussy punishment. Folks up there had the nerve to try to tie my tubes after I had LaQwana. Nurse come over to the bed before they give me my epidural talkin' 'bout, "The doctor recommends that a woman with your history try a surgical approach to birth control." She might as well said, "Nigger-bitch, we don't want y'all to be havin no mo' of y'all nigger children so we shuttin' down the reproductive power of yo' pussy!"

Crank Why you ain't call her out?

Toyia I did . . . I said, "Bitch, if you don't get them muthafuckin' papers out my muthafuckin' face I'ma stick a gun up in yo' muthafuckin' chest, and you won't be needin' no doctor after I'm finished witchu. You gone need a coroner." Hell, I raised the terror alert to red up in that bitch!

They give each other high-fives.

But she right though. I ain't got time for na'an one mo' child. And that why Cornbread on "pussy punishment." Put some red up in my head.

Crank Ghetto-ass.

Toyia Naw, bitch. I'm just expressive.

Crank Red weave does not look good witcho' complexion. 'Sides it's too expensive for yo' ass.

Toyia Hell, bitch, you be jankin' it half the time. Witcho' thievin' ass.

Crank Hustlin'-ass. Get it right! Did Cornbread give you my money for doing yo' head these past two weeks?

Toyia *goes into her pocket and hands it to her.*

Toyia (*sucking teeth*) You should be doin' my head for free –

Crank Bitch, please! (*She puts it in her bra.*) And Cornbread betta have my other money the next time he come up in here.

Toyia For what? She ain't his.

Crank He treat her like she is.

Toyia Bitch, so! Her real daddy here now, so you need go on down to that court, file them papers and get that back child support. He gone be gettin' a military check, too! Girl, don't play. You betta gone getcho own ATM – always *they* money.

Crank   I done done good so far without him.

Toyia   Well, get off Cornbread's dick, Miss Sojourner Truth. He already got enough to take care of – mine and then that other bitch baby out in South Memphis. You should be shamed of yoself.

Crank   You just a jealous bitch.

Toyia   Heifer.

Crank   Hoe.

Toyia   Skeezer.

Crank   Cunt!

Toyia   Oooo, I likes that one.

Crank   That's what them British folks say. I be watchin' reruns of *Are You Being Served?*

Toyia   Sippin' on sysyzurp?

Crank   Naw, bitch, *Are You Being Served?*

Toyia   What that is?

Crank   A British TV show. I'm real culture-like.

Toyia   How you be knowin' what them British folk be sayin'?

Crank   Bitch, I'm just jankin' Cornbread satellite.

Toyia (*under her breath*)   That ain't all you jankin'.

Beat.

Crank   Unlike you, I don't need nobody money. I gets mine own.

Toyia   Ain't nobody done no bit of good on they own.

Crank   How come I ain't? Ain't had to rely on not a na'an one niggah to get through. Been doin' shit on my lonesome for more than a minute. Even got clean . . . on my lonesome.

Been clean three years now, feel me? I done done good without any man. And I can do good without Buggy –

Toyia   Can I have him then?

Crank   NO!

Toyia   Hell, you don't want 'em, let somebody else get in where they fit in. 'Sides, I be lettin' you have a taste of my Cornbread. (*Beat.*) You thank I ain't know, huh?

Crank   Well, you be actin' like you don't want him.

Toyia   I don't, but I want that money. He only stay around me 'cause he afraid of this back child support I'll put on his ass – which is what *you* need to be doin'.

Crank   The baby daddy should be around for somethin' more than money, honey.

Toyia   Maybe. Maybe not. Hell, sometimes I wonder if I hadda had my daddy, how I mighta turnt out. Shit, even if he had laid up in a corner drunk, cracked-out, watchin' TV, at least he woulda been there, ya know . . . ya know what I'm sayin'? (*Pause.*) You know I saw him up on Auction the other day.

Crank   What Funky Ricky doin'?

Toyia   Same-ole, same-ole. Police had him hemmed up on a loiterin' charge. Like he different from any other niggah standin' around on the corner all day. They 'bout to cart him off. I went up to them and say, "My daddy was waitin' on me to bring him the Pamper money. Wun't no loiterin'. Just waitin' up on Auction." They took one look at me, let him go. Like they expected me to have a cracked-out daddy like that. I couldn' believe that shit came out my mouth. He ain't never said "that my daughter." Niggah, ain't even recognize me. Hmph . . . That lil' girl daddy here. Let her have that. Be grateful. Ain't shit wrong wit' 'em. He ain't no Funky Ricky. He seem a lil' white boy actin' sometime, but he always been that way. He ain't a total bastard.

Crank   He ain't come back for me. Fuck that niggah.

Toyia   At least he done come back.

Crank   She look just like 'em.

Toyia   Spittin' muthafuckin' image. Got his teeth. His attitude, his . . .

Crank *is visibly agitated. She starts throwing her cosmetology tools into their plastic containers.* **Toyia** *notices.*

Toyia   Look, bitch, like I say, put that niggah on child support, get them military benefits, 'cause I'm tired of you takin' my money. And you can get you a lil' dick on the side, too, then maybe you'll stop bein' so fuckin' cranky.

Cookie *enters through the screen door carrying a mason jar. She goes straight to the back room to put up her backpack.*

Crank   What, you gone come up in this house and not speak?

Cookie (*from offstage*)   Hey.

Toyia   Chillun just ain't got no kinds of manners nowadays, but I wouldn't say hey to yo' ass neither if you was my momma.

Crank *pulls her hair tight with a comb.*

Toyia   Ouch!

Cookie *comes back in.*

Cookie   They gave us a science project for the first week. I don't know how to do it.

Toyia   Don't look at me. I'm a puredee fool.

Crank   You'll figure it out, Cookie.

Cookie   I need some money for da posta board.

Toyia   You betta take one of them boxes, cut it up, and let that be the end of it, shee-it.

Cookie   But folk gone be comin' to school wit' dat nice posterboard.

Crank   'Cause they come from folk who can waste money on buyin' stupid shit like that. Like Toyia say, cut up one of them boxes and call it a day. What this is anyway?

Cookie   Fleas in a jar.

Crank   What in a jar?!?!

Cookie   It's fleas in a jar!

Toyia   I know you ain't brought no fleas up in here. Y'all already got roaches. Them niggahs gone breed and become fle-oches.

Cookie   That ain't gone happen.

Toyia   Watch!

Crank   What the hell this for?

Cookie   Science class. I gotta test my hypothesis.

Toyia   Hypothewhat? Is that the new project baby name? I need to write that down.

Cookie   Hypothesis! You gotta have an educated guess about yo' project. It mean, like, you guess how it gone turn out.

Toyia   Okay, whatcho hiphopcracy?

Cookie (*rolling her eyes*)   Right now, the fleas keep on jumpin' up and they keep hittin' they head, right? Look.

They crowd around the mason jar.

Toyia   Sho' nuff is.

Cookie   Afterwhile, they gone realize that if they jump so high, they gone ram they head into the lid.

Crank   Unh, hunh . . .

Cookie   So, it's nine fleas up in there now. Well, after 'bout a week the fleas stop jumpin' so high 'cause they know they gone bump they head. That's when you take off the lid. The fleas could jump out but because they done got tired of hurtin' theyself they won't jump no higher than the lid. Ain't nothin' holdin' them in, but they thank so. I bet if I leave the lid off, it'll still be nine fleas in there at the end of the week 'cause they ain't gone jump high enough to get out.

Crank   Sound like some shit to me.

Beat.

Cookie   I'm just testin' it out.

Crank   And yo' lil' smart tail testin' me. Gone to yo' room and do yo' homework.

Cookie   But I need help wit' it. They want me to write a report –

Crank   Git!

Just then, **Buggy** *and* **Cornbread** *enter the unit.*

Cornbread   What, you actin' up again?

Crank   She back talkin' as usual.

Cookie   No, I ain't.

Cornbread   Ay, girl, don't be back talkin' yo' mama.

Cookie   Shut up! You ain't my daddy! Unfortunately, he is. I hate all y'all!

She stands in the doorway of the back room, sulking.

Crank   Talkin' 'bout she need some help. She need to learn how not to axe nobody for no help. She need to learn how to depend on herself.

Buggy   If the girl need help, help her.

Crank   Why don't you help her then, Mr. Smartypants-I-done-went-to-the-military-and-I-know-everythang-God-know and then some?

Buggy   Awww, I forgot you wun't too good on homework back in the day.

Crank   I could help her if, if I wanted to.

Buggy   You don't even know how to help yoself. Cookie, I'll help you wit' it.

Cookie   Really?

Buggy   Yeah. We can do it later on.

Crank *stares the smiling* **Cookie** *down, who shrinks beneath her mother's gaze.* **Big Mama** *enters from the back room, rushing around. She is putting on her custodian outfit.*

Big Mama   This night shift is gone run me damn near crazy.

Crank   You is late as a mug.

Big Mama   Who you tellin'? (*Mumbling to herself.*) I can't never find shit 'round here. I'm supposeta be down there now. It's a Friday night. Gone be a lot of niggah blood to mop up. What, the boys ain't gone go on down to Beale Street? I hear somethin' goin' on down at the Pyramid.

Toyia   Cornbread on punishment.

Cornbread   Bitch, you don't run me.

Toyia   Niggah, you betta watch how you speak to me. See, just for that, I'm adding three more days to the pussy strike!

Big Mama   Can't find my ortho' shoes . . .

Buggy   Let me help ya.

Big Mama   Crank, you pack up my shoes?

Crank   Naw, I don't know where they at.

Big Mama   Oh Lord, I need to get out of here. Y'all heifers always holdin' me up!

Buggy   I'll help you find it, Big Mama.

Big Mama   Prolly in these boxes right here. Help me go through this goddamn thang.

They go over to a box. **Buggy** *lifts it and, as he does so, the bottom falls out.*

Big Mama   Goddamn it! Crank, clean this shit up!

Out has tumbled a red pair of platform heels and other various hooker clothes.

Cookie   Ohhh, weee, these so pretty . . .

She goes to pick up the red shoes. **Big Mama** *slaps her on the behind, and turns her around.*

Big Mama   Don't you ever put yo' feet up in a dead woman's shoes. You hear me? You liable to walk out yo' life the same way she did.

Beat.

Buggy   These was my momma's favorite shoes.

Big Mama   Well, you ain't got no favorites when you gone.

Beat.

Toyia   Here they go, Big Mama.

Toyia *hands* **Big Mama***'s shoes from under the couch.*

Big Mama   Where was you hidin' these? In yo' cooch?

Toyia   Big Mama, if you don't get yo' butt on to work . . .

Big Mama   How come I'm the only one goin' to work?

They all look their separate ways. Silence.

Y'all a cryin' shame.

Scene Four

Night time. Sweat. The crunk-drone bass from passing cars leaks into the unit from outside. **Cookie** *is tiptoeing in the darkness trying not to wake up* **Buggy**, *who is tossing and turning, on the couch. Then gunshots pop off, shattering the night.* **Buggy** *wakes up with a start as if he had been submerged under water about to drown. He seems to break through the surface for a gulp of air.*

Buggy   Mama?! Mama?!

Cookie   Nah, dawg. It yo' lil' mama.

Buggy   What the hell you doin' up?

Cookie   Shhh! Fo' you wake e'erbody up. I done peed in the bed. Need to change them sheets.

Buggy   Too much information.

Cookie   Well, you axed!

Pop. Pow. Pow. Gunshots echo.

Buggy   Do these niggahs ever go to sleep?

Cookie   They don't like to dream.

Buggy   Naw, they don't like to have nightmares.

Cookie   You sweatin' hard.

Buggy   Goddamn plastic on this couch make a muthafucka feel like he up in a sauna.

Cookie   Air conditioner prolly broke right before you went to sleep. Everythang always be breakin' 'round here.

She pours him some water out of the refrigerator.

Buggy   On the real though. Pass me my duffel.

She does. **Buggy** *digs into his bag and pulls out a bottle of pills. His hands are shaking uncontrollably. He's having trouble opening it.* **Cookie** *takes it from him and easily twists off the top.*

Buggy (*laughing it off*)   These things supposed to be childproof.

Cookie   I ain't no chile.

Buggy   Not no more.

He seems to see himself in her for first time. He gulps down the rest of the water. She picks up his medicine bottles.

Cookie   Nopramin . . . Paxil . . .

Buggy   You can read?

Cookie   Hell yeah, I can read!

Buggy   Well, keep on. Stay in school. Go to college.

Cookie   How 'bout I go into the military witchu?

Buggy   No need.

Cookie   I can get a scholarship, can't it?

Buggy   You watch too much TV.

Cookie   Naw, that what them recruits up at the mall be sayin'.

Buggy   At the mall? Hmmph.

Cookie   She hit me when I pee in the bed.

Buggy   You can't control that shit.

Cookie   Yeah, but I can't buy no new mattress either.

Buggy   What you wanna be when you grow up?

Cookie   What this bullshit is? Catch-up time?

Beat.

A rapper.

Buggy   Why don't you become a doctor?

Cookie   E'er niggah ain't gotsta be a Huxtable. Rappin' gone be my side-hustle. 'Sides, I really wanna be a flight attendant.

Buggy *laughs at her.*

Cookie   You sittin' over there laughin', but when I'm flyin'
in the friendly skies e'erbody gone be axin' me for a ticket.
I heard you could go anywhere you wanna. I'd go, maine . . .
I'dn know where I'd go, but I'd fly far away . . .

Beat.

I take pills, too. Birth control.

Buggy   You don't need to be fuckin' already.

Cookie   You wanna come up in here and be my daddy
now, huh? I don't see it though. I don't look nothin' like you.

Buggy   You might not be mine for all I know.

Cookie   You'd like that now, wouldn't you?

Buggy   You just like yo' mama.

Cookie   Yeah, that's what they say. What was you
dreamin' 'bout?

Beat.

Buggy   That I was driving in my humvee over there.
Regular mornin'. I'm rollin' through a quiet hood. Look just
like ours but real peaceful like. Smilin'. I'm bumpin' a lil'
Kanye West –

Cookie   Kanye West for faggots –

Buggy   Okay, Jay-Z –

Cookie   Mmmm.

Buggy   Wu-Tang?

Cookie *(high-pitched)*   MMMM.

Buggy   Eight-Ball & MJG? Three Six Mafia?

Cookie   *Thass* betta –

Buggy   On the speaker. All of a sudden this fireball come
up from between my legs. Roadside bomb. Next thing I
know, I'm lookin' down at my body. Well, half of it. My top

half blew out the humvee and hit the road. All my guts just spilled out into the dirt below my belly button. Eyes rolled up into the back of my head. All you could see was the white of my eyes, like I never had no color in them.

Cookie   Sound like muthafuckin' *Platoon* or some shit.

Buggy   Yo' mama let you watch that?

Cookie   Naw. Peaches 'nem be stealin' cable, too. See it over there.

Beat.

What was his name?

Buggy   Lt. Michael Bond.

Cookie   Y'all was close?

He nods his head.

Be grateful that shit ain't happen to you. Do they make it go away?

She points to the pills.

Buggy   Naw . . . Some things you just can't get over.

Cookie *takes a pill and pops it into her mouth. She chews it like candy.*

Cookie   I have.

Scene Five

AMERICA AIN'T SHIT

The unit. Next day. **Cookie** *is playing with her dolls' house in the corner. She is acting out a play with her dolls.*

Cookie (*male voice*)   "Oh, Princess Tequila Alizé Jenkins, will you throw down your hair so I can climb up and take you away?" (*Female voice.*) "Honey, this weave glued in, not sewed. You liable to pull out a patch of my hair you climb up like that! How 'bout I get you a rope?" (*Male voice.*) "Bitch, you betta just send down that weave. I ain't got time – "

Crank (*offstage*)   COOKIE!!

Cookie   What!

Crank (*offstage*)   Why it smell like piss in this back room?

Cookie   I don't know what you talkin' 'bout . . .

Crank *comes into the room.*

Crank   You do know what I'm talkin' 'bout .

Cookie   It might be Big Mama. You know how old folk be peein' in the bed –

Crank   Don't you lie to me, nah!

Cookie   I ain't tellin' no story.

Crank   She ain't that old to be peein' in the bed.

Cookie   I read it in a book. Folks wit' diabetes pee a lot. 'Specially in the mornin'.

Beat.

Crank   For real? You ain't lyin'?

Cookie   Swear fo' God . . .

Crank   I guess we gone need to get that bitch some Depends, then.

Cookie *starts giggling.* **Crank** *starts laughing, too. Beat.*

Crank   You finish yo' homework?

Cookie   Yeah.

Crank   You want me to check it?

Cookie   Uh. No.

Crank   How come?

Cookie   'Cause . . . you know . . . we doin' seventh-grade stuff.

Crank   Like what?

Cookie   English stuff . . . you know?

Crank   Well, I can speak English.

Cookie   It just grammar questions . . . I can check over it myself.

Crank   Just let me see it.

A hesitant **Cookie** *goes into her backpack. She gives it to her.* **Crank** *looks at it, blankly.*

Crank   That good.

Cookie   It's all correct?

Crank   Mmmhmm. From what I see.

Crank *hands it back to her.* **Cookie** *inspects it.*

Cookie   Ma, the first one wrong.

Crank   No it ain't. I looked at it.

Cookie   But it's wrong. I put down that it was a adjective and it a adverb.

Crank   What, you think I'm lyin'? That's right.

Cookie   No, it ain't. It ain't!

Crank *smacks* **Cookie** *in the back of her head.*

Cookie   I'ma tell Big Mama!

Crank   Tell her! I'm 'bout tireda you callin' me a lie!

Cookie   But you is. You can't read.

Crank   What, you thank I'm stupid? I ain't stupid. I'm like Maya Angelou up in this bitch, I'ma muthafuckin' genius. You get it from ya mama!

Cookie   I shoulda got Daddy to check my homework!

Beat.

Crank   "Daddy"? Since when he become "Daddy" allasudden.

She grabs her by the collar.

Listen, you lil' bitch, I'm yo' mammy, yo' daddy, yo' God, yo' everything. You bet not call him daddy again. If you do, I'ma get that electric cord . . . Believe that playa.

Big Mama *bursts through the door and surveys the room.*

Big Mama   Why y'all ain't finished packin'? I told y'all lil' bitches we need to be packed up by the end of the week. How come nobody listen to me? I just don't understand it! Nobody listen to me.

Crank *lets go of* **Cookie**.

Cookie   We gone pack it all up, I promise, it'll all be done, damn . . .

Crank   I just finished packin' all my boxes today. They say them men gone be here come tomorrow to give us some mo' boxes –

Big Mama *goes on a tirade around the apartment.*

Big Mama   Cookie, take that damn dollhouse in the back fo' I burn it. This food ain't packed up yet? Y'all just ain't gone listen to me, huh? Gotta tell y'all somethin' nine or ten times 'fo ya listen. WHY NOBODY EVER LISTEN?!

She throws a bottle against the wall. It shatters. Silence.

We ain't goin' nowhere.

Silence. She means it.

Them cracker-ass muthafuckas. If it ain't one thang it's another. I done worked hard all my life and this what they give me. Been to hell and back on wheels of fire and a seat of stone and what I got to show for it? Four raggedy-ass boxes and a toe-up-to-the-flo-up ass J.C. Penney catalogue full of check marks next to shit I ain't gone never be able to afford.

Cookie   Big Mama, whass wrong?

Big Mama   They actin' like they ain't gone put us up. Sayin' I'm makin' too much for the Section 8 housin' out in

Raleigh. Wit' my lil' rinky-dink job over there at the VA?
Say our application done got "denied." Now we ain't got
nowhere to move come next Friday – and WHY MY
MUTHAFUCKIN' 'FRIGERATOR DON'T WORK!

She kicks it, stubs her toe.

Lawd, when it rain it pour. I make $387 over. $387 put me
o'er the limit and they say it gone take two months for a
appeal! $387 dollars? Well . . . I ain't goin' nowhere. I'ma
chain myself to this bitch 'cause they can't tear it down wit'
me in it. Tell anybody who axe. Instead a' crackin' down on
welfare they need to crack down on how many of them
knuckleheads out there killin' folks. How lil' girls go outside to
play and get snatched up by some rapist. They don't care
about that. White folk always care about the wrong damn
thang.

Crank   What 'bout yo' sister in the 'burbs? Don't she got a
house out in Davies Plantation?

Big Mama   Niggahs done fought to get off the plantation,
and here this bitch done fought tooth and nail to get back
on it. Fuck her. She the most selfish bitch I done ever knownt.

Cookie   Big Mama, am I still gone be able to go to that
school?

Big Mama   Cookie, ain't nobody worried 'bout that right
nah! First we gotsta make sho' a roof gone be over our heads
come next week. We gone have to scrape up some money or
us 'n our boxes gone be out on the skreet. Livin' paycheck to
paycheck and this shit up 'n happen. I'ma have to go on
down to the welfare office. I can't stand goin' down to that
office.

Buggy *enters, a bit jittery.*

Big Mama   Where you been?

Buggy   Off.

Big Mama   I sees that much . . .

Crank   These white folk tryin' to do something horrible. We ain't got nowhere to move. Say we makin' too much money to live on Section 8.

She tries to read the letter.

"You have ex-cee-ded the a – "

Cookie *takes the paper out of her hand.*

Cookie   " – llotment for the head of household."

Big Mama   Well, at least my Buggy done come home. We can go live with him. Military take care of housin', ain't that the truth of it? We can just live off the military check he gone get.

Buggy   Uhhm . . .

Crank   You done come in the nick of time.

Big Mama   I know that's right. Now, we ain't gone have to scramble, but if you calls yo' lieutenant or the military or whoever we can be moved in somewhere by next Friday.

Buggy   That ain't the way it work.

Big Mama   How come it don't?

Crank   Well, how it work? We'll do what we gotta do to make it work.

Buggy   What y'all need to do, you ain't gone never do.

Crank   I'll do it with the quickness.

Buggy   The guvment ain't gotsta give you nothin'.

Big Mama   I can't tell!

Buggy   The city ain't gone have y'all livin' out on the streets. There are shelters.

Big Mama   I ain't gone live in no muthafuckin' shelta.

Buggy   Look at where you stayin' at, Big Mama. Look at this muthafuckin' hole! Hell, a shelta is a lot betta than this.

Big Mama   Them folk don't care nothin' 'bout us. They want us dead.

Buggy   Hell, "they" ain't got to care 'bout you, and who the fuck is "they"? "They." "They." Where "they" hiding at? I ain't never seen't no "they." "They" is you and you and you. "They" is them niggahs runnin' round outside sittin' around and ain't got shit else to do. That's who "they" is!

Big Mama   Oh, you just done went to wherever and got all siddity on a niggah, ain't ya?

Buggy   Naw, Big Mama. I'm just callin' it how I see it. It ain't no "they." You right. "They" don't care about us. "They" ain't got to care. And I ain't none of "they." I do care. If I had it, I would give it, but I can't and not 'cause I won't but cuz I don't got. I don't got, Big Mama.

Crank   Don't they give y'all a monthly check or is that the navy?

Big Mama   I tolja ya shoulda went into da navy.

Crank   Yeah, I think it's the navy that give you a check.

Buggy   That ain't the way it work!!

Big Mama   But folks down at the VA say –

Buggy   FUCK THEM MUTHAFUCKAS AT THE VA. I just been down there and they can't help me!

Big Mama   What you mean, they can't help –

Buggy   Folks like me can't be helped –

Crank   Then what we supposedta do?

Buggy *begins to tremble uncontrollably.*

Crank   You need to be the man of the house. You got a daughter that need to be took care of. Big Mama need to be took care of and I need to be took care of.

Buggy   I need my medicine. I need. I need my med –

Crank   What the hell's wrong witchu!

Big Mama   Buggy . . .

Buggy   I needs my medication. I need it . . . I need my pills –

Cookie *drops her dolls' house at the sight of it all. It makes a huge crashing noise.* **Buggy** *dives behind the boxes like a scared little boy. He is breathing hard and deeply from the bottom of his belly.*

Buggy   We been hit. Skywalker 16 been hit. Attack grid coordinate MB 4-3-0-6-8-niner-7-niner. DANGER CLOSE. Fire comin' over the sand dune west. We hit. Hit, hit, hit, hit . . . hit . . . hit . . . hit . . . hi . . . hii . . . hii . . . hi . . . h . . . h . . . h . . .

Silence. **Cookie** *walks over to her father. She reaches out to comfort, but her small hands startle him. For a second he doesn't know who she is. Once he realizes, he breaks down into tears, slouching against the boxes.*

Big Mama   Don't no military check in the mail come for folk like him. I done seen this down at the VA. Call it "other than honorable discharge." Call it "niggah crazy." I'm old enough to know betta. America ain't shit.

Act Two

Scene One

TONY C'S EMANCIPATION PROCLAMATION

Outside the units. "The Hurt Village is falling down" refrain is heard lightly in the background. In front of the wall spray-painted "Das Haus des Jammers," **Skillet** *and* **Ebony** *are smoking on a huge blunt.*

Ebony I don't even know what that shit say.

Skillet Niggah, 'cause you can't read.

Ebony Niggah, I passed the fifth grade three times. Bet. "Those hoes bes jammin!" See there.

Skillet That ain't it.

Ebony Alright then, niggah. You decode the ghetto hieroglyphics.

Skillet Can't. 'Cause I'm high as a MUFUCKA, maine!

Ebony Niggah, how come you ain't tell me you had more weed?

Skillet You know how weed make you forget; I forgot. Speakina" which, I forgot to tell you. This niggah down by the Pyramid gone axe me, which one I rather have. Pussy or weed? I say, "Niggah? Now what kind of question is that?" I'm the type a' niggah, can't live without neither, but I much rather have some weed than some pussy.

Ebony Niggah, you gay-ass-faggot-ass-bitch-ass niggah –

Skillet Naw, niggah . . . hear me out. Pussy and weed . . . got some similarities. Pussy and weed taste good . . . when they wet.

Ebony What bitch done let yo' ugly ass eat her out?

Skillet Yo' mammy, niggah – now listen! – they both . . . got a distinct smell. They both can have . . . you happy and

give you the munchies till six o'clock in the morning. They
both can burn ya if you get too close to the tip. They both
can turn yo' lips black, you suck on it too much. See, I likes
'em both, but . . . pussy leave you. Weed don't care nothin'
'bout yo' job, yo' credit or yo' car. Weed'll chill witcha . . .
anywhere and nowhere. Make everything real . . . slow . . .
motion like. Pussy speed shit up: the decreasement of the gas
in yo' tank, yo' bank account, and yo' . . . beloved weed.

Ebony   I like 'em when they both together. Now, I done
seen a pussy smoke some weed.

Skillet   Run tell that!

Ebony   This girl down at Pure Passion put a blunt up in her
chocha and smoked it. Swear fo' God!

Skillet   Hell muthafuckin' yeah! That's my next 'speriment.
I can make pussy-smellin' weed!

Ebony   Hell, don't nobody wanna come back home
smellin' like weed and pussy. It either one or the other. Yo'
girl sho' to put ya out on the humble if you come back
smellin' like both. But you wouldn't know nathan 'bout that
no way.

Skillet   Naw, dawg, I'm on a marketing grind: "Pussy
weed." Niggahs'll eat that shit up, you know what I'm sayin'?

Gotta make that money, cuz
I gotta get my own place
Can't stay wit' my cousin no mo
Gotta go. Gotta go
I stay high on the ya-yo –
Jump the boogie
Woulja puff puff pass that pussy to me.

Ebony   To me!

They laugh.

You a stupid-ass niggah.

Skillet   That was brilliant. I'ma have ta record that . . .
Three Six Mafia could use that verse.

Ebony   That shit's whack, niggah! I ain't never heard
nothin' like that in my life. No wonder Tony C don't give you
no work.

Skillet   Bet! Niggahs buy all kinds of pussy on the corner
anyway. Hell, let 'em buy mine.

Cookie *comes out of her unit.*

Big Mama (*offstage*)   Make sure you bring back two beers.
Colt 45. In a can. No bottles. 'Cause I'm liable to break it off
in somebody face. Yo' daddy need one and I need one. Take
yo' ass down to the liquor sto' and bring yo' ass skraight on
back. Gone, nah.

Cookie *walks down the street.*

Ebony   That little bitch look like she gone be finer than her
mama.

Skillet   Maine, she stout as a mug already, maine.

Ebony   She not too light, not too dark neither. Just that
right kinda brown, niggah. That shit right there, *that* shit right
there, that right *there* must be tight.

Skillet   I like her mind.

Ebony *smacks him upside the head.* **Cookie** *glares at them, then
jiggles the change in her pockets as she skips along.*

Skillet *and* **Ebony**   Hey, Cookie!

*There is the sound of Elvis coming from a car in the distance. Beep.
Beep. The car horn goes. The boys scatter and run. Beep. Beep.*

Tony C   Look, silly-ass girl. You see I'm tryin' to talk to
you.

She keeps walking.

Ay, Cookie!

Cookie *stops.*

Tony C   Come over here.

Cookie *stays where she is.* **Tony C**'s *car door slams. He walks up to her.*

Tony C   "It's a beautiful day in the neighborhood, a beautiful day for a neighbor. Won't you be mine? Won't you be mine?"

Cookie   Hell, naw.

Tony C   Whassup lil' playa. You headed to get a pickle from the candylady?

Cookie   Naw, a beer.

Tony C   Damn, that bitch sell beer now.

Cookie   Naw, she done moved out already. I'm goin' to the liquor sto'.

Tony C   Ride wit' me. I'll take you down there.

Silence.

I respect that. I guess we gone be neighbors since y'all movin' out to Raleigh.

Cookie   Ain't nobody movin' out to Raleigh.

Tony C   Why not?

Cookie   Crackers. I bet you got a big-ass house out in Raleigh.

Tony C   Four bedroom, two full bath, a living room –

Cookie   And a dinin' room?

Tony C   A businessman always need a muthafuckin' dinin' room for his guests.

Cookie   You got a extra room?

Silence.

Tony C   Naw, I got my moms, my sis and her four kids, my four wit' me at the crib. Ain't no mo' room at the inn, lil' bit.

Cookie   City say we make too much for help.

Tony C   That good, ain' it?

Cookie   Hell, naw.

Tony C   The city know they stay pullin' that shit. Learn this befo' you learn anythan' else. Crackers ain't gone give you shit. You gots to take it. That's one thang niggahs ain't never learnt, yet. Not stealin', but takin'. Like we got a niggah mayor, right – muthafuckin' Mayor Willie Herenton, right. But it's all fo' show 'cause that niggah don't care nothin' 'bout you or me. He gettin' boocoo bank from the guvment to "revitalize" these here projects. Millions! Movin' niggahs out like Hebrews to make room for who?

Cookie   Crackers!

Tony C   Thass right, niece! City use the guvment money to bulldoze this shit, then these private developers gone swoop in like roaches to rice, gettin' prime muthafuckin' real estate for free. End of the day Lil' Willie, this South Memphis lookin' ass niggah, gettin' paid millions to get paid more on the back end. 'Cause you know they just gone build some condos and Hurt Village niggahs ain't gone be able to 'ford that shit! It's a muthafuckin' conspiracy up in this bitch. He too busy makin' *his* dough, *his* paper. Hell, I shoulda been the mayor! But thass the politickin' of the projects, pure and simple. Getcho shit together, you gotsta always be on yo' job. See these Chink-ass mofos they got liquo stoes and check-cashin' stoes takin' twenty dollars outcho' check to give you yo' money.

Cookie   I know that's right.

Tony C   What kinda sense that make? What we got? Nathan! They make the money and take that shit out to wherever they at. We all gettin' fucked in the ass over here, niece. We all gettin' raped. But you got to get in where you fit in. Hell, I know my place. I sell that white to these niggahs so my lil' boy won't ever have to play on a playground got mo' crack vials than blades of grass. I'll be damned that happen.

I'll be damned. So . . . if I gotsta kill a couple niggahs who was on they way out anyway, so be it. It's for the greater good.

Beat.

Fuck Section 8. They was gone put y'all on the bad side of Raleigh anyway. Can you add?

Cookie   Yeah.

Tony C   Subtract?

Cookie   Betta.

Tony C   Lil' niggahs always betta at losin' than gainin'. You wanna be my lil' friend?

Cookie   If you stop playin' Elvis . . .

Tony C   Y'all lil' niggahs don't know nathan 'bout good music. Elvis grew up around the Hurt. (*Off her reaction of surprise.*) Ye'en know? These projects was built for white folks. Wun't no niggahs stayin' 'round here in the fifties. Just kykes, pollacks, wops, I don't know the bad name you use for Germans – ginks. Whatever. I bet they don't teach you that at school. Now Elvis, that's the original American idol. Came right from 'round the Hurt. I like his philosophy, too. The only thing a niggah can do for me is shine my shoes and buy my shit, too –

Buggy   Cookie, come on in this house.

Buggy *has come out of the unit onto the porch.* **Cookie** *doesn't move.*

Buggy   Cookie, I ain't gotta say it again, do I?

Cookie *smiles. He means business.*

Cookie   I ain't went to get the beer yet.

Buggy   Well, carry yo' ass on and be back quick fast.

She skips away.

Tony C   She a real sweet girl. You shoulda had named her after yo' mama. "Tiffany," a pretty girl name. You think 'bout what I toldja?

Buggy   Stay 'way from her.

Tony C   Can't. She too precious.

Buggy   I got a gun. I know how to use it.

Tony C   Whoa! Slow yo' roll, solja boy. Me, too, ye'en know?

Buggy   I ain't gone tell you again.

Tony C   Done come back to the cut and wanna shoot up e'rythang in sight. Be grateful you can walk skraight. Gotcho senses about cha. I said, did you think about what I told you?

Buggy   I ain't sellin' shit for you. I ain't gone sell this shit, period.

Tony C   Wha? The buck-ass business man gone? Just a lil' solja boy ra-pa-pummin' in his place. Where the fuck yo' drum?

Buggy   Right here. Who axin'?

Tony C   A maine. A maine that's proud of one of the Hurt's finest soldiers. You coulda been like me.

Buggy   But, I ain't you.

Tony C   You right 'bout that: You ain't. You too "good." You'll never be a kang like me.

Buggy   I don't wanna see you 'round this here porch again.

Beat. **Big Mama** *emerges behind the screen door and she stares at* **Tony C**. *He smiles.*

Tony C   And the boy comes back a man.

Tony C *walks away into the dusk. From the far distance shots echo.* **Big Mama** *comes out on the porch and sits on the rickety, rusty metal chair.*

Big Mama   You got a Kool on you?

Buggy   I thought you only smoked Parliaments?

Big Mama   I ain't got no Parliament money, so give me a muthafuckin' Kool. Ain't no rest for the weary. You aight?

Buggy   As aight as a crazy man can be.

Big Mama   You ain't crazy.

Buggy   I'ma be crazy if I don't get me no more pills. Niggahs down at the VA –

Big Mama   What they say when you went down there?

Buggy   That they can't refill me no more. I'm on my last script . . . Spend ten years goin' everywhere they tell you to go, doin' e'erthang. You make one mistake – *one* mistake and – they just kick you out.

Big Mama   Well, what you do?

Buggy   Nothin' nobody else ain't do.

Big Mama   Naw, but what *you* do?

Silence.

Well . . . that's how they do our boys. They use 'em for what they need, then they throw 'em away when they done. Like a man fuckin' a hoe for free. It's all old hat wit' me.

Buggy   I'm right back where I started. Worser off to boot. Can't get my benefits. Ain't gone be able to get no job. A bad conduct discharge like a damn felony for a niggah they sayin'. And I thought these stars and bars was gone set me free. Hell, maybe I should go work for Tony C.

Big Mama   Naw, naw, Buggy, you bigger than that.

Buggy   I can't have us livin' out on the streets. Y'all right. I got to take care of you, Cookie, then there's Crank –

Big Mama   You was surprised to see her, wun't ya?

Buggy   Yeah, but I was glad. Real glad you took her in..

Big Mama   Only reason I let Crank stay is 'cause she look just like ya mama. Beautiful girl, ain't she? Would be mo' pretty if she just smile a lil' bit mo'. Had a bit happiness in her heart. She did what yo' mama couldn't do. Quit. She woulda been forty years old this week. Tiffany woulda been forty years old . . .

Buggy   It's my fault momma died, Big Mama. I was the one brought that shit into the house that one day. Mama took it and she took it all. I 'member her layin' on the bathroom floor, and I went to get a blanket 'cause I thought she was cold. She wun't cold. She was dead.

Big Mama   Ain't no use in blamin' yo'self. Yo' mammy was a fuckin' crackhead. She was my daughter, but she was a crackhead. Plain and simple. Hell, some time I wonder if I wasn't so hard on her. Maybe she woulda done right eventually. If I hadna hit on her so much. If I hadna yelled at her . . . But coulda, woulda, shoulda give you gray hair and I'm too fine to be havin' some gray hair. Besides, you can't cry over spilt milk.

Buggy   Spilt blood different. (*Beat.*) I might have to sell. Big Mama. One last time.

Big Mama *pulls her letter out.*

Big Mama $387 . . . We niggahs on the cusp. Not too po', not too rich.

Buggy   Maybe this a good thang to not hafta rely on nobody but yo'self. Do for yo'self. All fo' yo'self. We might can do it. If I just sell a lil' bit . . .

Big Mama   I know . . . I know. I'll get you some gloves from the hospital. The Hurt ain't changed a bit.

Scene Two

THE LAST SHIPMENT

Cornbread's *unit on the upper level. Their hands covered with surgical gloves,* **Buggy** *and* **Cornbread** *are in the kitchen cooking crack.* **Buggy** *pours baking soda into a boiling pot.*

Cornbread   Niggah, that's too much!

Buggy   Niggah, that ain't enough!

Cornbread   You gone buy me some mo' bakin' soda you keep on dumpin' it in the pot like it's water!

Buggy   How you gone turn a profit if you don't really cut the shit?

Cornbread   Look, my shit be pure. I got customers been comin' to me for ten years.

He looks at his concoction boiling on the stove.

I'ma make 'bout a hundred cookies on this shit. And some pancakes at that.

Buggy   How much you thank we make?

Cornbread   We?

Buggy   Yeah, niggah, we . . .

Cornbread   At least two thou. Easy. In a week. Especially if . . . we run it together out in North and South Memphis. Hell, maybe sell it in the Hurt.

Buggy   Tony C wouldn't like that . . .

Cornbread   Hell, Toyia pocketbook would. So . . . whatchoo gone do, niggah? You gone run this wit' me or what?

Beat.

Buggy   One last time.

Cornbread   That's what I'm talkin' 'bout, niggah! We run that. Like we used to do. Like we used to *do*! I get these last couple of crates from my distributor dude, then I'll be out.

Buggy   Who you get yo' distribution from nah?

Cornbread   These Vietnamese niggahs live out over in Scutterfield. They shit be on that purdee white.

He takes a lighter and burns it for **Buggy**.

Buggy   Clearer than Tony C shit be.

Cornbread   He get his shit from them Mexicans off Jackson, but them Chinks make the besto crackos!

Buggy   We chop this shit up nice and clear make the money we need to make.

Cornbread   And be out!

Buggy   And don't violate Biggie crack commandment number four –

Buggy *and* **Cornbread**   "Never get high on yo' own supply!"

They laugh.

Cornbread   Only drug go up in me is a lil' bit of purple. And the Indians did that shit so it must be good for ya.

Buggy   That's that quarter Cherokee in you talkin'.

Cornbread   I'm everythang and nothin' at all.

They laugh like old buds.

Buggy   I owe you. You takin' care of Cookie like she yo' own and shit.

Cornbread   Yeah, you do. I ain't mind raisin' her like she was my own. Always feel good to step in yo' shoes. Even for a lil' while.

Beat. He stirs up the crack pot on the stove.

Hell, we make mo' than I thank, I just might stay up in it.
The Hurt might be lookin' at a new Kang afterwhile. Kang
Cornbread, how that sound!

Buggy   I thought this yo' last shipment?

Cornbread   Yeah, yeah, but thank about it? Me 'n you
together? We could quite possibly take over. They might be
tearin' down the Hurt, but it's some mo' muthafuckin' places,
maine. Build us up a empire. We could be partners, partnah!
We can have our house in the 'burbs and come check on our
crackhouses in the projects. That's real breezy-breezy fo' me.
Too bad you goin' back overseas, maine. That'd be the
dream wouldn't it?

Buggy   If I stayed . . . we would need more than me and
you to do the do.

Cornbread   Pull in Skillet. Pull in a lotta these lil' niggahs,
maine. We could push Tony C out of North Memphis! Take
over that Million Dollar Track. Do what we do. You can't
run from who you is, niggah.

Buggy   Sho'll can't. Sho'll can't.

Cornbread   Oooo, 'member when we was just lil' hustlers,
wun't nothin' 'bout fourteen years old? We was walkin' under
the train tracks on Lauderdale Skreet and ran into Tony C.
Auction Skreet hustlers. We was some lil' ass skinny-ass
niggahs then, maine. And one of them muthafuckas threw a
bottle down hit me in the face. Niggah lucky it ain't leave a
scar on my pretty-ass face. I'm cryin', but you ran after them
mofos, yoked 'em up. They ain't come after us no mo'. You
ain't scared of nathan, maine. You was everybody hero after
that, maine. You always get boocoo respect. I bet a hero like
you gets plenty respect over there maine.

Buggy *laughs uncomfortably.*

Buggy   Respect? Cornbread . . . I done did some thangs to
the point where . . . I ain't gone be goin' back over there. You
right. I ain't changed. Seem like the mo' I tried to run away
from who I is the mo' it follow me. Death for a niggah is

everywhere. Whether you in the projects or on the battlefield. Ain't no escapin' what God got for ya' or the devil. So you want me ta tell ya' 'bout the war?

Cornbread   Yeah, niggah. Tell me somethin' good.

Buggy   Every time I done shot somebody I put his face ontopa' theirs. Like mental Photoshop. Click, click. Eight-year-old boy wit' a AK – Tony C face. Sand niggah wit' a spooky eye – Tony C face. Bitch covered head to toe wit' a blue scarf – Tony C. Somehow it made it easier. Make them into the evil you know. I don't know how many folk gone 'cause of me. I lost count. I done seen some thangs, Cornbread, but my mind somehow can rub out those memories like bootprints in the sand. It shift the shapes. But I can't never forget that day, maine. My momma was the baddest bitch on the block.

Cornbread   Sho'll in the hell was, maine . . .

Buggy   Beautiful to the point it look like she didn't belong here.

Cornbread   Belonged in a Jay-Z video. "Big Pimpin' / spendin' cheese!"

Buggy   "Spendin' cheese!" You know what I'm sayin'? She didn't pay nobody no nevermind and that why Tony C wanted her. He was a persistent fuck, but she kept turnin' him down till that one day. He just . . . took her. Broke down the door. I'm standin' there in my pajamas. "Go to school Buggy. Getcho lesson," she said, but I wouldn't leave her. They pushed her into that back room and locked the door. I sat in that den all mornin' and listened to my mama bein' took by a whole gang of niggahs.

Cornbread   Yeah . . . I 'member that, too.

Buggy   At eight years old, I knew the world wun't right. Wun't gone ever be right. They left and Tony C said, "You a good boy." I went into her room, she layin' there, blood on her stomach and cum on her breath. "Close the door, Buggy, let Mama rest." She start hittin' that pipe hard after that.

World wun't right ever since. Nobody ever kill theyself, Cornbread. Till this day, I say Tony C kilt my mama.

Beat.

Cornbread   Let's do what we do then.

Scene Three

CORNBREAD IN THE OVEN

Cornbread's *unit.* **Crank** *is cutting* **Cornbread**'s *hair with clippers.*

Cornbread   I want you to line me up tight.

Crank   Where Toyia at?

Cornbread   Gone.

Crank   I sees that.

Cornbread   That's all you need to know.

Crank   Hmmph.

Cornbread   Can you line my beard up a bit?

Crank *sighs and slides in front of him to line his beard.* **Cornbread** *looks deeps into her eyes.* **Crank** *smiles and continues cutting his hair.*

Cornbread   I love to see your smile.

Crank   Well, sop it up, 'cause it don't come too often.

Cornbread   Seem like you only do it when I'm around.

Crank *smiles even wider, emitting a laugh.* **Cornbread** *puts his ear to her belly. Beat.*

Cornbread   I don't hear nothin'.

Crank   You ain't gone hear nothin' yet.

Cornbread   How long it take?

Crank   Long enough to know that you won't be around.

Cornbread   You act like I'm movin' to China. I'm just movin' to Mississippi. It ain't nothin' but a forty-five-minute drive.

Crank   Cornbread, I don't think it's yours.

Cornbread   Whatchoo mean? Who else you fuckin'?

Crank   Who else *you* fuckin'?

Cornbread   Toyia.

Crank   Exactly.

Cornbread   Awww, come on, maine. You knew from the git go that was the bizness!

Crank   I don't wantchoo.

Cornbread   You ain't ask me what I want.

Crank   'Cause you don't know what you want.

Cornbread   I know what I need.

Crank   Hmmmph.

Cornbread   You. I need . . . you.

Crank   Niggah, you is corny.

Cornbread   Wha?

Crank   You want too much, Cornbread. From me and everybody else.

Cornbread   What the hell wrong wit' that?

Crank   It ain't good to want too much. End up disappointed at the end of thangs.

Cornbread   I promise. I ain't gone disappoint you. I wanna make you happy –

Crank   You know she know.

Cornbread   She don't know nothin'.

Crank   Yeah, she know.

Cornbread   How the fuck she know?

Crank   I guess she called Cleo Psychic Friends, hell I don't know!

Cornbread   She don't know shit. She don't know nothin' 'bout this good lovin' right chere.

He leans in to kiss **Crank***. She pushes him away.*

Cornbread   Oh, I ain't him. That what it is?

Crank   No, you not. No matter how hard you try.

Toyia   Ahem.

Toyia *is at the door. They both straighten up.*

Cornbread   Do you believe in knockin'?

Toyia   I didn't know I had to knock in my own muthafuckin' house.

She carries in shopping bags.

Cornbread   Whatchoo done went done bought?

Toyia   Stuff fo' our new house. I done got the layaway out from Target (*pronounced Tar-zhey*).

Beat.

Crank (*to* **Cornbread**)   That'll be fifteen.

She holds out her hand.

Cornbread   Here.

He gives her a crisp fifty-dollar bill. **Toyia** *snatches it out of his hand.*

Toyia   Why you gone give this bitch a fifty? You ain't gave me nothin' but twenty-five dollars this morning.

Cornbread   Toyia, stay out my business.

Crank *quickly packs up her belongings.*

Crank   Keep it. Unlike you, I don't need na'an maine to take care of my ass.

Toyia   Needin' and havin' are two entire' different thangs, lil' mama.

Crank   If it was left up to me, I wouldn't come over here.

Toyia   Then don't, bitch. Ain't nobody done axed you to cut his head. You should be cuttin' it for free as much money he gives you for Cookie and that little cornbread muffin you got bakin' in the oven.

Beat.

What, y'all thank a bitch wun' gone find out about that, huh? Surprised he ain't make you go get that "fixed."

Toyia *has touched a nerve and* **Crank** *turns around, eyes brimming red with fury.*

Crank   I don't use abortion like birth control, like you.

Toyia   And I don't lose my babies over a little crack, like you!

Cornbread *steps in between the two.*

Cornbread   I know y'all ain't fightin' over me.

Toyia   You would like that fo' yo' lil' ego, wun' you?

Crank   This ain't got nothin' to do withchoo!

Toyia   Sho'll don't. But you should gone on and take it. Look like you gone need all the help you can get . . . partnah. Word on the skreets, y'all ain't got nowhere to stay. I would let you chill up in my cut, but . . . we need a maid not a mistress.

Toyia *looks* **Cornbread** *up and down.* **Crank** *snatches the money out of* **Toyia**'s *hands and walks out of the unit.*

Toyia   I'll be over to get my tracks pult out.

Scene Four

BIG MAMA'S PLEA (CASE AD1619)

The Welfare Office. **Big Mama** *has been standing in the welfare line for the past three and a half hours. There are crying children of all ages creating the kind of cacophony that causes a mother's migraine.*

A Voice   Case number AD1619.

Big Mama   Woohoo, my dawgs was just a' barkin'! You mind if I take off my shoes? Thank ya, darlin'. I been standin' in that hot-ass sun for what been like three hours. And y'all wonder why black folk like to riot. Excuse me, ma'am. Where a needle and thread to sew up my mouth? I'm one of them folks bein' moved out 'cause the city done won the HOPE grant. Yes . . . I live in Hurt Village, ma'am. Yes, ma'am. Who you tellin'? I been livin' there over thirty years and, yes, it has gone to hell in a hand basket, but it wun't always like that. I 'member a time when folks kept they porch clean, young men was respectful, didn't wear they shorts hangin' all down they ass, there wun' a liquo store on every corner and there was grass . . . Lawd, there was grass. Seem like after Dr King was shot this neighborhood went down faster than a two-dollar hoe for a ten-dollar bill, but I ain't here to give you a history lesson. Well, I done got this here, uhm, paper in the mail sayin' I's been denied Section 8 'cause I makes $387 ova this here, uhm, "public assistance maximum." Ma'am? I understand that that's here the rules, but we all know the law can be changed for folks who done done good. Well . . . I'm here 'cause we ain't got nowhere else to go. They said we was gone be moved out to Raleigh come this comin' Friday but 'cause I might have lied a little bit on the application here, well, we might be out on the skreets, and I gots a family to take care of – Ooooo! That nail polish look real good on yo' toenails. What that is? Electric lightnin' blue? Look real spiffy 'gainst yo' skin, ma'am. You got some creamy skin – Well, ma'am. Uhmm, I can't really go nowhere else. I gots my grandbaby. Done come back from the war and he . . . sick. Yeah and his girlfriend there, and they gots a beautiful smart

lil' girl – the best of both of them – and she gone be somethin'.
Already bein' bussed out to Raleigh, so, ma'am . . . ma'am . . .
Ma'am, LISTEN!! I don't mean to raise my voice, but ain't
no other office to go to but this one. What, I'm trying to do a
lil' betta for me and my family, and I gets punished for't?
What that is? Y'all say y'all don't want a niggah on welfare,
they get off it, they get them a lil' funky-ass job cleanin' up
piss and shit and vomit and other unmentionables and you
wanna drop 'em out the system faster than a hoe droppin'
panties on the Auction Street corner. We just tryin' to get by.
$387 ain't nothin'. It ain't enough money to even put a down
payment on a 'partment barely. It'll be gone takin' care of
what I needs to take care of. I'll quit my job if I need to, but
I need to be put back on the list. You see, ever since I was a
lil' girl all I could dream about was the day I'd have my own
room all to myself with a door that could close me off from
the sorrow of my home. That's all I eva wanted, ma'am, was
a lil' space of my own. I ain't like them other lazy niggahs.
And I ain't raised no chillen up that way. We good clean-
livin' people, and, when we ain't, 'least we tryin' to be. Please,
ma'am.

She gets on her knees.

Ma'am, I thank you for your kindness in advance if you do
me this one favor. I don't ever wanna be out on them
skreets like I been. Please . . . put me back where I belong.

Scene Five

THE UNTOUCHABLES

Night time. **Cornbread**'s *unit. The TV has on BET uncut. The
latest soft-porn videos are spilling into the living room.* **Buggy**,
Cornbread *and* **Skillet** *are chillin' in the cut.* **Cornbread** *is
counting money.* **Skillet** *is playing video games.* **Buggy** *is on the
phone.*

Buggy   Whatchoo' talkin' 'bout ? The ticket on that like $55 a piece. It been ugly out here. It's clear though. Chopped up and clear. Call me back when you get on Auction. Bet.

He hangs up the phone.

That gone take us to our $500 today. We on fire, playas.

Cornbread *puffs on some weed.*

Skillet   So you like it?

Cornbread   Pussy-smellin' weed, dawg? This shit tight, but I don't know how it gone be I come home smellin' like weed and pussy. Toyia already snoopin' 'round and shit.

Buggy   Yeah, we might have to put this on the backburner. But I likes yo' entrepreneurial spirit, lil' bra. You gone be a good businessman.

Cornbread   "Pussy-smellin' weed." I like this lil' niggah righ here.

They give **Skillet** *a pound and dap.*

Buggy   So this last shipment done turnt into the initial investment of Buggy Enterprises.

Cornbread   Buggy Enterprises?

Buggy   Yeah, niggah. Cornbread Corner sound too-too –

Skillet   Whack.

Buggy   Hell, yeah.

Cornbread   No, it don't.

Skillet   How 'bout Buggy, Cornbread 'n Skillet Associates?

Cornbread   Hell, Cornbread 'n Skillet sound better by itself.

Skillet   Cornbread in a skillet.

Cornbread   Shut yo gay-ass up. Ain't nobody puttin' they dick up in you.

Buggy   What the hell you talkin' 'bout ?

Cornbread   He comin' on to me and shit. Cornbread in a skillet.

Buggy   That purple got you paranoid.

Cornbread   Do not!

Buggy   Whatever, niggah. It need to be Buggy Enterprises 'cause I'm the boss of this operation.

Cornbread   How you gone come up and be the boss of this?

Skillet   You been gone for I don't know how long.

Buggy *and* **Cornbread**   Niggah, shut up!

Cornbread   Yeah, you have been gone for I don't know how long. I know the lay of the land betta than you. Follow a man who runnin' blind, we liable to catch a charge fo' real.

Buggy   I'm a natural born killer.

Skillet   I like that movie.

Buggy *and* **Cornbread**   Niggah, *shut* up!

Buggy   I'm tellin' you, niggah. I'm the smart one. That's how it always been. I'm the winner.

Cornbread   Oh, you the winner?

Buggy   I win everything. From the baddest bitches to e'er fight. You said so yo'self. I'm a untouchable niggah.

Cornbread   How you untouchable?

Buggy   'CAUSE I AM!! AND DON'T LET NOBODY TELL YOU NO DIFFERENT!

His hands begin to shake.

Silence.

Skillet   They say purple Kool-aid get rid of the shakes.

They look at him sharply.

Cornbread   I just wanna know why you thank you can come over here and put yo'self in a place you don't deserve to be. If anybody gone be the Kang of this op it should be me. Me. ME!

Buggy *catches another call. He takes it.*

Skillet   He do be gettin' mo' calls than you. And he just been here a minute.

Cornbread *stares at him.*

Skillet   But on the other hand . . . never mind.

Buggy *gets off the phone.*

Buggy   Take this to that crack house on Poplar and Keel. You know where that is?

Cornbread   Niggah, that's Tony C main house.

Beat.

Buggy   I know.

Skillet *takes it. Looks at his leaders who are staring each other down. He opens the door and leaves.*

Scene Six

SYNONYMS

Right after. Outside the unit. **Cookie** *is examining her science experiment on her porch. Applying cocoa-butter to his scars,* **Skillet** *looks down at her from* **Cornbread**'s *porch. He gazes at her a while.*

Skillet   I . . . like . . . yo' hair . . . like . . . that.

Cookie *ignores him. He cowers in slight embarrassment.*

Skillet   It sho'll is hot out . . . here.

Cookie   It's Memphis. It's summer. DUH!

Skillet   One of 'em jumped out.

Cookie   Impossible.

Skillet   Fo' real. I seen't it.

Cookie   It's nine up in there. Niggah, you can't count.

Skillet   I'm ugly, not dumb.

Cookie *counts.*

Cookie   Shit, one did get out. Fuckadoodle! My hypothesis gone be wrong.

Skillet   No, it won't.

Cookie   You don't even know what a hypothesis is! None of them supposeta get out. They ain't supposeta! Now, everybody gone laugh at me.

Skillet   It ain't bad when everybody laugh at you. That mean you matter, even if it ain't by much.

Cookie   How it get out? You musta came over here and knocked over my jar.

Skillet   I ain't come nowhere near yo' . . . porch. You ever thought 'bout the "exception to the rule," fool! Sometime shit go wrong for the right reason.

Cookie   Exception to the rule, my black ass!

Skillet   One of 'em just stuck wit' it a little longer then the rest, thass all. Didn't care 'bout bumpin' his bug head against the lid. 'Cause he kept on hittin' his feet on the jar bottom when he fell. And hell, one pain was easier to take than the other, so he kept on jumpin' 'cause he never stop believin' that one day that junt was gone be blowed off. If not by God, then by his own goddamn self, so he formed a helmet of scars that covered his head so it wouldn't hurt no more. When them other mofos stopped jumpin', he jumped higher till finally he blowed the lid off. When he jumped out on the other side, he had a harder head and a bigger heart 'cause he didn't give up when every other niggah did. Exception . . . to . . . the rule . . . Cookie.

Cookie   That's the smartest thing you ever done said.

Skillet   I 'member likin' science class – when I went. Like I said, I'm ugly, not dumb.

Cookie   You ain't ugly either.

Skillet   What, you got another . . . synonym for me?

Cookie (*she smiles*)   Naw, I got an antonym for you.

Skillet   Beautiful?

Cookie   Naw . . .

Skillet   Pretty?

Cookie   That for a girl.

Skillet   Handsome?

Cookie   That for a man. You . . . cute.

Skillet (*blushing*)   I'll take that. Well, Cookie . . . you . . . beautiful.

He means it. Uncomfortable silence.

Cookie   You lyin'.

Skillet   Have you ever knowed me to lie?

Cookie   You a niggah. You liable to lie to get some.

Skillet   I don't wantcho goodies. I just . . . I just . . . thought . . . that . . . that I could give you a present before we go.

Cookie   Where you movin' to?

Skillet   Nowhere. Nowhere like the somewhere you goin'.

He kisses her sloppily. She tenses, drowning in saliva. But then he kisses her softly. And softer still.

Cookie   That's how kissin' feel?

Skillet   Soft. Like that.

Being the socially inept being he is, **Skillet** *gathers himself, then runs away. Touching her lips,* **Cookie** *looks after him.*

Scene Seven

SAND NIGGAHS

Night. **Cornbread***'s unit.* **Cornbread** *and* **Buggy** *have Nintendo guns in their hands. They are shooting at the television screen playing "Duck Hunt." They are buzzed, dancing around with beer bottles in their hands.*

Cornbread
Get 'em high, get 'em loose off that fuckin' Grey Goose
Get 'em high, get 'em loose, tear the fuck up off this roof
We gone burn it, crunk it up, tear da fuckin' club up
Get 'em high, niggahs fly up to the sky

Cornbread *picks up the beat and* **Buggy** *flows with the chaotic frenzy of a man gone crazy.*

Buggy
I'm a solja, thought I tolja nota boast but
I'll stomp out any niggah who step too fuckin' close
Stomp! Stomp! in da face wit' my combat boots
I pop off e'er niggah, I don't care 'bout who I shoot
I'm Scarface, niggah!
Crates of cookies stacked high
If you step up to me, niggah
I'ma fly you to the sky

Cornbread *and* **Buggy**
Get 'em high, get 'em loose off that fuckin' Grey Goose
Get 'em high, get 'em loose, tear the fuck up off this roof
We gone burn it, crunk it up, tear da fuckin' club up
Get 'em high, niggahs fly up to the sky

They dance around.

Cornbread   Maine, where the fuck Skillet at? We gone drank all this shit up fo' he get back.

Buggy *shoots at the screen.*

Buggy   Take that, Tony C!

Cornbread Two caps to the brain and then it'll all be over.

Buggy Thass all you man 'nough to pop off? Shit, I'll put fifty-three bullets in that niggah dome. *Rat-tat-tat-tat-tat-tat-tat.* That's what we useta do. Anybody look at me funny they get it.

Cornbread *looks a little uneasy.*

Cornbread Yeah, right, niggah . . .

Buggy I ain't playin' witcho'. One straight to the dome. No problem. They pump yo' helmet full of that crunk music. It get 'side yo' head, bring that terror into yo' dome. Get you crunked up, fucked up, tear-da-club-up pumped. And pow. Pow. Pow. Shoot a muthafucka dead. You ain't never shot nobody?

Cornbread Hell, naw, niggah. But I gota gun though. Teach me.

Buggy What you wanna learn fo'? I'm the one that's gone do the do when it come down to it.

Cornbread I might need to protect myself.

Buggy Niggah, it's on me.

Cornbread Well, practice on me then.

Buggy Naw, naw, niggah.

Cornbread *mocks* **Tony C**'s *walk.*

Cornbread I'm the Kang! I'm the Kang!

Buggy *demonstrates with the Nintendo gun.*

Buggy Okay, first you get him in yo' sight line. Make sho' a vital organ come up clear in the circle window on the sight. Be quiet. Look at 'em. Look 'em in they eye if you can. Take a breath 'cause yo' finger gone be shakin'. Take another breath if yo' body shake. Then pull back and – pow!

Cornbread *pretends to fall dead on the floor.*

Buggy   Pink mist all across yo' sight. See, I loved to kill them sand niggahs. They looked just like you.

Cornbread   Whatchoo talkin' 'bout ? I'm black, niggah.

Buggy   Hell, they the new niggahs of the earth. They useta look at me crazy. Could tell they was talkin' shit 'bout me. Could feel they voices crawl up under yo' skin.

He mimics the sounds of the Arabic language.

Just knew what the fuck they was sayin'. You see, you get paranoid, Cornbread, of c'erbody and e'erthing.

While **Buggy** *speaks, he focuses his Nintendo gun on* **Cornbread***.* **Cornbread** *laughs uneasily.*

Cornbread   Niggah . . . you crazy.

Buggy   Am I?

Cornbread   I ain't a fan of poppin' pills, but if you need to take a chill pill, I'm all for it.

Buggy *draws closer to* **Cornbread** *with his Nintendo gun on him.*

Buggy   Naw, I'm chillin' right here up in the cut. You know what else we would do to sand niggahs like you?

Cornbread   I don't know.

Buggy   Take they daughters. Fuck 'em up the ass with a rifle. Maybe a broke beer bottle.

Cornbread   Niggah . . . thass disgusting.

Buggy *(laughing)*   Oh, what, you don't like to hear my freaky tales? You still like pussy, don'tcha?

Cornbread   I don't like cut-up pussy –

Buggy   Y'all all look the same. Couldn't tell if y'all was naughty or nice. Shit, 'least they got uniforms over here. If you a Crip or GD, you shoot the niggah wearin' red. If you a Blood, you shoot the niggah wearin' blue. Niggahs is real simple. They make they self easy targets. But over there, they just wearin' whatever.

Buggy *draws closer to* **Cornbread***'s head.*

Cornbread   I ain't nothin' like 'em . . .

Buggy *puts the Nintendo gun to* **Cornbread***'s head. Beat.*

Buggy   You are. Can I trust you, sand niggah?

Beat.

Cornbread   Yeah, yeah . . . partnah. We gone take down his set together.

Buggy *withdraws his gun. Beat.*

Cornbread   What they done done to you?

Buggy   "They" didn't do nothin'. I been trainin' for this my whole life.

He returns to his game of "Duck Hunt." **Cornbread** *stares at him.* **Buggy** *is oblivious.*

Scene Eight

THE BANK OF AMERICA

Later still that night. **Buggy** *walks into the unit.* **Big Mama** *is getting ready for work.* The Cosby Show *is on in the background.*

Buggy   You still here?

Big Mama   Gettin' ready to go to work.

Buggy   Constantly on that night shift grind.

Big Mama   I'm 'bout to go work a double.

Buggy   Here.

He hands her a roll of money.

Big Mama (*hesitantly*)   That fast, huh?

Buggy   Always one of the slickest hustlers in Memphis. That should tide you over for a bit.

She looks at the money balanced in her palm.

Big Mama   Thank you.

She puts it in her bra and starts shuffling out the door. **Buggy** *sits on the couch to relax his feet.*

Buggy   I told you I'd take care of you, didn't I? The boy is back. The good old boy is back to take over that "Million Dollar Track."

Beat. **Big Mama** *stops. She turns around.*

Big Mama   This ain't for long, Buggy, just till we get back on our feet.

Buggy   I know, Big Mama –

Big Mama   We ain't gotta do this forever.

Buggy   Don't worry, I'll do it till forever if I got to –

Big Mama   You like doin' this?

Buggy   I like survivin'.

Big Mama   Seem like you like doin' this.

Buggy   I like survivin'. Don't you?

Beat.

Big Mama   Buggy, I got down on my knees today for the first time in I don't know how long.

Buggy   You prayed?

Big Mama   Naw, I begged. But to me, seem like ain't no difference 'tween the two. Every time I done got on my knees I never hear what I wanna hear. Never get what I need to get. Guess it 'cause God only take care of fools and babies, the rest of us gotta get along by our damn selves.

Buggy   I must be a fool then –

Big Mama   Naw, you my baby, Buggy. The only thang I got left. The only thang I got left from her . . . We done had some hard times you and me. Me and you both runnin' in and out of crack houses.

Buggy Big Mama –

Big Mama Constantly bailin' her out of jail –

Buggy I don't wanna –

Big Mama Findin' her on her knees in alleys –

Buggy – hear this right now –

Big Mama Yankin' her out of the back of cars –

Buggy – PLEASE!

Big Mama My knees got rubbed raw from dealin' wit' that girl. You'd thank I was a fuckin' prostitute the way my knees got to lookin'. I musta did something wrong in another life, 'cause the more I talked to the sky, the more the moon laughed at me. When I was walkin' back home, all I could see was Tiffany . . . Tiffany. All these lil' Tiffanys wobbling they way down that "Million Dollar Track" trying to make they way to the sky. I don't know what gone happen now. I'm a fool to even dream it'll be different, but I can't take this no mo', Buggy . . . I just . . . can't . . .

She takes the money and gingerly places it in his hand.

Buggy Take the money, Big Mama.

Big Mama This money got blood on it. People tears on it.

Buggy Big Mama, what I say –

Big Mama It gone kill you.

Buggy No, it ain't –

Big Mama It kilt yo' mama. (*Breath.*) You used to be such a good boy.

Buggy Don't start.

Big Mama Such a good, good boy –

Buggy I AM NOT A GOOD BOY. QUIT CALLIN' ME
THAT! Good don't live here in the projects. Look out the
window. Just a bunch of niggahs and bitches runnin' amuck
havin' babies they don't need.

Big Mama You thank you betta than them? You ain't no
betta than them.

Buggy You right. I ain't. Thass the problem. This shit
can't be stopped.

Big Mama Buggy, things can be stopped. Now. You might
can't save yo' daughter, but you can save yo' grandbaby, you
my baby –

Buggy You can't save me. Nobody can save me.

Big Mama Yes, I can, if you just let me –

Buggy Oh, I see what it is. My glove-supplier gettin' all
guilty on me. You guilty? You feel bad about my momma?
Well, you should. Crack ain't kill her. You kilt her. Every
time you smacked, cussed her, downed her, you kilt her.
Everybody beatin' on her from Tony C to you to the whole
entire hood –

Big Mama *smacks* **Buggy**.

Big Mama Yo' soul so curdled up inside done got to
lookin' like buttermilk left out in the sun too long. (*Beat.*) I
wun't the best momma in the world, but who the fuck is. I'm
here, Buggy. I'm here. You done gotcho ass a second chance
at life, most niggahs don't get one. Take it. Take the right
way, not the left way 'cause you thank that's the only one you
got left.

Buggy Take the money, Big Mama.

Big Mama No.

Buggy Take it!

Big Mama I'm goin' to work. I'm gone works for mine.

Buggy   You think you can bring in five hundred a day? Two Gs a week? You ain't nothin' but janitor.

Big Mama *heads for the screen door.*

Buggy   Big Mama, you take this money, now. I been workin' all damn day to get this.

Big Mama   I said I don't want it.

Buggy   Cookie need that posterboard . . .

Beat. **Big Mama** *turns away.*

Buggy   So you done woke up and smelt the coffee, huh?

Big Mama   Yeah, bitches always do it faster than the niggahs.

Big Mama *walks out the door.*

Scene Nine

THE INSURRECTION

Later that same night. **Cornbread** *and* **Buggy** *are under the Auction Street sign.*

Cornbread   Where the fuck is that maine? He been gone all night. That niggah went and smoked all that shit up. Bet!

Buggy   He prolly just got held up with somethin'.

Cornbread   For three hours?

Buggy   Hell, I don't know!

Cornbread   Maybe he fuckin' some bitch.

Beat.

Buggy *and* **Cornbread**   Nah!

They laugh. Beat.

Buggy   Big Mama ain't take the money.

Cornbread   Hell, then give it to me.

Buggy   Naw, she just on that savior tip. But when she ain't got nowhere to go, then I'll be her muthafuckin' savior.

Ebony *walks in past them. He is shaking.* **Tony C** *is walking up behind him.*

Cornbread   What the hell wrong wit' that niggah?

Ebony *leans against a pole. Beat. He vomits.*

Cornbread   Drunk ass.

Buggy   Naw . . . he ain't drunk . . .

Tony C   Niggah, didn't I tell you! Aim at the side of his head. Don't listen to nothin' nobody tell y'all. Bitch-ass, niggah. Got that niggah blood all on my K-Swiss. Now, I'ma have to buy a new pair.

Ebony *vomits again.*

Tony C   Aww, just who I been lookin' for. Ran into y'all lil' boy. Down there. On Poplar and Keel.

Cornbread *looks at* **Buggy**.

Tony C   It's funny, when that niggah got a gun in his face, he sho'll do speak fast. Speak so fast he start stutterin' and shit. "T-tt-tt-on-n-ny C-c-c." I heard 'em loud and clear though.

Cornbread   Tony C, maine, we, um –

Buggy   Where Skillet?

Tony C   Unh, unh, unh . . . I ask the questions 'round here. What, y'all thank a niggah wun't gone find out? Buggy and Cornbread – what he say, Ebony?

Ebony   Associates.

Cornbread   It's Enterprises.

Tony C   Awww, my bad, niggah. Excuse me. That was a stupid move, Buggy. I ain't knownt you to be stupid.

Cornbread? Maybe. But you? You gone just up and ignore my proposition and hook up wit' this here twinkie-colored niggah, this South Memphis sellin' niggah on my muthafuckin' turf, niggah –

Ebony *dry heaves again.*

Buggy   Where Skillet at?

Ebony (*weeping*)   Gone.

Tony C   Niggah, if you don't be quiet, you gone end up where yo' friend is. We had to take him to the other side of the river, if you know what I'm sayin'. I don't take kindly to folk thankin' they can run me. I ain't no bitch. I can't be runt.

Cornbread   Tony C, maine, you know we was just –

Tony C   Fuckin' around, yeah, I know. Y'all gone have to come up off all that prof. Can't be sellin' shit to my customers on my turf tryin' to run me out. Y'all worser than these white muthafuckas. Thankin' they can come run me out of business. Can take over my muthafuckin' real estate. (*He screams to no one in particular.*) THIS IS PRIME MUTHAFUCKIN' REAL ESTATE. I'm the KANG. I can't be runt.

Cornbread   How 'bout we give you twanky-five percent?

Tony C   Niggah, is you crazy?

Cornbread   But, that's our money, niggah.

Tony C   My territory, my money, niggah.

Cornbread   That ain't fair.

Tony C   That's the politickin' of the projects. I RUN THIS BITCH!! Now give me that muthafuckin' prof.

Buggy   Take it.

Cornbread (*whispering to* **Buggy**)   Niggah, is you crazy?

Buggy   He can have it, only one thang. (*To* **Tony C**.) You gone have to take it from me, if you want it.

Tony C   I'm all about takin', niggah, ye'en know?

Cornbread   Maine, we don't want no problems.

He reaches in his waistband for a gun.

Tony C (*to* **Cornbread**)   Touché, niggah. You thank you fast enough.

Buggy   I am.

Tony C   Oh, solja boy, quit it.

Buggy   Ain't no hoe up in me.

Tony C   Yes, there is. Yo' mama.

Beat.

Buggy *charges toward* **Tony C** *and in one swoop lifts him off the ground with his bare hands. They struggle intensely.*

Tony C   You wanna kill me! Kill me! I double-dog dare you. KILL ME, NIGGAH!

Cornbread   Buggy, you ain't got the gun!

Tony C   Kill me! Please, kill me!

Buggy   I don't need no fuckin' gun.

Tony C (*hoarse*)   Kill me, niggah . . .

Buggy   You want me to kill you?

Tony C   Please . . . kill . . . me . . .

Buggy   You'd love that wouldn't you? The Kang can't stand to see his kingdom go.

Tony C   Kill me, niggah . . . Kill . . . me

Buggy *has* **Tony C** *up in the air with his bare hands.* **Tony C**'s *feet dangle trying to touch the crumbling ground.* **Buggy** *stares into* **Tony C**'s *eyes that are rolling into the back of his head. His huge hands are squeezing the life out of him. Police sirens can be heard.*

Cornbread   Niggah, leave his monkey-ass alone! Somebody done called the po-po!

Buggy   Naw, niggah. I'ma grant him his wish.

Buggy *squeezes harder.* **Tony C** *chokes, fighting to inhale.*
Beat. **Buggy** *lets him go.* **Tony C** *falls down to the ground.*

Tony C (*coughing*)   You thank I like doin' this shit? I got to!
Thass all we know. This all we know . . .

Buggy   Naw, niggah. Thass all *you* know.

Cornbread   Break out, niggah, now! Come on! COME ON!

Cornbread *runs off.* **Buggy** *stares at* **Ebony**. *Beat. He runs*
after **Cornbread**. **Tony C** *looks around and begins to gather*
himself together.

Tony C (*hoarse*)   Ebony, hand me my shoe. Ebony, hand me
my muthafuckin' K-Swiss.

Ebony   Kill yo'self fool, ole' Elvis Presley lookin'-ass niggah.

He busts out running as the police sirens engulf the night.

Scene Ten

ACE BOON COONS

Night. The unit. Gunshots pop off. **Crank** *is folding up clothes. There*
are police lights and sirens coming from the outside.

Crank   What the fuck is goin' on?

Bang. Bang. Bang on the unit door.

Who the fuck bangin' on my / muthafuckin' do' like they
crazy?

Toyia   It's me, bitch! Open up! It's me!

Crank *undoes the three locks to open the door.* **Toyia** *enters in a*
panic.

Toyia   This day is just fucked up from the rooda to da
tooda. First off. Girl, folk say they done fount Skillet wit' a
bullet in his head on the playground. And po po got
Cornbread down at the jail house on some trumped-up dope

charge. Cornbread call me say some deal wit' Tony went
awry like a muthafucka.

Crank   What!

Toyia   Girl, I'ma need some money for bail. He done fo'
shorely! $15,000, I need a $15,000 bail bond. Thass all our
scrilla! Say he had that pure*dee* white on him. I mean what
the fuck! Them cops call theyself investigatin' some shit all up
in the cut. God know what they gone find, you'd think
Cornbread be smarter than that. Hell, he half-white!

Crank   Just calm down, Toyia!

Toyia (*weeping*)   I don't know what to do. What the fuck am
I gone do? Cornbread . . . what about my Cornbread?

She falls down to the ground.

Crank   Bitch, pull yo'self together!

Beat.

Toyia   You my girl, right? You my ace boon coon, right?

Crank   Yeah, bitch.

Toyia   You'd be down for me like I been down for you,
right?

Crank   Yeah, yeah, yeah.

Toyia   Well, I need you to hold somethin' for me.

Crank   Like some money?

Toyia   Naw.

She passes a baby bag to **Crank**.

Crank   Hell, naw. I ain't keepin' LaQwanna all night!

Toyia   Bitch, quit actin' a damn fool!

Crank *looks in.*

Crank   Product.

Toyia   Cornbread say Tony C after him fo' sho. Tony C gone come for this product . . . or me . . . I gotta get gone . . . Come on, Crank. That niggah kill babies and shit.

Crank   No, I can't be by that.

Toyia   He bury folks alive and shit!

Crank   I can't be by that!

Toyia   He rape bitches with brooms and shit!

Crank   I said NO!

Toyia   Come on, you my *bitch*! What happen that time I kicked Mr. Stokley in the mouth for hemmin' you up in the PE closet? What 'bout that time, Crank? You owe me, girl.

Crank   I can't be by that stuff.

Toyia   Well, if you can't do it for me, then do it for him. Cornbread done took care of you and yours. You owe him. If you don't owe me, at least you owe him. Besides, you been off, like, three years, bitch. And plus you . . . ya know . . . you –

Crank   Pregnant.

Toyia   Yeah bitch, I know. I know . . . Look I wouldn't put you in a situation you could'n handle. That shit ain't got no hold on you. But if they find this shit on me, in that house . . . come on. We'd do it for you.

Crank   What if they come up in here and start sniffin' round here?

Toyia   We'd do it for you. Hell, we ace boon coons, ya know what I'm sayin'? Just hold it till this all ova wit'.

Beat.

Crank   You gone get it first thang?

Toyia   First thang in the mornin'.

She gives her a pound and a snap.

We ace boon coons fo' life, bitch.

Scene Eleven

THE LYNCHING

In the blue flicker of the television, **Crank** *stares at the diaper bag. Looks away. She tries desperately to occupy herself. Then she opens it. Tastes it.*

TV Anchor Voice   Breaking from Action News Five –
Memphis police units found the body of a young African-
American male, age fifteen years old, on Auction in the
infamous Hurt Village projects in North Memphis. Police say
the male was most likely the victim of a gang initiation. Police
charged an unidentified African-American male who was
caught fleeing the crime site with a concealed weapon –

Crank *turns off the television. She takes the antennae off the set. She then takes a crack cookie from the stash. She goes to the kitchen to get a spoon. Finds a lighter. Lights up. Begins to smoke it. As she smokes, she rises high in the air as if she's levitating.*

Crank
　　Dear Cookie, I hope you find this letter
　　You won't be able to because I can't write it
　　I can only spin the memories
　　Unwind the facts in my mind
　　As this rock makes my thoughts implode
　　Onto one another and hide behind
　　Prison walls of project cement
　　Stone the house we call home
　　If you only knew I thought in poetic slants, diatribes
　　That my mind held more words
　　Than the largest dictionary could ever find
　　That often I cannot heave my brain into my mouth
　　To impress redress the mask I die behind.
　　These are the thoughts of a druggie's
　　Coked-out choked-out wired mind
　　I can't seem to crack the safe I've hid my heart in
　　As I think about how I've never hugged you Cookie
　　My Cookie monster. I don't know how to begin
　　How to open my arms wide
　　Stretch my neck to a caving sky

Say those words my dictionary hearts
But my mouth fail to
"I love you."
Never heard those words said
Said them to niggahs as they fucked my brains out
Only to find the more you say it the less it means
Like sayin' niggah, bitch, or please
I need you to think that I'm a queen
Don't abide these diatribes
Just the thoughts of a dying druggie's mind.
My finger aches to wrap around your wrist
In a last moment mother–daughter tryst
I hope this body'll you'll never find
I wish you can capture my words as I think them into the sky.
I'll see you again beautiful girl as I vomit out
These last thoughts of a druggie's
Coked-out choked-out wired mind.

She has smoked the entire rock. Gone.

Scene Twelve

THE PLEDGE OF ALLEGIANCE

Next day. Inside the unit. **Buggy** *is rustling through the boxes, hurriedly packing his things.* **Crank** *enters with eyes rimming red. She drags* **Cookie**, *who has a jacket tied around her waist.*

Crank And get in that house!

Cookie   I don't wanna go there no mo'! Fuck school!

Crank Buggy, give me yo' belt.

Buggy What she done did?

Crank Actin' too grown for her damn good.

Cookie   I don't wanna do it!

Crank It don't matter what you don't wanna do, you do what that teacher say. You mind them. You stand when that teacher tell you to stand, nah. I ain't gone tell you no mo'.

Cookie   I hate you!

Crank   She sho'll is doin' a lotta hatin' lately. I need to send you back to Humes. Gettin' too opinionated. Don't worry. I'ma beat the opinions right out of ya. You say the muthafuckin' pledge of allegiance.

Buggy   What?

Crank   That teacher tellin' her to stand up and lead the class in the pledge of allegiance and this lil' heifer gone say, "Naw!"

Cookie   Id'n want to.

Crank   Tell him what you said. Tell it, Cookie!

Cookie   I ain't gone pledge allegiance to a flag that don't pledge allegiance to me.

Silence.

Freedom of speech –

Crank   Shut up, in the projects ain't no freedom of speech. You gone get it. I'm tired of all this goddamn back talk. You already know my nerves is bad. Get in that room. You gone strip down.

Buggy   You ain't got to do all that . . .

Crank   Naw, it's about time she learned her lesson.

Cookie *begins to sob uncontrollably.*

Buggy   Crank, she ain't did nothin' that bad.

Crank   She need to go to school and get her lesson. She don't need to be kicked out, 'cause she gone be somebody, now strip the fuck down. Take it off! Everything! And get in that room!

Buggy   Alright, Crank, you gettin' a lil' too crunk.

Crank   Niggah, I ain't got crunk yet! And shut up, fo' a beat yo' ass, too.

She goes into one of the boxes and she pulls out an extension cord.

Strip!

She goes over to **Cookie** *and starts pulling at her clothes.*

Buggy   Crank, you want me to beat yo' ass?

Crank   I'ma raise my chile the way I wanna, you gone come over here and stop me? You can't stop shit. As far as I'm concerned you ain't my babydaddy. You gone come up in here you been gone for God know how long and you thank you can say shit about my chile.

Buggy   She mine, too.

Crank   You sholl didn't act like it. Where you been? Where the letters from over there you said you was gone send us?

Buggy   If I sent them you couldn't read 'em no how.

Crank   Yo' mammy, niggah.

She continues to strip **Cookie** *naked.*

Buggy   Fuck you, you snagatooth bitch.

Crank   You ain't nothin' but a coward. You been a coward yo' whole life. You scared of Tony, you scared of this and that. You a pill-poppin' triflin' son of a –

She looks at the back of **Cookie**'s *school uniform. There is a deep crimson red blood stain on her bottom. She's sobbing so badly that she's hiccuping.*

Cookie   I didn't wanna stand . . . I didn' wanna stand.

Silence.

Buggy   Look what you done did.

Crank   Well, she just shoulda tolt somebody.

Beat.

Buggy   Go put you some clean clothes on. Gone to the back, nah. Gone.

Cookie *slowly gathers the clothes her mother ripped from her body and walks to the back room.*

Crank   So she just shoulda tolt somebody then I wouldn' have to whup her.

She stands there, shaking, twitching.

Buggy   You back on that white, ain't ya?

Silence.

You should be 'shamed of yoself.

Crank   How come? You 'shamed of yo' self? You sellin' it. Scllin' it to e'erbody. This shit got me on lock, maine. Ain't no runnin' from this shit. You walked out damn near ten years ago and now you wanna be here? For what? For what, *what*? Dangle a piece of candy in front of our heart? Make it break a lil' more. When Cookie was growin' up she would walk 'round here askin' me who her daddy was, where her daddy was. I almost wanted to tell her that I didn't know who her daddy was. I was willin' to label myself a hoe 'cause I couldn't get her daddy to love me enough to stick around to love her enough.

Buggy   I ain't have enough money back then –

Crank   Fuck the money, Buggy. "Why my daddy don't love me, Ma? Why my daddy don't send me birthday cards, Mama? Why I got his last name but I ain't neva seen his face?" Yeah, Buggy. Money don't answer them questions no matter how hard you try. I got to be makin' shit up. Did you see how proud she was of you? I'm sure you bein' a soldier satisfied e'er fantasy in her head. "That's why my daddy couldn't be there for me. That why, he was protectin' me from terrodom" – or terrorists or whatever the fuck you niggahs wanna call it. Her daddy was a fighter. Didn't know her daddy was a fuckin' doughboy, not no hero! Her heart's the spittin' image of yourn, but you don't see it, do you?

Buggy   Yes, I do.

Crank   Well, be the daddy yo' daddy couldn' be for you, my daddy couldn' be for me, e'er niggah daddy couldn' be for them.

Buggy   I can't be her daddy. I'm all messed up inside, Crank.

Crank   Maine, who you tellin'? She gone be messed up if she neva know the other half of her. Sometimes I look at her and I hate myself. Yeah, I just can't believe I done brought another lil' black girl into this worl'. This worl' ain't built fo' beautiful brown black girls. The worl' ignore her, kick her when it's suppose to love her, bite her when it's suppose to kiss her, tell her she ugly when she really pretty, rape her and blame it on her, piss on her stomach, cum on her face and say that the way to make a dollar, shake what ya momma gave you, not knowin' that what her mama gave her can't be bought. That her pussy is priceless. A lil' black girl got a hard load to carry. Sometimes I look at her and wish she ain't never been born. Not because I don't love her but because I love her with all my heart. Now is you gone be the worl' or her daddy? 'Cause I tell ya one thing, all her mama is is a lil' black girl who believed what the world done tol' her. Please take her from me.

Buggy   I can't. I can't. I gotta get gone, Crank. I gotta –

Crank   Yeah, I know. I just thought I'd ask.

Beat.

Buggy   Why'd you do it? Why'd you go back on it?

Crank (*shrugging her shoulders*)   That's the one thing that'll do a niggah in. Boredom and chaos, Buggy. Boredom and chaos.

Scene Thirteen

THE DOOR OF NO RETURN

Outside the unit. **Buggy** *goes outside.* **Cookie** *is on the electricity box, consoling herself.* **Buggy** *walks down to the box.*

Buggy   You mind I kick it witchu for a hot minute?

Cookie   Suit yo'self. I'm tryin' to kill myself. They say if
you sit on the box for two hours it blow up. Straight into the
sky. Like fireworks. I'll split in half. Like yo' friend.

Buggy   But you ain't gone wanna do that 'cause nobody'll
wanna look at you durin' yo' funeral.

Cookie *spits onto the ground.*

Buggy   That ain't befittin' a young lady.

Cookie   Oh, so now you wanna teach me how to be a lady?

Buggy   Actually, yes. I wanna tell you 'bout the birds and
the bees. I mean, since you a woman now.

Cookie   Don't worry. I know all about it. A boy put his
wee-wee in a girl mouth. She swallow his seeds and it go
down into her belly and then nine months later she blowed
up bigger than a house. That's why I won't let a boy nowhere
near these lips. Peaches be lettin' boys skeet up in her mouth.
I ain't 'bout to get preggers. Nozzir, not me.

Buggy   What you call it?

Cookie   Preggers –

Buggy   That ain't the way it happen. He don't put cum
inside her mouth to get her . . . preggers –

Cookie   Yes, he do –

Buggy   No, it's her legs.

Cookie   How it gone go inside her leg?

Buggy   Not inside, I mean between her legs.

Cookie   Like where the pee come out?

Buggy   Naw. See . . . there's another hole. Below the pee-
pee hole.

Cookie   I got two holes down there?

Buggy   In the front . . . yeah . . .

Cookie   Hmmph. That's interesting.

Buggy   That's the way it is. The birds and the bees.

Cookie   For real?

Buggy   Mmmphmm.

Cookie   For real! Then how come Peaches preggers then if she only let them skeet up in her mouth?

Buggy   Peaches prolly ain't tellin' the truth of thangs.

Cookie   Yeah, she is. She my bestus friend.

Buggy   "Best" friend.

Cookie   Oh, my bad. "Best friend." She tell me everything. Well, maybe not as much as she use to. I barely see her since I started getting bussed over there.

Buggy   To the white kids?

Cookie   I'm the only one there.

Buggy   I know how that feel.

Cookie   You was the only niggah up in yo' platoon?

Buggy   Yeap, bunch of cracker boys from Kentucky, Arkansas and a whole slew from Peoria, Illinois, for some reason.

Cookie   I'ma go them places when I become a flight attendant.

Buggy   Well, you gone have to learn how to talk right. 'Cause if you can talk right you can go anywhere you wanna. Be anything you wanna. Leave anytime you wanna.

Cookie   Like you, huh?

Buggy   Like me. Yeah, you can go to the Philippines, Germany, hell, Africa if you wanna.

Cookie   You ain't comin' back, is ya?

Beat.

Buggy   No.

Cookie *accepts his answer, then smiles to herself.*

Cookie   I'd be scared to go there.

Buggy   Where?

Cookie   To Africa.

Buggy   How come? I lived there for a hot minute.

Cookie   A real hot minute, I bet.

Buggy (*to himself*)   That's where it all started.

Cookie   You wun't rollin' 'round in the bushes with some cheetahs and apes, was you?

Buggy   Well, ain't no cheetahs up in Ghana and that's where I was. I was fully expectin' niggahs to have bones in they noses and shit, but naw. They look just like me. I blended right in, boy. Right in. I met one of them bougie-ass niggahs went on vacation there. Say they went to some museum called the "Door of No Return." I decide I'ma go. I go through this tour company, and they take us into this cave. Tour man say that they would have two thousand niggahs in a stone room no bigger than two of these mofuckin' units. Two thousand packed. You run yo' hands along the wall and there are these big-ass dents. Waist high. The tour man say that's how much shit had collected. Imagine two thousand muthafuckas walkin' 'round waist high in shit. Look up about two stories and there was three windows lettin' air come up in the cut. But cha can't git away from dat smell, maine.

Cookie   Least they had windows.

Buggy   Yeah, but they was so far away. See, the windows was for the ocean water. Now, if the ocean git high enough, water would splash in and rinse the shit away. Imagine mufuckas hopin' and prayin' water would somehow stream in to wash they hell away. Maybe even hopin' to drown. But then the tour man took us to a place for them unruly niggahs. The sun from the windows was sheddin' light on this hallway leadin' to a small openin'. It was a hole that come up to my waist. One foot in, you vanished into darkness. Nothin'.

Black. Pitch black. I placed my hand inside that hole and that when I felt somethin'. Like smooth scoops in stone. I asked "What this?" The tour man say, "The slave scratches." With my hand, I read them bumps and valleys scratched into those walls by fingers trying to break through stone. He said e'ey slave that went into that hole died there. That's where it all started. Been trying to claw our way out ever since.

Cookie   Seem like if e'ery niggah went over there and felt that wall, they'd live dey life a lil' different.

But **Buggy** *is not listening. He is staring at the graffiti tag. He reads it.*

Buggy   "Das Haus des Jammers."

Cookie   That's the Hurt Village code. When we tag other projects that's the letters we write. They say aliens came from out the sky and put them words outside the complex gate. Never knownt what it mean, though.

Buggy   It's German. It mean "the house of sorrow."

Epilogue

THE DEMOLITION

Outside the units. **Cookie** *stands beneath the Auction Street sign. She is playing with her beloved dolls' house on the ground. The "Hurt Village is falling down" refrain is heard softly beneath.*

Cookie   They ain't pick up Skillet body till the next day. Some of the kids was playin' outside that mornin' so we got to walk right up to the body. See it. They ain't even cover him up. Just left him like that. Policeman say, "Let 'em see it. Teach these lil' niggahs a lesson." He was black. Po po only come for the dead. They don't come for the livin'. They don't care about them folk. Just the dead. And they barely care 'bout them. Ashes to ashes, dust to dust. These project walls will crumble to the ground, and the tears and bloodshed will soon be forgotten. Big Mama got us back on the HOPE list, under one condition – my mama can't live wit' us since she got back

on that shit. So we movin' on to Raleigh. Big Mama my mama
now. Daddy – I mean, Buggy. He gone again. I try to act like
he was never here. Like them two weeks was a dream or
somethin'. Like it never happened. Some say it take a village
to raise a chile. Some time the child gotsta raise they
goddamn self. I believes that. But no matter how the Hurt was,
I'ma be a Hurt Village Hustler, for life, for LIFE! Whaaaa!
WHAAA! I ain't sad and all, but uhm . . . I'ma miss shit.

*As she says the other characters' names, a light comes up on them
standing in various places outside the project building, as if they are dolls
in the dolls' house of her imagination.*

Ebony checkin' niggahs on the corner. Toyia givin' her
coochie lessons. Cornbread, my real daddy. How Skillet
called me beautiful. Hell, even Tony C.

The lights slowly fade on them.

They all gone. I wonder how they gone be, but till we meet
again, *if* we ever meet again. I got 'em in my rhyme and in
my heart and in my mind.

*She begins a beat on the Auction Street sign pole. It rings with a metallic
clang, underscoring her chant.*

Cookie (*cont'd*)
   This be the war / ungh this be the war / ungh
   This be the war / ungh / this be the war / ungh, ungh
   This be the war / ungh / this be the war
   This be the war / ungh / this be the war / ungh
   This be the war / ungh / this be the war / ungh, ungh
   This be the war / ungh / this be the war

*The engine sound of construction trucks can be heard rising over the
refrain until it drowns **Cookie** out and all we see is her jookin',
floating, flying beneath a fading lamp light under the Auction Street sign.*

Christopher Shinn

Dying City

For E and L

Dying City was first performed at the Royal Court Jerwood Theatre Upstairs, London, on May 12, 2006. The cast was as follows:

Kelly   Sîan Brooke
Peter / Craig   Andrew Scott

Director James Macdonald
Lighting and Set Designer Peter Mumford
Sound Designer Ian Dickinson
Costumes Iona Kenrick

Characters

Kelly, *late twenties*
Peter, *late twenties*
Craig, *late twenties*

Craig and Peter are identical twins and played by the same actor.

The play takes place in January 2004 and July 2005.

No interval; blackouts should be avoided; sound between scenes should not be overdesigned.

The play takes place in Kelly's apartment. A combined kitchen and living room; doors lead to a bathroom and bedroom off. I imagined a design that lives in naturalism but suggests something beyond it. I've kept stage directions to a minimum, omitting obvious actions in an attempt to avoid clutter.

One

Night. **Kelly** *sorts through books. A cardboard box sits next to the couch. TV plays* Law and Order. *A bedsheet and pillow are scrunched up in the corner of the couch. The buzzer buzzes.*

Kelly Hello?

Peter's voice Hi – it's Peter!

Pause.

Kelly Hi!

Peter's voice I tried calling . . .

Pause.

Kelly Come up!

Pause. She throws the bedsheet over the box. **Peter** *knocks.*

Hi! Peter . . .

Peter Hi, Kelly – sorry!

Kelly Come in.

Peter You're unlisted now!

Kelly I am . . .

Peter I tried calling your landline, and then I tried your cell – I was wondering, I thought maybe it was a *work* thing, maybe one of your clients got your numbers or something and you / had to change –

Kelly It's – yeah, it's – I've been meaning to call you and – it's – I just haven't. I've been so / busy –

Peter Oh, no, of course –

Kelly I wanted to make sure I had the, that I had enough – energy, mental space, before I called . . .

Peter Did you, I wasn't – did you get my letter?

Kelly I did.

Peter   I was wondering, I wasn't sure if I had the right
address –

Kelly   I did. Yeah, and I just – I've been *meaning* to call —

Peter   No – of *course*.

Kelly   So . . .

Pause.

Well – sit down, please! I'll make some tea.

Peter   Oh, tea would be lovely.

Kelly   Were you – in the neighborhood or – you're in town
visiting . . . ?

Peter   – I know, barging in like this, I have to apologize.

Kelly   Well – I don't have a phone.

Peter (*laughs*)   Right. No, I didn't plan on – tonight – it's
actually a bit of a *drama* actually.

Kelly   Oh?

Pause.

Peter   I'm sorry, is everything – did I, is it a bad – a bad /
time or –

Kelly   No. No.

Peter   I just . . .

Pause.

Kelly   You know, honestly – when they come to tell you –

Pause.

When they came to tell me about Craig, they just showed up
– they just / show up, no warning, they don't call or –

Peter   Oh God. Oh Kelly, I'm so sorry. I'm so *stupid*.

Kelly   So I was just – a memory . . .

Peter   Of *course*.

Kelly   . . . of the buzzer – I'm fine.

Peter   God, I'm a total idiot.

Kelly   I'm fine.

Peter   And it's just about a year, right?

Kelly   Last week. Yeah.

Peter   Last *week*. Huh. I've been – the date was sort of floating around in my head but I've been kind of distracted because of these other . . . I've been thinking a lot about the *funeral*, actually.

Kelly   Uh-huh?

Peter   Just how weird it was.

Kelly   Yeah.

Peter   No one really talking.

Kelly   Mm. No one knew what to *say*.

Peter   About?

Kelly   Just – you know, the shock. Everyone was in shock.

Peter   Okay. I thought you meant – knew what to say, like, weren't sure what to say because it seemed like maybe what happened wasn't what the military was saying.

Kelly   Oh.

Peter   Did you feel that at all? I don't know, maybe I'm crazy, but I felt that underneath a little, that people kind of thought it wasn't an accident maybe, and that's why everyone was so quiet.

Kelly   Well. The way it was told to us – so many of his men saw it happen . . .

Peter   Yeah – I guess I thought maybe, because everyone there knew that Dad taught us, from the time we were little, how to shoot, how to handle weapons, that maybe some people didn't believe the story.

Kelly   Right. Well, the investigation was still going on at that point, it wasn't official, so some people might have felt that.

Peter   Yeah. And maybe it's a gun culture thing, we grew up around guns, you didn't, so it's something I would feel more than you . . . *Target* practice, I just . . . Craig would always write about how careful he was with his weapon – I still can't picture it.

Kelly   It's a hard thing to picture.

Pause.

Peter   Another thing that sucked was I could only be there for one *day*, remember? I had to fly back and do those stupid reshoots on my movie. The whole thing was so, it's like this *blur* – dealing with Mom, two years after Dad – and, like, the whole *gay* thing, do these people know, or not, and no one *talking* to me – except you.

Kelly   How is your mom?

Peter   Oh, the same. I don't know what it will take to pierce that woman's heart, but . . .

Pause.

Kelly   Well – I'm glad you're here. However. It's great to see you.

Peter   A bit weird maybe?

Kelly   Weird – a little. How you look.

Peter   Yeah, I always think of that . . . A relief, though, too.

Kelly   Uh-huh . . . ?

Peter   That's how *I* feel. Even though it's hard. To finally see you again. – Not since the funeral, God! Even *spoken*!

Kelly   *Time.* I can't believe so much time has passed –

Peter   It feels like yesterday, right? – I wonder if the
anniversary – because I wasn't aware of the exact date – if
that had anything to do with what happened tonight.

Kelly   What happened?

Peter   I . . . I did something sort of shocking.

Pause.

I'm sorry.

Kelly   What?

Peter   I know I've already said this, but I can't believe I just
showed up like this. Because – we talked, at the funeral, about
what it was *like* for you when they just showed up and buzzed
– and here I go do the exact same thing!

Kelly   You didn't have my number, what other way could
you have gotten in / touch?

Peter   I know, but still . . .

Kelly   It's fine. Really. Forget about it.

Pause. **Peter** *smiles.*

Peter   Oh, all right, if you *insist* . . .

Kelly *smiles.*

Peter   Was it – is everything okay, I mean . . . ?

Kelly   With . . . ?

Peter   Did you have to change your numbers because of a
client, did something happen?

Kelly   Oh.

Peter   I always worried something *stalkery* would happen to
you, you're so beautiful.

Kelly   Oh!

Peter I'm serious! Therapy, you know, two people alone in a room, it's very sexy! – Not that I've ever *done* it. In my fantasies – "the handsome Doctor . . . "

Kelly You take sugar, right? I only have whole milk –

Peter Plain is fine.

Kelly Plain?

Peter Yes – I'm playing this *assassin* in this movie I have coming up, I'm supposed to be getting in shape – I have this *trainer* . . .

Kelly He's tough?

Peter *She* – the guy-trainers I've had, it's weird, I think they've all been jealous of me – my manager thinks it's because I'm so handsome. – But yes, she is tough.

Kelly It's funny, you know, you say what you imagine therapy is like – when I first started I thought I'd get to hear people talk about sex, their sex lives? But it's food. People want to talk about eating – their *body* image, their *eating* habits –

Peter That's so pathetic.

Kelly It's really what people are obsessed with.

Peter Yeah, because nobody fucks anymore, they just eat like pigs instead!

Pause.

Kelly I don't know about that. Viagra's still pretty popular . . .

Peter That's true, I guess . . . Right! *There's* your problem – the people who would have gone to therapy and talked about sex are all just popping Viagra instead!

Kelly Huh . . .

Peter – Oh, but, what about fucked-her-so-hard-she? *He* wanted to talk about sex.

A moment. Then:

Kelly   – What?

Peter   It just came into my head, your client – we talked about him on Craig's last night. – That was what we called him, right? Fucked-her-so- / hard-she?

Kelly   Wow, you remember that?

Peter   We talked about him half the night, how could I forget?! Coming up with our little theories about him – *Tim* thought he should go on Prozac, of course.

Kelly   How *is* Tim? Nice to hear his name . . .

Peter   Tim's well, he's well. Just went back to Los Angeles, yesterday actually – school's starting in a month, month and a half, so . . .

Kelly   You guys were here . . . ?

Peter   He just came to visit – I've been here – I'm doing a play . . . ?

Kelly   *That's* right.

Peter   *Long Day's Journey into Night* –

Kelly   Of course – in the letter you – yes.

Peter   So . . . he was out for the opening in April, then came back after school got out . . . I've been here since *February*, God.

Kelly   I remember now. So you've been here a while!

Peter   Yeah, it has been . . .

Kelly   And Tim went back to get ready for school?

Peter   Another year of figuring out how to get inner-city eighth-graders interested in *Romeo and Juliet*. Hopeless . . .

Kelly   – You should go to his class, do a dramatic reading.

Peter   I suggested that! But he has this idea that it would be "disruptive." Since I'm "famous."

Kelly   I can see that.

Peter   Oh, please, my movie *tanked*. Did you see it?

Kelly   You know – I usually wait for the / DVD –

Peter   Oh God, it was *so* stinky – oh!

Kelly   Really? I've always been curious about that process – because I remember you said it was a good script. So how does it become a bad / movie?

Peter   Right – I was just about to start shooting, on Craig's last night, we talked about it . . . Why are we – who cares about my career, how boring!

Kelly   It's not boring to *me* –

Peter   To me it's like the least interesting – I guess we all get bored talking about work. Of course *I* want to know about fucked-her-so-hard-she, you probably find talking about *that* boring.

Kelly   I can't believe you remember that. You have such / a good –

Peter   We had such an interesting debate on how you should handle him! *I* thought he was lying just to sound interesting, Tim thought he was self-medicating – Craig didn't think he was *lying*, just that he wanted to torture you – and didn't actually want to get better.

Kelly   Craig the expert –

Peter   Fucked-her-so-hard-she . . . What happened with him, how did things turn / out?

Kelly   – I have to say, I hated that nickname Craig gave him. It was so crass.

Peter   But – wasn't that how the guy himself – didn't he, say, like –

Kelly   It was how he would phrase his conquests –

Peter   Which is all he ever would talk about, right? And he would always use the same phrase – "I fucked her so hard she came six times."

Kelly   Yes –

Peter   "I fucked her so hard she started crying." – "I fucked her so hard she – woke up my ninety-year-old hearing-impaired neighbor" –

Kelly   Well – he didn't go *that* far. – You know, it slipped my mind a second ago – but I have to say – I read a number of just incredible reviews for the play. You opened in April you said?

Peter *makes "masturbation" motion.*

Kelly   What.

Peter   It's a terrible production.

Kelly   No.

Peter *nods.*

Kelly   I had made a plan to come and just never got around / to it –

Peter   You're not missing anything.

Kelly   What's – wrong with it?

Peter   It's not true.

Pause.

Kelly   I'm sorry to hear that.

Peter   Yeah. "Oh well!" (*Smiles.*) The "drama" is actually – I'm still kind of in shock, I think – but the drama is that I walked offstage tonight – in the middle of the show.

Pause.

Kelly   Oh.

Peter Yeah.

Kelly I was going to – because I remember it being a pretty long / play –

Peter Yeah.

Pause.

Kelly Is your tea okay . . . ?

Peter No, it's because there isn't any sugar. I don't want to drink it.

Kelly Oh – would you like / some –

Peter No – I can't.

Pause.

Yeah. Right before the intermission – my dad is calling me from offstage, "Come on, Edmund!" I make my exit and there he is – Tyrone, John Conrad – you know him, right? Very big / man –

Kelly Mm-hmm –

Peter So he sort of beckons me over, like, with this look on his face like he has a joke to tell me, or some little piece of gossip. So I go over, I lean into him, he grabs my shoulder and whispers into my ear, "I have a piece of advice for you." He says, "You're never – "

Pause.

He says, "You're never going to be a good actor till you stop sucking cock."

Kelly Oh.

Peter Applause, act's over, I'm standing there *stunned*, he's looking at me and smiling this, this *smile*, and then he takes me, it's sort of like he's shoving me aside, but, like, *really* hard – I'm off balance and I go flying into the wall and really, *really* hurt myself, which he sees, and he just keeps walking off. Just goes.

Kelly   Oh, Peter.

Peter   I thought about going to the stage manager, telling her what happened, but she wouldn't be able to do anything until tomorrow, and John is the star, and no one else *saw*, so he can just *lie* and – you know, in rehearsals, with John, and Scott, the director – I talked about *Dad* dying of leukemia, I talked about *Craig* dying in Iraq, I – and so I'm in my dressing room at this point, all alone, imagining having to go back out there with this man and pour my heart out to him and – I looked in the mirror and I just grabbed my stuff and left.

Pause.

Kelly   You did the right thing.

Peter   I didn't, though – I should have gone to the stage manager. I fucked up the whole second half of the / show.

Kelly   You can do all the formal stuff tomorrow – I'm sure you have an understudy.

Peter   *Drew.* He like does coke and gets escorts, I don't even think he knows the lines.

Kelly   Well. You'll straighten it out tomorrow.

Pause.

Peter   Then the *other* thing is – I broke up with Tim last night.

Kelly   You broke up with / Tim?

Peter's *mobile rings, he checks it.*

Peter   I should . . .

Kelly *nods.* **Peter** *gestures towards the bedroom.* **Kelly** *nods again.* **Peter** *answers the phone as he moves into the bedroom, off . . .*

Two

Night. **Kelly** *cleans up.* **Craig** *comes out of the bedroom, helps.*

Craig   He's wasted.

Kelly   He's wasted? He didn't drink that much.

Craig   He's passed out . . .

Kelly   He just had two cups of coffee!

Craig   Yeah, with enough sugar to light up a room full of third-graders.

Kelly   Well, he *can't* be passed out for long.

Craig   It's ridiculous at his age. Ever since he was little – used to pour sugar on top of his Frosted Flakes, drove Dad crazy –

Kelly   *Ohhh.*

Craig   What?

Kelly   I bet he took a Xanax.

Craig   A Xanax?

Kelly   You were in the bathroom. Tim had Xanax for the plane, he hates flying.

Craig   What happened when I was in the bathroom?

Kelly   We were talking about Black Hawks –

Craig   Yeah –

Kelly   You got up to pee, and Tim said he couldn't imagine doing what you did because he couldn't even fly on a *commercial* plane without taking a Xanax. Then he took a bottle out of his pocket and shook it for effect.

Craig   "Shook it for effect"?

Kelly   It was cute.

Craig   So Peter took one?

Kelly   Not at the table – I'm just guessing – at some point.

Craig   But they're not prescribed to him.

Pause.

Kelly   *Well* . . .

Craig   That's a powerful drug! He's not a doctor. I bet this shit flows in Hollywood / like fucking –

Kelly   One Xanax, I mean –

Craig   Yeah, one Xanax and he's so fucked up he can't even talk, he's in there *drooling*.

Pause.

Kelly   So maybe he took two.

Craig   Why are you being flip? You're against these drugs.

Kelly   In my *work* – when people medicate so they don't have to look at their problems – not as a once-in-a-while / thing.

Craig   I'm going to Fort Benning in the morning and now I can't even say goodbye to him!

Pause.

Kelly   I'm sorry. How are you feeling?

Craig   A little agitated. I mean I'm *fine* . . . How are you?

Kelly   All things considered . . .

Craig   Yeah?

Pause.

I guess it was a nice night.

Kelly   It was.

Craig   He was nervous, but – I thought he'd be much worse.

Kelly   Peter or Tim?

Craig   Peter.

Kelly   You really do overestimate his attachment to you.

Craig   I know you think that –

Kelly   I think you need to be on the outside to see it. He's not seven anymore, copying the way you walk and talk. Look at when we were talking about Iraq – we really got into it!

Craig (*a realization*)   I think *I* was more nervous than I expected.

Kelly   Really? You didn't seem nervous to me.

Craig   No?

Kelly   At most I would say – you were a little more "animated" than usual.

Craig   I thought it got most intense when we were talking about his career. That's where I felt maybe I went too far.

Kelly   It's amazing, isn't it? Peter's gonna be a movie star! He's gonna be rich!

Craig   That movie sounded so fucking offensive.

Kelly   Yeah, but I agree with Peter, within the confines of what they / make today –

Craig   That's the thing. You start telling yourself / that –

Kelly   But think why we don't have any Brandos or James Deans anymore – they're not, it's all so corporate-controlled, nobody's writing parts that a Brando or a – imagine Marlon Brando doing *Titanic*. James Dean in *Lord of the Rings*, I mean –

Craig   But I'm talking about – yes, all the capitalist, corporate, I know Peter's not going to be in *Rebel without a Cause* his first movie out – but I'm talking about Peter saying he thought the movie was *good*. *That's* what makes / me –

Kelly   Within the *confines* of what they produce today.

Craig   But that's exactly what – why can't he just say, "It's a bad movie, it's a piece of shit, but I have to start somewhere"? What does that mean, "good within the confines"? You could say that about any movie, basically. Peter's too smart to start thinking that / way –

Kelly   Well, we don't know anything about the movie.

Craig   Yeah, but from what he said – "special forces" – "covert operations" – come on. I mean, do the movie, fine, but don't trick yourself about what it is.

Pause.

Kelly   I think it was a good night.

Craig   Yeah . . . Yeah. Why not? Let's call it a good night.

Kelly   It was.

Craig   Just . . . I wanted to say goodbye in a more formal way.

Kelly   So wake him up.

Craig   Nah, moment's gone.

Pause.

Kelly   You brought up fucked-her-so-hard-she, that threw me for a loop.

Craig   Oh God – it just came out . . .

Kelly   Out of *nowhere* . . .

Craig   I was thinking out loud. – I was pretty drunk there, till you put the coffee on.

Kelly   Why were you thinking about *him*?

Craig   Just – I don't know, you're seeing him in the morning –

Kelly   So?

Craig   Just – crossed my mind.

Pause.

Kelly I forgot for a second.

Craig What?

Kelly Morning . . .

Pause.

Craig At least it got Tim talking, finally.

Kelly What?

Craig Fucked-her-so-hard-she. Tim thought he was "clinically depressed."

Kelly He was very articulate, I thought.

Craig No, yeah – I liked him. Did you like him?

Kelly Oh, definitely! They're great together.

Craig Yeah . . . A little quiet . . .

Kelly I'm sure he was *nervous* – meeting his boyfriend's identical *twin* –

Craig No, I know . . . You didn't think anything was off with him?

Kelly No, not at all.

Craig I don't know, I had this little nagging, like – just this feeling that something was off. Like – like I couldn't picture them fucking.

Kelly Craig!

Craig Just, the vibe wasn't – whatever, he's better than The Psychopath.

Kelly Oh, Craig.

Craig I know you had a soft spot for him –

Kelly I actually didn't – but Adam was not a psychopath. He had *quirks*, he had *issues* –

Craig Quirks?

Kelly Whatever you want to call them. His personality was
affected by the abuse he suffered. That doesn't make / him a –

Craig The abuse he *claimed* to have suffered.

Kelly Well, we don't know if he did or not.

Craig Wait – I thought you told Peter it never happened,
the abuse.

Kelly I told Peter it was *possible* it never happened.
I / can't –

Craig That's not what he told me – he told me you told
him you thought Adam made it up.

Kelly Well . . . that's not what I said.

Craig So you think it's possible that Adam's older brother
forced him to give blow jobs to all the boys in the
neighborhood, every day after school for two years, when he
was six years / old –

Kelly I think it's unlikely. But what I told Peter is that the
memories could be an elaboration of something *less* severe
that *did* happen. Or a fantasy that he got mixed up with
reality because he was so young at the time / he –

Craig – Or a lie. Meant to make Peter feel guilty, so he'd
never dump Adam.

Kelly Or that. – The point is, even if it isn't in any way
literally true, the fact that Adam goes around telling people
that this happened means he feels that something traumatic
did happen to him when he was a boy, and that this "story" is
the only way he has of communicating that trauma. You
know, his parents were clearly very / disturbed –

Craig See – this is what worries me about you. You're the
same way with fucked-her-so-hard-she, you're so passive, or
finding / ways to –

Kelly Can you stop calling him that now?

Craig   What?

Kelly   It was one thing when it was just between us, but –
he's a human being.

Craig   I'm just saying – if you know someone is
manipulating you, then you should tell them, Look, I know
what you're doing, stop it.

Kelly   Even if he *were* manipulating me – if I said that, he
would never come back to therapy!

Craig   So what! At least this way he would know, he would
have to walk around knowing that someone knew the truth!

Kelly   The purpose of therapy is to help someone change,
not just / face the truth –

Craig   That's what I'm saying – people like that don't want
to change, they just want to see what they can get away
with –

Kelly   Stop.

Pause.

This always happens when we talk seriously about my work.

Craig   We don't talk seriously about your work.

Kelly   Exactly, / because

Craig   Okay –

Kelly   you treat me like I'm this ridiculous person. Which
does not make me feel *good*, or *loved*, / or –

Craig   Okay –

Kelly   Every time we talk about therapy or money, you get
revved up, you / start getting –

Craig   Money?

Kelly   Yes – like tonight, when Tim started talking about his upbringing, you did the exact same thing you used to do when Adam would talk about growing up on the Upper East Side, or skiing in Aspen –

Craig   Adam – / no –

Kelly   You turned off. You did. I think *that's* what was "off" to you about Tim – that he comes from money. It's why you have problems with my *dad*, it's why *therapy* / bothers you –

Craig   Problems with your dad?

Kelly   When you criticize his lifestyle, his / attitude –

Craig   My problem with your dad is that he didn't love you. And the thing that was off to me about Tim – was that they didn't leave together.

Pause.

Kelly   I did think that was weird.

Pause.

Maybe Peter wanted to say goodbye to you alone.

Craig   Then why did he . . . ? I don't know, something didn't feel right.

Kelly   I'm sure that's it.

Pause.

Craig   – I also thought it was weird how much his phone kept ringing. Agents and managers call so late? How many times do they need to call?

Pause.

Kelly   Speaking of late . . .

Pause.

Craig   Yeah . . .

Pause.

Okay. Do up the couch, I'll move Peter out / here –

Kelly   What?

Craig   What?

Kelly   He's *staying*?

Craig   On the couch . . .

Kelly   Craig – I said, if he comes, is this going to turn into an all-night thing? You said / no –

Craig   Kelly, he can't even –

Kelly   You said no. *Craig* –

Craig   Okay –

Pause.

Okay. I'll call him a car.

Pause.

Kelly   Thank you.

Pause. **Craig** *kisses* **Kelly**. *He goes into the bedroom, off.*

Three

Kelly *watches TV.* **Peter** *comes out of the bedroom.*

Peter   You painted!

Kelly   Oh – yeah.

Peter   White!

Kelly   Brighten things up . . .

Peter   It looks good. – I'm interrupting your *Law and Order*.

Kelly   Oh, I can watch it whenever.

Peter   Tivo?

Kelly   Yeah. I programmed it to record *Law and Order* whenever it's on – an endless / stream –

Peter   I see mine rerun all the time, it's so humiliating.

Kelly   You're kidding! Why have I never seen it?

Peter   Skater pothead: "Wha? Naw, man, I wasn't in the park that night."

Kelly   Very good!

Peter (*sitting*)   Please – the casting director just wanted to fuck me. I told him I couldn't skate, he said, "Oh, it's okay, there's not much skating" – they send me the shooting script, of course I'm on a skateboard in *every* scene.

Kelly   I used to not like *Law and Order*, but then it really started to grow on me.

Peter   Oh yeah?

Kelly   I have this theory about / it –

Peter   When did you start watching all this TV, I don't remember you being a big TV person.

Kelly   Yeah, I never was before.

Peter   Was it after Craig died?

Pause.

Kelly   Maybe – when I couldn't sleep I'd watch TV, I'd / watch –

Peter   I had trouble sleeping –

Kelly   – these shows –

Peter   The worst time for me was actually *months* after – when the official report came out that said it was an accident. After that I just couldn't sleep for some reason.

Kelly   Yeah, the grief comes at different times, it's so unpredictable. – But I came up with this theory – would you like to hear / it?

Peter   Oh, definitely!

Kelly   Well, I realized that all these shows, all the *Law and Order*s and all the rip-offs, have the same exact structure: someone dies, and a whole team of specialists springs up to figure out how to solve the mystery of the person's death.

Peter   Right?

Kelly   Which I think is a fantasy people have – that they won't be forgotten. That their death won't just be accepted and mourned, but that an entire *community* will come together, all these special people – lawyers and scientists and forensics experts, judges, detectives – who are devoted, who will not stop until the mystery of the death is solved. And therefore symbolically reversed.

Peter   Wow!

Kelly   Only took me six thousand episodes to figure it out.

Peter   Good use of *insomnia* . . . It's weird with me, lately – I've been *sleeping* fine, but then out of nowhere, doing the play, like – like the other night. I had this fantasy, this image almost, of a Black Hawk helicopter crashing through the ceiling of the theater.

Kelly   While you were onstage?

Peter   At the curtain call – and curtain calls have always been kind of weird for me, I sort of forget who I am – am I me, or am I the character? But lately, it's like – I feel like *Craig* in the curtain call. And I thought – well, it makes sense, that's how I started acting, when I was little, I would pretend that I was him . . . So maybe it's a delayed grief reaction, like?

Kelly   It may be . . .

Peter   Tim thinks I have post-traumatic stress disorder, keeps bugging me to see his shrink. But I'm like, no – if this is grief, these "moments" – then I should feel it, right? I don't want to medicate my grief away . . .

Kelly   I'm not a psychiatrist. But I think Tim is right, it does sound like you should see one.

Peter   Really, you think? Huh. That surprises me. I'll think about it then . . .

Pause.

I'm sorry – I feel a little silly asking this, but – are you moving?

Pause.

Kelly   You mean – all the boxes in the / bedroom –

Peter   Not that you wouldn't *tell* me, I / just –

Kelly   I felt like my life had a lot of clutter, that's all.

Peter   Oh, you're putting some things –

Kelly   In storage, clearing space . . .

Peter   . . . painting . . .

Kelly   So . . .

Peter   That's good . . . Hey, you know, I know I mentioned to you – I don't know if you remember – at the funeral? I mentioned Craig's emails? From Iraq?

Kelly   Yeah – I remember your mentioning them . . .

Peter   I just realized, I actually have them with me.

Pause.

Kelly   Uh-huh?

Peter   I keep them at the theater, I read them before shows, and I just grabbed them before I left tonight. Sort of instinctively . . .

Kelly   Right . . .

Peter   I know – I remember at the funeral your telling me you and Craig didn't email while he was over there, you just talked on the phone – something about the distance . . .

Kelly   Email felt weird to me – not intimate.

Peter   Hearing his voice . . .

Kelly   Felt more –

Peter   Right, yeah. But it must – do you ever – now that he's gone, do you ever wish you had anything down on paper, that you could look at, or . . . ?

Kelly   I have other things . . .

Peter   Yeah . . . I guess, too, you were used to distance. I mean – in a way it must seem like he might even be coming back. It's only been a year. He was on active duty four years after you guys finished Harvard, that's such a long time to be away from each other –

Kelly   Well, but I always knew that that would be over someday. There was a very definite timetable when he would be done. Plus he wasn't fighting. So it was always in the background that he'd be coming back . . . which – isn't the case anymore.

Peter   Right – and you were in grad school, and becoming a therapist, so you were also really busy then, you weren't as settled as you are now . . .

Kelly   Exactly.

Peter   I remember when he got called up again, I thought – because he had done his four years, it's like – I knew you go on Inactive Ready Reserves after, but I just assumed he was done. Starting his life finally, writing his dissertation . . . He never complained, though.

Kelly   He felt a lot of loyalty to the army – ROTC paid for school. He couldn't have gone to Harvard without it.

Peter   Well, he also believed in the war. There was that also.

Pause.

I think it's so sad he never finished his PhD. Do you still have all his Faulkner research?

Kelly   I sent it to your mom.

Peter   Really? She never told me that. Typical. God, for a woman who wanted both her sons to get out of the Midwest, she's never stopped resenting us for it. She hasn't come to see my / *play* –

Kelly   You think it's that?

Peter   What?

Kelly   You think she resents you because you left your –

Peter   Oh, the social-class thing, definitely, anything to do with being *educated*, *cultured*, makes her – I think that was a big reason she didn't – not that she didn't, doesn't *like* you, / but –

Kelly   But isn't it also – very generally, that she resents that her life didn't turn out the way she planned, her husband dying, her son – I mean, she pushed you and Craig very hard in school, didn't she? So you could / get out of –

Peter   Oh, and took us to theater, and took us to museums – but she didn't want us to be cultured so much as she just wanted us to be able to get away from Dad. When he got back from Vietnam I think she knew something was – even from pictures you can tell. But she wasn't going to leave him, they had us – so she pushed us to excel, go away to school . . . but once we *did* that – she resented / us.

Kelly   I see. I thought maybe she hadn't told you about the dissertation because it reminds her of everything – that hasn't turned out right.

Pause.

Peter   He was such a good writer. These emails – they could be published. I've thought about maybe trying to make them into a one-man show. I don't know if I'd play him. I guess it would make the most sense for me to, but – feels a little – also – they're so intimate, I don't know if I'd want to share them with people. I haven't shown them to anyone.

Pause.

I'd – love to share them with you if you . . .

Kelly   Oh. That's . . . you know, I just don't think I'm ready.

Pause.

Peter   I understand.

Pause.

You can really see in them how much he learned from you, I think . . . just, his emotions and . . . it's hard because, you didn't know him before you met him obviously, but – the way he blossomed with you – especially after you got married . . . God, it's just about three years, right?

Kelly   Just about. September . . .

Peter   Wow. I remember when you guys finally got engaged, him calling me up to tell me – God, I was so happy. Because I was getting – I was definitely, like, let's hurry it up here!

Kelly   We had always talked about it – he just wanted to wait till he was done with active duty.

Peter   – I also think Dad getting sick definitely – gave him some perspective . . . And 9/11 . . .

Pause.

It's so great that Dad got to see you get married. He looked so happy that day – so cute, so frail and gentle . . . Mom was such a cunt to you at his funeral, do you remember?

Kelly   Of course I remember. I was "too loud" in the receiving line – I barely said a word.

Pause.

Was that your director who called before? Is / everything –

Peter   No, I haven't called him back yet, he just left me a voicemail – I was talking to Tim, actually. He's emailing me all this information on PTSD, so . . .

Pause.

Kelly   I owe you an apology, Peter.

Peter   Uh-huh?

Kelly   I know how important it was to you that I stay in touch. I told you at the funeral that I would – and I didn't.

Peter   Oh, thank you . . . no, definitely, I mean – I'd be lying if I said . . . part of me, you know, definitely did the play hoping being in the same city would make us . . . you know, even if it meant going away from Tim, and pissing off my agents . . . make us close again.

Pause.

Kelly   Your letter really – it really did touch me. I should have responded.

Peter   . . . I knew it was a really big thing I was proposing, so I kind of – I expected you to say no, or at least – that you'd need time to think about it . . . But – yeah, you know? I asked you to have a *baby*, I mean, *some* kind of acknowledgment –

Kelly   I know.

Pause.

Peter   I hate to do this, but I should call Scott back before it gets too late, is that okay?

Kelly   Sure.

Peter   Thanks.

He takes out his mobile and goes back into the bedroom.

Four

Craig *comes out of the bedroom.*

Kelly   Hey.

Craig   So, I don't think Peter's gonna make it home
tonight.

Pause.

Kelly   Why not?

Craig   I've been trying to get him up for fifteen / minutes –

Kelly   Craig –

Craig   I don't know what else to / do.

Kelly   Wake him up.

Pause.

Call a car, I'll help you get / him –

Craig   What's the big deal if he just crashes on the couch?

Kelly   *I don't want him here.*

Pause.

Craig   You don't want him / here.

Kelly   I don't want him / here.

Craig   Why don't you / want him –

Kelly   All right, what's happening?

Pause.

Craig   What?

Kelly   Something is happening –

Craig   So say it then, what?

Kelly   You don't want to be alone with me.

Pause.

Craig   That's not true, Kelly. I'm going to *Iraq*, my brother
/ is –

Kelly   You're going to *Georgia*.

Craig   I'm going to Georgia, and then I'm going to Iraq. What, you think I'm being dramatic?

Kelly   Yes, I do.

Craig   Look, he's not – I don't feel right just throwing him in a car –

Kelly   Why not?

Craig   Because I think – he's scared, and I don't think he should have to wake up alone in the morning / like I –

Kelly   You keep saying he's scared – we talked about the war half the night, he didn't sound scared at all. He sounded very confident –

Craig   We were talking about politics, not me leaving.

Kelly   But if he was so scared, I really don't think he would have been able to disagree with you the way he / did.

Craig   That's not even – he was just putting on a show for Tim.

Pause.

Kelly   What?

Craig   Tim's against the war, so – whatever, the point is, whatever he said / when we were –

Kelly   No, what do you mean, "putting on a show"?

Craig   Tim's – that's actually not how Peter feels, Peter is not "against" the war, he was just saying that for Tim's sake.

Kelly   What . . . ?

Craig   He – Peter told me that because *Tim* marches against the war, and because all their *friends* are against it, it's just easier for him to keep quiet about how he really feels.

Kelly   So – everything he was saying – was / just –

Craig   His feelings are complicated. He's against the
administration, but the actual war he thinks is worth fighting.
Tim doesn't feel that way, *obviously*, / so –

Kelly   Wait – is *that* what this is about?

Craig   What?

Kelly   Are you acting this way because I agreed with Tim?

Pause.

Craig   Acting what way?

Kelly   Not wanting to be alone with me –

Craig   Kelly, I *do* want to be alone with / you –

Kelly   I could tell you were getting pissed, I just thought it
was something to do with Tim. Is that why you were so pissed
off? Because I was / saying that –

Craig   We *have* never really talked about the war in the
terms we did tonight.

Kelly   Yes we have.

Craig   *I* recall your saying to me that it would be good for
Saddam to be out of power – when the war started. You
disagreed with how we got into it, but you felt the Iraqis /
would benefit –

Kelly   What?

Craig   When we watched Tony Blair with Bush,
remember? You said how articulate he was –

Kelly   Craig, I said it was a *fake* war that they were *lying*
about to get us into –

Craig   You don't remember when we watched Blair?

Kelly   I was – *theoretically*, we were talking about human
rights in *general* –

Craig   And I remember you more or less agreeing with me.

Kelly   I was sympathetic – in the *abstract* – to the "idea" of human rights – I mean, what, did you expect me to argue for Saddam Hussein? Oh, this is ridiculous, you're purposefully / misremembering!

A mobile phone rings once. Both look vaguely to it. Pause.

Now I'm wondering what *else* I've said to you that you're unclear on.

Craig   What does *that* mean?

Kelly   I'm wondering about our having a *baby* . . .

Pause.

Craig   What about it?

Kelly   I don't know! I thought we were / clear about –

Craig   We just talked about it tonight – when I get back, when I finish / school –

Kelly   In front of *Peter.*

Craig   What . . . ?

Kelly   *Peter* brought it up, *Peter* asked if we were going to have a baby – were you saying it just to please him?

Craig   Kelly, we've talked about this a hundred times – I want to wait till I'm teaching, I don't want to take any more money from your father.

Kelly   I still don't see what the big deal is –

Craig   The big deal is, he's a *cock.*

Pause.

– Jesus! We talked about starting a family – sitting right on this couch, looking out at the *cloud of death* hanging over / the city –

Kelly   Please, please don't invoke / that –

Craig Why not? That day is seared into my – every single thing we said to one / another!

Kelly You know what? I'm tired, I want to go to sleep. I'll sleep on the couch – (*Goes to couch.*) Go sleep with your brother.

Craig Oh, fuck you!

He gets his keys, moves to apartment door.

Kelly Where are you going?

Craig For a walk.

Kelly Craig –

Craig *opens door.*

Kelly Craig – don't go –

Craig *stops. Pause.*

Kelly *approaches him. He shuts door. Turns. Pause.* **Kelly** *leans in, kisses* **Craig**. *Pause. He kisses back. The kiss grows . . .*

Mobile phone bleeps once. **Craig** *looks to it.* **Kelly** *keeps kissing him.* **Craig** *detaches himself and goes to the phone. Picks it up. Pause.*

Craig What?

Reads:

"Did Tim leave yet. Horny."

He looks up at **Kelly**.

Adam.

Pause.

Kelly You don't know what it means. It could just be a – like a joke or something.

Craig A *joke*?

Kelly Like he teases him by sending him texts like that.

Pause.

What?

Pause.

What?

Craig *looks at the phone again a moment, then puts it down. He gets up, goes to kitchen, opens cabinet, drawer . . .*

Kelly   What are you –

Craig *grabs a pot and a spoon, goes into the bedroom, off.* **Kelly** *stands.*

Offstage sounds of the spoon hitting the pot loudly. After some time **Peter** *comes out of the bedroom. Stumbles. Sees* **Kelly***, smiles.*

Peter   Hey . . . sorry . . .

He grabs jacket, starts to go. **Kelly** *sees phone.*

Kelly   Don't forget your phone.

Peter *(turns)*   Oh – thanks.

He goes to the phone. **Kelly** *moves to bedroom door.* **Peter** *puts phone in pocket, moves to door.* **Kelly** *turns to* **Peter***.*

Kelly   I think someone might have texted you while you were asleep.

Peter   Oh.

Pause. **Kelly** *goes into the bedroom, off.* **Peter** *takes phone from pocket, checks it. Then goes out the door, off.*

Pause.

The bedroom door opens. **Craig** *comes out, goes to the couch, curls into it. Grips himself tight.*

Pause. **Kelly** *follows.*

Kelly   Craig.

Pause.

Craig, what's happening?

Moves to **Craig**. *He curls more tightly into himself, burrows deeper into the couch.* **Kelly** *turns and goes back into the bedroom, off.*

Five

Kelly *watches TV.* **Peter** *comes out of the bedroom.*

Peter   Jon Stewart!

Kelly (*turns*)   My other Tivo favorite.

Peter   Yeah, he's funny. But it's weird – I was at a party a couple nights ago? And this guy starts saying Bush is as bad as Hitler. *Then* he starts talking about how hilarious *The Daily Show* is. And I thought – if you were in Germany in the 1930s, would you watch a show where some smartass made fun of Hitler? Little mustache jokes while he's throwing Jews in the ovens? I mean, if you really think George Bush is evil, then how can you laugh at "George Bush is dumb" jokes?

Kelly   It's the sensibility. The sensibility comes closer to conveying the truth than the real news does, I think that's what people respond to.

Peter   Yeah, but whose truth is being conveyed? Jon Stewart has so much privilege, I think it's a pretty small slice of the "truth" he's conveying. Like when I watch him make fun of evangelicals – if you really care about the truth, you can't just speak to your own tiny group, you have to figure out how to speak to the community.

Kelly   The community . . . ?

Peter   People who may not be like you but that you still have – something in common with. A basic humanity. Even if they *do* believe in God, or believe in the war in Iraq. Go to the Indiana State Fair – those are the people we need to figure out how to talk to. They're not going away, we can't just make fun of them. Don't you think?

Kelly   But aren't they beyond reach? These people think the Rapture is coming. They think people like us are going to burn in Hell – literally.

Peter   But that's the – that was one thing about Craig. He could talk to those army guys like – it didn't matter, Harvard, all the books he read – he never forgot where he came from. He knew that these people, whatever insane things they believed – he thought you could reach into the core of them, and find something deeper and truer than all the surface stuff, God and politics and all that.

Kelly   I don't know – God and politics go pretty deep.

Peter (*mostly conceding*)   Yes and no . . .

Kelly   He thought we could reach the Iraqis too. Do you think he was right about that?

Pause.

Peter   I hear you. I just don't want to write people off, I guess. I mean, how do you feel as a therapist? Someone comes to you with all these problems, doing all these bad things to themselves, to other people . . . you have to believe that there's a way to reach them, right? No matter how awful or crazy they seem . . .

Pause.

Kelly   No, I agree . . . What did your director say? Is everything okay?

Peter   I chickened out, I still haven't called him. I was just leaving messages for my agents, and my manager, and my lawyer.

Kelly   Your publicist is out of town?

Peter   I really should have gone to the stage manager.

Kelly   I think you're the last person who needs to be questioning his actions tonight –

Peter   I kind of – I don't know . . . Scott – the director – on opening night – God knows what I was thinking, but . . . Tim had left the party, he doesn't like staying out late – and I was really drunk, and Tim doesn't have much of a sex drive because of the Paxil and – I ended up following Scott into the bathroom – and – honestly – seduced him and – while it was happening, Drew, my understudy, came into the bathroom and saw – Scott blowing me, basically. So, I'm sure word got around to the company, I'm sure John heard . . .

Kelly   Oh.

Pause.

Peter   And – I might as well just put it all out there – I've been sleeping with Adam still. – So, basically, that's my life.

Pause.

You're moving, aren't you?

Pause. **Kelly** *turns off the TV. She looks at* **Peter***, nods.*

Peter   When?

Kelly   Next week.

Peter   Next *week*. Where?

Kelly   I have a good friend from school, in Ann Arbor. She's just been through a divorce. I'm going to go up there for a while.

Peter   What about your practice?

Kelly   I referred everyone.

Pause.

Peter . Why couldn't you . . . did I *do* something that made you not want to talk to me, / or –

Kelly   It's just me. I haven't wanted contact with anybody.

Pause.

I didn't know you were in this much pain, Peter. I'm sorry.

Peter   Oh, it's all – drama. I'm fine, really. I'm so sorry
you've been – I mean, I figured things were tough, that's why
you hadn't . . . I think I had the idea because, just, being in
the play made me – I had all these hopes going into it, but it
turned out to be like *Long Day's Journey to the Hamptons* – actors
constantly checking messages, luxurious spreads of pastries
at every rehearsal, Scott taking up all this time telling stories
about which Hollywood actors have big dicks – I wanted to
scream! The play is like being in a *war*, these people are trying
to kill each other – literally! My father won't spend money
on treatment for my TB, for the sanitarium! And no one was
taking it seriously . . . So I sort of – would retreat into my own
little world, and read Craig's emails . . . they were so
inspiring, I mean, just – this extraordinary thing of him
turning against the war, you know? And I kept thinking of the
two of you, how much you had wanted a / child –

Kelly   Turning against the war?

Peter   Yeah – Did you – ? I was wondering if that was
something he could even talk about –

Kelly   Not – there were limits to what he could say, he /
wasn't –

Peter   So you had no – Oh, Kelly – reading the emails is
like – this *awakening*, it's like the birth of this whole other
person! I know you said you're not ready – but if you ever
do want to read them – just – please – any time . . .

Kelly   Thank you – I might some day.

Pause. **Peter** *smiles at* **Kelly**. *Looks away.*

Peter   It's late, I should get going. Big day tomorrow, God
only / knows –

Kelly   Are you – where are / you –

Peter *goes to his bag.*

Peter   – If you have email in Ann Arbor, I really would like
to stay in / touch –

Kelly   – It's late, stay here.

She looks at **Peter**. *Pause.*

Peter   Okay!

Kelly   Take the bedroom. In the morning I'll make some pancakes.

Peter   Eeek, pancakes.

Kelly   Oh, right. What can you – I can make them without / sugar –

Peter   Ah, fuck it – pancakes! With *gobs* of maple syrup –

They laugh. Pause.

I'm – glad we could be honest with each other.

Kelly   Me too.

Peter   Yeah. – Just – gonna use the bathroom . . .

He goes into the bathroom, off. **Kelly** *takes the bedsheet off the box and goes to the couch. Sees* **Peter***'s bag. Goes to it, unzips it, looks in. Begins to reach in. Toilet flushes.* **Kelly** *zips up the bag, moves away.* **Peter** *comes out of the bathroom, takes his bag.*

Peter   You know – I really don't mind sleeping on the couch.

Kelly   Please – take the bedroom.

Peter   You sure?

Kelly   I'm sure.

Peter   Okay. – G'night.

He moves towards the bedroom.

Kelly   Can I – . . .

Peter *turns.*

Kelly   I think part of my hesitation with – the emails, your asking if you could share them with me before – I think because they were written to *you* I feel – that it's really not /my –

Peter   Oh, no, I'm *sure* Craig would have wanted me to share them with you.

Pause.

Kelly   Then I think I – I would like to / read them if it's –

Peter   Oh, of course, absolutely. (*Opens bag.*) There's one in particular I've most wanted you to . . . (*Picks one.*) I *think* this is the – they all blur together a little . . .

Sits down, as if to begin reading. **Kelly** *does not move to sit.*

Kelly   Oh.

Peter   Is it okay if I read it to you?

Kelly   It's not . . . I can read it.

Peter   Oh, you'd rather . . . I just thought it would be – I guess I'm so eager to *share* . . .

Pause.

Kelly   If you'd – sure.

Peter   Is that okay?

Kelly   Sure.

She sits.

Peter   Okay. If it gets to be too much or anything – just tell me, I'll stop.

Pause.

Lieutenant Conners.

Reads:

"Abu Ghraib is already a punch line; I'll spare you the jokes.
For about five minutes we all felt the truth of it but that
feeling got swept away in the hot desert wind like every other
emotion here." – A little Faulknerian. "From what I can tell,
it's not a big deal at home either. I think Abu Ghraib would
only hurt Bush if it were pictures of Americans jerking off and
smeared with shit; as long as it's Iraqis it can only help.
There's a real comfort in the images – that we're the powerful
ones, in control, alive, clothed. I had a memory the other
night of the time Dad put his fist through the car windshield.
Do you remember? I can't believe I forgot, and at times I
wonder if I made it up somehow. But I recall so vividly Mom
telling us when she was taking us to school the next day that it
was a Vietnam flashback. We couldn't have been older than
six. We were coming back from dinner, Dad was driving,
Mom was saying something to him – and suddenly there was
a crunch. I looked up and the windshield was like a
spiderweb, and there was Dad's bleeding fist, gripping the
steering wheel tight . . . I looked over at Mom and I
remember thinking that she was going to look a certain way,
upset or scared . . . but instead I saw her grinning. A little
creeping grin on her face. I looked over at you. You were
looking out the window like you hadn't noticed anything, so
I punched you in the arm. You said, 'Ow,' and Dad looked
back for a second, then turned back to the road. That's all
I remember. I think I've remembered this now, after so many
years, because what I learned in that instant – that to be
married to a man so powerful he could put his fist through
glass was what made our mother smile – is exactly how I feel
here: so powerful I can't stop smiling, while suffering a wound
I do not feel."

Pause. He looks up.

Kelly   Jesus.

Peter   No memory.

Kelly   You don't remember that at all?

Peter   Vague memory of Craig hitting me and Dad not doing anything. But that happened all the time.

Kelly   Craig would hit you?

Peter   It was weird. When Dad would hit me, Craig would yell at him to stop. But then Craig would hit me a lot too. When I would go tell Dad, he wouldn't do anything. And when I would go tell Mom she would say, "Go tell your father."

Pause.

Kelly   I'm sorry.

Peter   Oh, you know, everyone has a childhood. – Craig told me once – your dad abused you?

Kelly   Emotionally.

Peter   He was never really specific . . .

Kelly   Neither was my father.

Peter   You mean . . .

Kelly   He wasn't around, he was having affairs, he bought me lots of things I didn't want . . . my mother was on too much Valium to care.

Peter   I'm sorry.

Kelly *nods. Pause.*

Peter   Is this okay? Should I / keep –

Kelly   Please.

Peter   It's very eloquent, isn't it?

Kelly   It's beautiful.

Peter   A bit purple here and there . . .

He looks back at the paper, reads:

"The malaise among the men has taken a turn. It's clear to everyone now that we are not equipped to bring this country back to life. The city is dying and we are the ones killing it. Since the mission has no meaning, my men are making meaning for themselves. As you might expect, the meaning they are making is perverse. I can't bear to tell you what I'm seeing. I'm sure you can imagine. All I will add is that it is worse. But I do not blame my men. They were told they would be heroes bringing freedom, and instead have been told to invade people's homes and take their freedom. They are ordered to protect themselves from violence by actively doing violence, which leads to more violence to protect themselves against: no sane person could survive these tasks. I have begun to wonder if I myself will recover from who I have become here, in just a few short months. But then in quieter moments I find myself thrown back into memories of who I was before and am faced with the realization that the horror I feel here is not . . . " Hmm.

Pause.

This sort of goes on for a while, there was a part at the end –

Kelly   No, please, keep reading.

Peter   – Reading out loud, it's longer than I . . . there's a, where is the / part . . . ?

Kelly   Go back, what was he saying about the "horror" – "the realization that the horror I feel here"? – I want to hear that.

Pause. **Peter** *looks at the paper.*

Peter   "But then in quieter moments I find myself thrown back into memories of who I was before and am faced with the realization that the horror I feel here is not . . . something I fully understand . . . It is unclear which way the narrative of this war will twist next. Faulkner understood that the psychological legacy of war is that / the individual – "

Kelly   Are you skipping something?

Peter   No. No.

Kelly   The – read it again?

Pause.

Peter   I think – that part might have been something he meant just for me, actually.

Pause.

Kelly   What are you skipping?

Peter   It's not really –

Kelly *takes the email from* **Peter** *and reads it. She looks up. Pause.*

Peter   I think he – I think he meant just fantasies, or –

Kelly   *Fantasies?*

Peter   He says "need" – need's not – I mean, Fort Benning was probably anxiety, but –

Kelly *(reads)*   "In quieter moments I find myself thrown back into memories of who I was before and am faced with the realization that the horror I feel here is not just a consequence of the war, but is horror of the core of me, of who I have always been. In fact I have felt more clear-headed here than ever before. I haven't felt the overwhelming need to sexually demean women that has haunted me my entire life, and haven't fucked since leaving Fort Benning."

Puts down email.

Every night I let him fuck me – every night of my / *life*!

Peter   – I don't – I don't think / he's saying –

Kelly   – Did you know he fucked other women?

Long pause.

Peter   One time –

Kelly   I knew it –

Peter   We were – do you want me / to –

Kelly   Yes.

Peter   – we were in a bar, we were drunk, he went to the
bathroom – he was gone a while, so when he came back I just
said, "Are you okay?" Like, maybe he was throwing up . . .

Pause.

He said, "I think the bitch bit me."

Pause.

Kelly   "I think the bitch bit me."

Peter   I just thought he / was joking –

Kelly   I knew when he wouldn't apply for a deferment.
I knew –

Peter   – I think it's like, it's the violence just finally got to
him, you know? / The –

Kelly   It has nothing to do with – No – he said, it's who he's
always been –

Peter   No, that's what I mean – like – five years old, Dad
took us shooting, there's photo albums of dead animals / all –

Kelly   Don't blame this on your father, it's / not –

Peter   He loved you so much, Kelly –

Kelly   He was a coward!

Peter   He fucking shot his head off, right? He obviously felt
guilty!

Kelly   Guilt? Over *me*? No, that's not guilt, / no –

Peter   What is it then?

Kelly   He wanted to get *away* from me!

Peter   What?

Kelly   He wanted to get away from / me –

Peter   No –

Kelly   – so he went to Iraq and *shot himself* – *oh*!

She rises.

Leave my house, I need to be alone –

Peter   Kelly –

Kelly *goes into bedroom, off.* **Peter** *stays seated.*

Six

Craig *is on the couch. Near dawn.* **Kelly** *opens the bedroom door, comes out a few steps.*

Craig   Hey.

Kelly   You're talking.

Pause.

Craig   I have to leave / in a –

Kelly   I know what time it is.

Pause. She comes to the couch, sits.

Craig   Get any sleep?

Kelly *shakes her head "no."* **Craig** *smiles.*

Craig   Thinking about fucked-her-so-hard-she?

Pause.

Kelly   Why would I be thinking about him?

Craig   You're seeing him.

Pause.

Kelly   No. I am not thinking / about –

Craig   Call the bluff.

Kelly   What?

Craig   Tell him you know what he's doing. Every time you listen to him go on about one of these women he's getting / off on it –

Kelly   You have never met him. Yes, he is exasperating. But he is a human being, with a history, who is in pain – who is communicating his / pain –

Craig   He's *acting* like he's in pain –

Kelly   – in the only way he knows. He's trying to make me feel small, so I can know how *he* feels: small.

Craig   No, he's just trying to make you feel small. And he'll keep doing it until you crack, and then he'll leave.

Kelly   We have very different views of human nature.

Pause.

Do you love me, Craig?

Pause.

Craig   I don't think we should have a serious discussion right now.

Kelly   Why not?

Craig   I'm not capable of it. I'm stressed –

Kelly   Things have come up tonight. We can't / just –

Craig   I think saying anything is a bad idea.

Kelly   I think you should be able to answer the question.

Pause.

Do you love me?

Pause.

Did you?

Craig   Did I what?

Kelly   Did you ever love me?

Pause.

Craig   Of course.

Kelly   Of course?

Craig   Of course I loved you.

Kelly   Loved?

Pause.

When did you stop?

Pause.

When did / you − ?

Craig   After we got married. I knew it was a mistake. I knew I didn't love you.

Pause. **Kelly** *cries. She punches* **Craig** *repeatedly. She stops. Pause.*

Craig   I have to get dressed.

Pause. He goes into the bedroom, off. **Kelly** *hyperventilates. Calms some. Picks up her phone, goes to her phone book, dials.*

Kelly   Hi, this is a message for Bradley. It's Kelly Conners calling. I'm sorry to be calling so early and with such short notice. I need to cancel this morning's session. I'm very sorry. I'll see you at our regular time next week. Take care.

Seven

Peter *is on the couch asleep, a script open before him. Bedroom door opens,* **Kelly** *comes out. Pause. She looks at* **Peter**. *Goes into the kitchen and runs water, opens cabinets, makes noise.* **Peter** *wakes up. Sees* **Kelly**. *She sees him.*

Peter   Sorry . . .

Kelly *makes tea.* **Peter** *looks at the box of books.*

Peter   I was looking over one of my speeches – "It was a great mistake, my being born a man" – I got inspired by all of Craig's books. I must have passed out . . . Melville, Hawthorne, Hemingway, Faulkner . . . I remember in high school Craig was reading *A Farewell to Arms.* He said it was a war novel – I thought it was about a double amputee . . . God, America had so many great writers . . .

Kelly *continues making tea.*

Peter   Oh, shit, what time is it?

Kelly   Nine.

Peter   Phew – I have a company meeting at ten. Spoke to Scott – told him what happened, he talked to John, John I guess feels terrible . . . Sounds like we'll all kiss and make up.

Pause. He looks at **Kelly***.*

Peter   I'm sure this won't make – much of a difference to you, but – I'm really sorry about what happened last night.

Kelly   Thank you, I accept your apology.

She straightens things up in the kitchen. **Peter** *looks at the couch.*

Peter   I'm gonna miss this couch! I remember, on 9/11 – I had just moved to LA, and I remember calling here, all day, I couldn't get through till late in the night – Craig picked up the phone, and I remember this peace in his voice – telling me about how you two just sat on the couch all day – looking out the window, at the cloud, holding each other . . . When I think of 9/11, that's always the picture I have . . .

Kelly *does not respond.*

Peter   – *That's* what I forgot to ask you! Whatever happened to fucked-her-so-hard-she?

Kelly   He stopped coming.

Peter   Why?

Kelly   I had to cancel a session, and he never came again.

Peter   Huh. I had this whole fantasy that he was why you changed your numbers, like he was stalking you / or something –

Kelly *stops.*

Kelly   I changed my numbers because of you.

Pause.

Peter   Because of *me*?

Kelly   Peter, you've invaded my home, no warning, you come in here, you / read me –

Peter   I didn't have your numbers –

Kelly   – this email – say what you will, you did it. So please – just say goodbye, and leave.

Pause.

Peter   When did you change them, after getting my letter?

Kelly   I just want to start over.

Peter   I don't understand, what did I do?

Kelly   I just told you: I wanted to start over.

Peter   But – there was no one I could talk to about him, you were / the –

Kelly   There are therapists.

Peter   But – I love you.

Pause.

Kelly   Bye.

Pause.

Peter   *Fine.*

He grabs his bag, starts to go, then stops.

– For you.

He puts the emails down on the couch.

Kelly   How *dare* you – *no*!

Peter *goes, off. Pause.*

Kelly *turns to the window. The sun is shining, sounds of the city coming to life. She looks out of the window.* **Craig** *comes out of the bedroom, in uniform, with luggage.*

Craig   It's time for me to go.

Kelly *turns. Pause.* **Craig** *goes to the couch and sits. He cries.*

Kelly *goes to the couch and sits. After a time:*

Kelly   Listen. I think you were right. I think this stress is – it was a mistake to talk. I don't think this is who we really / are –

Craig   I have to go, I / can't –

Kelly   I know you do. We'll talk when – phone, email, whatever you're most comfortable with, whenever you – we'll find a way to understand what's / happening –

Craig   I don't – I don't think that's a good idea.

Pause.

Kelly   What's not?

Craig   Being in touch.

Kelly   Being in touch . . . at all?

Pause.

Craig   I have to go.

Kelly   Craig –

Craig *rises. He gathers his things and goes to the door.*

Craig   Goodbye.

Pause. He goes, off.

After a time, **Kelly** *gets up and pours herself a cup of tea. She returns to the couch, turns on the TV. Puts on* The Daily Show. *A moment* *passes. She looks at the emails sitting on the couch. Pause. She picks one up, begins to read.*

She stops, puts it down. Pause.

She goes to the box of books, opens it. Goes to the emails, picks them up. Places them in the box. Sits, begins placing books neatly into the box.

On the television, sounds of Jon Stewart, laughter, applause . . .

Dan LeFranc

The Big Meal

The Big Meal had its world premiere on February 7, 2011 at American Theater Company, Chicago IL (P. J. Paparelli, Artistic Director). Playwrights Horizons Inc. produced the New York City premiere of *The Big Meal* Off-Broadway in 2012.

About the Play

The setting is a restaurant in the Midwestern United States, or rather, every restaurant in the Midwestern United States. Some are popular chains, others are more homely; very few are fancy.

There are tables ready to be set. They may be brought together or apart depending on the size of the party at any given moment. Eight actors total. Three men. Three women. A boy and a girl. The server is probably a stagehand.

The actors play the multiple generations of one family as they glide through time (and the guests they pick up along the way). As the characters age, their "essences" pass from younger to older actors. These "passes" ought to be performed as simply as possible. They are designated in the script by the character's name sliding into a new column.

Shifts in time are designated by SHIFT. These shifts can be indicated as subtly or conspicuously as the moment demands, but please try not to overdo the theatrics. These are placed in the script primarily to help the actors, not the audience. We don't want the audience to get lost, of course, but it's okay if they're a little behind the play.

The food probably doesn't look very appetizing. Colorful. Glistening. Grotesque.

Except for a few key moments (and one long stretch towards the end), the play moves very quickly. Pretend the cast is an orchestra tasked to play a piece of music for a conductor whose pace is brisk and unrelenting. Or pretend they're sitting together at a player piano. Or getting their cues from a rapidly scrolling teleprompter. Regardless of which metaphor serves you best, play the action on the line. At performance speed, the play ought to run roughly eighty minutes.

Do your best to cast an ensemble who feels like a family, but don't break your back to make everyone look related.

Let the language carry us through time and space. Don't worry about representing the various restaurants literally. The scenography should probably be a little abstract, allowing our imaginations to leave the confines of a restaurant from time to time. Big scenic gestures should be kept to a minimum (or preferably, completely avoided). As a rule, there should be as few objects flying around the set as possible. The only plates in the play should be the ones that land in the script. The only consumables should be the ones on those plates. Feel free to rearrange the furniture when necessary, but let our imaginations do the heavy lifting.

Lines in parentheses (thus) are meant to be spoken to another character more privately than publicly.

A large generational gap between the actors is important to understanding the story. In other words, if possible cast children in the youngest roles, not teenagers.

The duration of the meals can vary depending on the needs of the production. The first and last meals should probably be the longest. The dialogue might begin over some of the later meals in order to break up the rhythm of the device. But see what works best given the circumstances.

There's a lot of cross-talk in this play and some parts of the conversations are more important than others. Make sure to highlight the parts that are most crucial to the story. It might be helpful to identify the "A conversations" and "B conversations" throughout.

Sound and light cues should be kept to an absolute minimum. There's a moment of dancing that might require a song, but that's about it for sound. Lighting may be used more often, but see how little you can get away with and take it from there.

This is key: all of the actors should be on stage for the entire play. When not in a scene, they are probably sitting in an area where they are removed from the action but can also observe it – actively waiting for their moment to jump in.

Characters

Woman 1 (Older Woman)
Nicole (*older woman*)
Alice, *Sam's mother*

Man 1 (Older Man)
Sam (*older man*)
Robert, *Sam's father*
Jack, *Stephanie's father*

Woman 2 (Woman)
Nicole (*woman*)
Maddie, *Sam and Nicole's daughter* (*woman*)
Jackie, *Robbie and Stephanie's daughter* (*woman*)

Man 2 (Man)
Sam (*man*)
Robbie, *Sam and Nicole's son* (*man*)

Woman 3 (Young Woman)
Nicole (*young woman*)
Jessica, *a gentle soul*
Maddie, *Sam and Nicole's daughter* (*young woman*)
Stephanie, *Robbie's wife* (*young woman*)
Jackie, *Robbie and Stephanie's daughter* (*young woman*)

Man 3 (Young Man)
Sam (*young man*)
Robbie, *Sam and Nicole's son* (*young man*)
Maddie's Adolescent Boyfriends (Steven, Marcus, Jeremy, Patrick, Michael)
Sammy, *Maddie's son* (*young man*)

Girl
Pesky Little Girl
Maddie, *Sam and Nicole's daughter* (*girl*)
Jackie, *Robbie and Stephanie's daughter* (*girl*)

Boy
Pesky Little Boy
Robbie, *Sam and Nicole's son* (*boy*)
Sammy, *Maddie's son* (*boy*)
Matthew, *Jackie's son*

W1 M1 W2 M2 **Woman 3**   **Man 3**   **Girl Boy**

Man 3

(He is sitting at a table by himself with a drink.)

Sam

Woman 3

(She is setting a table. Not interested in him.)

Nicole

Am I in your way?

(She cleans his table, ignoring him.)

Pretty much.

(He drinks.)

So what's up?

Um, side work.

Side work, huh?

Yeah, 'cause I work here.

Okay.

And I don't want to waste any more of my life than I have to.

(He drinks.) Then don't.

What?

Uh, If you don't want to waste your life, then . . . don't. It's pretty simple.

Yeah.

Is it?

I mean, no, it's really hard, but it's, uh . . . doable, I think.

Yeah.

Doable. *(Smiles.)*

. . . *(Smiles back uncertainly.)*

Is there, like, something on my face?

SHIFT   SHIFT

Hey. Sorry I'm late.

Hi.

W 1	M 1	W 2	M 2	Woman 3	Man 3	Girl	Boy

Man 3: It's okay. You wanna sit down?

Man 3: Here, let me get your chair. (*He does.*)

Woman 3: Oh yeah. Thanks.

Man 3: Okay –

Woman 3: Oh, you don't have to. Okay, wow, chivalry. That's intense.

Man 3: My? Sam, my name's Sam.

Woman 3: What's your name again?

Man 3: I'm pretty sure it's Sam.

Woman 3: I thought it was something else.

Woman 3: I'm Nicky.

Man 3: Oh yeah, I know.

Woman 3: My parents named me Nicole, but just look at what your mouth does when you say it. Nicole. It's weird.

Man 3: I think it's pretty.

Woman 3: Yeah, you would. You totally would.

Man 3: Okay.

Woman 3: Well, not, uh . . . All right. So not to be up front, but I, uh, I'm not really looking for anything serious right now.

Man 3: Oh, yeah. Did it seem like I – ?

Woman 3: No. No, no, no.

Woman 3: I just wanna be clear, 'cause I just got out of this long-term thing with this total, um, clingy narcissistic asshole, and I'm looking for, you know, someone to pass the time with or whatever, but not like "a relationship."

Man 3: No, I get it, it's cool.

Woman 3: You know what I mean?

Man 3: Oh, yeah, "relationships," they're so –

W 1   M 1   W 2   M 2   **Woman 3**   **Man 3**   **Girl**   **Boy**

Man 3: Yeah, it's like I look at my parents and they're, I don't know, intense, I guess, and, uh, hopefully you'll never meet them, so —

Woman 3: Yeah, I don't anticipate meeting your parents.

Man 3: Yeah.

Woman 3: This is totally casual.

Man 3: Yeah.

Woman 3: So that means if this goes anywhere beyond tonight, which I'm not saying it will, we should keep this as, uh, as anonymous as possible, you know? Like, I don't really wanna know about your life and I really, *really* don't want you to know about mine.

Man 3: Sure.

Man 3: Oh, okay.

(*Pause.*)

Man 3: Cool, that's cool.

(*Pause.*)

Woman 3: Oh, oh yeah, sorry, yeah. (*Smiles.*)

Man 3: But can I ask you what you like to drink? 'Cause I really wanna buy you a drink. (*Smiles.*)

Woman 3: Yeah, okay, let's have a drink. (*Drinks.*)

Man 3: Cool. (*Drinks.*)

Man 3: How is it?

Woman 3: Good.

Man 3: Yeah, I really like this one.

(*Pause.*)

(*Pause.*)

Woman 3: You wanna get out of here?

Man 3: Should we order —?

Woman 3: You wanna mess around?

Man 3: What?

W 1 M 1 W 2 M 2 **Woman 3**   **Man 3**   **Girl Boy**

Like right now? 'Cause, no offense, but this date is kinda painful.

> Uh . . . I am a male.

> Uh. Yeah, yeah.

Then let's go. .
SHIFT

> SHIFT

> Hey, Nicky.

Sam.

> Sorry I'm –

It's okay

> I'm glad you called.

Yeah, well, I was pretty bored, so . . .

> Did you order?

Just a drink. You want one?

> Sure.

(*Drinks*)

> (*Drinks.*)

> This is good.

It's kinda weak.

> Yeah. You know, my mom claims to have invented the Cadillac Margarita.

Oh yeah?

> Yeah.

Is that a margarita you order at a drive-in, or – ?

> No, ha ha, that's funny, but, uh, no. It's just like a normal margarita, but with, uh, a splash of Grand Marnier.

Cool. Cool.

> Yeah, she's really proud of it for some reason.

So is your mom like an alcoholic inventor?

> (*Smiles.*) Uh, well, maybe like casually alcoholic but no, she's just, she works in restaurants.

W 1 M 1 W 2 M 2   Woman 3   Man 3   Girl Boy

Man 3: You have a sister?

Woman 3: Yeah, so does my sister.

Man 3: Is that what you'd call it? A pickup? Like I just dragged you out of the bar by your hair back to your apartment?

Woman 3: Yeah. Actually the place where I work where you, um, picked me up – she's the manager, and pretty much the only reason I –

Man 3: (*Smiles.*) Yeah, yeah.

Woman 3: Ha ha, yeah, kinda. Yeah.

Man 3: Hey, do you think your roommate woke up?

Woman 3: Well, except I was the one doing the dragging

Man 3: (*Laughs.*) Why?

Woman 3: I hope so. I hate that bitch.

Man 3: What?

Woman 3: She's very, you know (*gesture*), very (*gesture*). Like this one time my sister came over to cook and she was, uh, wow, okay.

Man 3: Oh.
It's okay.
Totally.

Woman 3: I am telling you stuff about my life. I don't know why I am telling you stuff about my life, 'cause this thing is not –

SHIFT

Man 3: Nicky.

Woman 3: Hey, Sam.

(*They kiss*)

Man 3: *passionately*)

Woman 3: She's good. She left this morning.

Man 3: How's your sister?
That was fun, hanging out. She's cool.

Woman 3: Yeah, she liked you too.

W 1	M 1	W 2	M 2	Woman 3	Man 3	Girl	Boy
					You want a – (*drink gesture*)? (*Drinks.*)		
				What do you think? (*Drinks.*)			
					I know.		
				This is good.			
					You think so?		
				Your mom's a genius.			
					Yeah, she can definitely make a drink.		
				This drink's awesome.			
					What?		
				You're kind of awesome too. (*She makes a face.*)			
					(*Laughs.*)		
				SHIFT	SHIFT	SHIFT	
						(*The sound of a child crying in the restaurant.*)	
				Is that a kid?			
					Whoa.	Eeeeee	
				Yeah, have you ever heard a gibbon?		eeee	
					Sounds like some kind of freakish animal.	ee	
				You've never been to the zoo?		eeeeee	
					What's a gibbon?	eeee	
				Well, they're like monkeys, but they're apes.		ee	
					Yeah, but –	eeee.	
				Apes don't have tails.		Ee	
					What's the difference?	eeeee.	
				Listen to that.		Eeee	
					Really?	ee	
					Wow.	ee	
				Do you like kids?			
					They're okay.		

W 1	M 1	W 2	M 2	Woman 3	Man 3	Girl	Boy
				I hate kids. They're nothing but, like, snot and shit. Seriously, I think their bodies are literally powered by mucus.		eeeeeeeeeee	
					(*Laughs.*)	eeee	
					(*As if by accident.*) I love you.	eeee	
				What?		ee.	
					What?	Eeee	
				SHIFT		eeee	
					SHIFT	eeee.	
				Yeah, so I don't know what to do.	She still won't move out? Did you call the landlord?	SHIFT	
				No, she's a freak. (*Drinks.*) Yeah, I called the landlord, but the thing is she's on the lease and she hasn't technically done anything, so there's not much I can –	Okay.		
				Wait it – ?			
				No.	Do you think you can wait it out?		
				Sam, this is ruining my life, it is ruining my life. I hate her, I –			
					Okay, okay. So do you want me to talk to her?		
				Really? You'd talk to her?	Yeah. I mean it's worth a shot, right?		
				Okay . . . but I think she's kind of obsessed with you, so don't let her touch your hair or anything.			
					She's –		
				Yeah, a little . . .	whoa – seriously?		
				I mean, can you blame her? (*Makes a face.*)	(*Smiles.*)		
				SHIFT	SHIFT		

W 1 M 1 W 2 M 2 Woman 3   **Man 3**   **Girl Boy**

Man 3: So what do you think? Nice, right?

Woman 3: Are you sure we can afford this? It's pretty fancy.

Man 3: Yeah, I got it.

I mean my credit card's got it, but, whatever, it's our anniversary.

Woman 3: No, you can't pay for this. The glasses are like actual glass. (*Jokingly.*) Anniversary? Is that what this is?

Man 3: Uh huh.

Woman 3: Of what? The first time we, like, coupled?

Man 3: Um, no. Of our, uh, (*conspiratorial playfulness*) relationship.

Woman 3: (*Conspires back.*) Relationship? We're in a relationship?

Man 3: (*Keeps it up.*) Yeah.

Woman 3: (*So does she.*) Holy shit.

Man 3: I know.

Woman 3: How the hell did that happen?

Man 3: That's classified information.

Woman 3: I have clearance.

Man 3: Lemme see it.

Woman 3: (*She lowers a shoulder strap.*)

Man 3: Good enough.

Woman 3: Now tell me.

Man 3: Well, first we met.

Woman 3: Then what?

Man 3: Then we liked each other.

Woman 3: Interesting.

Man 3: Then we . . . coupled.

Woman 3: I liked that part.

Man 3: Me too.

Woman 3: And then?

Man 3: We fell in love.

Woman 3: Oh yeah. That was awesome. What happens next?

Man 3: I can tell you, but I'm gonna need to see some more clearance.

W 1	M 1	W 2	M 2	Woman 3	Man 3	Girl	Boy
				SHIFT	SHIFT		
				You want a drink?	That's cool.		
				. . .	. . .		
				So what's up?	Nothing.		
				Nothing's up?			
				We haven't talked in a week.	Yeah?		
				So is there something we need to talk about now?	Like what?		
				Like, I don't know. Anything. Everything.	Uh . . . (Pause.)		
				(Pause.)			
				What the fuck, Sam?	What?		
				Say it.	Say what?		
				(She starts to cry.) Oh my God, say it, say it, just say it!			
				SHIFT	SHIFT		
				(Shrugs.)	You want another? (Gestures.)		
				Look, I can't keep doing this.	So then do you wanna get outta here, or – ?		
				We're not involved, but then I see you and then we are and it gets confusing	Okay.		
				I don't wanna hear about your dad.	Yeah, well, my dad says this thing about healing, how it's like –		

W 1	M 1	Woman 2	Man 2	Woman 3	Man 3	Girl	Boy
					He's a smart guy.		
				You don't even like him.			
					Yeah I do.		
				Since when?			
					He's my dad.		
				You don't have to like your dad.			
					I didn't say I had to.		
				Right.			
					You're drunk.		
				Well, you're a waste of my fucking time.			
					Okay, then . . . forget it.		
				Forget it?			
					Yeah.		
				Is that what you want?			
					Sounds like it's what you want.		
				. . .			
				. . . asshole.			
				SHIFT	SHIFT		
			SHIFT				
		Nicole	Sam				
		Hey, Sam.	Nicky, wow, what are you doing here?				
		Can I sit down?					
			Uh, sure.				
		Sorry if I'm –					
			No, it's okay. You, uh . . . you look great.				
		Thanks. You look pretty much exactly like yourself, which is a good thing. It's totally a good thing.					
			Oh –				

Woman 2	Man 2
	Really? 'Cause I mean, it's been a while.
A little while, yeah.	
	How are you?
Good, I'm good. I'm, uh, here with this guy.	
	Oh yeah, me too. I mean I'm not here with a guy, I'm, uh –
She cool?	
	Yeah, she's great. She's very, um, peeing. She's peeing. What about your, uh –
He's very, um, peeing too.	
	Good. That's, uh, great. I'm really happy for you.
(Smiles.)	*(Smiles.)*
(Pause.)	*(Pause.)*
	Well, it was great to –
	What?
You wanna get out of here?	
	Whoa. Nicky, hey, look, this woman, she's –
This guy sucks.	
	No, Nicky, she's –
Oh.	
	She sucks, okay? She sucks, but she's nice, so I feel like I should probably not be an asshole, which I believe is the last thing you called me.
It's okay. I get it.	
Chivalry.	
	But, um, maybe later tonight you and I can, uh –
Yeah, something like that.	
SHIFT	SHIFT
Hey.	
	Did you order?
No, I just got here.	

W 1 M 1 Woman 2

W 3 M 3 Girl Boy

Man 2

MAN 2: You look, um, awesome as always.

WOMAN 2: Thanks.

WOMAN 2: No, there wasn't much time to do anything but, uh –

MAN 2: So, I didn't really have time to ask the other night – (*Smiles.*)

MAN 2: Yeah.

WOMAN 2: You got better.

MAN 2: Really?

WOMAN 2: Uh huh.

MAN 2: Well, I have been practicing.

WOMAN 2: Oh really?

MAN 2: Sure, but not – not like a lot. I mean, I did keep busy, but, uh, forget it. Reset, ha ha . . . um.

WOMAN 2: So.

MAN 2: How's your sister?

WOMAN 2: She's good.

MAN 2: Is she still working in, um, restaurants, or?

WOMAN 2: Basically. She's more, like, behind the scenes now . . . purchasing.

MAN 2: Cool, cool . . . is she, like . . . married?

WOMAN 2: Uh, no, no way.

MAN 2: Oh.

WOMAN 2: I mean, why would anyone do that to themselves? Like marriage is so – (*Gestures.*)

MAN 2: Yeah, yeah.

WOMAN 2: You know?

MAN 2: I . . . fully agree.

WOMAN 2: SHIFT

MAN 2: SHIFT

MAN 2: Hey.

WOMAN 2: Sam.

MAN 2: It's okay.

WOMAN 2: Sorry I'm –

(*They kiss across the table.*)

Man 2

Oh, hold on, Nic, you've got something in your hair.

Woman 2

What? I do?

Man 2

Yeah. Huh. What is it? Gee, where did this come from? *(He removes a small, shiny ring)*

Woman 2

What, uh, what is that? Sam? What the hell is that?

What are you doing? Sam.

Are you really fucking doing this?

Man 2

So I know it might seem a little, um, fast. I mean kinda fast but not really fast, 'cause, well, we have known each other for quite a while, and I know we both have, like, issues with the institution or whatever; but I figure some things are worth the risk.

Woman 2

Oh my God, Sam, seriously?

Man 2

Yeah.

Woman 2

I'm not wearing underwear.

Man 2

You're not?

Woman 2

No, this dress isn't – don't you think I should be wearing underwear for this?

Man 2

Uh, should we order you some? Ha ha.

Woman 2

Don't. Don't say things like that.

Would we have to have a "wedding"? 'Cause I really . . . I really hate weddings. They're so – *(Makes a face.)* You know?

Man 2

Right.

Woman 2

I don't know. Now there are people watching. I used to work here. This isn't exactly anonymous. Like that waiter over there? I think I maybe made out with that waiter once. Oh God, I can't believe he still works here.

Man 2

Uh, well, does that mean you're gonna say yes?

Woman 2

Yeah.

Man 2

I know. That's why I'm doing this here. It's where we met.

Really? *(He laughs.)*

W 1 M 1 Woman 2

Man 2

W 3 M 3 Girl Boy

Woman 2

At least don't do the knee thing.

Yeah, but then you're gonna be kinda looking up my dress and that doesn't seem like the most, uh – plus I always thought you might, if you did this, which I never expected you to 'cause that's (*Crazy gesture.*) and I'm not. (*Crazy gesture.*) If you did pop the thing, in my mind I thought you'd maybe

just, like, take my hand and . . . pop the thing but not the thing thing. You'd say something like the thing but better than the thing, way more interesting than the thing, 'cause it shouldn't be like a movie thing, it should be like –

like something real, um, beautiful? different? I don't know.

Oh Jesus Christ, yes! Yes! FUCKING YES!

(*They kiss across the*

SHIFT

(*They curl into*

A little.

Probably not.

Man 2

Nicky.

What are you talking about? I have to do the knee thing.

Yeah, okay.

What?

Like what?

So, um, how about this?

(*He takes her hand, maybe cautiously slips the ring on to her finger.*)

How's that?

table like maniacs.)

SHIFT

each other. Sigh.)

You think we're being, like, obnoxious?

Like maybe we shouldn't be making out in public like this?

W 1 M 1 Woman 2	Man 2	W 3 M 3 Girl	Boy
	(Smiles.) If I were in this place, I'd hate us. But we're us, so I'm into it.		
Definitely. *(Bites his ear)*	So what do you wanna do now?		
Mmm, everything.	Everything?		
Yeah. Well, except for kids.	Right.		
'Cause who would do that to themselves?			
Crazy people, our parents.			
I mean just think about it. A whole life with just each other. Think about how fucking rad that sounds.	Sounds pretty fucking rad.		
Yeah, we could like go places together.	You mean like Dayton, or –?		
No, dumbass.	Hey.		
(She takes his hand.) Like places that are really places – like, like Barcelona. *(She pronounces it in a fakey-funny-Castilian accent.)*	Barcelona. *(So does he. They keep this up.)* Wow, that is . . . exotic.		
It is.	What does one do in Barcelona?		
In Barcelona one can do everything.	Everything? That sounds like a lot.		
Yes, but in Barcelona, it is not so much.	*(Laughs.)*		
	What was that?		
Must be someone's kids.	It sounds like some kind of animal.		

W 3   M 3   Girl   Boy

Little Girl *(far away)*	**Little Boy** *(far away)*
Eeeeeeee eeee	Eeeeeeee eeee

W 1 M 1 Woman 2	Man 2	W 3 M 3 Girl	Boy
I think they're kinda cute.	You hate kids.	eeeeee	eeeeeee
Me? You're the one who hates kids.	When did I say that?	eeee	eeee
You know. (Gestures.)	Okay.	eeeeeeee	eeee
Yeah –	My body is literally shaking.	ee	eeeeeeeee
	You wanna get out of here?	eeee.	eee
		(Closer.) Eeeeeee	eeeeeeeeeee
		eeee	eee
		eeeeeeee	eeee
		eeeeeeeeee	(Closer.) Eeeeeeeeee
		eeeeeeeeeeeee	eee
		EEEEEEE EEEEE!	EEEEEEEEEE EEEEE!
SHIFT	SHIFT	SHIFT	SHIFT
Oh my God. Who is this? Whose child is this? Hello? Did someone lose a child?	Whoa.	Girl runs on.	Boy runs on.
	Hello?	She leaps into Nicole's lap.	He leaps into Sam's lap.
	Did someone lose a child? I've got a parentless child here! Hello? Anyone? Anyone?		
Hello? Anyone?			
Has someone lost a little booger monster? I've got a booger monster here.	I've got a Tasmanian devil who likes to get tickled.	Maddie Mom.	Robbie (laughs) Dad, Dad, no, no, Dad.
Look at all those boogers. (She tickles Girl some more.)	(He tickles Boy some more.)	(Laughs.) I don't have boogers! (Laughs.)	(Laughs.)

W 1 M 1 Woman 2	Man 2	W 3 M 3 Girl	Boy
	You guys hungry?	Yeah.	Yessss.
			Yessss.
	Yesssss? Yessss?		
Tamarin. Very good, Maddie, and what's a tamarin got that a gibbon doesn't?	What are you – a python?	I'm a tamarin.	Yessss. Yesssss.
All right, kiddo, you've won the grand prize.	What's a python sound like?	A tail.	Yeeessssss. Yeeessssss.
You don't like crayons?		Is the grand prize crayons?	Yeeessssss.
		That's what the grand prize was last time.	
Well, there's a limited selection of grand prizes these days.	Okay, that's enough python, buddy.		
Well, because of Congress.	Come here. Sit here next to your dad.	Why?	
The contest passed a bill.		Why? What'd the contest do?	Can I get a corn dog?
A bill's like a Band-Aid.	No.	What's a bill?	Why not?
	'Cause you had a corn dog last night	Okay.	So?
He wants a corn dog? No corn dogs.			Why?
You know what they're made out of?			Hot dogs.
No, they're made out of pigs, and not the nice parts of pigs.		Jennifer's mom has a pet pig	But I don't like anything else.

W 1 M 1 Woman 2	Man 2	W 3 M 3 Girl	Boy
You like tostadas.	I heard you, honey. What do you want to eat?	Dad, Jennifer's mom has a pet pig.	They're all right. I'd rather have a corn dog.
Sorry, kiddo, you're getting something else.		Jennifer says her mom likes to go outside and smoke and talk to her pet pig.	There's nothing else to get.
I'm sure you'll find something.	Well, that's what happens when you do what Jennifer's mom did when she was young. You end up talking to your pet pig.	I want a pet pig. Can I have a pet pig?	
	We don't have room for a pet pig. Now come on, honey, what do you want?		If we had a pig I bet we'd have bacon all the time.
Hey, Sam? Can I ask you something?	Yeah?	Pigs make bacon?	
You think you can maybe take off work on Wednesday?	Wednesday? Uh, maybe . . . hold on, Maddie.	No, they don't.	Yeah, they poo it out.
(Smiles. Laughs a little.) Robbie, that is very funny but very gross. Stop taunting your sister and figure out your order.	(Smiles.) Hey, Mom? Do pigs poo bacon?	Dad – . . . Daddy, do pigs poo bacon?	Uh huh, bacon poo.
It's just this wine-tasting thing – a promo for this new restaurant some of my girlfriends were talking about. It sounds fun.	What's on Wednesday?		Say yes.
I work on Thursday.	Okay.	Told you.	You're no fun.
Because a temp's coming in Thursday and I need to make sure he doesn't blow up the office	You can't do it Thursday?		She didn't say no. It's still possible.
	Yeah, I know, and I work Wednesday. Why can't you take off Thursday?	(She colors. Makes sounds.)	
		Wah.	
		Wah.	

W 1	M 1	Woman 2	Man 2	W 3	M 3	Girl	Boy
			So you want me to ditch work so you can get buzzed with your friends in the middle of the afternoon?			Wah.	
		It's a wine tasting.				Wah.	
		Maddie, honey, enough with the — (*Gestures.*)					
		It's fine. Just don't do it anymore, okay? Not all sounds are fun sounds.				Sorry.	
			Can't your sister watch the kids?				
		How many times are we gonna make her do that, Sam? Seriously. She's my sister, not our babysitter.	Make her?				
		Well, I think she's beginning to feel a little put out.	She loves the kids, and who wouldn't? Who wouldn't love you little rascals? Huh?				
							(*Makes a pig sound.*)
			(*Makes a pig sound back at him.*)				(*Pig sound.*)
						(*Pig sound!*)	(*Pig sound.*)
			Okay, okay. I'll take off Wednesday.			No, it's not. It's a pig!	That's wrong.
		Great. I appreciate it.	You know why? Because you deserve it, you really do.			You were so doing pigs! Dad! Dad! Dad! Daddy! Dad!	We weren't doing pigs.
		Thank you.	I'm sorry for arguing.				
		Just don't make me nag. I hate feeling like a nag				Weren't you doing pigs?	
			Yeah, honey, we were doing pigs.				
		I love you too.	I love you.			See?	I'm reading my menu. (*He does.*)

W 1	M 1	Woman 2	Man 2	W 3	M 3	Girl	Boy
		(They kiss the air,	*but not each other.)*			Fine.	
		Mwah!	Mwah!			*(She reads hers, too.)*	
		SHIFT	SHIFT			SHIFT	SHIFT
		What are you – a tamarin?	You guys hungry?			*(Monkey sounds.)*	
		What is it, Robbie?					Mom.
							What's an enchilada?
		Hey, you know what an enchilada is? It's a Mexican corn dog.					
		Yep!					It is?
		(They secretly high–	*five each other.)*				
							But I thought Mexicans only ate real dogs.
		Robbie!	Nicky –				
		Well, that's a bunch of crap.	Hey, watch your mouth around him, okay?				What? They do! Mexicans eat dogs! It's a fact!
		What?					
		No, listen to this. Where'd you hear that?					It's top secret.
		Robbie . . .					
		you wanna be grounded?					It is! I swore! . . . Grandpa.
		Of course, of course you did. Son of a bitch.	Nicky.			Grandpa told me something too. You wanna hear?	
		What?					

Woman 1	Man 1	Woman 2	W 3	M 3	Girl	Man 2	Boy
		He's polluting their minds, Sam. Your father is polluting their minds with this this (bullshit).				Not now, honey.	What's the big deal?
		Robbie, what your grandfather told you is a lie, a mean, nasty, terrible lie, and you can never, ever say it again. Is that clear?				I'll talk to him.	Okay, I'll have an enchilada.
SHIFT	SHIFT	SHIFT			SHIFT	SHIFT	SHIFT
	Robert						
	Don't listen to her, Robbie, the enchiladas are terrible.					Dad, come on, we're just trying to get through this meal.	
	Well, you're gonna want his meal to get through his asshole.						
Alice							
Robert. Jesus.	What?						
There are children at the table.	It's true. I had an enchilada here last time we came to visit and I was clogged up for a week an entire friggin' week!	He said apple.			What'd he say? What's so funny?	Dad.	
					(Laughs.)		
		Yes, he did.			Mom, what'd he say?		No, he didn't.

Woman 1	Man 1	Woman 2	Man 2	W3 M 3 Girl	Boy
Good God. No one wants to hear about your clog.				Why's he laughing about apples?	Apples of the butt.
		If you keep talking like that I'm gonna make you sit in the car.			Nuh uh.
It's so nice to see you again.		Yes, huh.		I'm gonna have a hamburger.	
You know what you need, Nicky? A Cadillac Margarita!		Oh, you too.		Mom.	
				I'm gonna have a hamburger.	
	I remember there being somewhere in the area better than this.	Thanks, Alice, but I've got wine.			
		Good. Just tell that to the server when she gets here.	Well, we wanted to take you to that place in the city, but with the kids it's not so easy.		
	Maybe you could get off?	(We work tomorrow.) What do we say when we order?	We have to work. I told you that.	Please.	
	It's not every day we come to visit.	And?	We can't. You guys know this.		
	(He peruses the menu.)	Robbie!	Guys, come on.		
Maybe you can take us there tomorrow? You talk about it so much.		Maddie, sit up.			
					Butthole.
Okay. Sorry.		Then pull them down.		But my socks itch.	What? Grandpa said it.
(She peruses the menu.)					

Woman 1	Man 1	Woman 2	Man 2	W 3	M 3	Girl	Boy
(Long pause.)	(Long pause.)	(Long pause.)	(Long pause.)			(Long pause.)	(Long pause.)
							Can I go to the game store?
						Yeah! Can I go too?	
							I wanna go by myself.
		I don't know.					
			You're not buying any more games.				
							Come on, it's just right there.
							I know. I just wanna look.
						Can I go?	
		You just wanna look?					
							I just wanna see what's new.
			You can go if you take Maddie.				
						Can I go?	
							I wanna go by myself!
		Do you wanna go or not?					
			Well, that's the deal.				
							That's so lame.
Oh, let him go.							
							Fine.
							Let's go.
	Hey Robbie.						
							What?
	You forgot something.						
							I did?
	Yeah, you dropped something under your chair.						
							No, I didn't.
	Why don't you look?						

Woman 1	Man 1	Woman 2	Man 2	W3	M3	Girl	Boy
							(He looks under his chair. He finds a simply wrapped box.)
	Open it when you get home.						Whoa. What's this?
						What is it? Do I have one? How come there's nothing under my chair? Why didn't I forget something, Grandpa?	Why can't I open it now?
		Great, just great. Look at her.					*(He opens the box. It's an old watch.)*
You know Maddie's asking a very good question, Robert. How come there's nothing for your granddaughter?	I don't have anything for her just yet. This one's for the boy. Maddie, no offense, darling, but I don't have anything for you.						Cool.
Robert.			Dad.				*(He puts it on his wrist.)*
			Dad.				
			Dad.				
	Maybe.		Hey.				
		(Hey, you think maybe your dad could consider Maddie sometimes?)	Don't screw around.			But will you next time?	
	I mean yes. Yes I will, Maddie, and it'll heal the world. It'll abolish prejudice. Are you happy?		These are my children.				Wow, it's got a watch inside the watch.
The sarcasm, always the sarcasm.	Oh, lay off.	Maddie, why don't you and Robbie go to the game store, okay?					
	Christ.					*(**Maddie** cries. The others take in this sad sight.)*	

Woman 1	Man 1	Woman 2	Man 2	Woman 3	M 3 Girl	Boy
See what you did? You see?	Alice –					
Robert.	(*Sighs.*) Darling . . . I . . . I'm sorry, I didn't mean any-thing by it, I just –	Oh, Maddie, honey, come here. That's not true.	Dad, apologize.	No one ever has anything for me.		
Young lady!		(*Laughs.*)	Maddie! Take that back – !	I HOPE YOU DIE!		
Sam, I hate to say it but we didn't drive nine hours for this kind of behavior. You've gotta get that girl under control. Oh, Robert, hold on, you just ate a whole thing of chips!	Let's just figure out what we want to eat so we can order. Can we order? Ah.	I'm sorry, but – (*Laughs.*)	Maddie! Come back here! (*He turns to* **Nicole**.) This isn't a joke. I know, Mom, I know. (*Back to* **Nicole**.) What is wrong with you?		(*She becomes embarrassed by what she has said and runs off.*)	Hey, wait for me. (*He runs off with her.*)
		Where . . . where did you people come from? (*Laughs.*)				
SHIFT	SHIFT	SHIFT	SHIFT	SHIFT	SHIFT	SHIFT
(*She continues to peruse the menu.*)	(*He continues to peruse the menu.*)		*At a separate table that is the same table.*	**Jessica** (*enters*)		
			Oh, hey, Jess.	Hey, Sam.		
				Where are the, uh, bambinos?		
			With Nicky's sister.			

Woman 1	Man 1	Woman 2	Man 2	Woman 3
				Oh yeah? What's Nicky up to?
			My parents are in town, so she's taken it upon herself to vanish. (*Drinks.*)	
				(*Smiles.*)
				Yeah, parents are intense. I mean, I'm sure your parents are great, but, um, you know what I mean. (*Smiles.*)
			(*Smiles.*)	
				But does she, uh, does she know we're all hanging out?
			Who?	
				Nicky.
			Uh, it's a work party.	
				Okay.
			(*Smiles, matter-of-fact.*) I'm allowed to have friends.	
SHIFT	SHIFT	SHIFT	SHIFT	SHIFT
	And so the guy says, "El barrio? Lo siento, senor! I thought you meant el baño!" (*Laughs.*)	That is funny, very funny. Sam? What do you wanna get?	(*Laughs a little.*)	
Huh.			I don't know.	

Woman 1	Man 1	Woman 2	Man 2
		You wanna split something?	Like what?
You think the mole sauce has trans-fats?	You've got to stop watching television.	I kinda want shrimp.	Okay.
It's not make-believe, Robert. Trans-fats are killers.	Well, then, let 'em kill you already.		Dad, come on.
Don't speak to me like that.	It's a joke!		
It's in poor taste.	It's in perfectly good taste!	(*Drinks.*)	
Sam, what would that counselor man say? Would he say your father's brutishness is in good taste?		Uh, how do you know about the counselor, Alice? (How does she know about the counselor?)	Let's not talk about the counselor right now, okay, Mom? (They asked. What am I supposed to do, lie to my parents?)
Did I say something wrong?	What's the matter? You don't like the guy? I thought you liked the guy.	(Yes!)	

Woman 1	Man 1	Woman 2	Man 2	W 3	M 3	Girl	Boy
			He's great. You don't like the counselor?				
		Not really.					
	Now I don't want to run my mouth, but you should know –						
And what are you gonna do? You're gonna run your mouth.							
	(Oh, pipe down.)						
		No, he's fine, he's – forget it. Why are we talking about this?					
	you should know that at this point in your marriage it is perfectly normal to be having problems with physical intimacy.						
	Now hold on, look, I know you kids love each other very much, but they don't call it the seven-year rash for nothing.						
			Dad.				
Robert.							
	What?						
Itch.							
		Oh my God.					
	Of course it is. What did I say?						
Itch. It's called the seven-year itch. You said rash.							
	Well, you know what? It feels a lot more like a rash. I think rash is better.						
			Twelve years, Dad. We've been married twelve years.				
SHIFT	SHIFT	SHIFT	SHIFT				

Woman 1	Man 1	Woman 2	Man 2	W 3 M 3	Girl **Maddie** (*runs in*)	Boy **Robbie** (*runs in*)
					Mom, Dad!	Dad!
					I need to tell you something.	She's lying. Don't listen to her, she's totally lying. Seriously, don't listen to her, she's not telling the truth. I would never do something like that! Why would I do that? I love her, she's my sister, I love her more than anything. She's my sister. Why would I do that?
		Hey.	Guys.		Robbie pushed me.	
	Wohoho.	You need to slow –	Calm down. What happened?		Yes, he did. I was looking at the princess movie and he told me you can see the princess's boobs in this other movie where she does it with a pirate who does it with other pirates and I said, You're lying, the princess wouldn't do that, and he said, No I'm not, and so I said, How would you know? Do you do it with pirates who do it with other pirates? And then he pushed me!	
		I can't understand. Hey.	Did you push her? Well, it sounds like –			No I didn't. Dad, you have to believe me!
Is she scraped? It looks like she's scraped!		We shouldn't have let them go.			He shoved me.	I didn't push you!
Are you sure?		She's fine. Yes, they fight, it's fine.				See? She's already changing her story. That means she's lying.

Woman 1	Man 1	Woman 2	Man 2	W 3 M 3 Girl	Boy
		Everything's fine.	Cut it out. Listen to me.		You're a compulsive liar and you're too dumb to even know what compulsive means.
			Hey! Both of you, calm down.	I hate you, Robbie, you're the devil and you have boobs.	
					Unlike you.
		Guys! Hey! Do you want to be grounded? 'Cause you keep acting like this, that's exactly what's gonna happen.		Take it back.	You told Grandpa you wanted him to die.
				You just like him 'cause he gives you stuff	
Ooooh, watch out, kids. Here comes big momma. *(Laughs.)*					
		(She's livid, but tries with all her might not to respond.) *(Pause.)*			
(Pause.)	*(Pause.)*		*(Pause.)*	*(Pause.)*	*(Pause.)*
				Where?	I'm gonna go play video games across the street.
				I'm coming.	At Lamppost Pizza.
					No you're not.

Woman 1	M 1	Woman 2	Man 2	Woman 3	M 3	Girl	Boy
						I have quarters.	Fine.
						(*She goes.*)	(*He goes.*)
						SHIFT	SHIFT
		(*Takes a drink.*)	(*Squeezes* **Nicole**'s *shoulder*)				
SHIFT	SHIFT	SHIFT	SHIFT	SHIFT			
			– and so the guy says, "El baño? Lo siento, senor, I thought you said . . . EL BARRIO."				
				(*Laughs.*)			
			(*Laughs.*)				
			Or, uh, maybe it's the other way around. I don't know.	(*Laughs.*)			
			Yeah.	That's good.			
			Thanks, yeah . . . Nicky thinks it's racist.	Barrio, that's funny.			
			Sure, a little. Yeah, I guess.	Well, it is a little racist.			
				But that's what makes it funny. I mean, it's racist, but it's not offensive or anything.			
			"EL BARRIO!"				
			No harm, no foul, right?	Ha ha.			
			(*Smiles.*)	Right. (*Smiles.*)			
			Why?	Lemme see your hand.			
			You're into that crap?	I wanna read your future.			

Woman 1	Man 1	Woman 2	Man 2	Woman 3
			Seriously?	Come on, hand it over. (*She grabs his hands. Studies them.*)
			What does it say?	Hold on.
			Well?	I don't know.
			What do you mean you don't know?	I'm new at this, okay? (*Laughs.*)
			Talk about a tease. (*Laughs.*) (*He lets go of her hand.*)	Hey, so I was gonna go to this show.
			Oh yeah?	Yeah. These friends of mine, they're supposed to be good.
			Cool. Sounds like your friends are pretty cool.	
			Tag along? Like go with you?	Oh yeah, big time . . . you wanna tag along?
			Oh, uh – (*Smiles.*)	Yeah.
			I know I don't have to but, uh – (*Smiles.*) uh –	You don't have to. (*Smiles.*)
		(*Drinks. She might absentmindedly pick some lint off his shirt. Something domestic, common, none too intimate.*)	I'm, um . . . I'm . . . married.	
(*Continues to peruse.*)	(*Continues to peruse.*)		Uh.	Yeah, I know.
				What's that have to do with –? Wait, what did you think I was asking?

Woman 1	Man 1	Woman 2	Man 2	Woman 3	M 3 Girl Boy
			(*Smiles, embarrassed.*) I didn't think you were – no, look, Jess.		
				It's a concert, Sam.	
			I know.	I'm not some slut.	
			Whoa, hey, I didn't say you were.		
				You're the one who started hanging out with me, so don't start acting like I'm the one doing something inappropriate here.	
			Sure.		
				What did you think was happening?	
			Hey, can we chill out? No one's doing anything.		
			(*Smiles.*) I, I didn't think anything was happening.		
				Oh?	
			Yeah.		
				(*A grin.*) Nothing was happening? Nothing?	
			(*Nervous, excited by her interest.*) No, what – was I supposed to think that?		
SHIFT	SHIFT	SHIFT	SHIFT	SHIFT (*Exits.*)	
	We're ready to order!				
Well, I'm not!	Come on, we haven't got all night.				
		I just need another minute.	Hold on a sec, Dad.		

Woman 1	Man 1	Woman 2	W 3	Man 2	Girl	Boy
	Well, then, I'm gonna order. I'm about to eat your mother's head.					
				Fine, if you feel like you can't wait.		
Hey!	That's exactly what I feel like.					
SHIFT	SHIFT	SHIFT		SHIFT	SHIFT	SHIFT
(At the same table but not in the same scene as M2 and W2.)	*(At the same table but not in the same scene as M2 and W2.)*				*(She runs in. She sits at the table. Colors. Same table but not the same scene.)*	*(He runs in. He sits at the table. Colors. Same table but not the same scene.)*
				So . . . uh . . . I was thinking maybe we could find some time to get away, just the two of us.		
		The two of us?				
				Yeah.		
		You hate vacations.		I love vacations.		
		All you did in Barcelona was watch TV.				
				Ohhh.		
		Why?				
				What?		
		Why? Why a vacation? Why now?				
				I don't know, I thought it'd be fun. I thought it'd be – We could have some time for just you and me, the two of us, and – what?		
		Uh huh.				
		I saw you.				
		Don't give me what.				
				What are you talking about?		
		At that restaurant with that, that girl.				

Man 2

What girl?

I don't know what you think you saw, but –

Okay, hold on.

Nicole.

Listen, please listen.

Nicole.

Hey,

I can explain, I can –

Hey, we're, we're in public.

It was nothing, honey, it was, hey, we didn't even –

I, I did not act on the –

not that there was anything to act on –

Okay, there were feelings. There were feelings, but feelings alone are not –

Hey, hey, no. My parents are coming in to town next week. This is not the time to –

No, so the kids can see their grandparents, so they –

That's not true.

That doesn't matter. What matters is –

Well, that's good; they should remember his birthday, he's their grandfather.

Woman 2

Oh, fuck you. What girl – fuck you.

With the jacket, the cute little – and the hands. I saw her holding your hand. I saw her whispering.

She's the one from work, right?

You had your hand on her thigh.

You are –

you are such an asshole.

Fuck you, fuck you.

I don't care.

Let the world know what a fuckin' asshole you are.

What? What were you so brave not to act on?

I'm taking the kids and we're going to my sister's.

Oh, so I can just grin and bear it through another fuckin' meal with that condescending fuckin' asshole and his miserable wife.

Oh, the kids don't like your parents either.

They're pests.

Your mother, last year she sat them down and made them write birthday cards to your father 'cause they forgot.

W 3 M 3 Girl Boy

W 1 Man 1

Woman 2

Man 2

Woman 2	Man 2
They're children.	That doesn't mean they don't have an obligation –
You don't like him either.	Yes, I have issues with my father, but those issues don't mean that my children –
Look, you've met someone. I . . . I've sort of met someone.	You don't –
	What? You what? Who? Who did you "meet"? Nicky? What is going on?
So let's just walk away and start over. Let's – (*Near tears, guilt-ridden.*) I'm sorry, Sam.	You can't do this.
My sister's agreed to let us live with her until I can find a job	No.
	No.
	Nicole, look at me.
I've made up my mind, Sam.	
No. No. I won't.	Come on, hey, look at me.
I, I'm miserable, Sam, miserable! No, I will not –	Listen, just listen.
	Nicole, Nicky, please.

CLANG.

(*Unbeknownst to everyone else,* **M1** (*as* **Robert**) *is served a big plate of food. It's heavy. It makes a big clang sound when it hits the table. The clang shakes the table.*)

Woman 1	Man 1	Woman 2	Man 2	W 3 M 3 Girl	Boy
	He begins to eat his food. Everyone else at the table notices him eating. They stop what they're doing. They avert their eyes. No one looks at **M1**. *He doesn't care. He keeps eating. He takes his time. He leaves the table when he's finished.*				
SHIFT	SHIFT	SHIFT	SHIFT	SHIFT	SHIFT
(Long, long pause.)	*(Long, long pause.)*	*(Long, long pause.)*	*(Long, long pause.)*	*(Long, long pause.)*	*(Long, long pause.)*
(Very, very shaken.)		I'm sorry, Sam. I'm so sorry.	*(He is very, very shaken. . . .)*	What's the matter?	What's the matter?
Robert . . . Oh, my dear, dear, dear . . .		*(She takes Sam's hand.)* I'm not going anywhere, okay? I am right here.		Dad? I'm sorry. I didn't really want Grandpa to die. Dad? I take it back. I really liked Grandpa.	
		Maddie, not now.			
		Why don't you kids color, okay? *(She keeps her hand on* **Sam**'s*.)*	*(He is staring off, not really noticing* **Nicole**'s *hand.)*	Grandma? You know I didn't mean to, right? I didn't mean to, I didn't mean to, I didn't mean to, I didn't – *(***Maddie** *runs off.)*	Hey, wait for me. *(***Robbie** *runs off.)*
SHIFT	SHIFT	SHIFT	SHIFT	SHIFT	SHIFT

W 1	M 1	Woman 2	Man 2	Woman 3	Man 3	Girl	Boy

Man 3: Robbie (*runs in*) Hey, wait. Dad, she is freaking out — I just brought up the car thing casually and she went off on me.

Woman 3: Maddie (*runs in*) Mom, Dad, is this true? Are you seriously letting this happen?

Woman 2: Hey, calm down.

Woman 3: With the car?

Man 2: Is what true?

Woman 2: Guys, we're in public.

Man 2: Yeah, what's the problem?

Man 3: I have a student-council meeting.

Woman 3: Oh my God, why does Robbie get the Nissan tonight?

Woman 2: Maddie.

Man 2: He's got a student-council meeting.

Man 3: What is this, Nuremberg?

Woman 3: And you buy that?

Woman 2: Honey —

Woman 3: Like you know what that is.

Woman 3: Come on, I have a thing tonight. Jennifer's mom let her have the car and he's lying.

Man 2: Robbie, do you or don't you have a student-council meeting tonight?

Man 3: Yeah, I do. Of course I do. I'm in student council, we have meetings. Why wouldn't I have a student-council meeting?

Woman 3: On a Friday night?

Man 2: Guys, come on, give it a rest. See?

Man 3: It's a social meeting.

Woman 3: Oh, okay, a "social meeting" —

Man 3: There's a swimming pool, there are parents.

Woman 3: More like suppliers.

Man 2: Hey! Robbie! That's your sister!

Man 3: Shut up, Maddie.

Woman 2: Watch your —

W1 M1 Woman 2	Man 2	Woman 3	Man 3	Girl	Boy
		See? He's an asshole. I don't get why he gets to have the Nissan whenever he wants.	I have meetings for my future.		
It's not whenever he wants.		Last time you had a meeting for your future you crashed the car.			
(He crashed the Nissan?)		(A scratch – he scratched it.)	I didn't crash the car.		
(I didn't know that.)		(It's not a big –)			
Robbie, you hit something with the Nissan?		Then what do you call it when your car runs into a fence? Is that like how people park in the future?			
		You smashed the passenger-side door.	I barely hit the fence.		
		Yeah, sure. My friends can't get in that way now. They have to climb over me.	No, Mom, I just dented it a little.		
		What?	More like climb on top of you. *(Gives his sister a knowing look.)*		
(Oh God, I don't wanna know.)	Maddie, cut it out.	Oh, okay. Hey, you guys wanna hear why Robbie crashed the car?			
		Why?			
Your brother is taking the car tonight. You get it tomorrow night. That's that.		But I'm not doing anything fun tomorrow night. I'm doing something fun tonight. Jennifer's mom let her go and			

W 1	M 1	Woman 2	Man 2	Woman 3	Man 3	Girl	Boy
				Robbie's lying. Look at him – he's a liar.	(*Victorious.*) Thanks, guys, gotta go. (*Gathers his stuff.*)		
			This isn't about Robbie.	That's a first.			
			Is the attitude really necessary? There's one car and two of you. What are we supposed to do?		I'm gonna be late. Later, Maddie. (*He exits.*)		
		Be careful!					
				Yeah, great. Don't die, 'kay? Cool, I like you so much.			
		(*Pause.*)	(*Pause.*)	(*Pause.*)			
			(*He turns to* **Nicole**.)	(*She seethes, having been left with her parents in a cheesy restaurant far away from her friends.*)			
		Huh, that's a drag.	Hey, did they raise the price on this sampler platter?	(*Rolls her eyes. Jiggles her leg. Growls.*)			
		SHIFT	SHIFT	SHIFT	SHIFT		
				Okay, guys.	**Steven** (*enters*)		
		Oh! Hey, Steven. Maddie's told us so much about you.		(*Sighs. Smiles. Hopeful.*) So this is, um, this is Steven.			
		Call me Nicole. (*Smiles. Drinks.*)	I'm Maddie's father. Sam.	It's Madeleine, Mom, not Maddie . . . Jesus.	It's really good to meet you, Mrs. –		

W 1	M 1	Woman 2	Man 2	Woman 3	Man 3	Girl	Boy
					It's so nice of you guys to take me out to dinner.		
			What? I thought you were paying.				
			(Laughs.) Ah, I'm just pulling your leg, Steve.				
			Sorry. I guess everyone's just growing up too fast for me.	His name's Steven.			
					It's okay.		
		(He's cute.)		(Mom.)			
			So what are your interests, Steven?	Steven's really talented –	Well, I'm really into music –		
			A musician.		Kind of –		
			Oh yeah? What do you play?		Guitar, mostly, but I can also play drums a little.		
			Cool, very cool. Well, it looks like you have yourself a pretty cool guy, Maddie.				
				Thanks.	Thanks.		
		How did you guys meet?		At school. A party at school for Spanish. We're in Spanish together. For Cinco de Mayo.	At a party.		
			Well, I met Maddie's mother while she was waitressing.				
		Sam.	It's true! We weren't much older than you two. You kids should've		Oh. Cool.		

W 1	M 1	Woman 2	Man 2	Woman 3	Man 3	Girl	Boy
			seen her. She was gorgeous, and I went right up to her. And lemme tell you, Maddie, your mother wasn't exactly looking to settle down. I mean, the first date alone was (*Laughs.*) well —	Okay, we don't need to hear about how you, like, conquered Mom.			
		That's not really how it happened at all. Maddie, don't listen to this. Sam, please.					
			All right, all right.				
			So, Cinco de Mayo, huh? Are you, uh . . . Latino, Seven?				
					Um.		
					I'm adopted, so I don't really know, but I sort of doubt it.		
			You know, my dad used to tell this joke about Latinos . . . it's not offensive, but it's a little racy —				
				Dad.			
			Okay, okay. (*Makes a whip sound as if he's fighting off lions. Laughs.*)				
	Sam.						
			Well, despite what these ladies might tell you, my dad was quite the comedian.				
					Wow, I, uh, I can't wait to meet him.		
			That's nice of you to say. But my dad passed away a long time ago.				
					Oh, I'm sorry.		
			It was a long time ago.				
					Still, that really, um, sucks.		

W 1	M 1	Woman 2	Man 2	Woman 3	Man 3	Girl	Boy
			(*Smiles.*) Yeah, well, we'll all get there someday.				
				Dad.			
			What?				
				You're being morbid.			
			Who's being morbid? Death's a part of life, am I right, Steve?				
			SHIFT	SHIFT	SHIFT		
		Where are your parents from, Marcus?		His name's Marcus, Dad.	**Marcus**		
			Then who's Steven?		Ohio.		
				That was — what is wrong with you?!			
			Buckeyes.		Okay.		
		SHIFT	SHIFT	SHIFT	SHIFT		
			Who doesn't like football?	Jeremy doesn't like football.			
			Oh yeah?	He plays tennis.			
				Jeremy's really talented, Dad.			
		SHIFT	SHIFT	SHIFT			
			What position?		**Jeremy** Um, there's kinda like only one position.		
		Don't listen to him.	Mm, well, what should we have to eat? Anyone want an appetizer?				
		(He's cute.)		(Mom.)			
			You want calamari?				
					Oh, I'm allergic. Sorry.		
			To calamari?				
					To shellfish.		

W 1	M 1	Woman 2	Man 2	Woman 3	Man 3	Girl	Boy
			Then why can't you eat calamari?				
		(*Laughs.*)					
		Oh, Sam.	Is calamari a shellfish?				
				Yes.			
			Excuse me, excuse me! Am I talking to you? No.				
			I'm talking to, uh, uh, Patrick, right?	Patrick.			
		Hey, don't talk to me like that! How dare you?		Oh my God.			
		SHIFT	SHIFT	SHIFT	SHIFT		
					Patrick It is, but –		
		Don't talk to me that way.	Now, Patrick, I thought calamari was a-a-a octopus.	It's squid.			
		Sam.	Okay, squid, but I don't see what a squid has to do with a clam or an oyster or what?				
		Sam. Apologize.	For what?				
		First of all, for your tone.	Tone. What tone?				
				Stop, please stop. We're in public. Oh my God, can't you guys be normal for just like one meal? I knew this would happen. This always happens.			
		The way you spoke to me and Maddie was totally disrespectful.	You were mocking me – both of you were mocking me and I'm supposed to respond in a respectful way when I'm shown little to no respect myself?				
		We were not mocking you.		This was a bad idea. I'm sorry, I'm really sorry they're being like this. But it's not okay. They're always like this.	It's okay.		
		Sam.			It's seriously okay.		
		We weren't the ones being disrespectful.					

W 1	M 1	Woman 2	Man 2	Woman 3	Man 3	Girl	Boy
			Then what do you call that "Oh, Sam," with the little laugh?	Maybe we should go.			
					We don't have to do that.		
			If that's not mocking, then I don't know what is. Wait, wait, did she —	I'm telling you I want to go.			
		Go? What do you mean, go?			Okay.		
			You can't go.	We're going. Yeah, we're gonna go.			
					It was really nice meeting you guys.		
				I mean me and Patrick are getting the hell away from this whole dysfunctional situation.			
					I think since we're going, I should really pay you guys for my meal.		
		Dysfunctional?	No, no. Patrick	Yeah. Dysfunctional.	**Michael** My name's Michael.		
		You think this is dysfunctional? God, you're spoiled, you know that?					
		SHIFT	SHIFT	SHIFT	SHIFT		
		You don't know a thing about dysfunction. Just take a look at all the terrible things happening in the world. Look at all the terrible things happening in the world and tell me that this, this is dysfunctional. If anything, you should feel blessed.	Right, right, right. Michael, you're not gonna pay, okay? This is on us.	Oh yeah, this is good. You're not dysfunctional 'cause there's like apartheid or something happening in some impoverished nation.	No, please, just lemme give you guys a little.		
			No, no. Thank you, but no.		It's okay. My parents gave me some money.		
			Well, that is certainly generous of them, but we've got it covered.	Blessed? Wow. Blessed. Okay.			

W1 M 1 Woman 2	Man 2	Woman 3	Man 3	Girl Boy
Yeah, get sarcastic. That helps.	It's very nice to meet you, and I want to apologize for the way my daughter is behaving, but –			
		Me? Why are you apologizing for me? Um. Okay . . . You're the one acting like a freak.		
	A freak.			
Sam, she's right, you were not –	Okay.			
What?	Why don't you just order another drink?			
	My mother's right. You're more fun when you're drunk.			
(Horrible pause.)	(Horrible pause.)	(Horrible pause.)	(Horrible pause.)	
(She is rattled . . .)	(. . . He is embarrassed.) Hey, ah, Nicky, I'm sorry. I didn't –			
Don't.		Seriously, Mom, I can't believe you let him talk to you like this after what he did to you.		
Maddie.	After what I did? What did I do?			
(Pause.)	(Pause.)	(Pause.)	(Pause.)	
	Nicole? What did I do?			
Sam.	You wanna fill me in here?			
Sam.	Huh?	I'm sorry, Mom. I didn't mean to – Mom – I didn't mean to – (She goes.)	(He goes.)	

W 1	M 1	Woman 2	Man 2	Woman 3	Man 3	Girl	Boy
			You wanna fill me in here on what I did? (*He slams the table with his palm.*)				
		SHIFT	SHIFT	SHIFT	SHIFT		
					Robbie (*enters*) Hey, Mom, Dad.		
		Hey, Robbie.					
					Um, well, this is Stephanie. *hands.*)		
				Stephanie (*enters, bright and cheery*) Oh my God, hiii!			
			stands up	*to shake*			
		(*And everyone*					
				It's so nice to meet you guys.			
		Oh, hey, Stephanie! I'm Nicole. We've heard so much about you.					
			Stephanie? What happened to Marissa? (*Laughs.*)				
					Dad.		
			I'm just pulling your leg, Steph. Marissa doesn't exist – well, at least not to my knowledge. Maybe Robbie's got a secret Marissa under the table. Watch out for this one. (*Laughs.*)				
					Robert. My name's –		
			Oh, I'm just having some fun.				
					Dad.		
			Call me Sam.	Thanks, Mr. –			
					It's not funny.		
				Thank you so much. Sam.			

Woman 1	M 1	Woman 2	Man 2	Woman 3	Man 3	Girl Boy
			(Hey, way to go, Robster) (*Sizzle sound.*)		(Dad.)	
SHIFT		SHIFT	SHIFT	SHIFT	SHIFT	
Alice (*enters*)						
I want a picture! Hello? Picture time!						
			Mom.		Grandma.	
Oh, shut up. I want Robbie and his new girlfriend for my wallet. Saaaay nacho!						
				Nacho.	Nacho.	
SHIFT		SHIFT	SHIFT	SHIFT	SHIFT	
		Oh, I like her, Robbie. I like her a lot.			Yeah, me too.	
You know, girls these days lack poise, they lack class. But Stephanie, that is a very classy young lady.						
		I don't usually like "girly" girls, but that Steph, she is something else. (*Laughs.*)			Okay.	
Absolutely adorable.					Cool.	
		Just don't fuck it up, okay? Men tend to fuck things up for themselves, especially when they're happy.			Thank you.	

Woman 1	M 1	Woman 2	Man 2	W 3	Man 3	Girl	Boy
Your mother's right.					Right.		
					Yeah.		
		God, I hope you're using condoms. You're using condoms, right? Sorry, I'm sorry, but I have to ask.			Mom.		
					Or not.		
SHIFT		SHIFT	SHIFT		SHIFT		
			So what's up?		(**Robbie** *adjusts his wristwatch nervously*)		
					Um, so what do you think of her, Dad? I mean, really.		
			Stephanie? She's great. She's a very nice girl.		And?		
			And, well, she's young.		She's just two years younger than me.		
			You're young too, Robbie.		You think everyone who's not old is young, I'm very professional for my age.		
			All I'm saying is now maybe not the time to be settling down.		Well, when's the time? When you say so? I've got plans, Dad. I've got ambitions. Play the field? Uh, wow.		
			No. I just think you should play the field a little. I mean, let's be honest, Robbie, you met this girl in high school.				

468

Woman 1	M 1	Woman 2	Man 2	Woman 3	Man 3	Girl	Boy
					And you met Mom at a bar. What's wrong with high school?		
			Restaurant. We met at a –				
					I love her.		
			Nothing, there's nothing wrong with it, it's just –				
			You – ?		Yeah.		
			Okay, sure, you love her and that's, that's real to you right now at this age, but –		It is.		
					No, at any age. It's real. This is what I want.		
			Sure, of course, sure, but –				
				SHIFT			
				(She clinks a glass.)			
				Excuse me!			
			Robbie.	Hi!			
			SHIFT	Excuse me! Um, hi.			
				So Robbie and I have a little announcement.	SHIFT		
			An announcement?				
				Um, you wanna?	Yeah.		
				Okayokayokay . . . WE'RE ENGAGED!	Go ahead.		
How wonderful! How absolutely wonderful!		Oh, honey! That's great! That's so great!	Wow, that is very . . . wow.	Thanks. Thank you.			
				(She runs over to the ladies.)			

Woman 1	M 1	Woman 2	Man 2	Woman 3	Man 3	Girl	Boy
		(Hugs her.)	*(And the*	*drinks start*	*flowing)*		
A wedding! I love weddings!		Welcome. Welcome to the family!					
				Thanks. Um, Mom? Is that okay? Can I call you Mom?			
		Mom? Wow! I guess I kinda am – Yeah, go for it!					
			Hey, I, uh, thought we were gonna talk about this some more, buddy.				
					Why? I've made up my mind.		
			Of course you have. I just want you to know that I'm always here to help you make your own decisions.				
					Dad, I'm getting married.		
		Oh, I love this girl. Don't you love this girl, Sam?	I know, I know. She's very nice.				
					She's the love of my life.		
		When's the wedding?	And why wouldn't she be?				
				We don't know yet, but we're thinking maybe Valentine's Day.			
Valentine's Day!			That is definitely a romantic day.				
		Wow!		Kissed.			
					Yeah it's the first day we, uh – kissed.		
Do you have a dress?		Oh, God, you should've seen mine. I don't know what I was thinking.		Not yet.			

Woman 1	Man 1	Woman 2	Man 2	Woman 3	Man 3	Girl Boy
When you order the cake, don't forget that I'm allergic to walnuts and marzipan.					(Dad, can you please say something?)	
			(Of course, yeah.) **Sam** *stands, toasts.*) Uh, Stephanie, honey, hey, congratulations.	*(She practically tackles* **Sam** *with a hug)* Oh my God, thank you, thank you so much. *(She is suddenly crying)* Yeah, it's just I'm so happy.		
			Are, are you okay? And your dad's footing the bill for this, right? It's a joke. I'm joking. TRADITION! Welcome to the family!			
		Sam.				
SHIFT	SHIFT	SHIFT	SHIFT	SHIFT	SHIFT	
	Jack *(enters with cigar)* Hey, who let all these handsome people in here? Huh?					
				Oh, hey, guys. Everyone, this is my dad, Jack.		
		(Everyone	*gets up*	*to shake*	**Jack**'s *hand.)*	

Woman 1	Man 1	Woman 2	Man 2	Woman 3	Man 3	Girl	Boy
	Great to meet you, Sam. Great to meet you.		Hey, Jack! Sam.				
I'm Alice.	You must be Robbie's mother.						
(*Laughs.*) Grand-mother, actually.					He's good, he's very good.		
Oh! (*Laughs.*)	Get out! With that figure? (*Laughs.*)	Hi, Jack, I'm Nicole, Robbie's mom.					
	An absolute pleasure. C'mere! (*He turns his handshake with Nicole into a sweet little twirl.*)	Whoa, ha ha!					
	Heck of a boy you raised.	Thank you.	Thanks Jack.				
	If I may say one little thing to the love birds?	Of course.	Sure.				
	Now Steph and I went through a lot, what with everything between me and her mother, so forgive me for getting sentimental for a moment, but if I've learned anything, kids, it's this:						
	Love is not California. With love there's a lot of storms and hail and sleet. We all know something about sleet around here now don't we?						
		(*Knowing	laughs	at the		table.*)	

Woman 1	Man 1	Woman 2	Man 2	Woman 3	Man 3	Girl	Boy
	But you know what? It passes. It might not seem like it, but it passes and it makes everything else a hell of a lot more beautiful for having braved the stuff. So please, whatever you do –						
	Steph? Robbie? You hearing this? Whatever you do . . . don't move to California! It's very far away and I can't stand the place!						
	Okay, enough of that nonsense. Let's have a party!						
(Laughs.)		(Laughs.)	(Laughs.)	(Laughs.)	(Laughs.)		
				We won't, Daddy.	You got it, Jack.		
		(Sam and Nicky	*look on with a kind of*	*(And the family*	*dance, dance,*		
		bewildered wonder, then	*begin to dance with*	*dances, stomping and*	*hollering with a*		
		one another. And just	*as quickly as the*	*a visceral celebration*	*of love and life.)*		
		dance began it's over.)					
SHIFT	SHIFT	SHIFT	SHIFT	SHIFT	SHIFT		
(Sighs.)	(Sighs.)	(Sighs.)	(Sighs.)	(Sighs.)	(Sighs.)		
		Oh, what an awesome wedding!	Can you believe this?				
		Can you?					
					(Drinks, stumbles a little.)		

Woman 1	Man 1	Woman 2	Man 2	Woman 3	Man 3	Girl	Boy
Where's Maddie run off to? I saw her with some man. Has anyone seen Maddie?			(*Castilian voice.*) Mmm, yes, yes, I can. (*They kiss.*)				
	God, she's beautiful. Isn't my little girl beautiful?						
My wedding night was something else, let me tell you. I had only been with one man before **Robert** – one! Oh, but thank God, thank God for that.					(*Clinks a glass aggressively, stands. Drunk.*)		
				Kinda loud, honey.	I want to thank my incredible family.		
					Mom: you're awesome. Dad: thanks. Thanks for everything. I mean I know you don't, like, condone our marriage or anything but it's fine it's a little (*gesture*) but it's fine.		
				I never said that.			
			Stephanie, honey, you have to know I never said anything like that. I adore you. I totally adore you.	I think my husband's had a little too much fun. (*Takes the drink.*)			
				What?	Hey!		
					Give it back.		

Woman 1	Man 1	Woman 2	Man 2	Woman 3	Man 3	Girl	Boy
				No way.	I love you.		
		(Pretty damn drunk.) Have another drink, Steph!		I love you too.	So can I have it back now or what?		
		(Drinks.) You're not drinking? You just got married!		Oh I'm not drinking			
(Pretty damn drunk.) Oh, pull the cork out of your ass and drink up! *(Laughs.)*				I know, but I really shouldn't.			
				Thanks, yeah, I would guys I would but I feel a little sick. Oh. . . .			
SHIFT	SHIFT	SHIFT	SHIFT	SHIFT	SHIFT	SHIFT	
					(He clinks a glass.) Hey, guys! Guys! Everyone! Hey! I wanna introduce you . . . to Jacquelyn.	**Jackie** *(enters)*	
			(Laughs and claps.)				
Oooooooooh.	Heeeeeey-oooo.						
		Oh my God, she's gorgeous, she's – Oh, Robbie, Stephanie, she's perfect, she's just perfect.	That's my boy! *(Laughs.)* Wow. Wow.				
You must be very proud, Jack.	You're damn right.				Isn't she?		

Woman 1	Man 1	Woman 2	Man 2	Woman 3	Man 3	Girl	Boy
				Say hello, Jackie.		**Jackie** Hello.	**Boy**
	Oooh, would you look at her? Look at those cheeks.	Oooooooh.	Aaahhhhhhhh. She's cute, she is very cute. You're a doll, Jackie. What a miracle.		Yeah, she's pretty much the best.		
Who wants another Cadillac Margarita?! Yeah, I invented this motherfucker!	(*Laughs.*)	Oooooooh!					
Aaaaaahhhh. (*Drunken.*) Picture time! Picture time!			Mom.		Grandma.		
Oh shut up. Saaaay nacho!	Nacho.	Nacho.	Nacho.	Nacho.	Nacho.	Nacho.	
SHIFT	SHIFT	SHIFT	SHIFT	SHIFT	SHIFT	SHIFT	
			(*He clinks a glass.*)				
			So I've heard a rumor, a teeny, tiny rumor that I'm . . . GONNA HAVE A GRANDSON!				
Oooooo! A picture! We need to take a picture! Where's my camera? Has anyone seen my camera?	(*Whistle and applause.*) That's my Steph. That's my little Steph.	What? Oh, that's incredible! That's so —!	A boy! A baby boy!	It's true, yeah, we're expecting again, yeah, isn't that great?	Yep, yep, thanks, ha ha. Yeah, sweetie?	Dad.	
	Hey, lemme buy you a drink, Alice.	It's so great!	Wow.		That's right.	I'm gonna have a brother?	
Oh for the love of God, Jack	(*Laughs.*)	When are you due?	WOW.	Pretty soon.			
		You've got to be thrilled.					

Woman 1	Man 1	Woman 2	Man 2	Woman 3	Man 3	Girl	Boy
	You're a spitfire, you know that?			I am, we both are, we're really excited.	Yes, your brother's gonna be very nice.	Is he gonna be nice?	
		I am, I am so happy for you.	Hey-ooooo! Ha ha ha ha!	*She holds* **Robbie**'s *hand.*	Of course.	Promise?	
							CLANG.
							(The boy enters and is served a plate of chicken fingers. The plate is heavy. It makes a big clang sound when it hits the table. Everyone stops what they're doing. They avoid eye contact. This will take the boy a long time to eat. He exits when he's finished.)
(Long pause.)	*(Long pause.)*	*(Long pause.)*	*(Long pause.)*	*(Long pause.)*	*(Long pause.)*	*(Long pause.)*	*(Long pause.)*
	Damn it.	I'm sorry.	Did they tell you what happened?				
	Goddamn it.	I'm so sorry.			Dad. *(He drinks.)*		
				(Sobs and runs off.)			

M 1   W 2   M 2   W 3   M 3   Girl   Boy

Woman 1

Alice

(She is shaken, as if reliving her husband's death all over again.)

When my husband died, I went to this man downtown, who worked in this little room with pastels on the walls, and I'd sit in a chair and talk to him. Only I don't remember myself talking; I only knew that I had talked because of the bill I got in the mail every month. And I wish I could remember what I said. I hope I didn't tell him anything terrible about your father, 'cause I loved him.

Yes, sometimes Robert was unkind to me, but at the core of him was a good person — one of the best people the world has ever known.

So what I've started doing is I've begun to write letters, and these letters are addressed to my husband, and I talk to him. I tell him how much I miss him, I tell him what's happening in your lives, and the baseball scores and the state of the yard, and I tell him how glad I'll be to see him.

And I've told him how he has a great-grandchild on his way to meet him there, and how, though none of us ever met him, he is a very curious person, a very kind person, and they will have lots to talk about.

Oh, my husband will have lots to tell your son, so don't be sad.

Don't be sad.

I was sad for a long time, but if you just get a little envelope and talk to him, it'll make you feel so much better.

Why, just try now. Just try writing to him now. Just write right here, say hello.

Just say hello.

Tell him you love him right now, right this moment. Just say hello. Go on, go on, go on.

Woman 1	Man 1	Woman 2	Man 2	Woman 3	M 3 Girl Boy
CLANG.					
(*Alice is served a big plate of food. She eats and eats. She exits when she's finished.*)					
(*Long pause.*)					
SHIFT	SHIFT	SHIFT	SHIFT	SHIFT	
		(*She takes **Sam**'s hand.*)	(*He is deeply shaken. He stares blankly.*)	**Maddie** (*enters*) It's okay, Dad. It's gonna be okay.	
	She was a great woman. Of course, I didn't know her as long or as well as the rest of you but she was a real	We're so glad you made it, Maddie.		Thanks, Mom. Yeah, they'll let me take my finals early so –	
	spitfire, and, sure, sure, well, who wants a drink?	Thank you, Jack. I'll take one.			
	That's the spirit! What'll you have?	Uh, how about a Cadillac Margarita? (*Laughs.*)	(*Smiles a little.*)		
	Alright! Now lemme track down that server. (*Exits.*)			Dad, if you need anything, seriously Dad.	

W 1	Man 1	Woman 2	Man 2	W 3	Man 3	Girl	Boy
		I'm not going anywhere you understand me? I'm right here. I'm here for you, Sam.					
			You know, Mom used to say you never really understand how alone you are until you lose 'em both.				
		SHIFT	SHIFT		SHIFT		
					Robbie		
		(*Exits.*)			Hey sorry I can't be at the funeral, Dad. (Yeah I'll –) Hang on, Dad. (Yeah, whiskey, thanks.) Dad, you there? (*Checks his watch.*) It's just my plane's about to leave for Orlando and – (Thanks thanks.) (*Drinks.*)		
			Orlando? What's in Orlando?		You there?		
			Robbie				
			Hey look Dad, I gotta go.				
	Sam I'm here.						

Woman 1

(*Nicole* alone. *She waits, peruses the menu.*)

Nicole

There you are.

It's okay, Maddie, sit down.

It's not a problem.

So what's up?

What? Maddie, holy shit.

Maddie.

With who?

I didn't, I didn't know you were seeing anyone. Darius?

A year? Okay, so what's, what's the story with Darius?

Man 1

. . . Orlando.

Yeah okay.

Well, lemme know if you change your mind, buddy.

Woman 2

Maddie

(*enters*)

Hey, Mom.

Sorry I'm late.

Thanks, um, thanks for meeting me. I know it's last minute –

(*She sits.*)

(*Hopeful.*) It's not, well, okay, um, I'm pregnant!

Yeah.

His name's Darius. It just, just sorta happened.

Yeah, for like a year now.

Well, he's a painter.

Man 2

I'd be there if I could.

It's just . . . too much.

(*Checks his watch.*) It's just a little too much.

(*Drinks.*)

Woman 1: Wow.

Woman 2: He's really talented, Mom.

Woman 1: So I mean, is that it? Have you covered, I don't know, every genre? I mean there was that video artist, then there was that string of musicians, that dancer, that actor, you had that chiropractor for a while – not sure that counts as an artist, but –

Woman 2: Painting is not a genre, it's a form of visual –

Woman 1: Oh lighten up. When did you get so serious?

Woman 2: Okay.
Okay, it's not like that, Mom.

Woman 1: Maddie, honey, trust me. I used to fall for these types of guys all the time – these scrappy, needy, narcissistic . . .

Woman 2: We're in love, Mom, okay? We're in love.

Woman 1: Oh, you know. I mean the guy I was dating before I met your father was –

Woman 2: Uh, hello.

Woman 1: Well, he was a freak, but he was a sexy freak – extremely attentive – so I get it. I get the thing you're going through.

Woman 2: Types? What types? Scrappy?

Woman 1: Remember Steven? Jeremy? Uh, uh . . . Marcus?

Woman 2: Uh, no, I don't.

Woman 1: Are you and Dario –

Woman 2: So now Darius is a freak?

Woman 1: Right. Are you and he planning to get married or –?

Woman 2: Okay, you haven't even met him.
I'm not going through anything. I'm in love.

Woman 1: Forget it. Forget I said anything.

Woman 2: Yeah, I've dated a bunch of guys – so what?

Woman 1: (*Small pause.*)

Woman 2: Darius

Woman 1: Alright, well you know what? You get older and you start to see things a little differently.

Woman 2: Married?! Oh my god, who are you? You and Dad barely had a wedding!

Woman 2: (*Small pause.*)

Woman 1	Man 1	Woman 2	Man 2	W 3	M 3	Girl	Boy
		Okay, so now I have to be like Robbie and his perky little wife, and everyone else in this fucking wasteland. Yeah right.					
This isn't about Robbie.							
		That's a first. And for the record: that wedding sucked. It was super cheesy.					
Oh get over it.							
		Hey, why don't you get a drink?					
I stopped drinking.							
		Oh, really?					
Yes.							
		When?					
When that alcoholic grandmother of yours finally kicked the bucket. (*Laughs.*)							
		(*Laughs.*)					
Wow, Maddie, another grandchild. Well, I'm – You know what? I'm ecstatic.							
		Really?					
Of course! You're my baby girl! Now come here! (*She hugs* **Maddie**.)							
		Thanks, Mom.					
. . . just don't fuck it up okay?							
SHIFT	SHIFT	SHIFT	SHIFT			SHIFT	
Nicole (*sings*) Happy, happy birthday from all of us to you.	**Sam** (*delighted*) You've gotta be kidding.	**Maddie** (*sings*) Happy, happy birthday from all of us to you.	**Robbie** (*sings*) Happy, happy birthday from all of us to you.			**Jackie** (*sings*) Happy, happy birthday from all of us to you.	

Woman 1	Man 1	Woman 2	Man 2	W 3 M 3 Girl	Boy
Happy, happy birthday, we're all so proud of you. Happy, happy birthday from all of us to you. Happy, happy birthday, may all your dreams come true. Happy birthday, SAAAAAAAM. (*Claps.*)	Happy, happy birthday, we're all so proud of you. Happy, happy birthday from all of us to you. Happy, happy birthday, may all your dreams come true. Happy birthday, SAAAAAAAM. (*Claps.*)	Happy, happy birthday, we're all so proud of you. Happy, happy birthday from all of us to you. Happy, happy birthday, may all your dreams come true. Happy birthday, SAAAAAAAM. (*Whistles.*)	Happy, happy birthday, we're all so proud of you. Happy, happy birthday from all of us to you. Happy, happy birthday, may all your dreams come true. Happy birthday, SAAAAAAAM. (*Claps.*)	Happy, happy birthday, we're all so proud of you. Happy, happy birthday from all of us to you. Happy, happy birthday, may all your dreams come true. Happy birthday, SAAAAAAAM. (*Claps.*)	Happy, happy birthday, we're all so proud of you. Happy, happy birthday from all of us to you. Happy, happy birthday, may all your dreams come true. Happy birthday, GRAAANDPAAA. (*Jumps a little.*)
	(*Laughs. He might take a picture.*)	(*Everyone is in	*a very jovial mood.*)		
	Now who hatched this little scheme?		I'm afraid that's classified information.	GRANDMA!	
Jackie, how could you?!	Nicky?				
I couldn't help myself. Happy birthday, Sam. (*She kisses him.*)	(*Big smile.*) Well there's nothing that works up the appetite quite like a public seruhm, uh, serum . . . Oh, Nicky, what is that word?	(*Hugs.*) Happy birthday, Dad. Dad –	(*Hugs.*) We love you, Dad.		
Serenade! (*Laughs.*)	(*Smiles.*)	(*Laughs.*)	(*Laughs.*)		
	Right right, serenade! So, uh, who wants an appetizer?		Bring it on.		

Woman 1	Man 1	Woman 2	Man 2	W 3	M 3	Girl	Boy
Uh, your daughter's pregnant, Sam.	How about calamari?						
	So? She's not allowed to eat calamari?	Dad –					
Sam –							
	I thought pregnant women ate everything.		Dad, it's a shellfish.				
	I've seen 'em at the aquarium and I don't buy it for a second.						
When have you ever been to an aquarium?			Well, I hate to break it to you, but science has a system, a classification system –				
	Robbie, it's cooked! How can it be bad for her if it's cooked?						
		It's okay, Dad, I'm just being careful.					
	(*Warm.*) There's being careful and then there's being crazypants, and I think you're being a little crazypants.						
			(*Drinks.*) Hey, it's tricky stuff. You know, Steph and I went through the same thing with –				
						Dad.	
						Daddy.	
							Hey, Daddy.

Woman 1	Man 1	Woman 2	Man 2	W 3 M 3 Girl	Boy
			Hold on, Dad. What's up, Jackie?	Can I get a corn dog?	
			A corn dog?	Yeah, they're the best.	
No way.					
	Oh Nicole, let her have the corndog.				
Now Jackie, what do you think your mom'll say when she finds out we let you have a corndog?				Um . . . did you get me one?	
(*Laughs.*) Somehow I don't think so.	(*Laughs.*) She's a doll. I always said she's a doll.	(*Laughs.*)	(*Laughs.*) No, no. Mommy will not be happy with Daddy if she comes back from her business trip and finds her little girl hopped up on preservatives. No, you'll get something else.		
				She would! Dad!	
				I'll only have a little, I promise!	
	So how's work, stranger?	Dad.	Uh, Steph's new venture's taking off so –		
	No, I mean your work –		You know, same old same old.		
		Uh, hello. Earth to Dad.			
	I'm talking to your brother.		(*Drinks.*)		

Woman 1	Man 1	Woman 2	Man 2	W 3	M 3	Girl	Boy
		Well I wanna give you a birthday present.					
	Can it wait?						
		No.					
	(*Closes his eyes. Opens his hands. Playful.*) Alright, lay it on me.						
		(*Takes his hand.*) I have decided to name him after you.						
	Who? What are you talking about?						
What do you think she's talking about, Sam?							
		Uh, him. My baby. Oh my God.					
	It's a boy?						
		Yeah.					
	And you're naming him after me?						
		Yes.					
	Well, hey, that's pretty cool! (*Laughs.*)						
SHIFT	SHIFT	SHIFT	SHIFT	SHIFT	SHIFT	SHIFT	SHIFT
							Sammy (*enters*) MEEERRRRY EX-MAS! MERRRRRY EX-MAS! (*He does a hyperactive ninja move.*)
Well, look who it is!	Sammy's back!						

Woman 1	Man 1	Woman 2	Man 2	W 3	M 3	Girl	Boy
		Sammy, honey, sit down next to your cousin. The food's gonna be coming out soon.					
	(*Kinda racist accent.*) Hoooo. Beware the Sammy-rai!						HO HO HO!
Very funny, Sam.							
	(*Laughs.*)	A little racist, Dad.					
							HI-YA!
						Ow! Don't yell in my ear.	
						Dad, make him stop.	
		Sammy, how many times do I have to tell you? Leave your cousin alone.	Maddie? Your son, can you get him to –				
							Fine.
		Now say you're sorry.					
							Sorry, Jackie. (*He kisses her cheek.*)
						Ew! Don't!	
						You got my cheek wet.	
	(*Laughs.*)		Buddy –				
	The kid's funny.	Come on, Dad, you're just encouraging him.					
							What? I'm saying sorry!
	So what were you up to out there, (*racist*) Sammy-rai?						
							I was making a snowman . . . WITH TITS.
		You what? No.					
	(*Laughs.*)		(*Weird look.*)				
Well, okay then.							
	Oh yeah? What size were her sno-cones? Huh?						Yeah!

Woman 1	Man 1	Woman 2	Man 2	W 3	M 3	Girl	Boy
Sam, grow up. He doesn't even know what he's saying.	(*Laughs.*) Come on, Nicky, it's a joke!						(*Laughs.*) Then a dog came over and peed on it, so it looked like the snowman peed while standing up, but girls don't pee standing up, only boys do. SO I PUNCHED HER TITS OFF!
							HI-YAH!
All right. Where's he getting this stuff?		God, okay. No, don't. Don't do that again, okay? You have to be nice to girls, even snowman girls.	He's got an imagination, I'll give him that.				
		Well, for starters, because your mother's a girl and you wanna be nice to me, don't you?					Why?
Hey!		Sammy!	You know, Mad, I know a guy, like a child-behavioral guy –			Sometimes.	
		Thanks but no thanks, Rob.	Are you sure?				(*He does something ridiculous.*) YAH YAH YAH.

Woman 1	M 1 Woman 2	Man 2	W 3 M 3 Girl	Boy
				PREEEESENTS!
You know what! Let's do some presents!	I thought we weren't doing Christmas tonight.		You're loud in my ear again!	
Well, now we're doing Christmas.	Come on, guys. I didn't know this was happening. I haven't done my Christmas shopping			
(*She tries to slow things down.*) Jackie, darling . . . since you have been so well behaved, you get to go first! (*Presents a box.*)			(*She opens it. Inside is a compass on a necklace.*) I don't know what it is.	
		It's a compass, honey. See, those are magnets and —	How's it do that?	
It can take you wherever you want to go.			And I can go anywhere with a compass?	
Yep! Anywhere! You can go anywhere!		It's a metaphor. Now what do you say to Grandma Nicky?		(Where's mine? Where's my present?!)
You're very welcome.	(Sammy.)		Thank you.	(What?) I wanna go next.
It's always on. It doesn't need to turn on.	(Be patient.)		How do you turn it on?	
			But how's it take me places?	

Woman 1	Man 1	Woman 2	Man 2	W 3 M 3 Girl	Boy
	Hey.	Whoa. Sammy.	Hold on. None of this. Hey –	You're being rude!	SHUT UP, JACKIE!
				I am not!	Well, you're being a spoiled little brat.
				Take it back.	That's what my mom says.
	Relax, Robbie. They're No. No. I don't know where he got that.	Sammy! Oh my God. Get over here!	What? Did you? Maddie, seriously? Did you tell him that?		*TWAT TWAT TWAT!*
Now where the hell did he learn that?			(*To* **Sam**.) Let me handle it, Dad. Say what? What did he say?	Daddy!	I heard you say it to Dad!
	The T word.	Nothing, he didn't – See? He didn't say anything.			Nothing.
	(You know, maybe your sister could watch him next time we go out.)				I was just making fun.
		I'm sorry, Rob, really. I don't know where he got that. (*She gives* **Sammy** *a look.*)	They're cousins. He needs to learn to respect his cousin.		
	(Can't hurt to ask.)	(*Sternly whispers to her son.*) Shut . . . up			(**Sammy** *grins at his mom, then hides it.*)
(My sister's not a babysitter, Sam.)					

Woman 1	Man 1	Woman 2	Man 2	W 3	M 3	Girl	Boy
SHIFT	SHIFT	SHIFT	SHIFT			SHIFT	SHIFT
						(*Exits.*)	(*Exits.*)
And of course your father insisted on taking a picture of every damn thing we came across, every, uh, church, painting, conquistador . . .	Matador.	(*Smiles.*) Big surprise					
What?	Conquistador's the soldier guy. The matador's the guy with the cape. Ho ho, toro! toro!						
All right. Whatever. You name it, Sam snapped it.	Pardon me for wanting to remember the things I've shared with the woman I love. (*Takes her hand.*)		(*Drinks.*) It sounds great, Mom. Sounds like Barcelona was really great.				
(*Smiles.*) Yeah, yeah . . . it was pretty fucking rad. (*Kisses* **Sam** *on the cheek.*)	(*Laughs.*)	(*Laughs.*)	(*Laughs.*)				
		Hey, guys, we're in public.	Well, there they are.				
						Jackie (*enters*) PEW PEW PUCKOOOO BAM BOOM EXPLOOOSION!	**Sammy** (*enters*) BOOM BOOM BANG BOOM BANG BOOM WWWW! POOOWWWW

Woman 1	M 1	Woman 2	Man 2	W 3	M 3	Girl	Boy
						(They do a kiddish karate-	*move high-five.)*
You know it was quieter when they were fighting.			Jackie, cut it out.				
						AND NIINJACKIE!	BEWARE THE SAMMY-RAI.
			Maddie, you think you can prevent your son from further corrupting my daughter?				
						YAH YAH YAH.	YAH YAH YAH.
						BRING IT. *(She scurries around.)*	You ready for chair battle?
							CHAAAAIR BATTLE. *(He scurries around.)*
		Uh, yeah, Rob, sure. Jackie's an innocent. Sammy's a – Hey, no. Uh, los ninos, no way.					
			Well, I'm gonna get another drink. Does anyone else want another drink?				
		(Gives a look.)					
			What? It's a holiday. This is what people do on a holiday.				
		Uh, wow, okay.	You know what, I've already got a wife, Mad.				
		Do you, Rob? 'Cause no one's seen her for a while.	Oh, so now I'm supposed to take relationship advice from you?				

Woman 1	Man 1	Woman 2	Man 2	Woman 3	Man 2	Girl	Boy
						(They start to	*chair battle.)*
						YAHHHH.	YAHHHH.
		Guys, hey, both of you, cut it out. Go back outside and play, huh?					
	Hey.	Too bad.					But we're out of firecrackers! *(Bangs the table.)*
Who the hell gave them firecrackers?	It's the Fourth! That's what kids do on the Fourth!	You're going.	Jackie.			Yeah, we blew 'em all up! BANG! *(Bangs table.)*	BOOM! POW!
		We'll come find you when dinner's here, okay?	Listen to your aunt.			Yeah, what about our corn dogs?	What about my corn dog?
		Bye! Byeeeee!				Dad?	
						BEEEEEOOOOO – SHAPOOOM – *(She runs after him.)*	BEEEEEOOOO – SHAPOOOM – *(He runs off.)*
SHIFT	SHIFT	SHIFT	SHIFT			SHIFT	SHIFT
				Jackie *(enters.)*	**Sammy** *(enters)*		
					Mom.		
					Hey, Mom.		
You're telling me.		God, it's just, they grow up so fast.	Speak of the devil. *(Drinks.)*	Hi, Daddy.	Mom. Mom.		
			It's okay, honey. Have a seat.	Sorry we're late. *(Kisses his cheek.)*	Hey, Mom.		

Woman 1	Man 1	Woman 2	Man 2	Woman 3	Man 3	Girl	Boy
		What is it, Sammy? I'm talking. You're interrupting me. Why are you always interrupting me?			I'm just letting you know I'm gonna be out past curfew. You told me to tell you if I was gonna be out past curfew so here I am telling you . . . Jeez.		
					You're such a spaz.		
	Hoo, big plans tonight, *(a little racist)* Sammy-rai?	Fine.			*(A little racist.)* Hooooo with your blessings, Grandpa Sam-sei. *(Laughs.)*		
	(Laughs.)		*(Weird look.)*				
			(He stands. Raises his glass. He may chime it a little too aggressively. Drunk.) Hey! Hello! In honor of Turkey Day, in the spirit of giving thanks, I would like to share what I am thankful for.				
		A little loud, Rob, a little –					
					(Snickers.) Booze.		
		Sammy.		*(Rolls her eyes.)*	What?		
Go ahead, Robbie.							

W 1	Man 1	Woman 2	Man 2	W 3	Man 3	Girl	Boy
			(*Holding it together.*)				
			Okay, well, uh, my family. I am so very thankful for my incredible family.				
					(*Snickers.*)		
			Excuse me?				
					You're excused.		
			Do you have something to say?				
					(*Gives a look.*)		
			Uh, (*Tries to laugh it off.*) now where was I?				
					Orlando.		
		Sammy.					
			What?				
					Uh, aren't you always in Orlando instead of with your incredible family? (*Laughs.*)		
			(**Robbie** *nearly explodes.*) Okay, listen to me, you ungrateful little shit. Your mother might not be interested in disciplining you, but that doesn't mean you get to do or say whatever you want. You have to learn some respect. You have to learn a little decorum.				
		Hey, Robbie, this is my son.					
					Hey, whoa.		
					(*Laughs.*)		
			This is your family, and you need to show them the love and patience they show you. No, no. You keep my wife out of this.		Like anyone knows what that means.		
	Hey, hold on.						
					Oh, hey, speaking of family, where's Aunt Steph? Yeah, hey, Jackie, where's your mom? What, does she not like hanging out with us anymore? Are		

Woman 1	Man 1	Woman 2	Man 2	Woman 3	Man 3	Girl	Boy
	Look, guys, it's Thanksgiving				we not all perky enough for her or something?		
					I'm just asking a question.		
				Grow up, Sammy.	Grow some tits, Jackie.		
					Whoa. (*Laughs.*) People are looking. I mean, you are totally embarrassing yourself.		
He's drunk. You're drunk.		This is unacceptable, absolutely unacceptable –	(*He grabs* **Sammy** *by the arm.*) (*Quiet.*) How dare you.				
			(*He lets go of* **Sammy**'s *arm.*) You know, it's no wonder your father left.	Dad, come on. He's just being a brat.	Seriously? Is that supposed to hurt my feelings?		
		Jesus Christ, Rob.	Look at what you're doing to your mother.		Me? Oh my God, you are so plastic.		
		Hey.					
		Hey.					
			You think this has been easy on her?				
		Leave him alone.			Yeah, leave me alone.		
		(*To* **Sammy**.) Don't you dare say another word.	God, Maddie, you have no idea how to handle anything, do you?				
				(There are people watching.)	(*Zip-the-lip motion.*)		

Woman 1	Man 1	Woman 2	Man 2	W 3	Man 3	Girl	Boy
							Mom?
Maybe Sammy should stay with Darius for a while.	Now, I'm not sure that's such a good idea.	No! No!	I'm just trying to help.				
Maddie, honey, I mean it. It might be for the best.		I don't need you. No. No. I can handle this myself!					
		I don't need help.					
		I'm not some damsel in distress. I am a grown woman! I don't care if you like the way I live my life. It's my life, okay? IT IS MY LIFE!					
		Ow. (*She feels under her armpit*).					
		(*A suspended*	*moment.*)				
		Why's it so hard?	Are you okay?				
		Why's it feel so hard?	It's gonna be okay.				
			Maddie, look at me. Hey, it's all gonna be okay.				
Maybe you should see a doctor.		I'm sorry, Robbie.					
		Mom. Dad.	No, hey, hey, just look at me.				
We're right here.		(*She turns to her son.*) Sammy . . .	Look at me.				
		Oh Oh! *CLANG.* (*She is served a giant, heavy plate of hot food. She eats and eats. She exits when finished.*)					

Woman 1	Man 1	W 2	Man 2	Woman 3	Man 3	Girl	Boy
SHIFT	SHIFT	SHIFT	SHIFT	SHIFT	SHIFT		
					Mom? Mom?		
(*Shattered.*) Maddie . . .	(*Shattered.*) (*He takes* **Nicole***'s hand.*)		(*Deeply shaken.*) No. God. No.		No. No.		
Sammy, here. Come here, darling.	I . . . I never . . .		Maddie.		Mom.		
				I'm right here, Sammy, seriously, if you need anything			
Sammy.					No. No. Mom.		
Honey, come here –					No, no, no, no.		
Sammy, please –							
(*She beckons the family to hold hands. They do.* **Nicole** *leads them in prayer.*)							
Our Father, who art in heaven, hallowed be thy name. Thy kingdom come, thy will be done, on earth as it is in heaven.	Our Father, who art in heaven, hallowed be thy name. Thy kingdom come, thy will be done, on earth as it is in heaven.		Our Father, who art in heaven, hallowed be thy name. Thy kingdom come, thy will be done, on earth as it is in heaven.	Our Father, who art in heaven, hallowed be thy name. Thy kingdom come, thy will be done, on earth as it is in heaven.	(*He very noticeably does not pray.*)	Our Father, who art in heaven, hallowed be thy name. Thy kingdom come, thy will be done, on earth as it is in heaven.	Our Father, who art in heaven, hallowed be thy name. Thy kingdom come, thy will be done, on earth as it is in heaven.

Woman 1	Man 1	W 2	Man 2	Woman 3	Man 3	Girl	Boy
Give us this day our daily bread, and forgive us our trespasses, as we forgive those who –	Give us this day our daily bread, and forgive us our trespasses, as we forgive those who –		Give us this day our daily bread, and forgive us our trespasses, as we forgive those who –	Give us this day our daily bread, and forgive us our trespasses, as we forgive those who –	You know what? You know what? You know what!	Give us this day our daily bread, and forgive us our trespasses, as we forgive those who –	Give us this day our daily bread, and forgive us our trespasses, as we forgive those who –
					(He stands. He berates the rest.)		
					You didn't care about her. None of you cared.		
			Sammy, buddy –		No, shut up, just shut up! She was my mom, okay? She was my mom and and none of you gave a shit.		
					You could have, like, tried to raise money or, like, given up your jobs to be with her. You could have, like, stopped your lives.		

W 1   M 1   W 2   M 2   W 3   **Man 3**   **Girl   Boy**

Is it so hard to, like, stop your life for just like a second?

It's like everyone goes back to their lives so quickly they barely take a breath before it's like, back to normal.

We should take the time, you know, we should take the time to, like, not be assholes. You're all just a bunch of assholes!

This whole, this whole country is just a bunch of fuckin' assholes!' Everyone's just sitting around and talking and not doing a fuckin' thing about all the hurt and pain and, like, bad shit that's going down all over the world, and I'm tired of just sitting here and talking, I wanna do something about it, I wanna go out there and do something about it – and if that means I have to, like, sign up and kill a few people, kill a few assholes to do it, then fine. Then I'll go sign up and kill a few assholes so people will understand that it doesn't have to be like this.

We can be better and I'm gonna show you, I'm gonna show all of you assholes.

She was my mother, so stop looking at me like that.

I'm going, okay?

I don't care what you say, I'm gonna make a difference.

'Cause I'm sick of it, I'm so sick of it I just want it to be different. That's it. I just want it to all be different.

CLANG.

(He is served a big plate of food. He eats and eats. Everyone averts their eyes. There's nothing to say really. He exits.)

(LONG, LONG, LONG PAUSE.)

Woman 1	Man 1	W 2	M 2	W 3	M 3	Girl	Boy

(Sam and Nicole *are left alone. Everything begins to move much, much slower now.*)

Woman 1	Man 1
SHIFT	SHIFT
(*She wears a tiny yellow ribbon.*)	
(*Pause.*)	(*Pause.*)
	What are you thinking of getting?
I don't know, Sam.	
(*Pause.*)	(*Pause.*)
	These menus keep getting bigger and bigger.
Mm.	
(*Pause.*)	(*Pause.*)
Robbie called.	Oh, yeah? What'd he say?
Not much. He was at one of Steph's conferences.	
(*Pause.*)	(*Pause.*)
	How's Jackie?
She got some kind of award at her high school.	
(*Pause.*)	(*Pause.*)
	Did he mention the pictures?
What pictures?	From their visit.
Oh, no. Why would they, Sam?	I thought he'd say.
Well he didn't.	(*Pause.*)
(*Pause.*)	
What?	Hm?
(*She shakes her head.*)	Did you say something?
	I think I might get the salmon.

Woman 1   **Man 1**   **W 2 M 2 W 3 M 3 Girl Boy**

Woman 1	Man 1
SHIFT	SHIFT
(*Pause.*)	(*Pause.*)
Robbie called.	When?
This morning.	(*Pause.*)
(*Pause.*)	Nicole.
What?	Why didn't you tell me?
You were asleep.	I was not.
I called to you.	(*Pause.*)
(*Pause.*)	Well, what'd he say?
He's got a new job.	Oh yeah? Does he like it?
He hasn't started yet.	(*Pause.*)
(*Pause.*)	How's Jackie?
She's fine.	Did she get our present?
I don't know, Sam.	SHIFT
SHIFT	(*Pause.*)
(*The yellow ribbon is now gone.*)	Hey how's your sister?
(*Pause.*)	Yeah – she still in restaurants?
My sister?	(*Pause.*)
She's . . . she's gone, Sam. You know this.	
(*Pause.*)	

Woman 1	Man 1	W 2 Man 2	W 3	M 3	Girl	Boy
(*Smiles at Sam. Takes his hand.*) Why don't we order? (*Pause.*) SHIFT	Then who's gonna watch the kids? (*Pause.*) SHIFT	SHIFT				
		Robbie (*enters*) Sorry I'm late.				
We're good. We're just so happy to see you.	Whoa, ho ho! Robbie!	How are you?				
		Hi, Mom. (*Kisses her cheek.*) Dad. Uh, happy anniversary . . . what a run, huh?				
	How long are you staying?	(*He adjusts his watch. Smiles.*) You know how it is. Can I get you guys something to drink?				
I'm fine.	Well, we'll make the most of it, won't we? Where's, uh, where's Jackie?	(*Drinks.*) She's, uh, backpacking with her friends in Norway, then Iceland next week.				
Wow, exotic.	I hear they eat whale there. Now don't tell me that's a shellfish! (*Laughs*) Whoa, ho ho!	Uh huh.				
It's very exciting	Big change of scenery from Massachusetts. Are you sure?	Connecticut, Dad. She goes to school in Connecticut.				

Woman 1	Man 1	W 2	Man 2	Woman 3	M 3	Girl	Boy
			Yeah, I write the checks, so –				
(Pause.)	*(Pause.)*		*(Pause.)*				
Have you heard from Steph?							
			(Bristles.)				
			Mom, please.				
			(Drinks.)				
SHIFT	SHIFT		SHIFT	SHIFT			
				Jackie			
				(enters, wearing her compass necklace)			
				Hey. Hi.			
Jackie! Oh, darling! Look at you all grown up! My God! You're so beautiful!	Whoa ho ho!						
And you're wearing the necklace I gave you! How wonderful!				Thanks.			
	Well, have a seat.						
				This? Oh yeah, huh.			
	At least have some coffee, Maddie, or –		Dad.	Oh, sorry, I can't stay. My boyfriend's plane just got in, and he lost his luggage so he's – *(Gestures.)*			
	What?		This is Jacquelyn.				
	Of course it is! What'd I say?						
You said Maddie.							

Woman 1	Man 1	W 2	Man 2	Woman 3	M 3	Girl	Boy
	So? What's wrong with that?			Shit, I'm already late. Sorry – it's so nice to see you guys.			
				(She leaves.)			
Sam.	Now Madeleine . . .		Dad.				
Sam.	I'll say what I want. Leave me alone! Lemme be. Lemme be.		Dad.				
	Uh, what –						
Here, let me –	What, what, uh, don't touch me!						
Here.	I can . . . don't . . .						
Sh.	Leave me alone.						
*(She tucks a napkin into **Sam**'s shirt.)*	I don't want you touching me.						
	(Nicole *feeds* **Sam.** *She takes her time.)*		*(He watches this for a long while.)*				
			So, look. I know this is bad timing, Mom, but uh –				
			(He stands. Finishes his drink.)				
			Hey, let me pay for this, okay? That helps right? If I pay?				
			I don't know.				
			(He adjusts his watch.)				
			Things are pretty crazy, what with the lay-off, and uh, well, I met this woman, this amazing woman. Maddie would've . . .				
When are you coming back?			. . . Maddie would've loved her.				

Woman 1	Man 1	W 2	Man 2	W 3	M 3	Girl	Boy

Woman 1

That's wonderful.

I'm sure it is.

(*Long pause.*)
(*The pace slows down considerably.*
Nicole *continues to feed* **Sam**.)
My God, where does the time go?

(*A little laugh to herself.*) Where does it
all go? Oh, Sam. I will never forget
the day we . . . the day we . . . I will
never . . . ever . . .

Oh, Sam. Sam, my Sam.
(*She watches him eat.*)
Sam, Sam, Sam.

(*Long pause.*)

SHIFT

Man 1

(**Sam** *begins to eat by
himself.*)

(*And* **Sam** *slowly recedes
from view.*)
(*Long pause.*)

SHIFT

Man 2

She's got a lotta spunk, and uh, kids. And
they're great family, so . . .

It's all a little too much right now, but you
should really come out and visit sometime.

It's nice –

Well . . . hey . . . soon, okay? I'll be home
again soon. I love you.

(*He kisses* **Nicole**. *Turns to his father.*
With regret . . .) Bye Dad.
(*He leaves.*)

SHIFT

Woman 1	M 1	Woman 2	M 2	W 2	M 3	Girl	Boy

Matthew
(enters)

Jackie
(enters wearing necklace)
Grandma?

Is that . . . Is that Jackie?

Hey, grandma.

My God, look at you, Jackie. You look just like your mother.

(Smiles) Yeah, thanks.

It's been so long. How are you?

I'm good. I'm, well –
I want you to meet someone. This is Matthew. Matthew, this is your great-grandmother, Nicole. She gave me this when I was little like you.
(Gestures to necklace.)

Hi.

He's a little shy.

He's precious.
(She touches the boy's hair.)
Oh! A great-grandchild! My God! To see the day!
(She is upset.)
We started something, didn't we?
We really started something.

(She stares off.)

Are you okay? Grandma?

Hey why don't we eat, huh? Grandma? Oh now, where – Where's that server?

She's probably hiding from you, Mom.

W 1 M 1 Woman 2	M 2 W 3 M 3 Girl Boy
	'Cause she's playing a trick on you?
Oh yeah? Why's that?	
	A funny trick.
And what kind of trick might that be?	
	Funny like a surprise.
Funny how?	
	Yeah, she's maybe hiding on a shelf in the kitchen while you're, like, "Where is she?" "When's she gonna get here?" until you think about it so much that you forget, and once you forget she's gonna sneak up on you when you're not thinking about it in her special server sneaking shoes.
Oh yeah?	
	Really slowly, sneak, sneak, sneak, sneak.
	Mmm. Then she's gonna take your order.
Then what?	
	Mmmm, everything.
And what am I gonna order?	
	Yeah, 'cause it's been so long and you're so hungry that when you finally get the chance to order you're gonna get everything on the menu.
Everything?	
	Well, it seems like a lot, but when you really think about it's not so much.
That's a lot.	
Yeah, I guess not. I think you might be right.	
	I know I'm right.
I love you.	
	You don't have to get cheesy, Mom.
(*Cheesy voice.*) I love you so much.	
	(*Laughs.*) Mom.
Now say goodbye.	
No, honey. Steph's my mom like I'm your mom. This is my grandma Nicky, like grandma Steph's your grandma.	
	Bye, Grandma Steph.

Woman 1	M 1	Woman 2	M 3	W 3	M 3	Girl	Boy

Boy

It's a lot to remember.

Goodbye, lady.

(He begins to recede from view.)

Goodbye, lady.

(Fainter and fainter.)
Goodbye, lady.

Goodbye, lady.

Goodbye, lady.

(He's faded away . . .)

Woman 2

That's okay. Say goodbye.

(Laughs.) Goodbye, lady.
(She begins to recede from view.)
Goodbye, lady.

Goodbye, lady.
(Fainter and fainter.)

Goodbye, lady.

Goodbye, lady.

. . . Goodbye
(She's faded away . . .)

Woman 1

(But **Nicole** *remains. The table is
hers and hers alone.
She waits and waits and waits.
But the wait is

so,

so

long . . .)*